THE MEETING SPECTRUM

The Guide for Meeting Professionals

Second Edition

RUDY R. WRIGHT, CMP
with E.J. SIWEK, CMP

HRD PRESS, Inc.
Amherst, Massachusetts

Copyright © 2005, Rudy Wright.

All rights reserved. No part of this publication may be reproduced or transmitted in any form or by any means, electronic or mechanical, including photocopying, recording, or use in an information storage or retrieval system, without prior written permission from the author.

Published by:
HRD Press
22 Amherst Road
Amherst, MA 01002-9709
800-822-2801 (U.S. and Canada)
413-253-3488
413-253-3490 (Fax)
www.hrdpress.com

ISBN 0-87425-839-1

Editorial services by Suzanne Bay and Sally Farnham
Typeset by Wordstop, Madras, India
Cover design by Eileen Klockars

Printed in Canada

Contents

Preface v
Acknowledgments ix

Part One
MEETINGS AND MEETING PROFESSIONALS 1
1 Meetings: A Medium for Communication 3
2 Quest for Professionalism 9
3 The PCO as Part of an Organization 17

Part Two
PLANNING 29
4 Initial Planning 31
5 Program Development 53
6 Program Elements 69

Part Three
ADMINISTRATION AND LOGISTICS 89
7 Budgeting and Fiscal Management 91
8 Getting There: Air and Ground Travel 101
9 Event Promotion and Marketing 111
10 The Function of Functions: Food and Beverage 119
11 Registration and Housing 141

Part Four
OPERATIONS 155
12 Communication and the Meeting Environment 157
13 Meetings and Event Technology 191
14 Planning and Managing Exhibitions 219
15 Pre-Meeting Coordination 235

| 16 | On-Site Operations | 259 |
| 17 | Emergencies, Safety, and Security | 303 |

Part Five
INTERNATIONAL CONFERENCES AND
MULTICULTURAL AUDIENCES — **315**

| 18 | Managing International Events | 317 |
| 19 | Organizing and Hosting Multicultural Events | 349 |

Appendix A: Organizations in the Global Meetings Industry — 363
Appendix B: Industry Web Sites and Software — 365
Index — 369

Preface

The term *PCO* has been used for several decades—initially outside North America—as an acronym for *Professional Congress Organizer*. These professionals are highly-skilled specialists, thoroughly versed in the techniques of international conference management, who interface between the corporation, association, or society sponsoring the event and the facilities, hotels, transportation, and related suppliers at the meeting venue. Their professionalism, knowledge, attention to detail, and management skills assure the meeting sponsors of a successful, well-run event that achieves its purpose. A "PCO" is commonly referred to as a *Professional Conference Organizer*, using "conference" in the generic sense. The author has expanded the scope of that term by bestowing that designation on those for whom the book is intended: professionals who facilitate, manage, and service meetings (i.e., corporate or association meeting executives; independent event managers; conference service managers of hotels, conference centers, and convention and exhibition facilities, and the like).

Asia, Australia, Europe, Canada, and the United States now recognize meeting management as a specialty—one that has taken on the semblance of a profession albeit still lacking in the clear definition, job description, and career opportunities that characterize other professions. Nevertheless, the terms *meeting planner* or *event planner* are widely recognized in the business world and there is some consensus as to what those functions entail. Less clear is the job description. The position of meeting *manager*—preferred to *planner*—has emerged as a middle management role (and only in a relatively limited number of organizations). Associations heavily dependent on meetings generally have a staff member serving as convention manager, or they assign the additional responsibilities to a staff executive. Corporations consider meetings to be a function of management and an important part of the total corporate communications picture. That recognition notwithstanding, meeting management may represent but a small percentage of such individuals' corporate responsibilities. Whether employed by corporations or associations, most of these meeting executives have achieved a marked degree of professionalism in this exacting, highly specialized field. Concurrently, the industry worldwide has coalesced as organizations devoted to event management and support services form alliances to collaborate. The industry consists of services in four main components: Meetings, Incentives, Conventions, and Expositions, referred to as the acronym MICE. It is a mouse that roars! In the United States alone, it was estimated in 2002 to be a $120 billion industry.

In the 1990s, as corporations downsized, the industry witnessed a proliferation of *independent* conference consultants possessing skills comparable to those of corporate and association meeting managers. These consultants provide event management services to organizations without a "meeting executive." Some have been eminently successful and are highly regarded by their clients and suppliers; others are emerging to fill a perceived need and are developing that expertise or bringing it with them from their previous employment. As organizations outsource a variety of staff services, this segment has continued to grow. The role of independents and Professional Congress Organizers is covered in detail in Chapter 3.

Concurrently, a third specialist has emerged, indispensable to in-house meeting managers and consultants, but employed by the hotel or conference center: the convention coordinator, conference manager, or convention services manager (CSM). Many convention managers were formerly facilitators in banquet or catering departments. They are now essential parts of the management team at those venues, demonstrating skill, professionalism, and a serious commitment to the meeting market. Airlines and convention bureaus have likewise designated and trained individuals to assist their clients in planning meetings. They and the CSM, whose primary responsibility is meeting support, seek to master the same body of knowledge as the meeting manager and are, therefore, equally entitled to be called professional conference organizers. In recognition of this professional development and competence, the term *PCO* will refer also to those facilitators whose primary function is meeting support and service.

Although the prime focus of this book is the meeting professional, readers and students new to event planning will likewise find it a comprehensive and valuable reference. It has been recognized as such at a number of universities that include event management courses in their curricula.

For experienced event planners, the operative word is *professional*. Those meeting executives whose responsibility is the management or support of conferences, exhibitions, and conventions will find this book a valuable asset toward achieving a higher degree of professionalism in those disciplines. The book's more advanced chapters are intended for those who have mastered the *mechanics* and seek to better understand and manage the *dynamics* of those activities generic to meetings. In that respect, the information contained in this work is equally applicable to the corporate or association executive, the independent consultant, or the organization that is thinking about adding professional event management to its existing activities.

What follows is a compilation of the knowledge and acquired skills of many meeting professionals. It is also a summary of the author's own three decades of experience in event management, as staff director of a major audiovisual production company, division vice-president of a Fortune 500 corporation, president and chairman of an international meetings industry association, and, for twenty-five years, head of his own international event management firm.

This new edition of *The Meeting Spectrum* reflects the significant participation of E.J. Siwek, CMP. His wide-ranging contributions to the understanding of meeting technology are manifested in the extensive references to this omnipresent influence on all aspects of today's events.

The authors are acknowledged professionals—PCOs in the full sense of the term.

Acknowledgments

It is virtually impossible to recognize all of the people who influenced or contributed to this book or who have helped by their comments, their teachings, and their examples: There are the 19,000 members of Meeting Professionals International, who provide an indispensable-network and resource, as well as my many colleagues and acquaintances in the meetings industry worldwide who have helped me attain professionalism and maturity in what was an emerging career field thirty years ago. They created a global industry and articulated a body of knowledge, and in so doing, identified a need for a work of this kind. Some, however, need to be singled out for recognition and appreciation.

Ray Hall, whose commitment to professional education and leadership style served as a role model for my own career development. Jimmy Jones, who first provided the inspiration for this book and continued to encourage me when the obstacles seemed insurmountable. The late Mel Hosansky, who set a sterling example with his provocative articles and encouraged my own writing efforts. I feel privileged to have known them and call them friends.

When it became clear that the escalating development of event technology and accepted practices had outpaced the original work, others came to my aid. My son Chris Wright, whose career in business theater provided a valuable insight into meetings and exhibitions, began the effort with a thorough review of the first edition. He identified obsolete practices, pointed out changes in technology, and updated complete chapters. We had some arguments over the need for gender neutrality, but his common sense prevailed.

To ensure that the second edition encompassed the current body of knowledge in event technology, I was fortunate to have as my co-author E.J. Siwek, the most knowlegeable meeting professional in the field. E.J. not only contributed his considerable expertise, but he went out on a limb to predict tomorrow's technological developments—thus ensuring that the book would circumvent the obsolescence of its previous life.

Crucial to this work were the acknowledged leaders of the events industry who willingly responded to my call for input: Terri Breining, Tony Carey, Jim Daggett, Roger Dow, Christine Duffy, Joe Jeff Goldblatt, Bill Grusich, Tom McDonald, Rodolfo Musco, Patti Roscoe, and Diane Silberstein. To save space, I did not include the professional qualifications following their names. Suffice it to say they lend new meaning to the term *professional.* Thank you dear friends.

I cannot emphasize enough the value of the contributions my sons made. While pursuing their own careers, they took on much of the burden of reviewing the first edition and finding where new data was needed, allowing me to concentrate on writing. Chris, a professional industrial theater writer/producer, also rewrote much of the text related to program elements and exhibitions. The chapter on communication benefited from Andrew's experience as head of his own video production company.

Finally, perhaps the quintessential influence was my wife Sarah, who started all this in 1987 with the innocent comment, *"Why don't you write a book?"* Little did she realize that the project would demand as much of her as it did of me. Her love, patience, sacrifices, and unselfish support are very much a part of this book.

Rudy R. Wright, CMP
Boulder, Colorado

Part One:

Meetings and Meeting Professionals

Chapter One
Meetings: A Medium for Communication

Corporate and association executives recognize the importance of getting input from ad hoc committees consisting of managers from each department or membership segment. This group functions as a task force, coordinated by the PCO, and comes into being only after the key executives and the meeting professional have answered the following questions:

- What is the purpose of the meeting? Education? Problem solving? Incentive? Recognition?

- Who will attend? From the staff? From the field? From the membership?

- Is there a behavioral change that management would like to see as a result of this meeting?

- What impression should attendees have when they leave the meeting?

- Should timing coincide with other related events?

These are management decisions, and they can influence the course an organization takes in its relationships with its management, shareholders, members, employees, associates, and ultimately its public.

Clearly defined objectives will influence the meeting venue, the program content, and the "style" of the meeting, as well as how it is perceived by those in attendance. The locale, the business and social agendas, the very ambiance of the function rooms are all part of the medium and the "message."[1]

THE AUDIENCE IS THE PRIME FOCUS

Successful meeting executives understand that organizational objectives are only half of the communication process. One reason meetings fail, even though every device is incorporated to support the objective, is because the planners were not cognizant of audience expectations. They failed to address the participants' needs, which are not always congruent with those of the organization.

The late Mel Hosansky, editor-in-chief of *Successful Meetings* magazine, had this to say: "The attention of the delegates must be engaged immediately and then held for as long as the meeting lasts—whether two, three or four days. The prime enemy of good meetings is boredom and planners will do anything to counter it. For that, dramatic techniques must be employed, which means that the natural tendency to go for a climax at the end of the meeting must sometimes be sacrificed in order to rivet delegates' attention from the outset."

A regional manager who had transferred from another company summed it all up in his post-meeting evaluation:

> The program was certainly informative, he wrote. But what impressed me most was that the company recognized the importance of the field sales force by bringing them to an attractive location and communicating its message in an exciting, professional manner. That says a lot about my company!

A dramatic example of this attitude came out of Chrysler Corporation's 1998 crisis. Management stipulated that shows and meetings escaped the company's budget axe. "Our salespeople and dealers are our front-line troops," one executive reported. "That made our meetings a top priority." And *that* is the bottom line!

WHAT MAKES A SUCCESSFUL MEETING?

"One reason the potentials of a meeting are not often achieved," writes Dr. Myron Gordon in *Making Meetings More Effective,* "is that we know more about the *theory* of good meetings than about carrying it into practice." Gordon focuses on two elements of meeting management:

- *Centering.* Gordon defines *objective* as a method of achieving the clearest focus on the task of a meeting.

---

1. McLuhan, Marshall, *Understanding Media* (New York: McGraw Hill, 1965).

- *Balancing.* He uses this encompassing term to describe the flow of energy made possible by alternating shifts of concentration from one element of a meeting to another. Meeting professionals and performers will recognize this as "pacing."

There is a third element. While addressing a meeting-industry conference, the chief executive of Provident Life Insurance Company used a show business expression to refer to what successful meeting professionals must have: "the ability to keep the wires from showing." Their goal is to give the audience a smooth-running, polished performance without revealing all the crises that may be breaking loose backstage.

To achieve such perfection at meetings, all of the participants must understand the dynamics of the medium and be willing to subordinate their positional power and ego demands to the expertise of the meeting professional, who can then orchestrate a flawless, well-paced meeting program much as a director does in theatrical production. The event manager must have the assertiveness gained from confidence in his or her own abilities and nurtured by supportive management. A meeting professional, for example, should have no compunction about telling the chairman of the board that his presentation is too long and doesn't scan.

If this paradigm seems somewhat euphemistic, it is only to emphasize the ideal. How closely reality will resemble the model will be determined by management's attitude and commitment. This was important in the past, but in today's accelerated information flow, attitude and commitment are paramount if an organization is to achieve its objectives through effective use of the medium.

What of the Future?

Futurists John Naisbitt and Alvin Toffler concur that strategic planning requires strategic vision. "Management must know exactly where it is going, with a clarity that remains in spite of the confusion natural to the first stages of change," said Naisbitt in his popular *Megtrends*.[2,3]

We have already seen dramatic shifts as the private sector assumes some of the responsibility for adult learning that has been abdicated, some say, by academia. Noted educator Dr. William Boast points out that ". . . on any given day there are more adult learners sitting in hotel meeting rooms than in all the universities in the nation."[4]

Nowhere has this emphasis on education been more dramatically apparent than in the proliferation of medical, technical, and scientific society meetings and in the gradual but inevitable shift in priority of professional,

---

2. Naisbitt, John, *Megatrends* (New York: Warner Books, 1982).
3. Toffler, Alvin, *The Third Wave* (New York: William Morrow, 1980).
4. Boast, William M., Ph.D., *Masters of Change* (Provo, UT: Executive Excellence Pub., 1993).

trade, and even fraternal associations. Gone are the days when conventions consisted of a group of men getting away from home for a good time, and generally indulging in adolescent behavior. Today's convention and congress delegates—men and women—are generally interested in program content, and determine their attendance on the basis of value expectations in terms of their own professional, social, or business benefits.

Naisbitt predicted a new era of university-industry cooperation and a new concept of what a university is. Today's information economy demands that management be as cognizant of educational philosophy as it is of economic theory. Technology and the Internet have allowed us to impact more people, to disseminate information more effectively, and to learn without attending classes. Asynchronous learning allows people to become proficient in their field by attending virtual classes through distance learning programs. Indeed, through the medium of Web conferencing, we can now attend meetings without getting up from the computer.

That is not to say that people will attend fewer meetings. The dynamics of human interaction will not be replaced by technology. Teleconferencing and Web conferencing augment—not supplant—kinesthetic communications, the mano-a-mano contact that is a key motivation for attending events. Indeed Toffler and Naisbitt agree that increasing high-tech emphasis elicits a commensurate "high-touch" need that can only be fulfilled by the social and interpersonal relationships that are experienced at events where people can interact freely.

Continuing advances in technology will generate a quantum adjustment in people's perception of meetings. But it can be readily assumed that technical developments will enhance rather than replace face-to-face meetings. Daniel Burrus represents a newer generation of futurists. He foresees real-time desktop conferencing growing to rival e-mail by the end of the first decade. But like his predecessors, Burrus agrees that technological advances in interpersonal communications are an added dimension to face-to-face meetings.[5]

Dr. Tom McDonald, a noted meetings industry speaker and author, is even more enthusiastic about the potential of this industry segment. "There is evidence which confirms an imminent revolution in the meetings industry. Forecasts are that meetings in some altered form will become one of the fastest growing sectors of the economy." But McDonald also foresees a metamorphosis to events wherein adult learning is preeminent and a proliferation of smaller regional and local meetings, focused on more narrowly-defined, specific tasks and objectives.[6]

The expanded emphasis on international meetings with their more esoteric logistics and dynamics—simultaneous interpretation, protocol,

---

5. Burrus, Daniel, *Technotrends* (New York: HarperCollins, 1993). office@burrus.com
6. McDonald, Tom, Ph.D. tom@drtommcdonald.com

cross-cultural sensitivity—places an even greater demand on the organization as well as the PCO. Both must become more knowledgeable and professional in their approach, planning, and implementation. In recognition of this aspect of event management, the last two chapters of this book are devoted to international events.

Chapter Two
Quest for Professionalism

Take any number of professionals at random and examine how each measures degrees of competence in their discipline and you will find a high correlation in the following areas:

- Compliance with predetermined standards of professional conduct and competence
- Educational criteria encompassing basic, advanced, and continuing education
- An examination of knowledge and experience requirements leading to some form of certification

The need for some measure of professionalism in the field of event management has never been greater. Meeting management evolved and developed from a loose-knit body of planning skills, grew through an "adolescent" period involving more sophisticated techniques and technology, and eventually matured into a reasonably well-defined career field.

THE MEETINGS INDUSTRY CAST LIST

Event management in its broadest sense involves a wide range of people, disciplines, and services. They fall into two main categories: people who manage events, and people who facilitate events by providing essential support services, facilities, or products.

The Managers:
- Meeting planners, convention managers, incentive managers
- Independent planners, PCOs, travel agents

The Facilitators:

- Producers, speakers, entertainers, speakers' bureaus, agents
- Exhibitors, exhibit managers, designers
- Exposition service contractors
- Convention service managers and staff
- Destination management companies
- Convention and visitors' bureaus, national tourist organizations
- Facilities: hotels, resorts, convention centers, conference centers, auditoriums
- Transportation: airline, motor coach, car rental, special
- Technology: ISPs, software providers, Web sites, Web designers
- Services: Audiovisual, graphics, special events, staging, security, caterers, interpreters

WHAT MAKES A PROFESSIONAL?

Associations and professional societies long ago defined the function of the convention manager or congress organizer with some variance in terms of responsibilities. Organizations whose membership and programs are devoted to association management, such as the American Society of Association Executives (ASAE), the Union of International Associations (UIA), and the Professional Convention Management Association (PCMA) (see Appendix A) have long recognized that meeting management is a specialized field with its own body of skills and have designed their educational programs accordingly. In many associations, the meeting executive is in a management position, often but a step from the top, and occasionally succeeds in making the ultimate move. Not so in the corporate area!

Most progressive companies have qualified meeting managers heading conference departments. But in the past, meeting planning was often considered an additional duty. It was a task given, perhaps, to an already overburdened middle management executive, rotated year-to-year among directors of sales, marketing, or advertising, or delegated to some administrative assistant with little or no training or experience. In other companies, the task was assigned to an ad hoc committee whose members lacked the qualifications but had done it before—however good that may have been. These methods produced mixed results and they took away key staff people from their primary responsibilities.

Enlightened management recognizes that the primary job of professional meeting managers is to make it possible for other professionals within their organizations to devote 100 percent of their time to what they know best: their jobs!

Most meeting veterans and some progressive corporate executives agree that the professional planner provides a service that permits others to maximize the value of their time.

Because of the wide range of knowledge, skills, and talent that is required —much of it specialized—the PCO must be expert in multiple disciplines. Aside from basic management skills essential to any executive, consider the wide spectrum of expertise that helps define meeting management:

- *Communication*, with particular emphasis on group dynamics, behavioral psychology, and adult learning theory
- *Communication technology*, from an understanding of graphic design and print media to sophisticated audiovisual techniques encompassing film, multi-image, video, teleconferencing, theatrical production, and electronic/digital media
- *Program design*, content as well as such esoteric concepts as needs analysis, motivational psychology, continuity, multicultural skills, and nominal group methods

Add these less-complex elements of meeting planning:

- Attendance promotion and registration
- Group travel
- Graphics and printing
- Food and beverage planning
- Destination and venue selection
- Hotel negotiations and contracts
- Meeting room setup and equipment
- Union regulations
- Exhibit and trade show management
- Protocol and security

Now you have a job function that calls for a multi-disciplined individual who is at once a generalist and a specialist. Columnist Mauri Edwards, former vice-president of communications for a major corporation, describes this individual as "... a true renaissance man or woman, equally at home with Proust and Plath, as well as menus and venues."

MANAGER OR ADMINISTRATOR?

Pivotal to any conception of professionalism is one's self-image and the perception of one's peers. Without getting hung up on job titles, it is safe to say that the *perception* of the PCO's function is more meaningful than the title. That image of professionalism is formed by the responsibilities and authority that go with the position; those are the parameters that determine position status and, consequently, salary. Whether you are considered an administrator or a manager, you have an insight into management's evaluation of your position.

Most meeting planners are seen as administrators. There is nothing wrong with that; good administrators and facilitators are worth their weight in Beluga caviar. But it is an accepted principle of business that compensation and advancement potential are influenced by the candidate's management orientation. Thus, for PCOs intent on consolidating their status and gaining the attention of the organization's hierarchy, it is necessary to seek increased management responsibility.

The Administrative and Management Society[1] identifies five components that differentiate administrators from managers:

Component	*Manager*	*Administrator*
Planning (forecasting)	Plans strategies. Incurs greater risk.	Plans tactics; little or no adverse consequence.
Controlling	Establishes long-term objectives.	Sets up short-term goals.
Organizing	Determines organizational structure to fit tasks. Recommends policy.	Works within existing organization and policies.
Staffing	Recruits and develops staff to meet long-term objectives.	Hires personnel as needed for immediate tasks.
Innovating	Recommends changes with some risk. Accountable for results.	Works within established guidelines. Analyzes changes recommended by others.

---

1. Joint study by the Administration and Management Society Foundation and Drexel University.

EDUCATION EMPHASIS IS GROWING

The good news is that these unique skill needs have been recognized and are being met. Meeting Professionals International (MPI), the 19,000-member professional society, conducts week-long institutes as well as semi-annual educational conferences and periodic seminars in some fifty geographic areas in North America, Europe, and Asia. The Professional Conference Management Association (PCMA) likewise conducts extensive educational events for its members.

The annual Conference Management Program sponsored by the International Congress and Convention Association (ICCA) and the Seminar on Professional Congress Organization presented annually by the International Association of Professional Conference Organizers (IAPCO) provide PCOs with valuable opportunities to learn from their peers and advance their professional development.

Other organizations offering educational programs in the United States and Canada are the Society of Corporate Meeting Professionals (SCMP), Association for Convention Operations Management (ACOM), and the International Special Events Society (ISES). Overseas are European Society of Association Executives (ESAE) and the Association of Conferences and Events (ACE) in the United Kingdom, and Meetings Industry Association of Australia (MIAA).

Though much of the educational emphasis has been directed at meeting planners, there is a proportionate effort at developing professional competence on the part of facilitators.

Roger Dow, vice-president of Marriott Corporation, has this to say: "Professional education in event management is becoming a major emphasis in the hospitality industry. In the past, event management was virtually learned by hands-on experience. The expertise was shared by many areas, from sales to catering to convention services. At Marriott we are implementing a career in event management, with all the appropriate training, professional development, and growth opportunities."

Universities and colleges recognize this important career field. While only a few offer a four-year curriculum in Hotel, Travel, and Meeting Management, some 300 schools include aspects of this specialized discipline in their offerings. They include Cornell University, George Washington University, University of Hawaii, Metropolitan State College of Denver, and Sir Stafford Fleming College in Toronto. All have expanded their curricula to include event management.

Nor is all learning confined to traditional venues such as meeting rooms and classrooms. Such tutorial methods are defined as synchronous instruction: The instructor and the students share the same time frame as well as physical space. With the proliferation of computers worldwide has come a form of asynchronous instruction. Distance learning—also called *online learning*—allows a student to access courses by computer at a time and place of his or her choosing. Thus, a hotel banquet staff member in Alexandria, Egypt, wanting to learn the finer points of servicing meetings can sign up for an online course in event management offered by George Washington University. The student learns the body of knowledge, completes assignments and tests, and interacts with the instructor much as he or she would in a traditional course, except that this is all done by computer at times that are convenient for the student. As early as 1995, the author proposed an online learning course to the MPI Foundation. Online learning is now an essential part of the association's professional curriculum.

RECOGNITION FOR PROFESSIONALS

In response to the need for well-defined levels of competence in the meeting management field, several associations have instituted certification programs to designate individuals who have met the requirements and demonstrated high standards of experience and knowledge.

In North America, the Convention Industry Council, an umbrella organization comprising thirty national and international industry associations, adopted in 1984 a certification program designed by an MPI task force on which the author had the privilege to serve. The first candidates received the designation of "Certified Meeting Professional" (CMP) in 1985. The CIC/CMP Board of Trustees identifies the professional body of knowledge by the following functions:

1. Establishing meeting design and objectives
2. Selecting sites and facilities
3. Negotiating with facilities
4. Budgeting
5. Handling reservations and housing
6. Choosing transportation options (air and ground)
7. Program planning
8. Planning guide book/staging guide/documentation of specifications
9. Establishing registration procedures
10. Arranging for and using support services: convention bureau, outside services, hospitality committee

11. Coordinating with convention center or hall
12. Planning with convention services manager
13. Briefing facilities staff (pre-meeting)
14. Shipping
15. Planning function room setups
16. Managing exhibits
17. Managing food and beverage
18. Determining audiovisual requirements
19. Selecting speakers
20. Booking entertainment
21. Scheduling promotion and publicity
22. Developing guest and family programs
23. Producing and printing meeting materials
24. Distributing gratuities
25. Evaluation and post-meeting responsibilities

In 1995, a task force composed of members of MPI's European chapters proposed a level of certification beyond that of CMP. The rationale was based on the need to learn and understand the principles and dynamics of global event management.

Dr. Rodolfo Musco, CMP, a veteran PCO based in Milan, spearheaded the project. The MPI Board approved and funded the development. A year later, the first Certified Meeting Manager (CMM) designations were awarded and Rodolfo Musco was among the first to add that distinguished title to his name.

The global Certification in Meeting Management (CMM) is the first university co-developed global professional designation for meeting professionals. The global CMM focuses on strategic issues and executive decision making and offers advanced level meeting professionals the opportunity for:

- Education in strategic thinking and acting
- A global certification and industry recognition
- Potential career advancement
- A networking community of other advanced-level people

By focusing on management issues that are critical to the meeting industry, the course can benefit all senior meeting and event professionals—whether they seek the prestige and career rewards that come with the CMM designation or the training in advanced management processes and inspiration that improves strategic planning skills.

PROFESSIONAL DEVELOPMENT

> The whole point of conferences is communication, and that communication needs to start from the first day that the meeting is conceived. In these days of heavy competition for people's time, conference organisers have to work hard to persuade people that they should spend precious hours or days at their event.[2]

This attitude expressed by Oyez Training Ltd. of London, a highly respected training organization, suggests what should be a very basic tenet:

> The meeting is a medium for COMMUNICATION!

The PCO must be a consummate communicator, not merely a facilitator or logistician. The industry has come to accept the premise that meeting planning is more than menu planning: The task encompasses setting objectives, negotiations, administration, fiscal management, computer automation, theme and program design, interpersonal relations, and communication skills—in short—all of the functions associated with management in any field. For some PCOs, the responsibilities of the position also include exposition/trade show management, international congresses, protocol, group and incentive travel, transportation, and special events planning.

For the individual who is able to master these skills, career advancement can be attained through lateral mobility, such as moving from corporate/association meeting management to conference service and vice versa. Another career option is establishing one's own event management firm or affiliating with an existing one. Many organizations outsource the meeting function, so there are more independent event managers. Among those remaining executives with proven and demonstrated leadership and communication aptitude, the skills and experience gained in the field can become steppingstones to higher corporate or association management positions.

---

2. Oyez Training Ltd., London.

Chapter Three
The PCO as Part of an Organization

Early in his career, meeting veteran Jim Jones, then Director of Conference Planning for a major life insurance company, was asked by a management consulting firm to provide a concise job description. He replied: "I'm an investment counselor!" When the interviewer appeared puzzled, Jones elaborated: "A meeting is an investment in terms of direct costs and *people time*. My job is to ensure that management maximizes the return on its meeting investments." Jones is well-equipped to expound on management philosophy by virtue of his MBA from Harvard University, and some thirty years' experience in meeting management. Statements on his views of management philosophy are replete with such phrases as "value analysis," "resource optimization," and "organizational credibility."

Jones was an industry pioneer in the career field of event management. In the beginning, like any new career, it sought to find a clear definition and consensus. Early meeting managers' primary concern was that meetings and conventions be recognized as management tools in the total corporate communication spectrum. Thanks to the efforts of pioneers like Jones, event management has gained the status of a profession. Knowledgeable corporate executives now appreciate the fact, long understood by association managers, that the meeting is one of the most effective forms of group interaction and communication.

Asked to define the role of the meeting professional in an organization's internal and external communications, Christine Duffy, president of McGettigan Partners, responded:

> I attended a meeting where Michael Schraeg, a *Fortune* magazine writer, described the meeting professional as the company's Chief Interaction Officer.

That description clearly defines the meeting executive's role. We facilitate the interaction between internal and external constituents on behalf of our client if we are suppliers, or on behalf of our company or association if we are planners. This role is an integral part of all organizations' communication strategy as they seek to educate, motivate and communicate to customers, suppliers, employees and members.

As far back as the late 1980s, Jack Miller, then CEO of Providential Mutual Insurance, invoked the philosophy of Marshall McLuhan, oracle of mass media, that "the medium is the message." "Nowhere is this truer than in a meeting," said Miller. "Meeting objectives are served by a certain ambiance. Meetings are tools for CEOs. They are major investments that we and our senior staff make in managing our companies."

Miller emphasized that because meetings are investments, their planning and execution must be entrusted to competent, knowledgeable professionals who are cognizant of the organization's objectives. The meeting manager or PCO needs to have access to top management and to have the authority, staff, and budget to produce an event consistent with those objectives.

Job descriptions for PCOs now reflect the important position they hold in their organizations. However, a caveat is in order so that the reader does not conclude that a PCO alone holds the answer to any organization's meeting needs. One should keep in mind that meetings are a *management* tool. Therefore, all levels of management must have some understanding of the medium and its dynamics as a corollary to the meeting manager's function.

Considering the monetary investment in a meeting—from $20,000 for a training seminar to $1 million or more for an international congress—this vital function must be placed in the hands of trained professionals. No organization can afford to delegate the responsibility to "good old Charlie" who is due to retire soon. There are far too many "Charlies" planning meetings. Jim Parr, the executive-search consultant, described such people as having "a residue of goodwill from earlier performances, which keeps them in their positions of incompetence."

SECTION A: THE PCO AND THE MANAGEMENT TEAM

MANAGEMENT ATTITUDE

Corporate management has no trouble recognizing and delineating traditional functions such as sales, engineering, accounting, personnel, advertising, or even the somewhat arcane Management Information Systems. These departments tend to be specialized and have a narrow focus, with well-defined job descriptions for each staff member whose role in the company's mission is readily understood and articulated.

Not so for the professional who is responsible for meeting management. The PCO, who by definition must be the consummate generalist, views the function through a wide-angle lens that encompasses a broad range of seemingly specialized skills and esoteric practices involving matters from menus to venues. The meeting manager often falls into an amorphous role with few parameters and no clear-cut lines of communication. Consequently, he or she may be subject to the whims, demands, and direction of every vice-president and department head in the company.

Can you picture an organization that would permit its sales manager to tell Accounting how to keep its books? Or one that would allow its executives to overrule its medical director or legal counsel? We must wonder, then, why some corporations allow their executives to plan meetings that incorporate vast amounts of time and people—their most important assets—without the benefit of professional event management. Or where that resource is available, without deferring to the PCO's expertise.

Associations, on the other hand, are more sensitive to the valuable contribution a competent meeting manager can make to the organization's objectives. Meetings and conventions are a major source of non-dues revenue for associations. Indeed, the convention manager usually fills the number two leadership position and occasionally moves up to chief executive.

A frequent complaint from corporate meeting managers is that they lack visibility. They are taken for granted by the corporate hierarchy until something goes wrong! This may be because the meeting planner plans meetings part of the time, and other duties have greater priority. In most cases, however, the fault lies with them for not having made the effort to educate their superiors about the skills and time commitments involved in planning and executing a successful meeting.

General Electric is one company that emphasizes that recruiting and training competent people is the key to effective central meeting management. Here are the qualities and skills they seek in their event staff:

- Is analytical, resourceful, flexible, and detail-oriented.
- Possesses excellent negotiating skills. Understands hotel economics and operations and legal aspects of meeting facility agreements.
- Demonstrates superior people skills that elicit cooperation from others.
- Is knowledgeable about meeting technology, computer usage, audio-visual techniques and equipment, and how they relate to function space.
- Possesses basic accounting skills to understand folios and master accounts.

- Is able to master specialized aspects of meetings, such as food and beverage, exhibits, air and ground transportation, program design, VIP protocol, guest programming, security, speakers, and entertainment.

To assist the meeting facilitator and the meeting manager or PCO in developing and maintaining management credibility and awareness, here are some pointers:

- Maintain a professional image. Your self-image and demeanor will be reflected in the perception of others. Seek opportunities to make recommendations and suggestions to improve meeting content and format by sharing your knowledge and expertise. A conviction that meetings are an essential tool of management and the communication of that belief to those in power will enhance your position.

- Seek to grow and develop professionally. Take advantage of association educational opportunities and professional certification. Seek peer recognition through speaking and writing. Acquire broad management skills outside your own field. Then communicate your achievements to your superiors.

- Be assertive in your relationships. Having achieved a measure of experience, knowledge, and self-confidence, let others in your organization know that you are the expert in meeting operations. Present your ideas and recommendations in a positive manner and take a strong position defending them when meeting management principles are at stake. Respect and acknowledge others' opinions, but don't allow yourself to be intimidated by others if you are right.

- Protect your organization's meeting investment. The PCO is a *financial* manager. Seek to maximize the return on your company's investment in terms of *time* as well as funds. Maintain accurate budget figures, revise them as needs change, and stay on budget. Then communicate the results to your superiors.

- Strive to upgrade your position. Learn how higher level staff positions are evaluated. Seek to increase your status and that of your staff by offering creative solutions to problems even though they may be out of your area of responsibilities. Strive to be known as a troubleshooter. Study ways that your function impacts organizational goals and report on your findings. Place in your superior's hands the ammunition for a favorable evaluation.

ACCESS TO THE CHIEF EXECUTIVE

CEOs tend to make a distinction between meeting *facilitators* and meeting managers. As one corporation president pointed out in an interview, "Managers report to me; facilitators report to my staff." He added, however, that it is important for the chief executive to have a voice in establishing meeting objectives. The PCO should understand how top management thinks and follow proper staff procedure to gain access to key executives.

Most CEOs seek information essential to decision making. The PCO's responsibility is to organize his data and structure specific questions that elicit the right answers. Instead of just saying to the boss, "Let's talk about the meeting," prepare a memorandum something like this:

> It is my responsibility, as your meeting manager, to assure you the greatest return on our meeting investments. (That gets his attention.) The clearer I am on the purpose and objectives of this meeting, the better I will be able to ensure maximum return and effectiveness. Please let me know when it might be convenient for us to meet.

KEY FUNCTIONS OF A MEETING MANAGER

While responsibilities and functions will vary in every organization, the following list provides an overview that will apply to most association and corporate meeting managers, whether the position is full-time or an added duty:

- Plan and manage meetings, conventions, and special events.
- Develop a meetings policy for top management to review; update as needed.
- Negotiate with hotels, airlines, conference centers, and other suppliers and facilities. Establish favorable company/vendor relationships.
- Develop systems and procedures for department administration and operations.
- Implement and maintain budgeting and cost-control procedures.
- Plan, manage, and/or provide expert advice on program content and formats.
- Conduct post-meeting evaluations; compile and distribute the findings to top management and appropriate departments.
- Prepare periodic management reports and analyses on meeting activities.
- Design and administer staff training programs to ensure professional competence and performance in meeting management.

In addition to these basic functions, the PCO may also have responsibility for travel management, coordination of in-house meeting space and services, incentive programs, training, administration of company aircraft and autos, and other related activities.

MEETING DEPARTMENT MANAGEMENT

An organization's meeting department may consist of a meeting manager and a secretary, or it may be a full-service professional department that is fully staffed. In the latter case, the person in charge has general management responsibilities as well as those related to meeting functions. Like any manager, the meeting division head has an obligation to make sure that the department's function is understood, evaluated, and rewarded by management. The following is a plan and strategy for implementing a departmental policy:

1. Formulate a mission statement, such as "To provide the resources and services to facilitate achieving the specific meeting objectives of *(organization)*."

2. Delineate types of meetings and services to be performed.
    Types of meetings: Conventions, management conferences, annual meetings, sales meetings, seminars, user meetings, workshops, training meetings, etc.
    Services: Site research and selection, contracts and negotiations, program development, logistical and operational support, database management, coordination and execution, budgeting and fiscal management, liaison with other departments/committees, and post-meeting evaluation.

3. Research and propose optimum organizational structure and staffing:
    - Personnel—duties and compensation
    - Facilities and equipment
    - Staff development
    - Operating budget, systems, and procedures

4. Maintain good relationships with other departments and associates. Seek to be of service in your area of expertise.

5. Request a clear statement of authority to include:
    - Contract authority and limitations
    - Purchasing limits

- Enforcement of meetings policy
- Lines of communication and control
- Access to corporate resources (facilities, data bank, printing, transportation)

SECTION B: CENTRALIZED MEETING DEPARTMENTS

RATIONALE FOR CENTRAL CONTROL

Should an organization's meetings be managed by the executives responsible and the various departments who initiate them, or by a central conference department that has the responsibility for all meetings? As meetings, travel, and exposition activities increase, corporations and associations are finding that one central department for these activities is beneficial. The management rationale for central control is:

Cost reduction
    Greater efficiency
        Enhanced productivity

The larger the enterprise, the more valid the concept of centralization. The three foregoing advantages increase in value as size and scope increase.

The corporate world's greatest concern is *productivity*. "As our (meetings) department has grown," said the CEO of Merck Pharmaceutical, "so has the productivity and effectiveness of our meetings." Evidence of this positive management attitude is the fact that Merck operations in North America and Europe include fully staffed meeting departments. Ralston-Purina's top management looks to its Meeting and Travel Management department " . . . to get optimum value for our meeting and travel dollars and to handle meeting arrangements efficiently and economically, allowing other executives to concentrate their efforts on their full-time tasks."

An important argument for centralization is that you are better able to negotiate favorable rates based on heavy usage of facilities and services. As a dramatic example, AT&T, prior to the divestiture, booked all hotel rooms through a central meetings department—an average of 3 million room nights per year! Can anyone doubt that AT&T had clout when they negotiated for hotel space?

Associations with substantial room blocks have discovered the same benefits. Following centralization of its meetings, the American Bankers Association (ABA) estimated a net savings of $1.5 million in just one year. ABA meeting business under contract contributes more than $1 billion in revenues to the meetings industry!

Association PCOs often encounter the problem of room block splintering: the practice of attendees to seek less expensive accommodations. To counter this habit, some associations pass on the savings. Others add a supplement to the registration fee, which is credited to those who book through the association's housing bureau. Thus, the organization is able to maintain the integrity of its hotel contracts.

Corporate planners are hampered by the need to change venues from one meeting to the next, thus diminishing the advantage of repeat business as a negotiating strategy. Centralization permits the corporation to return to a facility—even several times in one year—to hold meetings by other divisions or departments. This strategy pays additional dividends, such as becoming familiar with the service staff, maintaining cordial relations, and saving time in site inspections. Dick Rudkin, past travel and convention manager for Bristol-Myers Company, estimated that an organization needs to be able to leverage a million or two million dollars in meeting and travel costs to justify central control.

In spite of well documented, favorable bottom-line results, proponents of centralization have encountered resistance. This might be because department heads are unwilling to relinquish autonomy and control, or it might be due to management inertia. There might be reluctance to surrender the perquisites and VIP status, perceived or real, that hotel personnel have traditionally extended to meeting executives. Some opponents to centralization argue—perhaps justifiably—that one simply cannot grind out a large volume of meetings like so many widgets, and that meetings by their very nature demand a high degree of customization, personal attention, and knowledge of the marketplace. As one department head stated in opposition to centralization:

> If my department and I are rated on how effective a meeting is, then I have a very strong motivation to continue to be personally involved in that meeting, and not to turn over any substantial reins to someone else.

ORGANIZATION AND FUNCTION

A central meeting department, in charge strictly of meetings and conferences or one that is also responsible for travel, needs to be staffed according to its workload and its mission. Figures 3-1 and 3-2 illustrate staff organization for small and large meeting departments. Some departments will have a nucleus of trained, permanent staff and a policy of hiring supplemental independent PCOs and temporaries for each meeting. Other departments, especially in associations that derive most of their revenue from meetings and expositions, may have an extensive permanent staff. The qualities and skills enumerated earlier in this chapter serve as valuable guidelines for staff recruiting and training.

To make the transition to centralized meetings and maintain the value of the concept, the department should establish a client relationship with the entities it seeks to serve departments, divisions, and chapters. As with independent PCOs, the meetings manager must *sell* the benefits of the department, continually advising "clients" of the availability and benefits of the service, keeping them involved in the planning and progress, and reporting on the results.

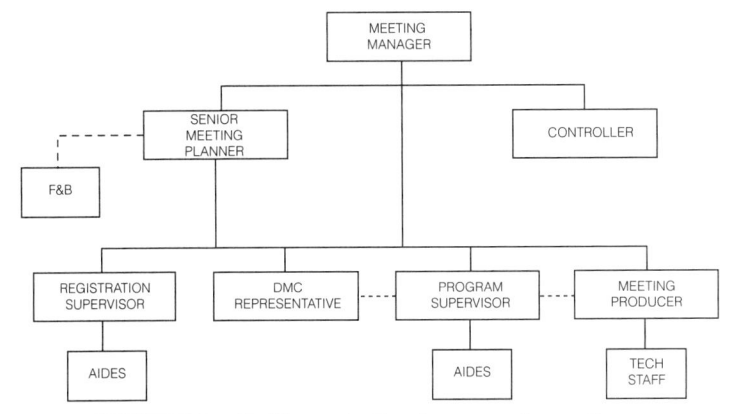

FIGURE 3-1 Staff organization for corporate meetings.

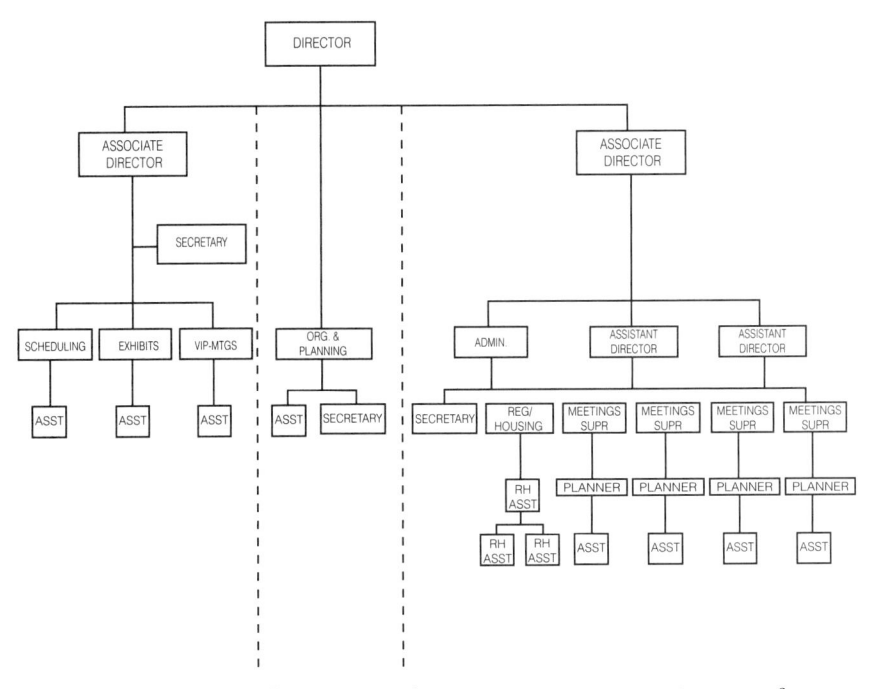

FIGURE 3-2 Staff organization for association convention. Courtesy of American Bankers Association.

The extent to which meeting managers or their staff will be involved beyond making travel arrangements and booking facilities will vary from one organization to another, according to management philosophy. As previously mentioned, PCOs who are perceived as facilitators do not receive the respect accorded to *communicators*. The litmus test for acceptance is the extent of involvement in planning the business agenda or program.

INDEPENDENT MEETING PROFESSIONALS

Back in the dawn of history—sometime in the 1970s—there arose a different approach to event management started by a few talented entrepreneurs with an aversion to hierarchical organizations. They called themselves "independent meeting planners." Some began as providers of meeting-related services such as audiovisual or show producers. Others spun off from corporations and associations, where they had learned and perfected their planning skills.

In Europe and Latin America, the *PCO* or Professional *Congress* Organizer has long been an established and highly regarded profession. These specialists are accredited by the International Association of Professional Congress Organizers (IAPCO) and are required to participate in continuing education in order to maintain their designation.

Independents became a significant career segment as companies recognized the value of outsourcing certain functions. Management asked itself whether it was feasible to devote time and resources to activities unrelated to their primary business. While meetings were an essential function of, say, an electronics manufacturer, the logistics of meeting management were not. They could be better handled by a subcontractor experienced in that field: an independent meeting professional.

Today there are hundreds of independent event managers in Europe, in the Americas, and in most industrialized countries. Some are generalists, able to assist their clients with all aspects of event management. Others serve a particular niche such as corporate meetings, medical conferences, incentives, association conventions, expositions, special events, or seminars.

Terri Breining, a highly regarded and successful independent who holds both the CMP and CMM designations, believes this proliferation accelerated when corporations were downsizing and meeting planners were among the first cuts.

> Corporations realized sometime later that they still had to produce meetings—if for no other reason than to explain the downsizing—but that they didn't have anyone left with the requisite skills. Some contacted their former employees to run the meetings, and new independents were born. Those planners, in turn, found that they could utilize their planning skills outside the box of a highly-structured corporate environment and put their creative talents to work.

Breining's professionalism and stature in the industry were recognized when she was named MPI's Chairman.

While most independents operate as a small business with limited staff, others have grown in both size and scope of operations. Conferon, Inc., has seven offices in the United States. They have been providing a broad client base for three decades with meeting planning and trade show management. As a result of CEO Bruce Harris's dedication to professional development, more than sixty of their event managers have earned the CMP designation. "The Internet had a significant effect on the dramatic growth of the independent sector," Breining adds. "That development made it possible for entrepreneurs with limited resources to reach a broader client base and provide them with the full range of event management technology."

A measure of the importance of independents in the meeting spectrum was borne out by MPI's 2003 study. It showed that planners who categorize themselves as independents lead the budget category with more than $4.8 million in annual spending, almost $800,000 per year higher than corporate event managers.

MANAGER OR FACILITATOR?

Another study by the MPI Foundation revealed several differences between meeting facilitators and meeting managers. Among these was the point that managers are rated on whether the meeting met the organization's objectives. Facilitators are rated on whether the meeting was "glitch-free." The study also found that meeting managers possess more than fifty skills and attributes in five domains:

1. Cognitive style
   - Perceives and exploits opportunity; risk taker, entrepreneurial
   - Has a sense of limits
   - Stays well informed on industry trends and programs; curious
   - Possesses ability to apply objectivity
   - Is detail oriented, yet conceptual and able to grasp the whole picture

2. Interpersonal style
   - Professional but friendly
   - Good sense of humor
   - Confident; somewhat cocky
   - Diplomatic; gets along well with others

- Relatively unflappable
3. Work habits/work organization
    - Well-organized; thorough
    - Documents
    - Strong time-management skills
4. Organizational style/power relationships
    - Functions as catalyst for timely decision making and can communicate decisions to different audiences
    - Understands office politics and image projection; savvy
    - Develops leadership, management, and supervision skills
    - Applies principles of group dynamics and team building
5. Technical knowledge and skills
    - Principles of adult learning
    - Advanced computer and Internet competence
    - Health and fitness trends and requirements
    - Entertainment trends, requirements, and options
    - Budgeting and financial management
    - Goal and objective setting
    - Structure and inner workings of hotels

The study concludes that those who claim the most authority as meeting managers are also most likely to have serious input and/or sole responsibility for budgeting, meeting program, establishing objectives, and evaluating results. Reflecting a need for even greater management credibility, almost half of the MPI respondents claiming full authority attributed to managers also noted that their authority is limited in one or more of these key functions.

Organizations recognize the importance of the meeting as a marketing medium, as a management communication tool, and as a human resource vehicle for keeping people informed and motivated. This heightened awareness calls for a broadened competence on the part of the PCO. The meeting professional must become an expert in creative programming, and be familiar with current audiovisual techniques and technology, special events planning, and adult learning methodology.

In short, the role of the PCO is that of a "generalized specialist": a man or woman for all seasons.

Part Two:

Planning

Chapter Four
Initial Planning

Every military campaign, business enterprise, and building starts with a plan. So does every meeting or event. Even meetings arranged by people with no prior experience follow some sort of plan, though some seem to achieve their goals by chance rather than by design. The professional conference organizer must be a consummate planner with a good measure of manager, strategist, educator, creative director, financial manager, and diplomat thrown in. The PCO will need to call on all those skills. At the initial planning phase, the PCO and the meeting staff—perhaps in concert with other executives—will have to accomplish these tasks:

- Define and establish the objective.
- Determine whether or not the meeting is needed.
- Establish a time frame and agenda.
- Develop an overall theme.
- Prepare a task analysis and a master timetable.
- Determine the number and the profile of attendees.
- Set up appropriate internal and external communication procedures.
- Prepare an initial budget and get it approved.
- Formulate a tentative program in concert with participating departments.
- Prepare a meeting profile and a prospectus.
- Research, inspect, and select a destination by using Web sites and/or personal visits. Identify and evaluate hotels and other facilities to fit

the type of meeting, paying particular attention to conference facilities, services, rooms, and food service.

- Prepare and convey Requests for Proposal (RFPs) to likely venues.
- Negotiate hotel rooms, food and beverage (F&B) rates, facilities, and services.
- Negotiate and arrange for air and surface transportation; appoint official airline (if appropriate); and screen destination-management companies.
- Research and evaluate support services, and verify by networking.
- Design and implement a promotion program. Produce promotional materials.
- Refine business and social agendas; contact speakers' bureaus for recommendations; arrange for speakers; request confirmation and outlines, etc.
- Determine entertainment needs; audition and book acts and musicians.
- Select audiovisual and exhibit contractors and other support services.
- Plan F&B functions; review menus; review beverage controls.
- Formulate a shipping plan for freight, exhibits, meeting materials.
- Follow up and confirm all arrangements in writing.

Considering this immensity of detail, it's difficult for the meeting professional to realize that not everyone looks at meetings with the same reverence.

The late comedian Fred Allen defined a meeting as "... a group of men who individually can do nothing, but as a group decide nothing can be done."

Regrettably, far too many corporate managers share this cavalier attitude, viewing the meeting as an infringement on executive time, even while recognizing its necessity. Often this biased perspective filters down to middle management and field staff, who sometimes resent being pulled off the firing line. (Though one would not suspect this, judging from their copious consumption of spirits and iced shrimp at the meeting site.)

Seasoned PCOs counter such negative influences by insisting, sometimes to the point of irritation, that valid objectives be set before the planning begins. In spite of their efforts, a surprising number of organizations call a meeting "... because it's June and we always have our meeting in June." Given that "always" factor, it can be argued that as long as there's going to be a meeting, wouldn't it be nice if it was in support of some organizational objective?

SETTING OBJECTIVES

Detractors notwithstanding, the Merriam Webster dictionary defines a meeting as, ". . . an assembly for a common purpose."

Adopting that guideline, and at the risk of oversimplification, a meeting's purpose can be fairly broad: to inform, to educate, to change attitudes, to solve problems, to generate ideas, to motivate, to persuade. Objectives, on the other hand, need to be more narrowly defined and related to organizational goals. They must be clearly articulated, easily understood, and readily achieved. Some examples might be:

- To introduce the company's product line for the coming year
- To inform members of the impact of tax reform on our industry
- To explain the benefits of the merger and ensure a smooth transition
- To acquaint attendees with current advances in state-of-the-art
- To achieve a 10 percent increase in convention attendance

Having defined and articulated the objectives (there can be more than one), it is the PCO's and management's responsibility to ask this pointed question: "Can this be achieved by means other than a meeting?" It takes a great deal of fortitude and integrity for a meeting planner to talk management out of having a meeting. But if one accepts the stated premise that the PCO is also a financial manager, that decision must at times be made.

THE MEETING PROFILE

The character and nature of the meeting and its various elements are determined by the objective and are formulated in the Meeting Profile, the PCO's blueprint. In its simplest form, it covers the journalist's "Five Ws":

WHAT? Type of event: annual convention,
        incentive meeting, exhibition, seminar,
        Web conference, symposium, etc.
WHY?   Objective: Rationale for holding the meeting
        and expected results.
WHO?   Participants: Brief description of who will attend,
        such as corporate and sales staff, association
        membership, delegates, presenters, dealers, field managers,
        spouses/guests, non-members, user groups.
        (Includes estimated accommodations required.)
WHEN? Proposed dates: Targeted month or range of
        dates, to include arrival departure pattern; specific
        dates, if known.

34 Planning

WHERE? Destination: Domestic or international; city hotel or resort; conference center or specific venue, if established.

Ideally, the WHEN and WHERE at this stage should be as broad as possible to afford the organization maximum discretion and negotiating leverage.

It is possible to begin some of the initial planning using the meeting profile as a guide. The PCO can start researching sites and facilities, since the time of year and rooming needs are known. But at this point, one may have to speculate on the program and, consequently, the required meeting space. Meeting history can be a valuable guide in estimating space requirements.

THE PROSPECTUS

Carrying the blueprint analogy further, the meeting profile is no more than a rough floor plan. As decisions are made and information is gathered, the profile is refined to resemble an architect's rendering, with elevations and detailed diagrams until it becomes the "Meeting Prospectus" (some call it the "Meeting Specifications"—yet another allusion to architecture). See sample in Figure 4-1.

The Five Ws are expanded as the planning continues. These elements are added:

- *Theme.* Usually reflects objective or locale or both.

- *Subject matter.* A list of topics in support of meeting objectives.

- *Format.* Method of presentation for each topic to achieve optimum results and efficiency, such as plenary sessions, breakouts or discussion groups, seminars, panels, workshops, case method, etc.

- *Business agenda.* The program continuity, from opening address to closing session. The agenda delineates types of sessions and presentation formats, meeting enhancers, bridges, continuity links, and presenter names or profiles (if known) (e.g., "financial analyst").

- *Social agenda.* Receptions, meal functions, recreational events, and organized and optional leisure activities.

- *Guest agenda.* Special programs for invited guests, spouses, children.

- *Budget.* Tentative overall budget showing projected, fixed, and variable expenses. Projects registration fees and income, if applicable.

- *Registration and reception.* Registration forms, policies and fees, deadlines; online registration; on-site reception and registration of attendees, exhibitors, speakers, guests, etc.

- *Transportation.* Plans for transporting staff and participants to and from site, official airline Web site, transfers and surface transportation; shipment of freight, exhibits, products, and meeting materials.
- *Support services.* Resources required on-site, such as clerical staff, telecom and computer systems, audiovisual equipment and technicians, exhibit contractor, decorations, security, convention aides, photographer, ground operator, and volunteers.

MEETING PROSPECTUS

Organization: Proposed Dates:

Site: Proposed:___ Confirmed:___

Type of Event: Attendance Range:

Event Manager: Phone: Fax:

Address: E-mail:

Accommodations: <u>Date</u>   <u>Single</u>   <u>Double</u>   <u>Suites</u>   <u>Special</u>

Meeting Rooms: <u>Date</u>   <u>Capacity</u> <u>Rooms</u>   <u>Purpose</u>   <u>Setup</u>

Functions: <u>Date</u>   <u>Type of Event</u>   <u>Guests</u>   <u>Requirements</u>

Leisure Activities:

Special Requirements:

Remarks:

FIGURE 4-1 Meeting prospectus.

Collectively, volunteers working on behalf of the APEX Initiative have developed and identified best practices in the areas of terminology, history/post-event reports, requests for proposals, résumés, work orders, meeting and site profiles, registration and housing, and contracts. To obtain more information about APEX or to obtain a copy of recommended best practices and their forms, visit www.conventionindustry.org.

These key planning elements are covered in greater detail in Chapters 5 through 17.

THE MEDIUM AND THE MESSAGE

Before proceeding with initial planning details, the PCO should pause and reflect on the impact of the decisions about to be made on the meeting and their consequences for the organization. As earlier stated, a meeting is a medium for communication. Further, it is an investment in effective communications. The reason companies and associations convene people at exotic sites away from "the office" and wine, dine, and entertain them is because someone has a message to communicate.

Meeting professionals understand this. They are also cognizant that the message is far more than words on a script or a presentation from the podium. Indeed, everything about the meeting conveys a message in some *gestalt* manner. The whole is greater than the sum of its parts! It reflects on the organization, on the importance of the event, and on its pertinence to the audience. It makes a statement about the stature of the participants and the sponsor's appreciation of their needs and personal agendas. This perception applies to all of the meeting elements: the quality and reputation of the venue, the caliber of presenters and relevance of their topics, the pacing and timing of sessions, the sensitivity to interpersonal needs beyond the business agenda—right down to bottle labels in the hospitality suite.

In contemplating and designing the various meeting elements, the meeting manager takes on the role of an impresario, as well as that of an architect and financial manager; he or she orchestrates each component and each performance to create maximum impact. But even the theatrical producer must address the mundane yet essential questions of budget and finances before the magic can happen. The PCO prepares a cost analysis that will afford the organization the proper medium for its message.

SITE SELECTION AND INSPECTION

Some may call it snob appeal, but the reason venues such as The Greenbrier, The Broadmoor, Boca Raton, and Colonial Williamsburg enjoy a preeminent image and consistently high bookings is because they reflect favorably on the organizations that meet there year after year, and they lend their imprint of quality to the meetings.

Stated another way, the choice of the meeting venue enhances the event and the organization. This tendency has given rise to a large number of five-star quality hotels and resorts that aggressively pursue meeting and incentive business. But by no means does the conscientious meeting organizer overlook the potential of more economically priced venues. In a tight economy or when cost-effectiveness takes precedence over image (as is often the case with some associations and small companies), selection of such cost-effective sites is necessary. For every super-deluxe, blue chip event, there are literally dozens of others less demanding. For these, location, facilities, and price take precedence over status and ambiance when all other factors are equal. These "lesser" events, too, have a profile consistent with their objectives and their attendees' perceptions.

Factors Influencing Destination

A well-defined meeting profile and budget suggest a certain category of destinations. Before a site inspection takes place, the PCO applies the criteria to all venues in this category in order to reduce the number of venues under consideration. In real life, most planners have a mental "tickler file" of places they have visited during orientation tours, or places where they have held successful events, or places known by reputation. Very few start with Anaheim and go through to Zanzibar on a directory or Internet list, although they may refer to these resources to identify destinations for further research.

The first consideration is the geographical area, which is sometimes left to the PCO's expert opinion. More often it is articulated in a general way by management. Many factors can influence the selection of the geographical area, such as time of year, climate, and attendee originating points, and possibly, tax, safety, or political implications. Other options are considered: distances and accessibility; tax and organizational factors; sun belt or snow belt. Is the season a factor? Budget and attendee profile? Domestic? Canada? Asia? Europe? The location might depend on where they went last time. Above all, the choice should be the one that enhances the meeting objectives, promotes attendance (if it is not mandatory), and encourages increased participation.

Once the destination is selected, additional criteria are applied to determine specific cities or areas to be considered:

- Does the city/region have a wide choice of conference hotels and facilities?
- Is there a selection of airlines and sufficient lift capacity?
- Is the area politically stable and relatively crime-free?
- Do climate and seasonal factors favor the preferred meeting dates?

- Are there adequate support services and ground transportation?
- Does the area offer a variety of recreational and cultural attractions?
- Is there a counterpart organization in the vicinity? (This is sometimes a valuable asset.)

Site Selection on the Internet

One of the key ways that meeting professionals use the Internet is when conducting site research. Thankfully, a number of highly useful Web sites can assist the PCO in finding a site and with submitting online Requests for Proposal (RFPs). Today, varying degrees of information and functionality can be found on sites hosted by convention and visitor bureaus, hotel chains, and third-party providers. The potential cost and time savings in utilizing site selection Web sites can be dramatic. Use of these sites is indeed a win-win scenario for both planners and suppliers.

Site selection Web sites provide users with free access to all online information with a user name and password. Some will query users on their organization demographics and meeting-specific information. In addition, third-party providers offer functions beyond site selection and RFP planning. On these multifaceted sites, registered users can participate in online auctions of available space, submit meeting specifications for third-party processing, participate in chat rooms, catch up on industry news, and more.

All sites offer a search utility of one design or another. In general, one can find a property by clicking on a map or region of the world or by providing a brand name, city, or region in which to search for suitable venues. On some Web sites, secondary filters allow visitors to select a facility based on variables such as the number of guest rooms, the size, and amount of meeting space. Other criteria may include airport, downtown, campus, resort location, or close vicinity to a convention center.

The end result is that meeting professionals can quickly identify potential space that meets their primary needs. Added functionality allows visitors to analyze a facility in depth—to review room diagrams, menus, site and venue amenities, and nearby attractions. Advanced Web sites even provide virtual tours of select properties and 3-D views of function space. These virtual site inspections afford an efficient way to assess public space and general facility amenities.

These site-selection utilities identify potential venues, and reporting options allow users to build comparison reports so as to quickly align properties that meet primary needs and then document them for review by other staff or decision-makers.

Is one Web site better than another? Are some more complete than others? Is information better kept up-to-date on one site, compared to the next? In general, yes! However, the unique needs among meeting managers also vary greatly. What may be useful to one is not so with the next. The ultimate criterion is whether a specific Web site meets one's own individual needs.

Hotel Selection Criteria

Once the destination or destinations have been identified, the PCO will usually schedule a site inspection trip, unless he or she has recently visited the area and is familiar with it. Before the trip, additional research is needed to target specific properties. An important consideration is access, such as travel time from the airport to the hotel. Very often, the desirability of a venue will outweigh any travel inconvenience. Often, the facility will help ease the strain of transfers and long trips.

A survey of full-time meeting planners in *Successful Meetings* magazine cited the following hotel selection criteria, in order of importance:

Factor	*Percentage*
Location	23%
Service	18%
Price	16%
Quality Reputation	15%
Staff Attitude	11%
Hotel Staff	6%
Amenities	5%
Sales Staff	3%
Chain Affiliation	1%

The International Association of Professional Congress Organizers (IAPCO) offers these criteria for a conference hotel:

- Staff must demonstrate flexibility and adaptation of routine governing normal service of hotel guests.
- Management and staff are familiar with special needs of conference organizers.
- Information provided must be truthful, and commitments must be honored.
- Convention manager must be available to PCO during coordination and operation phases. Individual must have full authority over hotel departments.
- PCO and delegates must be accorded the courtesy and service of important guests.
- At least one meeting room of agreed maximum capacity must be available. Additional smaller rooms must be available as program requires.

40   *Planning*

- All meeting rooms must be equipped with proper lighting, electrical service, in-room controls (e.g., dimmers), adequate electrical outlets, a good sound system, and high-speed Internet access.
- Rooms must be capable of being blacked out for projection.
- Adequate ceiling height and clear sight lines for projection are necessary.
- Main meeting rooms must be equipped for sound amplification with in-room controls.
- Adequate supply of staging elements, risers, podia, and lecterns.
- Suitable number of outlets for electricity, telephone, and high-speed data access.
- In-house inventory or ready access through outside contractor of most frequently required projectors, including LCD, screens, video, and audio equipment/accessories.
- Availability of technicians trained in working with conferences, in ready communication for fast response to speaker needs.
- Office or room for conference organizer near main meeting rooms.
- Complete business center, with photocopying services available at reasonable prices.
- Room dividers (air walls) of sufficient density for acceptable sound isolation.
- Availability of secure storage, with keys restricted to PCO and security staff.

One important criterion that will immediately eliminate several candidates is capacity, or more specifically, committed capacity—the number of rooms a hotel will commit for a group at any given time. This is particularly important for seasonal resorts, and most PCOs have learned to take this variable into consideration. Whatever other criteria may apply, there is no point spending time visiting venues that cannot accommodate the program, no matter how many stars they have been awarded by the you-know-which oil company.

Another major limiting factor is budget. No, Virginia, there is no Santa Claus in the comptroller's office! Price can be a shut-out factor, regardless of date flexibility, value seasons, and the PCO's negotiating skills. If an organization has never spent more than US$150 a day European Plan, the PCO will not bother contacting any property with a net group rate of $200 or more. Certainly, there may be that much room for negotiation, but the true professional negotiates for service, not room price alone, because he/she knows that the hotel makes most of its profits on sleeping rooms. It stands to reason that if room rates are unprofitable for the hotel, service is likely to suffer.

Many meeting professionals have delegated housing negotiating to independent hotel representatives, thus relieving themselves of some of that burden. Bill Grusich heads a successful firm that acts as an intermediary between select independent hotels and resorts and meeting clients. He offers a rationale for using a hotel representative firm:

> Since they are non commissionable, hotel reps have an incentive to secure favorable rates and suitable accommodations and to push hard for their association and corporate clients. Representative firms know their clients' business, their strengths and requirements and are thus able to place the event at a venue which achieves the sponsor's objective. It's a win/win situation for both parties.

Grusich offers this further advice for hotel negotiations: "Know your group's patterns and preferences. Be flexible and document your meeting history."

SITE INSPECTIONS

Virtually every meeting professional agrees that a site visit prior to the meeting is essential. Even in cases of repeat venues, it is important to inspect the facility to be assured that it is satisfactory and to review essential coordinating details. There is some ambivalence concerning announcement of the site visit. As a rule, planners announce their intent, send advance information, and set appointments. Some prefer to arrive anonymously, in the belief that the reception thus accorded them reflects how their attendees would fare on arrival. There is merit to both positions.

Pre-Inspection Preparation

Most PCOs prefer to notify the hotel and provide advance information in order to utilize their time on-site more efficiently. They generally agree on the following suggestions:

- Review site selection checklist and decide on service standards.
- Provide information on meeting history and total value of your business.
- Schedule meetings with the sales staff at their convenience, but avoid evening and weekend meetings. (Salespeople have families, too.)
- Ask the general manager to meet with you, preferably away from the office. A breakfast meeting or a brief ten-minute conference is adequate.

- Do not ask to be picked up at the airport. Use the same type of transportation that attendees will use when they arrive.
- Don't ask for complimentary accommodations, but accept them if they are offered.

It is best to schedule site inspection visits at approximately the same time of year as the meeting time in order to observe conditions of climate, traffic, service, etc. There is, however, a caveat on this point. The meeting may fall during the hotel's peak season. If the site inspection coincides with high occupancy, it is customary to pay for accommodations, even if complimentary ones are offered. It is a sign of integrity and professionalism.

Similarly, the PCO has a right to expect the hotels under consideration to be equally obliging in supplying information in a timely manner. The letter advising the hotel of the inspection visit should include the following requests:

- Complete floor plans of all meeting rooms
- Confirmation of a firm hold or first option on rooms and public space during the dates being considered
- Information on other organizations holding space at that time
- A list of preferred suppliers (AV, florist, decorator, photographer, etc.)

The Site Inspection Trip

The PCO and any sponsoring organization officials attending the site visit customarily stay at one of several hotels to be evaluated. Personal preference, however, would prevail in this regard. It is entirely feasible, with a detailed checklist, to conduct a thorough inspection and evaluation of a hotel without staying overnight. The PCO will ensure that the host hotel understands that it enjoys no favored status, and that selection will be based on objective analysis.

On arrival, observe the airport layout with particular attention to baggage handling, lounges and club rooms, and available ground transportation. Verify cost of taxis, buses, and limousines, and check travel time from airport to hotel.

Plan to arrive at each hotel an hour or more before any scheduled meetings. Wander around and get the feel of the place. Seek out hotel staff at the reception and bell desks or the concierge. Note the appearance of staff members and their attitude in responding to questions hotel guests might ask. Are they helpful? Patient? Courteous? Anxious to please? Proud of their hotel? Observe the quality of housekeeping during the makeup of vacant rooms.

Look at public rooms when meetings are not in progress. If a meeting is taking place, ask the meeting planner about the quality of the hotel and service staff. (Knowing the pace a meeting planner keeps, keep questions brief and to the point.) Look for group registration locations, airline and car rental desks, shops, and guest services in the lobby and adjacent areas.

Now it's time to meet the sales representative and get down to cases. A site inspection checklist is essential at this time. Figure 4-2 at the end of this chapter illustrates such a form compiled from those developed by veteran PCOs and industry experts. It is not the ultimate or even the most detailed checklist, but it covers the essential points and will help planners develop their own.

The meeting with the sales staff should begin with a brief summary of the prospectus. (Some prefer to send it ahead of time.) Verify that the dates are available, that meeting space has been reserved, and that rates quoted will be in effect at the time of the meeting. It is a good idea to inquire about rack, tour, and corporate rates for comparison. Ascertain that the sales representative has the authority to commit the hotel. One way to do this is to ask the general manager to attend the first part of the meeting.

Request a walk-through inspection of typical sleeping rooms, suites, meeting rooms, exhibit areas, and other guest facilities. If key meeting rooms are in use and you cannot take an unobtrusive look, ask to visit them during meal breaks. Many of the questions on the checklist will be answered during the walk-through. In guest rooms, judge the quality of housekeeping, condition of the furniture, carpets and drapes, space utilization, lighting, and decor. Note special conveniences such as a writing desk, a portable or extension telephone, fax/printer/server access ports, an alarm clock, remote lighting and TV controls, a smoke alarm, a mini-bar, and a room safe. See whether baths are equipped with amenities, hair dryer, coffee-maker, and convenience outlets.

The recognition that events are part of sustainable tourism goals has led to a growing emphasis on "green" meetings. Ascertain the property's commitment to sound environmental practices, such as recycling and use of earth-friendly products. MPI has published a Resource Guide (see Resources) that lists the following criteria for meeting venues:

- Energy and water conservation programs
- Towel and sheet re-use program availability
- Donation of edible food not consumed during the meeting to a local food bank
- Paperless check-in, checkout, and billing

Inspecting Meeting Rooms:

- Observe ceiling height, colors, furnishings, staging, room shape, and size.
- Check type of lighting and light controls.

44 Planning

- Note barriers and distraction, such as obtrusive chandeliers and columns.
- If the meeting room has windows, check drapes for blackout capability.
- Note the number and placement of electrical outlets. Verify power capacity.
- Check location and verify type of data outlets (DSL, T1, etc.) See Chapter 12, Voice and Data Communication for more tips.
- Determine room acoustics. A room can be too live, too dead, or too suitable. Clap your hands and note whether the sound reverberates or is muffled.
- Inspect room dividers for density to evaluate sound isolation. Listen to activity, especially amplified sound, in adjacent rooms. Check divider tracks and panel storage compartments.
- Note audio and public address controls, including type, number, and placement of speakers as well as speaker controls. Check audio, video, computer, and telephone outlets. If centrally controlled, ask to see the control room.
- Evaluate the room for projection using front- and rear-screen formats. Check the projection booth if one is provided. Inquire about AV equipment inventory. Ensure availability of high-resolution data projectors for graphic-intensive presentations.
- If the facility offers simultaneous interpretation, check interpreter booths for isolation and ventilation. Inspect receivers and headsets.
- Note the type and condition of lecterns, platforms, chairs, tables, linens, and drapes. Worn or damaged furnishings reflect poor maintenance and attitude.

(A sample meeting room survey form appears at the end of Chapter 12.)

Safety Inspection

The rash of hotel fires in the early 1980s made meeting organizers more sensitive to the safety of their attendees. Hotels responded by upgrading fire protection features and posting emergency instructions in guest rooms and public areas. Nevertheless, during the walk-through, look for the following key safety features:

- Automatic sprinklers in all hallways, guest rooms, and public areas.
- Smoke alarms in the guest rooms. A minimum of one window that can be opened in case of smoke penetration.

- A minimum of two fire exits on each floor, remote from one another. Do exits lead directly outside? If not, are there two sets of doors?
- Exit signs that are illuminated and clearly visible. Directional signs to exits posted in all hallways.
- Emergency lighting in all meeting rooms, hallways, and stairwells.
- Signs at elevators directing use of stairways in case of fire.
- Extinguishers tagged and inspected regularly.
- Manual fire alarms accessible on each floor.

Meeting participants who are single parents or whose partners also work have expressed a need for competent child care at professional conferences and events. The growing desire to travel with children to out-of-town conferences and the resulting program and security concerns are responsibilities that meeting professionals need to be aware of and assume. Having an appropriate plan for child care assures peace of mind for the parents, thus enhancing their meeting experience.

Meeting Services

Meet with the convention service manager and coordinators. Determine the extent of their authority and judge their level of training and knowledge with a few strategic questions. The success of the event will depend on their expertise. If the CSM acts as overall coordinator for all hotel departments, review all food and beverage (F&B) needs. If not, meet with the F&B director or manager to ascertain policies, beverage plans, and service standards for various types of functions. (See Chapter 10 for specifics.) Request current banquet menus and determine the average price increase in a given period of time. Ask for an estimate of proposed price adjustments and the lead time for F&B price confirmation. Try to get a feel for the chefs' creativity and their willingness to depart from standard menus. If not volunteered, inquire into the executive chef's schooling, qualifications, and awards. Schedule a tasting meal of menu items approximating what will be ordered for the banquet or primary meal function.

The Ethics of Site Inspections

A minority of alleged meeting executives chronically tend to abuse site visits, viewing them as perquisites or free vacations at best and outright bribery at worst. For this reason, PCOs must be circumspect in their attitude and painstakingly ethical in their behavior. It is essential to keep in mind that site visits are *business* trips, not holidays or fringe benefits. Unless there are valid reasons for a spouse to attend—and there well may be—leave the family at home! Children have no place on site inspections, though inclusion of spouses may be justified if they are given meeting-related duties. Repeat: offer to pay room and meal costs. If the hotel is at full occupancy, insist on it! You may be displacing a paying guest.

There is also the question of who besides the meeting planner should make the site inspection trip. If the inspector is an independent consultant, it is appropriate for a client representative with decision-making authority to go along. In the case of an association meeting or corporate meeting, there may be a site selection committee. In such cases, the following guidelines apply:

- Limit the number of participants (and spouses, if appropriate) to committee leaders. Three or four perspectives are usually adequate.
- Offer to pay room and meal costs, and budget accordingly.
- Emphasize the business nature of the trip, and schedule full days of activity. All members of the delegation should have specific tasks.
- Insist that participants attend all meetings. Judgment should prevail; however, it might be more appropriate to hold negotiating meetings in private.

Not all PCOs agree on this last point. Some say that they can accomplish their inspections and meetings more effectively without a committee. In that case, plan to have the "entourage" attend the introductory meeting and walk-through only. Then assign specific tasks to the appropriate committee members. Such tasks might be evaluating various guest services, shops, and recreational facilities; observing check-in procedures; touring the city and attractions that will be on the upcoming meeting agenda; visiting with counterpart organizations; and giving media interviews if the event justifies it.

Follow-up Details and Obligations

Occasionally, even when several venues are inspected, the selection can be made on-site. More often, the PCO reviews all notes and checklist entries after the trip to compare them to the meeting prospectus, analyze impressions of each site before and after the inspection, and finally focus on the most likely choice. At this point there may be a need for validation with the client or with peers who have used that property, and you might need more research and negotiation.

The PCO then prepares a report to management, to the client, or to a selection committee, setting forth recommendations and rationale, and requesting approval to proceed with contractual arrangements. Some professionals prefer to use visual aids to make their report. This is a good way to convey the "feel" of a site or hotel to those decision-makers who did not attend. Photographs, videos, Web site, CDs, and brochures are readily available that add a valuable dimension to the report.

Once the recommendation has been accepted, the PCO advises the selected facility and confirms in writing all conditions agreed to during or following the site inspection. After the selected facility confirms these arrangements, the PCO notifies in writing or by electronic communication the other sites under consideration and releases any options held by them.

MEETING INSURANCE

Meetings and all major events involve hundreds of people and thousands of details, offering a fertile field for the dynamics of Murphy's Law. Add to such high-risk potential our concerns about terrorist acts and the climate of litigation for fun and profit, and meeting planners become paranoid about liability. Some put it out of their minds and keep their fingers crossed; professionals take out insurance.

Event Cancellation

One source of stress for PCOs is the possibility of cancellation or attendance attrition due to causes over which they have no control. Since 9/11, concern about acts of terrorism has motivated a substantial number of planners to seek insurance protection. Though such threats are a significant concern, more conventional perils such as natural disasters, riots, strikes, and other calamities are more likely to cause an event to be cancelled or postponed. A meeting cancellation policy is designed to compensate the insured for losses arising from:

- Penalties imposed by hotels and other facilities as a result of event cancellation, curtailment, or postponement
- Loss of revenues and/or deposits stemming from attrition or early termination of the event
- Charges resulting from an organization's inability to vacate the conference premises, as scheduled
- Failure of a principal speaker or entertainer to appear
- Cost of relocating a meeting in case of hotel overbooking, a labor strike, or a natural disaster

It should be emphasized that the loss must be a direct result of cancellation for valid reasons or an unexpected cause beyond the control of the organizers. There are a number of exclusions, such as financial insolvency and currency fluctuations. On the positive side, a broad all-risk meeting insurance policy can cover the following:

48   Planning

- Damage to leased property arising out of activity on the part of meeting organizers, staff, attendees, or guests
- Loss of registration receipts, cash, checks, tickets, or other negotiable instruments as a result of fire, theft, embezzlement, etc.
- Damage to, destruction, or loss of personal property that the insured owns or rents (furniture, fixtures, equipment, materials)

A risk assessment by a qualified security service can be a valuable document when applying for such insurance. This service assesses the sponsoring organization's potential exposure, and recommends measures to minimize risk. (See Chapter 17 for details.)

Professional Liability

This is a form of errors or omissions policy that may be issued independently of event coverage. It protects the PCO from suits arising out of loss or damages incurred in the performance of his or her duties. Most such plans cover liability for accidents and injuries arising from inebriation. (See "Liquor Liability" in Chapter 10.)

Insurance Plans

The organization's broad liability insurance policy can include the above coverages or cover them through policy riders. In addition, insurance specifically designed for the meeting industry can be obtained from Meeting Professionals International (MPI). Developed for MPI, it is known as ExpoPlusCCI. The plan provides coverage for cancellations, terrorism, strikes, and attrition. The American Society of Association Executives (ASAE) in North America and the Association for Conferences and Events (ACE) in Europe and Australia also have similar plans. The latter is called ACEPLAN, underwritten by ExpSure Ltd. Appendix A provides addresses and Web sites. Other sources are listed at the end of this chapter.

In subsequent weeks, establish lines of communication between the PCO and the meeting site for further pre-meeting coordination. Develop a planning timetable covering key planning elements and tasks, their interrelationships, and deadlines for critical actions. The initial planning phase overlaps into the coordination phase, and the difference is sometimes hard to distinguish. For the purpose of this book, however, the decisions on meeting venue concludes the initial phase.

Resources:

MPI Green Meetings Resource Guide: www.mpiweb.org/resources/green-meetings/

Hotel Representation: Bill Grusich, CMP bgrusich@hinton-grusich.com

Insurance Plans

http://www.asae-aon.com

http://www.specialeventinsurance.com

http://www.insurexpo-sure.com

http://www.expoplus.net

http://www.hennenpublishing.com/timeline.html

Site Selection Checklist

Meeting Requirements
Ask these preliminary questions:

Are meeting objectives best served by a resort, metropolitan hotel, or conference center?
From where are most attendees coming?
Should site be regionally rotated?
What kind of accommodations can attendees afford?
Should site be considered a jumping-off point for pre- and post-convention trips?
What are anticipated needs for hotel rooms, other facilities, and services?
What are projected convention dates?
What is anticipated attendance?

Convention History
- Number and types of hotel rooms reserved
- Number of no-shows
- Types and number of functions guaranteed
- Actual attendance at each
- Arrival and departure patterns
- Promotional assistance from hotels, convention centers, bureaus
- Association's payment history
- Exhibit program (if any) details

For each year, calculate expenditures on:
- food and beverage
- hotel rooms
  -exhibits
  -hotel room service, restaurant
  -other on-site activities

Convention Bureaus/Hotels
For bureau or hotel contacts, find out:
- name, title, address, phone number (services bureau will provide)
- How long hotel contact has been with the hotel
- names of general manager, director of sales, convention services manager, reservations manager, banquet manager

Site Inspections
Check hotels for:
- number of singles, doubles, suites
- rack rates for each
- complimentary room policy
- housekeeping/appearance
- adequate public space
- meeting room capacities/dimensions
- lighting, ventilation, temperature controls
- soundproofing
- sound system
- obstructions
- staging area
- exhibit facilities
- drayage policy
- available equipment, services
- access to banquet kitchens
- elevator service
- security/fire safety
- facilities for handicapped
- distance from convention center, airport
- renovation plans
- overlapping conventions
- recreation, entertainment, parking facilities
- credit, gratuity, liquor policies
- theme parties
- union requirements
- concierge

Investigate local:
- food, beverage, entertainment taxes
- alcohol laws, special licenses
- public transportation
- overflow housing options
- entertainment
- accessibility

- promotional assistances
- climate
- holidays

Negotiations/Bookings
Be sure to research:
- facility's pricing structure
- other planners who have met at site
- dollar value of your meeting
- complimentary-room policy
- rates at comparable area facilities

Negotiate reasonable group rate:
- flat rate
- sliding scale
- other

Obtain food and beverage quotes or determine date to negotiate them.

Possible negotiable items:
- staffing
- exhibit space, setup
- cut-off dates
- complimentary rooms
- credit, deposit arrangements
- recreational facilities
- gratuities
- function-room fees
- parking
- decorating, cleaning, security
- other

Make tentative bookings and agree on option date.
Put all agreements in writing:
- proposal
- letter of agreement

FIGURE 4-2 Site selection checklist.

Meeting Planner Timeline

18 Months Out
- Set objectives, meeting/exhibit dates and locate
- Set preliminary budget
- Set registration fees and policy
- Conduct site visit
- Check site references from other meeting planners
- Negotiate fares with official airline
- Select ground operator
- Select official car-rental agency
- Define promotional strategy
- Assemble potential exhibitor lists
- Prepare first calendar notices and press releases
- Contact CVBs, hotels, and conference centers

16 Months Out
- Establish meeting theme and objectives
- Negotiate hotel rates and blocks, sign hotel contracts
- Select freight company
- Select exhibit service contractor
- Produce exhibit floor plan
- Establish exhibit space rates
- Arrange insurance coverage
- Contact speakers' bureau to check on availabilities/fees

14 Months Out
- Prepare budget/receive approval
- Invite and confirm key speakers
- Determine preliminary food and beverage requirements
- Prepare and mail first meeting announcements and promotional materials to prospective attendees
- Prepare program agenda
- Mail first exhibitor promotion

12 Months Out
- Select and contract with audiovisual supplier
- Develop logo/graphics theme
- Get speakers' audiovisual needs
- Adjust exhibit floor plan
- Issue new media release
- Produce and mail new promotion to prospective attendees

6 Months Out
- Create checklist for all meeting segments
- Order and confirm delivery date of materials/giveaways
- Select photographer, entertainment, and security vendor
- Arrange for on-site office and communications needs
- Begin processing registration forms
- Determine participants: facilitators, dignitaries etc.
- Solicit sponsors and confirm in writing
- Book your headliner entertainment

- Develop meeting requirements and times for meal functions, receptions, special activities, exhibits, and tours
- Mail next promotion piece to prospective attendees

4 Months Out
- Issue new media release
- Refine program and agenda
- Select photographer, entertainment, and security vendors
- Determine materials shipping arrangements
- Order and confirm delivery date of giveaways
- Assign speaker locations/times
- Confirm audiovisual requirements
- Plan meeting sessions that include topics and rooms
- Determine transportation needs of participants
- Determine meal selection and pricing
- Finalize the specific meeting rooms and layouts required
- Have all decisions finalized in contractual form

3 Months Out
- Determine what materials need to be reproduced
- Obtain permission for any material you intend to copy
- Plan and arrange airport arrival needs for meet-and-greet
- Mail new promotional piece to prospective attendees
- Send invitation letters to VIPs
- Determine materials needed in registration packet
- Determine meeting room setups and notify site
- Order necessary signs, banners, and room signage

2 Months Out
- Adjust budget again
- Open host-city bank account
- Finalize session schedule and room assignments
- Produce and mail exhibitor services kits
- Finalize F&B schedule
- Determine on-site staff needs
- Determine security needs
- Compile exhibitor directory
- Review processing and billing activity with hotels
- Plan social events with local clubs and restaurants
- Confirm agenda with speakers and presenters
- Confirm presentation needs with site manager
- Mail speakers and/or presenters their travel and registration information and preliminary agendas
- Finalize meal selection/confirm site details
- Reconfirm with all external vendors
- Send attendees information regarding meeting attire, agenda, hotel and travel arrangements
- Mail final promotional piece to prospective attendees

FIGURE 4-3 Meeting timetable.

Meeting Planner Timeline

1 Month Out

- Print final program and conference guide
- Print workbooks
- Check cut-off date for sleeping room bookings at hotel
- Request room pick-up list
- Submit daily schedule to hotels
- Produce badge and ticket stocks
- Contact all speakers to confirm
- Submit final room list to the site manager
- Arrange business center for participants, if appropriate
- Create tent cards that have daily agendas on the back
- Create name badges
- Create meeting handouts in hard copy and electronic
- Send attendees information about the meeting, participation requirements, and facilities
- Mail final registration information, travel plans, and updated agendas
- Cut off date for guarantee numbers for special activities such as golf outings or family tours
- Organize registration materials

2 Weeks Out

- Ship materials to meeting site and confirm delivery
- Prepare name badges for all attendees
- Make pre-event preparations on-site
- Prepare registration list with count of registrants
- Finalize food arrangements
- Mail press release to all local press
- Review any updates or changes with site manager
- Confirm number of attendees with hotel and caterer

1 Week to 1 Day

- Check inventory of materials shipped in advance
- Hold a pre-convention meeting: Review last-minute changes to conference résumé, including guarantees, and remind facility staff of importance of meeting
- Meet with facility accounting department to confirm procedures for daily review of charges to master account and prepare final accounting and auditing report of all charges
- Confirm information to be posted on reader boards
- Meet with security and review procedures
- Review rooming list with front desk and confirm all pre-registered attendees and procedure for check-in; inspect rooms assigned to VIPs and to attendees requiring rooms meeting ADA standards
- Check weather reports for arrival delays and review alternative plans; coordinate airport meet-and-greet plans
- Coordinate specific times for guest room delivery of any meeting materials and/or gifts for VIPs
- Set up private office space and separate registration area
- Review any updates or changes with site manager
- Set up registration tables with attendee materials
- Re-check accommodations list and meeting room needs
- Set up signage, banners, and tent cards in the meeting rooms
- Check audiovisual equipment

Meeting Day

- Post direction signs and large posters outside rooms
- Set up a registration table one hour before meeting
- Appoint staff to greet speakers as they arrive
- Appoint staff to greet press members
- Appoint clean-up committee
- Welcome attendees
- Distribute name badges, final agendas, and materials
- Check audiovisual equipment before presentation begins
- Distribute giveaways
- Confirm meal timing
- Plan separate post-meeting follow-ups with your own staff and facility staff and issue specific gratuities

Post Meeting

- Reconcile finances
- Do a post-budget performance review
- Ensure all costs have been covered: food, printing, etc.
- Finalize budget report, including actual costs and revenues
- Complete payment for site, speakers, and other services
- Prepare invoices for sponsors and unpaid attendees
- Pack and inventory materials
- Have leftover materials shipped back to office
- Send thank you notes to speakers and presenters
- Send thank you notes to facility and to personnel who went above and beyond to ensure success of meeting
- Send thank you notes to VIPs for their attendance where appropriate
- Review meeting evaluations
- Document meeting notes, prices, vendors, and suggestions for future meetings
- Print final registration list including on-site registrants
- Request a sleeping room pick-up summary from hotel

The Meeting Planners Timeline is a combination of information obtained through various meeting planners, publications, magazines, and Internet research.

The Meeting Planners Timeline is meant to be used as an abbreviated general guide for the decision-making timeline process. The guide should be modified depending on experience of planner and size of meeting.

FIGURE 4-3 Meeting timetable (concluded). For a more-detailed meeting timeline, contact Hennen Publishing, publishers of *Midwest Meetings Magazine:* www.hennenpublishing.com/timeline.html.

Chapter Five
Program Development

Program development is piecing together the content, agenda, and selected formats into a design that is compatible with the meeting objectives. The degree of involvement in planning and implementing the program, particularly the business agenda, distinguishes the meeting *manager* from the facilitator. In some organizations, the meeting executive is instrumental in determining content, but generally speaking, program subject matter is the responsibility of management or the program committee. Whatever the role, the PCO provides professional help as an expert *communicator*, since, as previously stated, a meeting is essentially a medium for communication.

For seminars and association conferences wherein a fee is charged, organizers have come to understand that content is the vital ingredient. Attendees are seeking return on their investment of time and money, and that means that they want more than one-way communication. The time-honored paradigm of a speaker dispensing knowledge to a receptive but static audience is giving way to innovative, interactive learning methods and such radical models as participant-controlled content and agenda. In this changing environment, the event organizer plays a vital role.

The PCO orchestrates the program, much as the conductor would a musical score, beginning with an attention-getting overture, proceeding with links and bridges, appropriate crescendos for emphasis, and moments of quiet and rest to ensure proper pacing. A cursory knowledge of stage direction and an understanding of the skills of the playwright and musical arranger are as valuable to program design as are the most esoteric disciplines of group dynamics, adult learning theory, and behavioral science. Only with the proper application of all these skills will the meeting program achieve that critical pacing and smooth continuity that ensures a receptive, involved audience and effective communication of the essential message.

ELEMENTS OF PROGRAM DESIGN

Clearly defined goals are essential to program design. Articulated by management, the meeting goals and objectives serve as master criteria against which all elements are judged before acceptance of the program. Too often program committees "shoehorn in" a speaker or an audiovisual presentation based on personal taste rather than relevance. Meeting professionals' roles become that of devil's advocates. They must eschew favoritism and personal preference, stick by their convictions, and advise the program designers to evaluate all elements in terms of objectives. It takes considerable courage, though, to explain to the chairman of the board why his annual message is too long and does not scan.

Time Frame

Adequate planning time is a must for a program that is to reflect polish and professionalism, particularly when complex elements such as electronic media and video are involved. As programs become more sophisticated, more lead time is needed. A typical timetable for program development is illustrated further on.

Validation

Before the first speaker is named or the first topic selected, the following factors must be validated:

- What are the program goals?
- Who will attend?
- What will they gain from this program?
- How much planning time is needed?
- How much program time is allocated?

To validate goals, they must be measured according to the participants' needs as well as those of the sponsors, for example:

- To increase personal income by aggressively expanding prospect list and acquainting prospects with our new products.
- To increase sales by introducing sales force to new marketing support programs and sales tools.

Audience validation varies with the type of meeting and is directly related to organizational goals. Thus the question of who will attend will require a far different approach for an incentive meeting than, perhaps, a technical conference. But the decision must be made before proceeding with the next point: What will they gain?

In order to determine what attendees will derive from the program, some idea of their expectations is needed. The meeting sponsors can afford to speculate on expectations when they know their participants well. But even then, program designers find it valuable to poll potential participants for their input and suggestions. An understanding of audience expectations is essential when attendance is voluntary.

Program Content

Having validated the goals of the program and drawn certain conclusions about the audience, the PCO guides the program committee in selecting and positioning specific topics. They focus on the participant's perspective and they adhere to the following principles:

- Emphasize *need* to know, not *nice* to know.
- Recognize that attentiveness is highest at the beginning of the program and position elements accordingly.
- Strive for quality, not quantity.
- Integrate the meeting theme wherever possible.
- Position topics and bridges for effective pacing and continuity.
- Ensure understanding and retention by using audiovisual support.

Communicators and educators have established the relationship between retention/understanding and sensory stimuli. It is illustrated in Figure 5-1.

	We understand	We retain
What we hear	11%	20%
What we see	57%	30%
What we hear and see	87%	60%

FIGURE 5-1 Use of AV for understanding and retention.

STEPS IN PROGRAM DEVELOPMENT

Designing a meeting program calls for a logical sequence of steps:

Step 1: Define meeting objectives and secondary goals.

Step 2: Designate and organize program committee and appoint chairperson.

56 Planning

Step 3: Prepare needs assessment, task analysis, time frame, and budget.

Step 4: Analyze audience and define learning objectives (where appropriate).

Step 5: Prepare initial program proposal to include:

Objectives	Theme
Scope	Needs assessment
Broad content	Resources
Areas for research	Tentative budget

Once these preliminary planning steps have been accomplished, the program committee follows a timetable based on the complexity of the program and the lead time required to accomplish their task. The following lead times are typical for most meetings.

Six to Eight Months Out

Issue call for presentations if program requires that procedure. Prepare program outline covering the following:

- Final meeting theme and theme design
- Major topics and allotted times
- Presentation method and format
- General topic content
- Proposed presenters, where known
- Audiovisual scenarios for theme and program continuity
- Production and staging requirements
- Method of validation
- Guidelines for speakers

Four to Five Months Out

- Select presenters and assign topics.
- Invite and contract speakers.
- Establish deadline for return of speaker outlines and AV requirements.

Two to Three Months

Develop program content:

- Prepare script and produce AV presentations. Add continuity segments.

- Review and edit speaker outlines, handouts, case studies, etc.
- Produce speaker support materials.
- Determine AV and other staging arrangements and contract.
- Finalize formats, session chairpersons, and program logistics.
- Review and analyze for timing, pacing, and balance.
- Incorporate social and recreational agendas and print program highlights.

One Month Out

- Finalize and print program.
- Post to Web site if applicable.

PROGRAM DESIGN AND FACILITY REQUIREMENTS

One frequently asked question concerns the timing of facility selection and program design. The program determines meeting room requirements. Selecting facilities only after the program is designed and meeting room needs are determined makes sense. But the PCO rarely has that luxury in real life. Organizations anxious to use popular sites will book one to five years in advance of the meeting, long before a program has even been discussed, much less formulated. In practical terms, then, site selection will be based on previous meeting experience or educated estimates. What follows is a typical PCO projection to determine public space needs for a three-day program:

PROGRAM OUTLINE

Assumptions
Participants: 260, guests: 140

ACTIVITY	SETUP	NUMBERS	
Day 1: Arrival			
Cocktail Reception	Reception	400	
Rehearsal for General Session	Stage	n/a	(1)
Day 2: A.M.			
Opening of General Session	Theater (rear projection)	350	(2)
Luncheon	Round 8s	400	

58 Planning

	P.M.			
	Breakout sessions	Classroom	3/80 2/60	(3)
	Guest Programs	Round 8s	100	
Dinner (TBD)				(4)
Day 3: A.M.				
	Breakfast	Round 10s	300	
	Guest Breakfast	Round 8s	140	
	Table Discussions	Round 10s	300	(5)
	General Session(?)	Theater	300	(6)
	Luncheon	Round 10s	300	(8)
	P.M.			
	Breakouts	Classroom	3/80 2/60	
	Reception	Reception	400	
	Banquet, Dance, & Show	Round 10s	400	
Day 4: A.M.				
	Regional Breakfasts	Round 8s	2/100	
	General Session	Theater	400	
	Luncheon Buffet	Round 10s	250(8)	

Notes on Program Outline:

1. The PCO reserves the room where general sessions will take place for staging, audiovisual setup, and rehearsals. A fee may be incurred when additional time is needed for complex setups. This advance reservation is particularly essential when exhibits are involved.

2. Stage and rear projection may take up as much as one-third of the room. (See Figure 12-3, Seating for AV Projection, in Chapter 12.)

3. Three meeting rooms for eighty people and two rooms for sixty. Since exact attendance at each session is unknown, adequate space is reserved to ensure flexibility.

4. Dinner TBD (to be determined) may mean an off-site event, or may be the type of function contingent on weather conditions.

5. Attendees stay at their breakfast tables for table discussions. (Based on previous group practice.)

6. No general session is planned this day, but the PCO reserves the room and will release it when it is determined that the room will not be used.

7. Dimensions allow for a stage and dance floor.

8. It is assumed, based on previous meetings, that a substantial number will leave after the morning session.

PROGRAM SESSIONS AND FORMATS

Recognizing that most meetings involve adult learning, the PCO guides the program development process by selecting the appropriate format for each topic. The following principles of group dynamics and communication are applied:

- Proceed from the tutorial (imparting information) to the participative (applying information).

- Recognize that adults possess a background of experiences and provide opportunities for sharing ideas.

- Select a format and introduce techniques that ensure maximum participation (e.g., case studies, triads, buzz-groups, game shows, role-playing).

- Provide opportunities for frequent feedback.

- Solicit a variety of viewpoints through the use of panels, focus groups, and dissenting opinions (devil's advocate).

- Strengthen marginal presenters with supportive devices such as panels, and interactive or prerecorded audio and video.

- Program some free time for participants to share knowledge and discuss what they learned at structured sessions.

It is assumed that most readers will be familiar with the various meeting structures and formats. A brief review of two of the most common ones follows.

General session (plenary session). All participants in attendance. May or may not include guests. Presentation may be a lecture, demonstration, or panel. The term "plenary" is used if resolutions are to be presented; "general assembly" is used if association business is to be conducted.

Formats used within the general session structure include:

- Symposium. A panel discussion by experts
- Forum. A panel discussion by experts taking opposing sides of an issue
- Lecture. A formal presentation by a single speaker, frequently followed by Q&A

Breakout session. Usually several run concurrently. Denotes a smaller group structure, using the following formats:

- Seminar. Face-to-face group focused on a single topic and guided by an expert discussion leader
- Workshop. Small groups training each other to gain new knowledge, skills, or insights; can include hands-on application
- Clinic. Similar to workshop, but under the supervision of an expert trainer
- Conference. Face-to-face group with high participation and multiple topics; focused on discussion, planning, fact finding, problem solving, sharing of ideas; includes buzz groups, roundtables, T-groups, seminars
- Colloquium. Participants determine topics; equal emphasis on discussion and instruction

In the early 1990s, Harrison Owen, a management consultant, developed a unique format he called Open Space Technology (OST). It is an unstructured meeting wherein the attendees determine the agenda and goals. OST participants must be willing to give up control, ego, and preconceived ideas; under the guidance of a facilitator, they develop "outside the box" ideas and methods to achieve the meeting's objective.

Virtual Web conferencing is gaining ground and meeting many needs. Online forums, bulletin boards, and so on are commonplace, and people are comfortable communicating electronically. But the isolation of such interaction in today's business and social worlds compounds the desire for social interchange. An intangible, yet vital reason for people to convene is simply to share, to renew friendships, to exchange ideas, and to strengthen relationships *in person*. These are essential human needs that cannot be met through correspondence, telephone conversations, computer interface, or other exotic media.

The opportunity to interrelate and to "press the flesh" is an essential byproduct of any meeting. The knowledgeable meeting manager finds ways to facilitate these interpersonal relationships within and beyond the business agenda. Some of this need is served by social activities, and some by utilizing various formats that encourage group interaction and often generate a synergistic effect that exceeds the objectives.

Because the program is the core and rationale for the meeting, it behooves organizers to settle on program elements, if only in outline form, as early as possible. These are the components that will determine the logistical needs, program resources, and support services data that are essential to productive site negotiations. Having prepared a general program outline in order to identify facility needs, the PCO will encourage the program committee to provide specifications for the business agenda as soon as possible. All these data are then entered on a worksheet such as shown in Figure 5-2.

THE BUSINESS AGENDA

Whether the meeting is an international congress, a corporate sales meeting, an educational conference, or any organizational event at which people convene for whatever purpose, there is a core program called the "business agenda." (In technical meetings, this may be called the "scientific program" or "educational program.") It generally reflects the event's objectives.

The PCO will usually work with a program committee typically consisting of the general chairperson, the program chairperson, and select members, though composition changes with usage. The committee may also include a producer who is responsible for audiovisual and staging elements, paid speakers, entertainment, and other enhancements. The PCO, as the authority on communication, advises the committee, suggesting how various program components should come together to achieve balance and pacing. Generally, the program committee determines content and the PCO advises on technique, continuity, environment, and logistics. In some organizations, he or she may advise on content as well.

A primary responsibility of the program chairman, aided by the PCO, is to evaluate each suggested program element in light of how it contributes to the meeting objective. Of course, in real life one seldom finds a meeting dedicated solely to one objective. There are other subordinate goals that are important to the members and management of the sponsoring organization.

BUSINESS AGENDA WORKSHEET

Meeting dates _____

TOPICS (In order of priority)	FORMAT	INPUT SOURCES	AUDIENCE	PRESENTERS	DAY/TIME	REMARKS, SPECIAL REQUIREMENTS
(Corporate Meeting)					DAY 2	
Industry Overview	Gen. Session	Annual Report Trade Publications	All (incl guests)	Industry Spokesman	9:00 a.m.	AV support
New Product Preview	Gen. Session	Product Development	All	VP Sales	10:30 a.m.	Special staging, AV, live models, lights
(Scientific Congress)					DAY 2	
State-of-the-Art Review	Plenary (Symposium)	Proceedings Panel Journal	All	Moderator, panel	10:00 a.m.	
Application in Geothermal Data	Workshop	Speaker Journal	Per sign-up roster	Authority	1:30 p.m.	Lab equipment, AV support
Regulating Nuclear Fusion	Seminar	Speaker Intl. Assn.	Per roster	Regulatory Agency (France)	3:00 p.m.	AV support, Display
(Association Convention)					DAY 1	
General Assembly	Gen. Session	Board Report Comm. Chairmen Exec. Director	Membership	President Comm. Chairmen Exec. Director	9:00 a.m.	Slides, Video augmentation Awards for outgoing officers
Keynote Address	Gen. Session	Speaker	All	Cabinet Officer	10:30 a.m.	Protocol, flags, security
Concurrent Sessions	Seminars	Journal, Educ. Comm., Speakers	Per sign-up	Selected Speakers	11:00–12:30 p.m. 2:00–5:00 p.m.	Individual room setup and AV per speaker requests

FIGURE 5-2 Business agenda worksheet.

GUIDELINES FOR PROGRAM DESIGN

Meeting programs vary greatly according to organizations, objectives, and audiences. It is difficult to apply the same guidelines to, let us say, a medical congress whose aim is continuing education and a sales meeting with the goal of market penetration. Nevertheless, people tend to react much the same way, whether they are obstetricians, financial planners, or sales executives.

Leo Rosten, renowned author and educator, put it this way:

> There is a myth that communication is a fairly common phenomenon which involves a fairly common set of skills. I submit that communication is extremely rare; that we really don't know very much about how to get an idea from one head to another. Because in all of our talk about communication we make a fatal assumption: that there is somebody trying to communicate something to somebody who wants to listen. I submit that most people have a strong resistance to being communicated with. Most people do not surrender self-autonomy easily and the skillful communicator is one who reassures people that it is safe to listen; that . . . "I know what I am doing and you may comfortably give me control."[1]

Following that philosophy, these basic guidelines apply to program design:

Guideline A. Begin the program with *IMPACT!* Recognizing that barriers to communication exist, the skillful communicator leads into the message, lowering the barriers by piquing the listeners' interest. Successful speakers begin with a humorous anecdote to open up the channels of communication. Some use dramatic multimedia productions, video, live actors, and other entertaining devices. Others get carried away with the lead-in, giving rise to the term "dog-and-pony show."

Guideline B. Establish and reinforce the theme. A good theme is to a meeting what a cover is to a book. Good covers incorporate two necessary elements: a memorable title that tells something about the subject, and a graphic design that reinforces the subject and provides visual impact. Often a subtitle will explain further the book's subject.

A meeting theme should do the same, as shown in Figure 5-3.

---

1. Rosten, Leo. 1984. *Myths by Which We Live*. Remarks made to the 20th National Conference on Higher Education.

Colorado Tourism: Coming Together

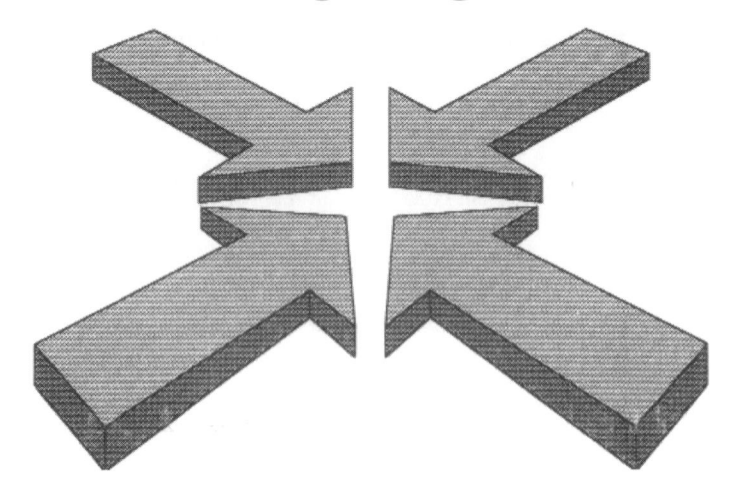

October 27-29
Colorado Springs Marriott

Organized by
Center for Sustainable Tourism, University of Colorado
and the
Colorado Travel & Tourism Authority

FIGURE 5-3 Sample meeting theme.

In this case, the title suggests the subject of the meeting and identifies the author: the sponsoring organization. The graphic restates the theme in a dramatic, easily recognized visual.

Guideline C. Incorporate the theme throughout the meeting. The opening segment—audiovisual or otherwise—establishes the theme and provides a rationale related to the organization's activities and meeting objectives. Presenters, both internal and paid speakers, should be made aware of the theme and be encouraged to include it in their presentations. With the use of a little imagination and creativity, all program elements, business and social, can reinforce the theme visually by means of graphics, decorations, program titles, gifts, etc. A dynamic theme gives the meeting a sense of cohesiveness and unity of design.

Guideline D. Control timing and pacing. A person's attention span tends to decline after the first ten to twelve minutes of a presentation. People have mental and physical slumps around the third hour of a four-hour program. The PCO understands these reactions and encourages speakers to utilize various pacing devices in their presentations. For example:

- Musical, audiovisual, and multimedia bridges
- A pre-recorded or live actor or an audience advocate interacting with speakers
- Alternating speakers at dual lecterns
- Use of a "talk-show host" who interviews the speaker
- Demonstrations, questions, and skits that change the focus from the primary speaker and break up a long presentation

Consider the fact that the person in the third row from the back may have partied until the wee hours, another is worried about the mortgage payment, and several are engaged in sexual fantasies. They need periodic nudges from the podium to bring them back to the here and now.

The skillful program planner also varies the timing and format of the sessions for diversification. Tony Carey, a veteran meeting professional based in the United Kingdom suggests the following:

> Variety is key. People need constant stimulation, so it is a good idea for messages to be served up in different ways. Programmes should take unexpected turns. Humour, if used intelligently, can be very useful. Planners have access to an arsenal of effective audiovisuals that can be used to enhance a speaker's performance.

David Seekings author and conference organizer recommends this:

> Whenever you can, mix the type of sessions so that there is movement from the main hall to group rooms and back—but do allow adequate time.

The physical act of moving to break up periods of inactivity is helpful. A periodic shift from passive listener to active participant is also important. Therefore, use discussion groups, case studies, simulation games, and other program techniques for group involvement.

Guideline E. Utilize enhancements, lead-ins, breaks, and bridges. Closely related to the previous guideline is the use of techniques that increase attention span, provide a sense of continuity, and reinforce the theme. Program enhancers are those resources that may not necessarily support the meeting objective but are used to lower the barriers to communication. Generally, they are entertaining devices, using film modules and other types of visuals, actors, humorists, and "put-on" speakers. No one ever goes to sleep while laughing! Not all enhancers are humorous, however. A dramatic appeal to pride, achievement, patriotism, or self-esteem can be a powerful stimulant and may be effective in changing or reinforcing attitudes.

Lead-ins and bridges are continuity devices used to introduce a topic or bridge from one to another. They range from elaborate films, multi-image spectaculars, and theatrical production numbers to simple video clips. Or they can consist simply of up-tempo recorded music as one speaker leaves the podium to be replaced by another. One veteran PCO starts the opening general session with a Dixieland band playing in the foyer or a high school marching band trooping down the aisles to open the program. Some meeting managers make use of the many excellent rental films and video modules to position the theme, condition the audience, introduce the next speaker, or announce the coffee break in a humorous or dramatic manner.

Guideline F. End the meeting on a high note. There is an old show business adage: "Leave them wanting more!" That certainly applies to meetings. Some PCOs save their best speaker for last as a wrap-up. Others employ a motivational speaker, humorist, or celebrity to provide that high note (and to encourage attendance at the closing function). Whatever technique is used, the meeting manager who is a skilled showman realizes that the final impression is a lasting one. The meeting will end with a strong, dynamic statement that leaves the audience in an enthusiastic mood.

As the program elements are developed and move from general to specific, the PCO expands the meeting prospectus into an event schedule. This is a highly fluid document, expanding as program details become known or undergo changes (see sample event schedule at the end of Chapter 6).

Resources:

Carey, Tony CMM tonyccma@itl.net (UK)

```
                    SPEAKER CONFIRMATION

     SPEAKER:

     EVENT:                                    DATE:

     TIME:              PROGRAM LENGTH:        ROOM:

     TITLE/TOPIC:

     SESSION CHAIRMAN:                         AUDIENCE SIZE:

     TRAVEL ARRANGEMENTS:

     ACCOMMODATIONS:
_____


SPEAKER REQUIREMENTS:    Please complete the following and return to
     this office no later than: _____.
     (   )        Flipchart
     (   )        Blackboard              (   )  Screen (size) _____
     (   )        Lavalier Microphone     (   )  16mm Film Projector
     (   )        Overhead Projector      (   )  35mm Slide Projector
     (   )        Video Cassette Player (Type or format) _____
     (   )        Audio Cassette Player (Type or format) _____
     (   )        Other:
     Special Room Setup:

                      RECORDING AUTHORIZATION
     I, the undersigned, hereby authorize _____
     _____ and its assigns to tape-record my presentation.
     It is understood that audio cassette reproductions of the recording will be
     sold to attendees at this event.

                         SIGNATURE _____
```

FIGURE 5-4 Speaker confirmation.

SPEAKER GUIDELINES

- In order to be successful, carefully plan the presentation. Decide what you want to get across and follow up with an outline.
- Think about specific ways to involve your audience.
- Check out the audiovisual equipment before your presentation.
- Practice. Practice. Practice. Be familiar with the material you present.
- Begin your presentation with a discussion of the program's objectives. This ensures that everyone is on the same wavelength.
- Make sure your handouts include only the most important points you want your audience to remember. Our audiences react negatively if the handouts do not relate readily to the presentation and overheads.
- Allow flexibility in your session to provide for discussion of issues of special concern.
- Please don't sell. Sessions should not be used as vehicles for advertising—this always results in very negative feedback. Even speakers who simply over-emphasize the positive characteristics of their company receive poor evaluations. (This includes the selling of books, tapes, or other products.) We permit promotional materials to be placed in the back of the room, but please do not refer to these items during your presentation. Promotional materials may not be included in handout materials.
- We encourage you to be comfortable and down-to-earth in your presentation and to use humor if it adds to the program. However, remember that there is a broad mix of people in your audience. Do not use profanity or off-color humor.
- A very important issue that you will be evaluated on: Please make sure that your audiovisual materials are neat, clear, and readable *from the back of a meeting room*. Remember, they must enhance your presentation.
- It is generally easier to develop rapport with the participants if you do not stand firmly in one place or behind a podium.
- Seek feedback during and after your presentation. Be sure you pick up on nonverbal signals.
- Murphy's Law lives—have backup plans.
- **HAVE FUN!**

FIGURE 5-5 Speaker guidelines.

Chapter Six
Program Elements

The proper utilization and management of various elements of the program, such as speakers, audiovisuals, presentations, and entertainment, is as much a concern for the PCO as is program development. If the program and the principles of design are the blueprint, then the elements are the brick and mortar, lumber, and structural members that result in sound construction. To extend the building analogy further, the PCO, like the building contractor, must be familiar with specifying those elements, purchasing them, and managing them after they arrive at the site. Indeed, many PCOs may not be involved in program design and content but are responsible for the administration and logistical needs of presenters, audiovisual elements, entertainers, and other program enhancement components.

SECTION A: THE CARE AND FEEDING OF SPEAKERS AND PRESENTERS

If the meeting is a medium for communication, good speakers are as essential to the success of the meeting as good performers are to the entertainment medium. Frequently, the PCO will be personally involved in the actual speaker selection and invariably responsible for administration, communication, and support.

The term "speaker" is used in the generic sense for:

- *Professionals.* Humorists, celebrities, and motivational speakers who speak for a fee on specific or general topics
- *Recognized experts, and leadership and political speakers.* Educators, industry or scientific experts, top executives, and government leaders who usually receive an honorarium

Executives and experts who are part of the sponsoring or affiliated organization are generally termed "presenters." They normally do not receive compensation.

SELECTING THE RIGHT SPEAKER

Whether the responsibility for speaker selection is the program committee's, the PCO's, or a joint effort (as is more often the case), the choice is based on meeting objectives, the organization's personality, program format, and audience composition. It can be most embarrassing to have a person with impeccable credentials make an excellent speech, but offend the audience with raunchy jokes or sexual slurs. To avoid such pitfalls, take the following precautions:

- Preview the speaker in person at a preceding engagement. If this is not practical, ask for a disk or a videotape or audiotape.

- Request references. Check with a speakers' bureau or other meeting organizers.

- Whenever practical, request a transcript or a detailed outline of the presentation. Check it as well as handout materials for content and relevance.

- Prepare all speakers. Make sure that they understand the makeup of the audience, the meeting objectives, the nature of the organization, and exactly what is expected of them.

SPEAKERS' BUREAUS

Some conference organizers have mixed feelings about whether or not the use of a speakers' bureau, a producer, or a booking agent is justified. Most professionals agree that it is. Many of the top speakers have exclusive agreements with a bureau and can only be booked through them. Competent speakers' bureaus can provide a number of other benefits.

The bureau or agent will handle administration, contracts, expenses, and scheduling. They will know in advance their clients' itineraries and can offer potential fee savings for a speaker who has an engagement in the vicinity at the same time as the meeting. They will guarantee a backup speaker of equal stature in case of illness or other circumstances that preclude the principal speaker's appearance.

PCOs who have ongoing relationships with one or more bureaus can often depend on these professionals to recommend a speaker who will meet the organization's criteria for relevance, quality, name-value, and budget. As one meeting executive puts it: "I don't have time to research, contact, and screen every speaker we use. I look to the speakers' bureau to recommend those who will fulfill our needs and depend on their professional judgment to select the right ones."

The speakers' bureau and booking agent—in some cases the producer—each receive a percentage of the speaker's fee, paid by the end user. Many independent PCOs will negotiate a commission from the bureau and credit that amount against their fees.

SPEAKER CONTRACTS

Whether working with a bureau or directly with an agent or a speaker, the PCO protects the organization by entering into a contract. Some key contract elements are:

- *Speaker's fee.* Amount, when paid, and in what currency; details on deposits and royalties on disk/cassette sales or waiver thereof.

- *Travel arrangements.* Party responsible for ticketing, mode, and class of travel. Speakers who spend hundreds of hours in airplanes ask for and are entitled to first- or business-class transportation to the meeting site.

- *Expenses.* This is one area that can cause embarrassment if it is not spelled out in detail. If accommodations are provided, state category of room and number of nights; whether or not speaker will be included in group functions; and whether or not a per diem allowance is to be paid. Also spell out those incidentals (tips, laundry, telephone, bar, etc.) that will be reimbursed by the sponsor and those that won't; in addition to limitations on accompanying persons. High level business and government executives and celebrities often travel with an entourage of staff and security people; the contract details their expenses as well. Unless these details are spelled out, an unscrupulous speaker might take advantage of the situation and run up several thousand dollars in entertainment, bar bills, lavish meals, gratuities, and even a variety of "personal" services.

- *Billing details and stipulations.* Specify fees, to whom paid, what expenses are prepaid or reimbursed, how fee is invoiced, and any commissions due. Stipulate that the speaker is an independent contractor and not an employee. If a waiver on recording rights is called for, it should be included.

DETAILED INFORMATION IS ESSENTIAL

The PCO needs to furnish the speaker with additional details at the time, or shortly after the contract is drawn. Some prefer to provide this as an attachment or follow-up; others incorporate the details in the contract. This information should include the following specifics:

- *Meeting details.* Location, dates, hotel or meeting facility, phone number and address of sponsoring organization, theme or meeting name, business and social agendas, names of key executives, program chairman, and name of speaker liaison.
- *Presentation specifics.* Title of presentation, date/time/duration, meeting room name, setup, and location (enclose hotel floor plan). Rehearsal or speaker briefing information, location of speakers' lounge, audience number and composition, AV/data support equipment, projection format. This last item is particularly important: The speaker may be part of a set staging with horizontal or multiple screens. It can be embarrassing if the speaker shows up with vertical visuals.
- *Speaker data.* Request for the speaker's photo and biography, form of introduction, AV requirements, special staging or room setup, protocol, script or speech outline, handouts that will be needed or supplied, and recording and publicity release forms.
- *Other information.* Meeting professionals recognize that the more the speaker knows about the audience, the more effective the presentation will be. Thus, they will include additional pertinent information in the initial or follow-up mailing. They place the speaker on the mailing list to receive all meeting participant materials. They will also provide:

    1. Speaker guidelines, such as audience expectations at this meeting; topics to avoid (e.g., politics, economic problems, "commercials" for speaker's organization); certain types of humor if inappropriate; expected dress and platform demeanor
    2. Information on the industry or field, as well as on the sponsoring organization (annual reports and descriptive literature are useful)
    3. Other speakers on the program and their topics
    4. Invitations to social functions or other sessions preceding appearance (if speaker is to be seated at a head table, an escort is provided)
    5. Name of aides, room captain, session chairman, etc.
    6. Security arrangements, if applicable
    7. Media coverage—any press conferences that the speaker is expected to attend; clearance on subsequent press releases

RESPONSIBILITIES OF THE PCO

As a representative of the sponsoring organization, the meeting executive has certain responsibilities to the presenters and guest speakers. Several of these overlap and apply to both; others have to do with the PCO's relationship with guest speakers:

- *Statement of expectations.* The speaker guidelines should state how the speaker fits into the program and what he or she is expected to accomplish in terms of the audience.

- *Arrival and departure.* If the speaker is scheduled for a morning session, it is essential that arrival be on the previous day, especially at foreign destinations. The PCO advises the speaker accordingly, states anticipated departure times, and makes any necessary arrangements for extending the stay.

- *Fees and expenses.* As previously stated, clear, concise, and written confirmation of compensation and covered expenses needs to be provided so that there are no misunderstandings. Prompt settlement is also an obligation.

- *Subject matter.* The subject and content of the presentation, determined previously, are reconfirmed.

- *Audience and organizational profile.* Detailed information on the audience composition, age group, gender mix, function, and economic status will help the speaker maintain rapport. The speaker can customize the presentation if he/she understands the nature of the organization, its goals, products, services, and position in its field.

- *Format and timing.* It is essential that the speaker know the meeting format and allotted time for the presentation. A 45-minute speech delivered at a general session is far different from a two-hour seminar or workshop in terms of content, methodology, and scope of coverage.

- *Protocol and security.* This is of particular concern when the speaker is, let us say, a political leader, a high-level official, or a head of state. Protocol can usually be coordinated through the protocol section of the official's government. Security arrangements are coordinated between local law enforcement agencies and the dignitary's security detail.

- *AV support.* The PCO solicits the speaker's AV requirements and arranges to provide any and all equipment, accessories, and AV technicians.

- *Travel and reception.* Unless otherwise agreed, the PCO will make all travel arrangements and assign an aide to meet speakers and escort them to the hotel, to functions, and to the meeting. VIPs and high-level speakers should be met by an officer of the sponsoring organization.

- *Receptive audience.* Nothing is more disturbing to a speaker than to have to address a group of delegates who have been out partying all night, unless it's appearing on the podium after a heavy meal served with three courses of wine and preceded by a two-hour cocktail party. The PCO has an obligation to schedule important speakers and social activities so as to avoid such situations. Menus that complement the nature of the program can be designed. (See Chapter 10, Food and Beverage).

- *Suitable environment.* The PCO must recognize that a meeting room is an environment for communication. The room should be set according to audience needs and the speaker's requirements. It must be free of distractions and noise, and be properly lighted and acoustically sound, with a first-class amplification system. If visuals are to be shown, the room must be capable of being darkened and lights should be equipped with dimmers.

SECTION B: ENTERTAINMENT AND SPECIAL EVENTS

Many meeting professionals have heard the reference to their jobs ". . . it's almost like show business." And it is! The meeting executive is frequently called on to be an impresario, working with producers, musicians, specialty acts, and professional entertainers. It is the glamorous side of the business. Entertainment might not be scheduled at seminars and educational events, but is common at corporate meetings and most association conventions.

Funds designated for entertainment and special events can be a substantial percentage of the meeting budget (someone the caliber of former New York Mayor Rudy Giuliani commands as high as $100,000 for a single appearance), so it is essential that the PCO be cognizant of the potential pitfalls surrounding this function. Entertainment, like the meeting itself, is an investment in communication. It adds enjoyment and excitement to a meeting. It helps people lighten up. As with any investment, meeting professionals need to understand and be familiar with the rules, procedures, and the potential risks.

SPECIAL EVENTS

Joe Jeff Goldblatt refers to this next dimension as "The Art and Science of Celebration." He should know! "Dr. Event," as he is called in the industry, has produced events for the White House as well as scores of meetings, fairs, grand openings, and other celebrations. And the "Dr." designation is authentic, since Joe has an Ed.D. after his name. He has also earned the designation Certified Special Events Professional, conferred by the International Special Events Society (ISES) for which he served as founding president.

In his book *Special Events, Twenty-first Century Global Event Management,* Goldblatt suggests that human beings have, in addition to basic needs such as food and shelter, a vital need to celebrate. EPs specialize in events such as themed events, fairs, tours, and awards ceremonies.

Goldblatt advises organizations considering special events—either as part of a meeting or as an isolated occasion—to engage a professional event company. "By using an outside expert to plan, stage and manage the event, internal staff will be able to concentrate on their primary responsibilities."

Event specialists are able to use elements such as entertainers, décor, props, and other components with several clients, thus reducing cost. If you are about to contract for special event management, get two or three proposals. Final selection should be based on event-specific experience and creativity, as well as price.

RESEARCHING AND SELECTING ENTERTAINMENT

The selection of appropriate entertainment, like speaker selection, is influenced by meeting objectives, the organizational profile, and audience composition. A fourth criterion is the nature of the specific function.

Music for Ambiance

We have all been innocent victims of cocktail receptions where a large orchestra or hyper-amplified instruments and vocalists impair the event and its objective. The intent of a reception is conversation—the opportunity to renew old acquaintances, make new ones, and share experiences. It's a waste of entertainment funds and a disservice to attendees to drown them out with loud music.

There is certainly a place for vocalists and amplified music, but a reception or dinner is not it! Vocalists, one or many, demand attention and are, therefore, inappropriate. Music at meals and receptions should be background music only, a subtle and unobtrusive part of the ambiance. That does not necessarily mean "elevator music" or classical music (although a harpist or string quartet can provide a touch of class at a reception or banquet). The repertoire should include soft-rock, jazz, light classics, blues, and show tunes. Rap and hip-hop are never appropriate.

It's Showtime!

Conversely, when entertainment rather than just ambiance is what you want, the PCO must select the artists or acts that attract and hold the audience's attention. These usually fall into the following categories:

- *Program enhancers.* Instrumental ensembles to start or end the meeting or live actors, singers, dancers, and interactive personalities in a "business theater" production integrated into the business agenda
- *Celebrity speaker or humorist.* The popular roasts, celebrity "look alikes," and the so called "put-on" speakers who begin on a serious note and gradually allow the audience to realize they've been had
- *Dinner and dance entertainment.* Vocalists and orchestras who conclude a meal and provide dance music
- *Show acts.* Musical groups, choruses, comedians, revues, and specialty acts (magicians, acrobats) who stage a show, usually following a meal

HOW TO BOOK MUSICIANS AND ARTISTS

While speakers' are generally contracted directly or through speakers' bureaus, music and entertainment are normally booked through a producer or agent. (See Figure 6-1 for various options.)

When entertainment is a significant element of the meeting agenda (such as business theater), a professional producer or event planner is essential to the success of the meeting. The PCO has far too many details to supervise without being concerned with rehearsals, stage crew, music, wardrobe, lighting, sound, and all the other impedimenta that accompany a theatrical production. The producer is responsible to the meeting executive for these aspects of the production: scripting, creative supervision, auditioning and booking artists and musicians, AV production, and compliance with union regulations.

A Word about Unions

Many unwary meeting planners have found themselves faced with budget overruns because they did not know enough about this one area. The PCO

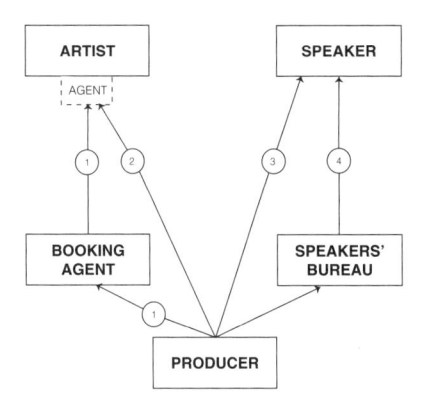

```
                ARTIST              SPEAKER
                  ↑                    ↑
                ¦AGENT¦                ↑
                  ↑                    ↑
              (1)   (2)           (3)    (4)
                                  
            BOOKING              SPEAKERS'
             AGENT                BUREAU
                ↖                   ↗
                  (1)
                 PRODUCER
```

1. Through booking agent
2. Direct to artist (or personal agent)
3. Direct to speaker
4. Through speakers' bureau

FIGURE 6-1 Booking speakers and entertainers.

should be aware that certain hotels have agreements with musicians' unions specifying the number of band members for various ballrooms. Uninformed meeting executives who bring along their favorite quartet may end up paying six standby musicians not to play because they neglected to ascertain that the Chippendale Ballroom requires a ten-piece band.

Cities throughout the world will be affected differently by the jurisdiction of several entertainment industry unions that regulate, among other factors:

- Musicians and vocalists
- Actors and other performers
- Stage hands, scenic artists, carpenters
- Lighting and sound technicians
- Projectionists and video technicians

Even supervisory people such as directors, stage managers, orchestra leaders, and conductors are sometimes represented by unions.

Meeting executives are well advised to ask the hotel or auditorium staff what union jurisdictions apply and what performance rules must be followed. In some cities, unions are so powerful that hotels require a projectionist to be present when any audiovisual equipment is employed—even if a speaker is simply using a projector! Forewarned is forearmed!

Stars in Your Eyes

Occasionally the importance of the meeting and size of the budget will suggest the use of "name talent." This responsibility requires yet another set of skills, and invokes certain potential pitfalls. The PCO unfamiliar with the vagaries of star-caliber performers may wish to call on the services of a professional producer.

Celebrities come in all sizes, types, and price tags. From "singles" such as magicians, actors, political and sports figures, popular recording artists, and comedians to the Vienna Boys' Choir or the Cirque du Soleil, name entertainment can be found throughout the world. The determining factors are availability, budget, and the needs of the meeting sponsors.

If the sponsor's budget allows for star-caliber entertainment, it is best to make a list of perhaps ten artists or acts that fit the audience's expectations and the budget. The emphasis here is on the attendees—not the organizer's preferences. Then the list is narrowed based on availability and best fit, and three or four choices are presented to the program sponsors.

Role of the Professional Producer

As with celebrity speakers, knowledgeable PCOs will seek professional help—usually a producer with proven performance and integrity. If the event is in a foreign country, it is usually best to find a qualified local production company or events manager, if one is available. Producers can assist the meeting manager with the following services:

- Ascertaining the function of entertainment in the meeting and advising on its integration in the overall program.
- Researching, recommending, and arranging for auditions of acts that fit the PCO's needs and budget.
- Negotiating with and contracting entertainers on behalf of the buyer.
- Arranging for accompanists and/or orchestra and technical backup, such as lighting, staging, audio, etc.
- Arranging transportation and accommodations for artists and entourage.
- Briefing performers on the meeting, the organization, and the industry or field, and introductions to key people. This may include custom scripting to integrate the sponsor's message, special recognitions, or key phrases into the artist's repartee.

- Supervising performers, musicians, and technical staff; serving as liaison with in-house technicians and engineers during rehearsals and performance.

- Providing contract fulfillment and compensation to performers and staff (i.e., settlement of travel expenses, shipping, and equipment rental charges).

A Few Pointers

The PCO needs to possess a basic knowledge of entertainment, even if a professional producer is engaged. This does not call for an education in theatrical production or entertainment management. However, in order to be able to communicate with performers and technical staff, it is advisable to enhance one's vocabulary with some of the specialized terms and language of the theater. Staging terms (see Figure 6-2), an understanding of contract provisions, and sound and lighting basics are valuable supplements to the PCO's stock of knowledge.

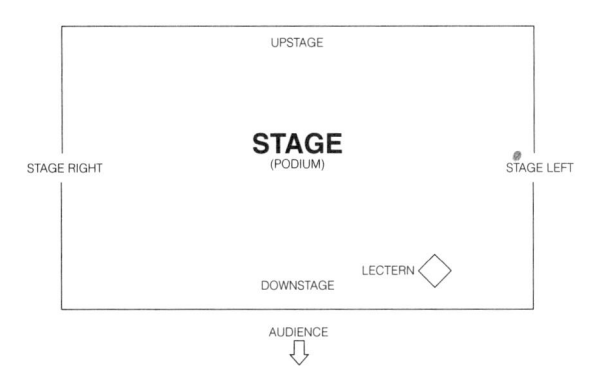

FIGURE 6-2 Staging terms.

The meeting executive should make it a point to meet with celebrities and performers and to introduce them to the organization's executives and key personnel. He/she should not be intimidated by an artist's reputation or stature or the amount of his or her compensation. After all, the PCO is the professional to whom most performers will look for guidance in those areas that relate to the meeting and program. In this respect, the PCO is much like the director or producer of a film or theatrical event. Performers depend on him for references to key people in the organization, the integration of specialized language pertaining to the industry, the so-called buzz words that can provide an added dimension to the performance and elicit an empathetic response from the audience.

It is common practice to ask performers to join attendees during social events and meals. Most of them are willing and anxious to do so in order to develop a "feel" for the audience. If such is the case, the PCO should be sure that the artist is escorted, is appropriately seated with other VIPs, and is introduced. It is also essential to be sensitive to the need of entertainers and speakers for some quiet time for preparation and meditation prior to the performance.

Many performers use copyrighted material, and prefer not to be recorded. The audience should be alerted to this restriction before the performance commences, unless other arrangements have been made and are specified in the contract.

As with any element of a successful meeting, communication is the key to effective and enjoyable entertainment and a smooth show. Professional entertainers are as anxious as the PCO and the organization's management that the performance will go on without a flaw and that the audience will be pleased with the results. Communicating each other's needs and wishes and creating an atmosphere of mutual respect will ensure that both objectives are met.

TECHNICAL SPECIFICATIONS

Most celebrities or name groups will have a staging specifications or technical rider as part of their contract. Some of these are fairly straightforward and simple; others are quite detailed. One Italian recording artist's agent even specifies the name and vintage of the wine to be served in the star's dressing room. But generally, the specifications will include:

- Stage size and dimensions (if stage is not fixed)
- Quality and capacity of sound system, including:
  - amplifier power rating
  - number and type of microphones for vocalists and instruments
  - number and types of speakers, including monitor speakers
  - microphone cables, microphone stands, and accessories
- Stage (technical and special staff specifications)
- Stage lighting, follow-spots and operators, color "gels" in spots
- Headset communications from stage manager to orchestra leader, lighting, spot operators, curtain, sound, and other staff
- Dressing room facilities and amenities
- Orchestra or accompaniment requirements, if not provided by artist— music stands, lights, electrical outlets, risers, piano, piano tuning
- Special security staff and procedures for artists and dressing rooms

Where complex staging and technical requirements are involved, the PCO may want to compare known costs for staging with the expense of renting a theater and busing attendees, all else being equal.

THEY COULD HAVE DANCED ALL NIGHT

At functions where dancing is scheduled, the PCO is responsible for advising the set-up supervisor of that fact and also of the size of the dance floor. To be able to do so, he needs to calculate the approximate percentage of attendees who dance at any given time.

The table in Figure 6-3 suggests a method for estimating dance floor size and its relationship to total room capacity.

Banquet seating requirement:
 60" rounds of 8   124 sq. ft. per table
 72" rounds of 10 156 sq. ft. per table

Bandstand:
 5-piece combo and vocalist (12 × 16)   224 sq. ft.
 12-piece orchestra and vocalist(s) (16 × 24) 384 sq. ft.
 12-piece orchestra and entertainers (24 × 24) 576 sq. ft. or more
 Staging for awards   128–256 sq. ft.

Dance Floor:

Percentage of audience dancing at any time	30%	40%	50%	60%
Dance floor needed (per person)	1½ sq. ft.	2 sq. ft.	2½ sq. ft.	3 sq. ft.

COMPUTATION:
 For 400 people at 60" rounds of 8
 Banquet seating, aisles, etc., for 50 tables   6,200 sq. ft.
 Bandstand for 12-piece orchestra   384 sq. ft.
 Awards stage   128 sq. ft.
 Dance floor to accommodate 60% maximum   720 sq. ft.
 (240 people × 3 sq. ft.)
                                    Total area   7,432 sq. ft.

Request an 8,000-square foot ballroom!

FIGURE 6-3 Dance floor capacity formulas.

The PCO briefs the orchestra leader on the type of music to be played and the scheduling of breaks, speakers, presentations, and recognition ceremonies, and reviews introductions, fanfares, closing, and related details.

Music and entertainment can provide an important added dimension to the meeting. Attendees are increasingly more sophisticated and demanding. They know what they like, and the successful event manager understands their desires and caters to them within the limits of the meeting budget.

AWARDS AND RECOGNITION

At a meeting convened to raise company morale during a poor fiscal year, an entertainer, following a seemingly endless succession of awards, remarked: "Why don't you guys go into the plaque manufacturing business? Your own consumption would guarantee a profitable year!"

The award ceremony, meticulously planned and effectively staged, has become a tradition at most corporate and association conventions. There is an adage that applies to awards: "Do it right or don't do it at all." The recipients must perceive the awards as milestones in their careers—recognition for extraordinary effort. The presentations in front of peers is a significant emotional event and deserves to be dramatically staged. Consideration for the audience, those who merely observe the ceremony, must also enter into the equation. A recognition program should not be seen as an obligatory ceremony to be endured before the entertainment can begin. Properly produced and staged, it can be the entertainment, and its impact can motivate this year's spectators to be next year's winners.

PCOs are constantly challenged to come up with new formats and new ideas to make the ceremony exciting and keep it from becoming tedious. To solve that dilemma, creative meeting managers have developed some reliable and innovative techniques. For the award ceremony itself, the following guidelines are offered:

- Script the entire ceremony from start to finish. Supply scripts to the master of ceremonies, presenters, and the technical staff. Rehearse thoroughly.

- Use a professional organization to produce the event. It deserves the same emphasis and dramatic impact as your opening session.

- Produce a program book with photographs or line drawings and a brief biography of the winners. This becomes a valued keepsake and serves to shorten the ceremony. Less important categories and honorable mention designees can be recognized in the program, rather than on stage.

- Utilize all of the entertainment devices available. An orchestra can provide fanfares, play-up, and play-off. Multi-image, digital or video projection, and special effects enhance the award and portray in visual format what is otherwise described in the narrative, thus shortening the presentation.

- Maintain good pacing by positioning the winners close to the podium in a "winner's circle" near the stage or on a dais. Keep introductions to a minimum, and discourage acceptance remarks except in the top categories.

- Alternatively, seat key recipients and guests with the organization's top executives or VIP guests.

- Highlight key awards with greater fanfare and special effects. Save them for last to build a sense of anticipation.

- Present lesser awards at functions other than the awards banquet. An upscale luncheon for service longevity or a president's reception for special achievement awards provides the desired recognition and sense of worth without lengthening the prime award program.

- Use a competent photographer or team of photographers to take pictures as the award is presented. Having each recipient pose for the shots imposes a delay. Print and distribute photographs to winners at the meeting.

- Consider a roast in place of the traditional recognition for the top recipient. It is entertaining for both the audience and the subject. But make sure that the target is a good sport and supply presenters with extensive background information. Most speakers' bureaus can supply professionals who specialize in this type of entertainment.

There are ways other than the award ceremony to give special recognition at the meeting. Here are some that meeting professionals have found to be effective:

- Provide special transportation benefits. Air fare upgrades, limousine reception at the airport, or the use of a car at the site are but a few. One veteran meeting manager has the winners arrive in the ballroom in individual golf carts driven by attractive male or female models.

- Assign key recipients to suites or a VIP floor designated as such. Pamper them with special amenities such as fresh flowers, bathrobes, cordials and wines, gourmet desserts, and newspapers. Have the hotel provide a concierge, a winners' lounge with free drinks and snacks, complimentary breakfast, and quality room gifts. The hotel gift shop can offer suggestions.

- Provide winners with a distinctive lapel pin or badge device that identifies them to hotel staff as "distinguished guests" entitled to special services, free use of health facilities, complimentary massages, etc. Arrange these with the hotel and be sure staff is alerted to recognize the device.

84 *Planning*

- Post oversized photographs or posters of the recipients in the convention lobby or main meeting room.

- Arrange press conferences with the trade press to interview winners. If a convention newspaper is published, feature award recipients.

- Acknowledge the importance of family support with VIP treatment and special amenities for spouses and children accompanying winners.

As an alternative to the traditional gold watch or diamond ring, award post-meeting tours of a duration and luxury consistent with the importance of the achievement. Travel is a great motivator, and the nostalgia of a memorable trip lasts long after the jewelry is consigned to a dresser drawer.

COMMUNICATING PROGRAM DETAILS

Once the program begins to take shape, the PCO prepares an event schedule, listing all program components from staff arrival to post-conference critique. This document goes through several stages of development as new information is received, loose ends are tied up, and changes are made. Because changes are inevitable, the event schedule is best generated as a computer document.

One component of the event schedule is the heading, which includes the name of the event and a revision date. A typical schedule's column headings are Day/Time, Location, Event, Number of attendees, Setup (theater, schoolroom, etc.), Audiovisual and Staging, Remarks. (See the sample event schedule at the end of this chapter.)

The event schedule is communicated to the hotel or center and changes or additions are sent as they are documented. This schedule becomes the basis for the facility's own document, the event orders (formerly Banquet Event Order, and still called "BEO.")* Each event is numbered and listed on a separate BEO; this serves as confirmation to the meeting executive and as an internal control form, communicating meeting details to all departments and the banquet staff. In addition to the information from the event schedule, BEOs list details of room setup, special staging, equipment, food and beverage selection, and charges. These records are also dated (they tend to change as new information is received). Reviewed and signed by the PCO, they become the backup for final billing.

---

* Note: One form that is part of the Meeting and Exhibition Specification Guide developed by the APEX Terminology Panel referred to in Chapter 4 is key: the Event Order (EO). This document provides specifications for each function that is part of the overall meeting or event. It is expected to replace the time-honored Banquet Event Order in use, if not in name.

The theatrical or film director is accountable for assembling the many elements called for in the script and for directing the actors and crew to achieve a memorable production. The Professional Conference Organizer does much the same thing: He or she makes certain that the program's design, pacing, and elements are blended into a smooth-running, high-impact event that achieves the meeting's objective.

Resources:

Goldblatt, Joe Jeff. *Special Events, Twenty-first Century Global Event Management* (New York: Wiley & Sons).

SAMPLE STAGING SPECIFICATIONS RIDER

EVENT: AAA Convention Banquet

PURCHASER: American Accounting Assn.

ARTIST(S): New Christy Minstrels   **PRODUCER:** Howard Lanin Productions

In addition to the terms and conditions provided in the attached contract, it is further agreed by the parties that Purchaser shall arrange for and provide at his sole expense for this engagement, the following:

1. A professional quality sound system with sufficient speakers to provide clear, undistorted sound reinforcement evenly distributed throughout audience area. Said system must include a minimum of 12 professional quality microphones consisting of:

   A. Seven (7) vocal microphones on straight stands with removable heads and 25 feet of cable per microphone.

   B. Five (5) instrumental microphones on boom stands.

   C. System shall include a high-quality bass amplifier.

2. Two (2) follow spotlights in good working condition capable of illuminating artists on stage with full stage light, and two (2) experienced spot operators. The following gels will be required:
   flesh pink, lavender, red, blue, light amber, or straw.

3. An intercom system with headset communications between stage manager and sound man, both spot operators and lighting control.

4. A stage area not less than 24 feet wide and 16 feet deep. (See attached sketch for dimensions and microphone placement.) If stage is a non-permanent or rapidly constructed type, it is critically important to check the performing area for microphone stand stability and foot vibration. Purchaser shall provide carpeting if required.

5. Separate, clean, private dressing rooms for men and women, equipped with bathrooms, that are climate-controlled, inaccessible to the public during and after performance, and under lock control by the troupe manager.

6. Purchaser shall guarantee proper security at all times to ensure the safety of artists, instruments, and personal property.

THIS RIDER IS A PART OF THE ATTACHED CONTRACT BY REFERENCE.

ACKNOWLEDGED: _____   (PURCHASER)

FIGURE 6-4 Staging specifications rider.

Program Elements **87**

GOVERNOR'S TOURISM CONFERENCE   EVENT SCHEDULE   Revised: _____

Day/Time	Room	Event	Number	Setup	Audiovisual	Remarks
Wednesday						
11:00	(suggest)	Pre-conference meeting		conference		
1:00	Pre-conference area	Registration setup		Two 8' tables; One 6' table	One house phone; one outside phone	3 chairs, wastebasket, 2 easels
1:00	Vail/Steamboat	Exhibit area setup		8'×30" draped tables	SEE NOTES	Pipe and drape to be determined
4:00	Silverton. Breck	AV setup/Rehearsal	350	Theater, staging	Agency supplies AV	Details to come
6:00	Vail/Steamboat	Opening Reception	150	Reception	Standing microphone	
Thursday						
7:30	Pre-conf. area	Registration				
7:30	Vail/Steamboat	Continental Breakfast	150	Buffet Exhibit area		Exhibits/Auction open
8:30	Silverton. Breck	Opening Ceremony	350	Theater, Stage	Agency provides AV	Flags, lectern, table for 20
9:00	Silverton. Breck	Praeco presentation	350			
9:45	Silverton. Breck	Tourism promotion	350			
10:30	Vail/Steamboat	BREAK				
11:00	Silverton. Breck	CTO panel discussion	350	Panel seating for 20	6' table; 4 wireless microphones	Mixer
12:30	TC Room B	Luncheon	275	Podium, lectern	lectern microphone, lavalier microphone	Round 10's (See BEO for Menu)
2:00	Breckenridge	US Travel Trends	200	Podium, lectern	lectern microphone, data projector	
3:00	Telluride	Customer Relations	60	Classroom		
3:00	Aspen	Transportation Issues	75			

(*Continued*)

88 Planning

Day/Time	Room	Event	Number	Setup	Audiovisual	Remarks
3:00	Silverton	Cultural Tourism	125	Classroom		
3:00	Breckenridge	Training and Education	125	Theater	Data Projector, screen	
4:00	Vail/Steamboat	BREAK				See BEO for Menu
4:30	Telluride	Customer Relations cont'd	60	Classroom		
4:30	Aspen	Shopping and Tourism	75	panel table for 5	Table microphones (5)	
4:30	Silverton	Outdoor Recreation	125	Classroom		
5:30 -7:00	Vail/Steamboat	Reception	125			
Friday						
7:30	Pre-conference area	Registration				
7:30	Vail/Steamboat	Exhibits				Auction closed
7:30	Silverton/Breck	Breakfast	125	8' rounds, stage TBA	TBA	
		Future of Skiing				
9:00	"	Sustainable Tourism	150		Data Projector, screen	
10:00	TBA	BREAK				Reset (See BEO for Menu)
10:30	Silverton	Sustainable Tourism				Turn room (but keep rounds)
10:30	Breckenridge	Marketing on Internet	60		TBA	
10:30	Aspen	Message to Media	60		TBA	
12:00		Conference ends				
1:00	(CSM suggest)	Staff Critique		conference		
NOTE:	Phones, power outlets, easels, AV, and special equipment charged to exhibitors' account					

Part Three:

Administration and Logistics

Chapter Seven
Budgeting and Fiscal Management

Responsible fiscal management is essential to any event and is among the meeting executive's most important responsibilities. For corporate meetings, staying within budget is a gauge of the planner's competence; for association events, budgeting to generate revenue is a critical measure of success. The process for managing revenues and expenses can be automated using off-the-shelf spreadsheet software programs such as Quicken. However, most PCOs prefer meeting-specific software that is part of a suite of event-management applications (see Appendix B). Custom programs simplify event-related calculations such as registration fees, break-even, and changes in variable expenses based on number of registrants.

An initial working budget can be prepared once the meeting prospectus with its basic assumptions has been completed. The working budget is not cast in concrete; in fact, it must be revised periodically to reflect changes in attendance, costs, and added requirements. PCOs who conduct the same type of meeting year after year rely on the simple expedient of analyzing last year's meeting and then budgeting 10 to 15 percent more. (After all, has anyone seen meeting costs go down?) They are thus able to estimate accurately by identifying areas where savings can be achieved to compensate for overruns in other areas.

MAJOR BUDGET ITEMS

Costs for accommodations differ according to site, season, occupancy, class of hotel, and room distribution. Given those variables, one constant that seems to have become an immutable law is that this year's price will be higher than last year's. Occasionally, overbuilding or a catastrophic event forces hoteliers to reduce prices in order to attract business. The

92 Administration and Logistics

logical approach is to establish a range of dates and a variety of acceptable choices that fit the budget. A principle of negotiations to keep in mind at this stage is that it is not the hotel's responsibility to provide a product at a price the organization can afford. It is the company manager's responsibility to budget realistically and then approach only those hotels that can satisfy the service standards within budget limitations. This is especially crucial for association meeting planners whose attendance, and hence revenue, can be adversely affected by hotel room rates beyond the attendees' means.

Transportation costs can vary greatly in this age of aggressive competition. Some PCOs have found it advantageous, before site selection procedures begin, to ask their travel agency or travel department to provide an air fare cost analysis, comparing several potential destinations. It is advisable to budget for full coach fare and lock in a guaranteed discounted group fare, thus creating a budget reserve. Vouchers for limo or motorcoach transfers from the airport to the hotel are less expensive alternatives to per-person airport reception. Other ground transportation for off-site activities is budgeted as part of recreational and leisure events.

CONTROLLING EXPENSES

Most meeting managers create some kind of a budget worksheet. Figures 7-1 and 7-2 show two examples with fixed and variable expenses. *Fixed* expenses cover those items that are the same regardless of attendance.

The meeting budget and the post-meeting budget reconciliation are often viewed as the PCO's report card—a measure of competence. Consequently, careful budgeting by line item, constant monitoring, and meticulous accounting are vital in order to avoid budget overruns. Here are some additional guidelines:

- Update and revise the initial budget as requirements and numbers change. Forward copies to management.
- Provide a detailed master account instruction document for the hotel, limiting and specifying the persons authorized to sign banquet checks, equipment orders, and cash payouts.
- Specify which executives are authorized to charge rooms, hospitality services, and incidentals to the master account.
- Advise speakers on which expenses will be covered by the organization, which can be charged to the room folio, and expenses for which they are responsible.
- Prepare detailed function control forms for each event, listing all approved charges, guarantees, and methods of validating guarantees.

Budget Planner

Time and Budget Control

Meeting Cost Estimate

Facility Services			Actual Costs
Rooms (Administration)	No. _____ @$ _____	$ _____	$ _____
Rooms (Guests)	No. _____ @$ _____	$ _____	$ _____
Meeting rooms	Ballroom		
Conference rooms or breakout rooms	No. _____ @$ _____	$ _____	$ _____
Hospitality suite		$ _____	$ _____
Complimentary rooms	No. _____		
Food	No. of persons	Rate	
Breakfast	_____	$ _____	$ _____	$ _____
Lunch (brunch)	_____	$ _____	$ _____	$ _____
Dinner	_____	$ _____	$ _____	$ _____
Coffee breaks	_____	$ _____	$ _____	$ _____
Beverage	No. of bottles	Cost	
Cocktail party	_____	$ _____	$ _____	$ _____
Hospitality suite	_____	$ _____	$ _____	$ _____
Reception	_____	$ _____	$ _____	$ _____
Dinner	_____	$ _____	$ _____	$ _____
Transportation	No. of people	Avg. Cost	
Plane or railroad fares	_____	$ _____	$ _____	$ _____
Taxi or bus transportation	_____	$ _____	$ _____	$ _____
Cartage and freight	_____	$ _____	$ _____	$ _____
Wages			
Planning salaries	_____	$ _____	$ _____
Staffing salaries	_____	$ _____	$ _____
Security services	_____	$ _____	$ _____
Other outside services	_____	$ _____	$ _____
Audio/Visual Support			
Labor costs		$ _____	$ _____
Equipment rental		$ _____	$ _____
Production costs		$ _____	$ _____

Total estimated daily cost $ _____   Total actual cost $ _____

FIGURE 7-1 Budget worksheet—corporate.

Copy staff members responsible for the event. Request hotel setup and banquet orders well in advance, and compare their specifications with yours. Correct discrepancies.

- Keep track of guarantee adjustments, additional orders, and catering replenishment orders. Record these on your control forms.
- Request that banquet checks be presented promptly. Compare with control form and discuss discrepancies with captain or catering manager.

BUDGET WORKSHEET

Meeting: **Dates:**

Participants: **Guests:**   **Cost per head $**

FIXED EXPENSES	PROJECTED	MISCELLANEOUS	
PROGRAM: $ Speaker fees Speaker expenses Audiovisual production AV rental, staging, staff Program elements Guest program Entertainment		Decoration Theme support Signate Board and committee expense Gifts, awards Shipping Photography Special gratuities Management fees	
PROMOTION: Production and printing Translation Mailing Advertising		**Total Fixed Expenses** $ **VARIABLE EXPENSES** Unit cost Extension	

REGISTRATION:
Materials
Lists, labels
Mailing
Processing
On-site administration
		Air fares $
		Ground transport
		Food and Beverage:
		   Meals
		   Breaks
		   Receptions
		   Taxes and gratuities	

STAFF: Staff travel Housing, meals Clerical staff On-site transportation		Program materials Badges Room gifts, favors Recreational	
FACILITIES: Meeting rooms Hospitality suite Exhibit space Other		Miscellaneous **Total variable expenses $** **contingency** **PROJECTED TOTAL:** $	

FIGURE 7-2 Budget worksheet—association.

- Ask for a daily accounting of master account charges for the previous day's functions. Resolve disputed charges promptly. Request copies of backup vouchers on disputed items with final accounting.
- During the pre-conference meeting, review function control forms and identify potential problem areas. Schedule a meeting for after the conference with the hotel accounting office to review charges.

- Analyze and allocate expenditures that properly belong in operating budgets or overhead, though they may occur during the planning phase or at the meeting (e.g., postage, telephone, certain travel expenses).

It would be nice to have a financial crystal ball that accurately predicted all meeting expenses. Lacking that, most budgets include a percentage for contingency. After all, you can hardly end a four-day meeting on the third day by telling everyone to go home because the budget ran out. PCOs who manage multiple meetings or central meeting departments customarily work with an annual budget. This allows them to average costs among meetings. But even they need to have a contingency fund, if for no other reason than to cover those short, unexpected meetings that are invariably called. The budget has to be considered a flexible document that will undergo adjustments between formulation and reconciliation.

Veteran meeting authority Bill Grusich cautions planners to consider unforeseen charges:

> Meeting planners report charges for pitchers of water, notepads and pencils, or even such necessities as table linens appearing on hotel fees. One planner was shocked to discover that it cost more to have meeting materials delivered from the hotel's storeroom than it did to ship them across the country. Since such extras are rarely discussed at contract time, planners are understandably upset when unforeseen charges appear on the hotel bill and they are unsure about how best to handle such matters.

Grusich, president of the hotel representative firm of Hinton and Grusich, cautions that such clients' "killer extras" will make a shambles of the budget.

DETERMINING FEES

The first priority in establishing a fee structure is to analyze all meeting elements outlined in the initial budget and determine fixed expenses. The example shown in Figure 7-2 lists those expenses, though they will vary from event to event. If income to offset fixed and variable expenses is derived primarily from registration fees, there is a greater need for accurate projection than where other sources of revenue exist, such as exhibitor fees, sponsorships, and advertising.

Next, the organizers project minimum and optimum attendance figures based on previous events. If there is no history, this step becomes a critical procedure and budget planning must include provisions for interim funding, a substantial percentage for contingency, and a higher promotional expense. Planning might also provide for a break-even point and a decision to cancel if that point is not reached within a reasonable time. (Fees will be refunded and the organizers will absorb the losses represented by fixed expenses.)

Based on attendance projections, the PCO computes cost per-head, taking into consideration those variable expenses listed in Figure 7-2. Registration fees are determined by applying the following formula:

$$R = \frac{V+F+C}{D}$$

R = Registration Fee
V = Variable, per capita costs
F = Fixed costs
C = Contingency
D = Break-even projection of delegate attendance

In determining the fee for accompanying persons, most planners omit the fixed costs on the assumption that these are covered by the delegate's fee. However, those fixed costs that specifically apply to guests, such as entertainment and transportation, should be factored into the variable costs. Compute these, and use this formula for guests:

$$R = \frac{V+C}{A/P}$$

A/P = accompanying person or guest

REVENUE PROJECTION

Once these formulas are applied, the PCO computes anticipated income and expense by creating a reasonable income model that projects:

- Early registrations for:
    - Delegates only (number) × (fee)
    - Delegates with guests
- Non-member registrations and other fee-paying categories
- Late registrations for the same three categories
- Cancellation penalties
- Other revenues

Then, fixed and variable expenses (plus contingency) are entered and deducted from total revenues to arrive at a desired profit or surplus. The surplus, if there is one, becomes the safety margin. By building in a contingency—10 to 15 percent of the fixed cost (which some organizations call a profit margin)—the PCO safeguards a revenue sufficient to satisfy the budget in case the actual numbers fall short of the projections.

There are, however, other considerations in setting fees. Foremost of these are market and economic conditions and attendee profile. Indeed, the success of the event might hinge on whether the fee is perceived as being reasonable. A high fee will reduce the number of attendees, whereas a fee too low may still not attract the requisite number of attendees, and thus place the organizers in jeopardy. Some knowledgeable meeting professionals address this dilemma by soliciting attendee viewpoints on their evaluation forms or by circulating questionnaires. Others abide by the formulas and factor into their planning cost-cutting methods that can be applied if attendance falls short of the desired level.

Incentives for early registration benefit cash flow and increase planning time. The most obvious is an early registration discount. (The average attendee views this as a late registration penalty.) Other incentives for registering early might be one or more nights of free lodging (utilizing complimentary room allotments), room upgrades, a drawing for complimentary registration, drawing for a free airline ticket to the meeting or a post-conference destination, and special amenities at the meeting site. With the incentive carrot, however, there must be a stick to avoid attendee attrition and hold cancellation refunds to a minimum. Most PCOs apply a staggered formula that reduces the amount of the refund as the meeting date draws near. To ensure fairness, the refund policy must be strictly adhered to, though unusual circumstances, handled case by case, may be given special consideration. The cancellation penalty must be clearly stated in the registration information.

Unless there are other sources of revenue such as exhibit booth rentals or sponsorships, it is important to be sure that the early registration fee or discounted fee is adequate to cover all variables and a proportionate share of fixed costs. Since this is the base fee derived from the formula, the "late" fee does indeed carry a penalty—bad news for procrastinators but good news for the organizers, since these penalties help supplement income and increase safety margins.

EXHIBITS

Exhibits can be a substantial source of revenue. They can be a financial failure, however, if the expenses related to marketing and managing them are not carefully planned and constantly monitored. The basic premise is that the show organizer rents the hall or room at a gross rate, determines total booth capacity based on net saleable space, and arrives at a per-booth price that includes rental cost, certain services, and a profit margin. If that seems overly simplistic, it is. Obviously, there are other considerations. A

INCOME MODEL—ANNUAL CONVENTION

Revenues

Early registrations:

Delegates only — 200 @ 275	$ 55,000
Delegates w/guests — 150 @ 400	60,000
Non-members — 50 @ 350	17,500

Late registrations:

Delegates only — 100 @ 350	35,000
Delegated w/guests — 50 @ 475	23,750
Non-members — 30 @ 425	12,750
Cancellation Penalties — 30 @ 100 (avg)	3,000
Exhibit booth sales — 100 @ 650	65,000
Extra exhibitor registrations — 30 @ 275	8,250
Educational product sales (estimated)	4,000
Sponsorship off-sets (estimated)	40,000
Total Revenues	**$316,000**

Fixed Expenses

Administration	30,000
Operations	36,000
Program	22,000

Variable Expenses

580 registrants @ 180	104,400
200 guests @ 110	22,000
230 exhibitors @ 130	29,900
Total Fixed & Variable Expenses	244,300
Contingency	36,600
TOTAL	280,900
Anticipated surplus	35,100

FIGURE 7-3 Revenue projection.

realistic analysis of potential exhibitors will determine the size of the show and the facility. The scope of the show is further influenced by the venue and other industry events that may be in conflict. Cities and halls, which have a reputation for high labor costs and inflexible union regulations, tend to discourage exhibitors. (Further details on exhibit costs are covered in Chapter 14.)

RECONCILIATION

Once the meeting is concluded and all the charges and disputes have been resolved, the PCO prepares a budget report reconciling, by line item, the initial budgeted amount and adjustments with the actual expenditures. The report designates items charged to contingency and includes an overall summation reflecting whether the event was over or under budget (see Figure 16-3 for an example of this report). This document serves as a measure of performance and fiscal responsibility and is a valuable planning and negotiating instrument for subsequent events.

RESIDUAL REVENUES

The chief executive of an association presided over a conference notable for the value of its educational content and the caliber of the presenters. In a closing statement, he drew applause by announcing that an unprecedented 38 percent of the association's members attended the meeting.

But what of the remaining 62 percent?

If the content was valuable enough for the attendees to pay the registration fee, transportation, and lodging, wouldn't it have residual value for those members who didn't or couldn't attend? Astute association executives have discovered that bringing the meeting to the absentees not only affords them a value-added dimension to their membership, but also provides the organization with a collateral revenue source.

Research by the On-Line Publishers Associations (OPA) reveals that people are willing to pay for online educational content. Since 2001, Internet users have gone beyond surfing and are putting their money where their mouse is. Web casting is now largely accepted and many of those association or corporate absentees recognize that the information they missed out on may be important to their careers or businesses. Even those delegates who attended might benefit from a refresher course.

This trend is being recognized as an added member benefit as well as a source of revenue. Organizations are now documenting key presentations and Web casting them during or after the conference or offering copies on tape, CD, or DVD.

There are no magic formulas for budgeting. Sound fiscal management is the end result of the PCO's cumulative experience, analysis of the organization's meeting history, understanding of facility pricing structures, and sound financial controls, tempered by a good deal of common sense.

Chapter Eight
Getting There: Air and Ground Travel

Airlines are generally the primary form of travel, but some attendees will drive or go by train if the site is within convenient travel distance. It is rare to find a meeting sponsor who takes a "let them get to the meeting on their own" attitude, even among associations whose members traditionally make their own travel arrangements. They, like their corporate counterparts, charge the meeting organizer with the responsibility of researching, negotiating, and disseminating information on convenient, economical air travel. Indeed, association meeting executives have become enthusiastic air negotiators upon discovering the promotional benefits airlines offer—often at no cost.

Travel planning starts with a distribution analysis. Where are people coming from? That information may be available from travel patterns of past meetings, the organization's geographic dispersal, or the registration list. However, the PCO must not wait until registrations are in to begin travel negotiations because travel information should be included in promotional mailings. Most PCOs review past history and demographics, and then formulate a list of primary originating points.

PLANNING AND NEGOTIATING AIR TRAVEL

There are several resources available to assist the planner in developing a comprehensive transportation plan. Travel agencies experienced in commercial and group travel can research fares and provide an analysis of cost-effective destinations, as well as handle ticketing and administration. Caution is in order here, however; check the agency's credentials and experience. Small retail travel agents often lack experience in commercial and group travel. Another resource is the airlines themselves. In recognition of the market's potential, most major airlines have established convention sales departments staffed by meeting specialists. Begin by contacting the convention staff of the airlines serving your destination, provide the essential information about your meeting, and request a proposal.

Meetings have become a major market segment for most carriers. Increased competition and the efforts of industry associations, such as Meeting Professionals International, have resulted in more latitude in negotiations and marketing support. You can obtain the best service and fares for your meeting attendees by learning and understanding fare policies, airline nomenclature, and basically, what airlines can and cannot provide.

Be prepared to supply the travel agency or airline representative with as much detail as you have on meeting objectives, dates, venue, and estimates on how many people will be traveling by air. Compile a list of probable originating cities and a likely percentage departing from each. Since airline lift capacities (the number of passengers that can be carried on any given day) vary among airlines and destinations, information about your group is essential. Conversely, knowing their lift capacities can assist you in selecting the airline best qualified to transport your group.

Fare Structure

A knowledgeable travel counselor can be a valuable asset for keeping track of the roller-coaster world of airline fares. The negotiated group discounted fare may not be the most economical when actual ticketing occurs. A phenomenon called "zone pricing," which provides discounted promotional fares between two cities, or sudden price wars in certain destinations can have a substantial effect on fares. Professional travel counselors and airline meeting staff are able to keep up with these changes in this mercurial marketplace. Understanding restrictions and their effect is also essential. For example, the PCO can qualify meeting attendees for a reduced fare by encouraging them to travel on Saturday instead of Sunday for a Monday meeting start. This can be tied in to a reduced "early bird" room rate at the hotel if Saturday is traditionally a low occupancy day for that property.

Negotiating with Airlines

In order to negotiate effectively, it is important that you understand that airlines set their fares using a revenue management system. Under this method, demand at different fare levels is estimated based on current and historical booking data, and inventory is allocated accordingly to get the best mix of revenue with a view to cover operating costs, overhead, and—hopefully—a profit. Financial reports showing losses in the billions attest that such is not always the case. An airline seat is a perishable commodity; carriers overbook to cover potential shortfalls. Revenue management allows airlines to estimate the number of seats that can be discounted on any given flight. A cursory understanding of revenue management can be helpful in negotiating group fares.

The choice of an airline for a destination served by more than one carrier is usually determined by reputation for service and safety, frequency, scheduling, and lift capacity. Experienced travel planners will contact several carriers that meet the desired criteria and focus on the eligible ones, weighing their advantages and limitations. The object is to select one official airline, thus maximizing negotiating position. As in any meeting activity, the prime consideration is service rather than price.

There are two primary fare concessions the PCO can negotiate. The most common is a percentage discount off standard coach fare. (Most carriers do not offer discounts on lower published fares, since these are already discounted, and discounts are subject to change.) The percentage discount off coach might not be the best fare, but it does guarantee a discount for all attendees, even those originating in cities where there is no promotional fare. The option of changing to a lower promotional fare, if offered, is usually available, though there may be restrictions. The second concession is a guaranteed fare contracted well in advance and backed by a deposit that is usually paid by the sponsoring organization. The latter offers less opportunity to take advantage of new promotional fares, and usually requires a minimum number of passengers (making it more of a group fare). An organization that guarantees repeat business and volume can enjoy substantial benefits. The National Passenger Traffic Association (NPTA) is a valuable source of information on special fares and other aspects of air travel.

As in all negotiations, there is a quid pro quo. In return for the reduced fares, the meeting organizer agrees to designate the airline as the official carrier, and, if air travel is paid by the organization, will ticket all or most travelers on that carrier. Travelers originating from points not served by the official airline may be eligible for reduced fares when the airline enters into a reciprocal arrangement or a partner status with another airline. The meeting organizer agrees to promote the official airline (or designated travel agency) publicizing the Web site and toll-free telephone number to travelers making their own arrangements.

Fare negotiations are usually centered on a 10 to 30 percent discount off full coach fare. It may be offered to all attendees, regardless of point of origin. Depending on the time of year and size of the group and whether or not there are airlines serving the destination, the PCO might have significant leverage in fare pricing. Yield or revenue passenger miles determines the profitability of a specific flight. The negotiating parties seek a balance between reduced fare seats and the higher yield full fares.

104 Administration and Logistics

Ask the airline representative to describe their peak periods, blackout periods, low load factors, and the percentage of empty seats on given flights. Knowing when the airline needs group business will influence the percentage of discounts, group fares, and other concessions.

WHAT AIRLINES CAN DO FOR MEETINGS

Lower fares are not the only inducements offered by air carriers. It is useful for planners to understand what airlines can provide and how these concessions can often surpass the benefits of fare reduction. Some valuable services to assist the PCO in planning, promoting, and staging the event are also open to discussion. Benefits to be negotiated with the official airline are:

- Complimentary or reduced-fare tickets for meeting staff used for site selection, pre-conference coordination trips, and other meeting travel. (Rare, but some airlines may allow this concession.)
- A percentage of complimentary seats for staff members accompanying the group. (Also rare.)
- Credits that can be redeemed by the trip organizer or meeting planner for free tickets, lounge passes, lounge memberships, onboard "currency" for drinks or headsets, and upgrades. *These credits are earned post travel.*
- Restriction waivers on incentive and promotional fares and subsidies on joint fares from originating cities to gateways and hubs.
- Seat blocks, permitting the group to sit together as a group.
- Promotional assistance such as mailing shells imprinted with the organization's message, mailing assistance, complimentary tickets and upgrades to be used to promote attendance, site videos, and literature. Advertising in association publications (paid or traded).
- Single invoice billing for all tickets, regardless of the originating point.
- Special in-flight amenities: a group welcome by the captain, free beverages, customized comfort or convenience items such as flight bags and luggage tags, etc.
- Ground conveniences: use of club lounges at departure and transit terminals, early boarding, group holding area, first-off baggage handling, welcome banners, assistance with ground transportation, etc.

- Freight assistance and special rates for meeting materials and equipment. Special freight rates can effect substantial savings if a large volume of materials must be shipped to the meeting site. Some airlines offer as much as 300 pounds of complimentary air freight for every 50 passenger seats booked.

Event-oriented airlines also have staff assigned to help with planning, site research, and liaison. Typical of these is Continental Airlines' MeetingWorks, which is staffed by knowledgeable meeting professionals who have Web sites and dedicated toll-free telephone lines to provide meeting information to delegates and attendees. At the operation phase, the PCO can request updated manifests listing attendees' flight numbers and arrival times—a valuable tool for ground arrangements and for verifying room blocks. However, this feature can only work if travelers make their arrangements using the event code assigned by the official airline.

At the time of this writing, a new entity has entered the meetings market: online travel agencies such as Travelocity, Orbitz, and Expedia. They have built loyal customer bases with online retail and business travel, but plan to offer group travel services shortly. Some are affiliating with event-technology companies or third-party organizations that offer site research services. How this strategy plays out and what impact it will have on the airline industry and travel agencies remains to be seen.

GROUND TRANSPORTATION

Ground transportation is the other component of travel planning and management. Whatever the size or location of the event, some form of ground transportation is involved; airport transfers, car rentals, hotel shuttles, and other modes of surface transit move groups to attractions and off-site activities. The PCO needs to have a thorough knowledge of available resources such as destination management companies (DMCs), bus companies, and car rental firms.

In planning for attendee arrivals, the meeting manager may work with a DMC or ground operator, coordinate with the airline or hotel, or let attendees arrive at the hotel on their own. In the latter case, travelers should be given detailed information on distance and directions from the airport to the hotel; cost of taxis, limos, and mass transit; and availability of car rentals. Some meeting organizers will designate an official car rental agency and negotiate a reduced convention rate.

The cost of providing reception services at the point of arrival is returned in tangible dividends. Everything about the meeting creates an impression, starting with arrival at the airport. A greeting by a guide or a welcome banner or perhaps a group of young people in regional costume imparts a warm welcome and feeling of importance. It is remembered long after the proceedings are over and souvenirs have started to gather dust.

At most events, what is desirable for the average attendee is essential for VIPs. See "Handling VIPs" in Chapter 15 for more on this topic.

SELECTING A DESTINATION MANAGER

Many meeting organizers prefer to work with a ground operator or destination management company (DMC). With their intimate knowledge of the venue, they bring an added dimension of service and creativity to the meeting. They relieve event managers of some of the burdensome mechanics, allowing them to concentrate on the dynamics. A good DMC is said to be worth its weight in gold. PCOs returning to a venue tend to use the same company again and again; companies that earn their clients' respect are those that pick up attendees as a group, treat them as individuals, and deliver them on time, but also add creativity and a friendly attitude to their efficiency.

Patti Roscoe, Chairman of PRA Destination Management, offers these benefits of working with destination professionals:

- A qualified, well-connected DMC is a planner's prime asset in any destination—domestic or international.

- DMCs have the experience and knowledge to use local resources creatively and cost-effectively to meet and exceed a program's objectives.

- Destination professionals have a client's best interest at heart and will be blatantly honest about what works and doesn't work in a given destination.

- The DMC's strength and buying power go a long way in meeting budget parameters, without jeopardizing quality and service.

- Because of their business volume, they can bypass long lines at cultural facilities and attractions.

Roscoe recognizes the VIP status of meeting and incentive attendees. "DMCs provide the trained, professional staff to insure that a program is handled efficiently and that it provides a cordial, memorable experience for all."

Finding competent DMCs is no problem at most meeting venues. Ask the airline, national tourist office, ConVis bureau, or hotel sales staff to recommend at least two established and stable companies. Ask about the groups they have serviced recently, and call those prior clientele. Their experience is a valuable yardstick for gauging the DMCs' competence, creativity, performance, and integrity. Interview each one, providing precise details on your support requirements, and request a proposal. Do not feel compelled, however, to accept the low bid unless there is a wide discrepancy in pricing. Consider the following questions before final selection:

- Is the quotation all inclusive, or are there other charges such as gratuities, tax, and surcharges?
- Does the proposal reflect flexibility and willingness to tailor the program to accommodate your group's special needs? Are they responsive to the PCO's ideas?
- If charges are on a per-head basis, is it more economical to compute per hour or per vehicle, with a fee to cover staff and special services?
- What are the number, type, capacity, and condition of vehicles? Are they being used to service another meeting the same day, possibly incurring delays?
- Will DMC staff accompany each vehicle and act as tour guides, if such a service is called for?
- Will the staff be readily identifiable at the airport (signs, badges, uniforms)? Are there provisions for delayed flights?
- For international events, can DMC provide multilingual staff?
- What gratuities are paid and how? By cash or master billing?
- Does DMC have adequate liability insurance; what are the limits?
- What special services are included or available at additional cost (refreshments, signs, baggage handling, entertainment)?

Patti Roscoe adds these further suggestions: "Ensure that the DMC is well connected, not only within the industry, but also the community. Those affiliations offer the client valuable contacts. Be sure the chosen DMC has the financial capacity to manage the program and has an emergency security plan in place."

BUSES, VANS, LIMOUSINES

Some PCOs choose to contract directly for ground transportation or use a DMC for some events and contract for others. In addition to the above guidelines, apply these criteria when working with motorcoach and car hire companies:

- For minimum rental period and cost of additional hours, does rental begin at spot time, or is dead time charged? If the latter, what is driving time from garage to pick-up and drop-off points?

- Can minimum rental be split into two short runs the same day?
- Is there a surcharge for mileage? How is it computed?
- Will all vehicles be uniform? Are they company-owned, or subcontracted?
- Is back-up equipment available in case of breakdown or added loads?
- What are minimum and typical turnaround times for each event?
- Are some events more suitable to one-way transfer rates, rather than minimum charter? If so, how are charges computed?
- How are vehicles dispatched? Is there two-way radio communication?
- Does the company provide a coordinator for the event?
- What is the deadline for cancellation or reduction without penalty?
- Are coaches air-conditioned? Equipped with PA systems? Toilets (for long-haul trips)? Are there provisions for the handicapped?
- What types of vehicles are available for VIP, special transportation, and staff needs? What are the rates for various categories?
- Are there parking or access restrictions at pick-up and drop-off points?
- Ascertain what hotels have shuttle services.

If time permits, drive the routes to be used, preferably with a local guide and under similar traffic conditions to verify distances and turnaround times and to spot potential hazards and bottlenecks. It is also advisable to plan for contingencies such as inclement weather and delayed flights. The airport reception plan should be flexible and cost-effective. (For example, release buses after peak arrival times and augment with stretch vans for smaller numbers of people). Use the less expensive vans, a rental car, or courtesy cars driven by a staff member or hotel staff to pick up late arrivals. Check with the convention and visitors' bureau during site inspection. These organizations often offer to provide or share the cost of ground transportation.

The event sponsors can also help simplify the attendees' travel experience. Some of the gimmicks the author has used to ease the burdens of air travel are:

- Provide attendees with distinctive buttons, tags, or decals bearing the conference theme. They identify passengers to one another at the airport and on the flight.

- Send share-a-cab or rental car information for people arriving on the same flight if transfers are not offered.
- Conversely, furnish sign-up and departure schedules for cab or car sharing from hotel to airport.

CAR RENTALS

Meeting planners and business travelers considering car rental frequently encounter an overwhelming array of rental prices, categories, and discounts. Many car rental companies, having discovered the potential of the meeting market, have established convention and group departments, staffed by specialists who can help the hapless buyer through this bewildering maze. Rental companies may also supply complimentary cars for site inspections. The major car rental firms can offer the PCO a group or convention rate usually equal to a corporate rate, and will consider extending those rates several days before and after the meeting if asked. Except in high-density metropolitan areas, car rentals offer many advantages. The organization can benefit by qualifying for free staff cars based on the ratio of cars rented (customarily one for every twenty). This benefit is especially valuable for association meetings.

One point to keep in mind during negotiations: Auto rental companies have come under criticism for the excessive rates charged for collision/damage waivers. Most of their customers are covered under their own or their companies' policies for damages to rental automobiles; the rates charged by car rental agencies will thus be redundant, and may be as high as 30 percent of the daily rate. Have attendees verify their insurance coverage and advise them to decline CDW if covered. In your negotiations, see if the collision/damage waiver can be provided free of charge.

Car rental firms will assist the meeting sponsor in publicizing availability of convention rates by providing a special group code, rate schedules (mailed to attendees or included with registration kits), special group IDs, and amenities. Other negotiable services include personalized welcome and directional signs at airports, one-way drop-off fee waivers, an on-site rental desk if large numbers are involved, and post-meeting utilization reports. PCOs who customarily make use of the same company are afforded year-round special rates comparable to a travel agency rate. Volume users may also be able to negotiate rental company vans and buses (the vehicles used for airport shuttle service) to augment their shuttle requirements.

Chapter Nine
Event Promotion and Marketing

MARKETING THE EVENT

Promotion is as vital to the ultimate success of any meeting as any other planning element. Some industry gurus call it "marketing" rather than "promotion," implying with some justification that the event must be sold. This is true not only of association conventions at which attendance is voluntary, but even for corporate meetings, since an audience that wants to attend will be more receptive and inspired than one attending "because the boss said so!" A company hoping to attract independent dealers or representatives to a sales meeting must employ marketing techniques. And for incentive meetings, where attendance demands an extra effort to qualify, the promotional materials help recipients decide whether the reward is worth that effort. For such events, a dynamic, motivational marketing program is manifested in positive bottom-line results. The task goes beyond getting people to attend: A proper marketing program creates a sense of anticipation and delivers an audience that is prepared, informed, and receptive to the sponsor's message.

Most meeting executives feel that the one aspect of the planning process that contributes to the success of the meeting is the Advance Meeting Information Release. This is a document sent by mail or electronic means well in advance of the event alerting potential attendees and advising them of the dates and venue. A well-designed program of promotion and publicity gives participants everything they need to know about getting to the meeting from home and back, as well as details on the venue, and what they can expect and what is expected of them when they arrive.

Whether you are marketing breakfast cereal or seminars or conventions, the principles are essentially the same:

- Analyze market demographics, perceived problems, and needs.
- Design a program or "product" that addresses those needs.
- Create a dynamic theme or "package design" in marketing terms.
- Determine the most-effective media to reach the target audience.
- Communicate the message with effective advertising and publicity.

MEDIA ANALYSIS

Direct marketing by mail or e-mail is the most common and effective medium to promote a meeting, but it should be reinforced with other methods when the budget allows. The PCO determines other types of appropriate media for the target audience (such as dedicated Web sites) and uses them selectively to augment the primary medium. For example:

- Trade publications and professional journals are logical conduits for publicity. Display advertising can be effective if used with some frequency.
- In-house publications and newsletters offer a low-cost medium for a targeted audience.
- For certain types of events, the business press (magazines and newspapers) might be effective, but analyze cost and market reach.
- Posters can be useful for a well-defined, closely targeted audience such as employees, community groups, and institutions.

A marketing medium that is often overlooked is the venue itself and the various contractors who supply goods or services in support of the meeting. Many of them have Web sites that can be used to call attention to the event particularly helpful for exhibitions open to the public. Others can provide amenities related to the destination and its attractions. These may be used in direct mailings to attendees or as room gifts.

INITIAL ANNOUNCEMENT

The initial announcement, whether electronic or paper, announces the meeting theme, site, and dates, and outlines the program content. Some organizations, particularly in the incentive field, make effective use of "save these dates" teasers or other pre-announcement pieces stating the theme and giving the dates and site. These help to build suspense and anticipation and reinforce the theme. Others will send only a site brochure with, perhaps, an invitation letter as the announcement piece. Some organizers have letterheads and envelopes imprinted with the meeting theme. Graphics, paper, and text should be of a quality consistent with the stature of the event and its sponsor, since these mailings reflect on the organization. Many organizations take advantage of the proliferation of computers, by using e-mails linked to the organization's homepage or, budget permitting, create a dedicated homepage for the event.

Corona Ware from Cardinal Communications, a Web-design software program geared to non-technical users, can generate e-mail promotional elements and online brochures for a targeted audience and tabulate responses. Unlike some registration software having marketing applications, Corona Ware is not a registration program.

> **Fax Solicitation**
>
> The Federal Communications Commission changed its rules governing facsimile transmissions to members of trade associations in August of 2003.
>
> Associations now need to have express, written permission from their members to send an unsolicited fax that advertises goods or services, convention registrations, etc. "Unsolicited advertisement" means "any material advertising the commercial availability or quality of any property, goods, or services which is transmitted to any person without that person's prior express invitation or permission."
>
> It is no longer sufficient to rely on an "established business relationship" with the member (such as paying dues or having ordered or attended meetings in the past). Furthermore, associations can no longer use an "opt out" device whereby the member could simply ask not to receive any more faxes. A member who has given the association a fax number does not comply with the rule. The association must obtain a signed written consent (including the person's fax number) before sending a fax that promotes goods or services. Faxes for informational purposes only, such as committee meetings or pending legislation, are NOT subject to the new rule.

FOLLOW-UP MAILINGS

A minimum of two mailings is suggested for most events, the final one containing links to Web sites, detailed program information, travel arrangements (including luggage tags, if used), and any other materials and data to get the participant to the site. But be mindful of the marketing aspect of promotion: Meeting sponsors may want to create repeat impressions, especially if participants attend of their own volition. Some recognize the benefit of spouse influence, particularly for more romantic destinations by stressing social and leisure programs in mailings sent to the home. Pre-meeting mailings may also include concurrent sessions, special events, pre-post-conference tours, case studies, and related information.

Some organizers expand their market universe beyond the membership, particularly when exhibits are involved. Rented mailing lists, if properly targeted, can be an effective way of expanding market reach. If used, it is advisable to maximize rate of return by asking recipients who opt not to attend to provide or indicate:

1. Names of colleagues who may be interested
2. Whether or not they wish to receive other mailings
3. Whether or not they desire information about the organization, reports, videos, discs, etc.

Greater market saturation can also be achieved by enlisting cooperative promotion from other interested parties. When exhibits are part of the event, provide exhibitors with promotional materials and Web site links to their own communications and encourage them to promote the event in their advertising and publicity campaigns. Airlines, hotels, and convention bureaus can also augment the promotional effort; if the revenue is substantial, they might provide cooperative advertising funds.

PUBLICITY

Publicity is a valuable marketing tool if it is used properly. Some events call for a professional publicist or media relations expert. The event, depending on scope and content, may attract coverage by business editors, columnists, talk show hosts, trade press, and local, national, and international mass media. Some organizations won't want to attract attention to their meetings because of confidentiality, the nature of the audience, potential civil disturbance, or destination characteristics. But for most meetings, publicity is an important part of the promotion and public relations effort.

The Convention and Visitors' Bureau can be instrumental in generating local news coverage. If the event is of sufficient scope, it will provide staff to coordinate media coverage or host a pressroom. The PCO or PR staff assists the bureau by supplying updated press kits, parking passes, name badges, and contact names. For advance publicity, media kits should be mailed to city editors or assignment editors and to news departments and TV stations four to six months before the event. Then submit periodic news releases on meeting theme, program content, prominent speakers, industry issues, innovative special events, and newsworthy developments in the organization. Your submissions won't always result in articles, but they will remind editors of the upcoming event. It's a good idea to retain a local clipping service to track coverage.

When news conferences and interviews are scheduled during the meeting, give assignment editors and talk show producers one month's notice, and remind them again two or three days before the event. Follow up with a telephone call the day before. Post a schedule of press conferences in the press room and distribute to media representatives. Provide diagram books to the trade press covering the proceedings. Ask speakers to go to the pressroom after their sessions, and advise the media beforehand that they will be available for interviews. If a pressroom is to be set up, include it on your facility checklist. (For pressroom requirements and operations, see Chapter 16 on "Media Relations and the Pressroom.")

A TYPICAL CONFERENCE MARKETING PLAN

One year out	Announce the dates and site of next year's meeting during the current meeting. Establish Web site.
Eight months ahead	Decide on theme and design graphics. Determine preliminary agenda. Analyze prospective audience and prepare marketing plan. Draft announcement letter. Obtain draft and design approval.
Seven months ahead	Design registration forms and systems, or contract for electronic registration services. Prepare mailing labels and/or order lists. Alert mailing service. Obtain bids on printing and Web hosting. Submit first mailer elements to printer. Prepare mailing labels.
Six months ahead	Deliver mailers to mailing service. Send out first mailing. Prepare second mailing elements. Establish registration controls. Design and produce ads for trade publications. Contract for space. Prepare news releases.
Five months ahead	Fine-tune business and social agendas. Design second mailing elements and obtain approvals. Contract Web services. Deliver second mailing materials to printer. Include registration forms. Submit ads, insertion orders, and initial news releases to trade media and Web sites.
Four months ahead	Send out second mailing. Continue news releases. Track registrations. Design final mailing and registration kits. Fine-tune program.
Three months ahead	Track registrations. First ads appear. Send final news releases to trade media. Determine need for additional

	mailings based on registration. Finalize program. Deliver mailing elements to printer.
Two months ahead	Confirm speakers. Send out final mailing. Deliver program book to printer. Prepare press kits. Contact talk show producers.
One month ahead	Contact assignment editors and follow up. Order staff and equipment for pressroom. Generate signage and name badges; assemble registration kits. Schedule press conference. Arrange for officers and spokesmen to arrive early for talk show appearances.

When it comes to promoting an event, there are too many variables to permit a magic formula; every meeting is different. The foregoing includes general guidelines, some or all of which may apply. But one principle does hold true: As with any activity requiring specialized knowledge, leave it to professionals.

TIPS FROM A PRO

Dan Herbers, an industry professional who is well qualified to counsel on event marketing, has this advice:

> When it comes to successfully promoting your event, there is no "one size fits all" plan or magic formula that works every time. Every event is different—the audience you're promoting to, the location, the agenda, the season, and the economy can all play a critical role in the success or failure of your event.
>
> One principle holds true: As with any activity requiring specialized knowledge, seek professional advice and counsel. Seasoned professionals are many times the secret ingredient who can best teach you the techniques and practices that can ensure success. They can help show you the how, when, and where to target your marketing dollars for maximum return.
>
> Finally, always *test*. You'll never improve the outcome by doing the same thing the same way. Never stop searching for that breakthrough concept, that new mailing list, fresh offer, or unique mix of marketing media to touch your prospective attendees in a novel and distinct way.

For detailed information on marketing meetings and seminars, one of the foremost and highly respected authorities in the world is Marketing General Incorporated. MGI is North America's largest direct marketing agency servicing the association community.

Resources:

The global event marketing agency George P. Johnson Company and the MPI Foundation have joined efforts to provide the industry with important information. The study, "2003 MPI/GPJ Trends in Event Marketing Research," uses first-of-its-kind research to capture current data and projected trends relating to event marketing in the United States, Canada, United Kingdom, Germany, and Asia-Pacific. Contact www.mpinet.org for more information.

Cardinal Communications and Corona Ware: www.coronaware.com
  Rodman Marymor, CEO, Cardinal Communications

Marketing General, Inc. Dan Herbers, Senior Director:
  dherbers@marketinggeneral.com

Chapter Ten
The Function of Functions: Food and Beverage

FUNCTIONS AND THE MEETING AGENDA

Ask any left-brained, analytical efficiency expert if there are more-effective ways to convey a message than bringing people together from great distances, housing them in expensive hotels, and wining and dining them. The answer you will no doubt get is a resounding affirmative. Nevertheless, it has long been established that there is a dimension to meetings, generated by the synergy and chemistry of human interaction, that cannot be as effectively achieved by electronic or other media as hospitality events, refreshment breaks, and group meals. They provide more than sustenance: they are opportunities for social interaction. People bond together as members of an organization, renew past acquaintances, rekindle friendships, and make new ones. Such functions also play a vital role in the dynamics of the program. Attendees can exchange ideas and viewpoints, analyze what speakers have presented, and reinforce the benefits of the meeting experience.

The PCO and food service personnel understand that these functions serve the very essential purpose of providing nourishment, reward, and refreshment for the mind as well as the body. There is a psycho-physiological relationship between food and mental activity, a sort of "gastro-intellectual tract." It is a relationship that knowledgeable nutritionists and meeting managers have come to recognize: "What you eat is how you think!" They have known for some time that it is counter-productive to serve heavy meals and alcoholic beverages before sessions requiring mental alertness and receptivity. In the past two decades, nutritionists and event professionals have refined the concept and correlated specific types of food and metabolic processes with mental and physical activity. This concept is covered in depth at the end of this chapter.

The PCO must also balance the needs of the program with the social and psychological aspects of food functions as perceived by the audience. Meals and breaks offer a change of pace from intellectual activity, from sitting for long periods, from responsibility and concentration, or from sheer boredom. They are a change from the cerebral to the sensual; from the demands of thinking and concentrating to the sensory pleasures of smell, taste, and sight. Indeed, meals can be perceived as rewards for effort, a throwback to childhood when good behavior was rewarded with a treat. Time after time, meeting evaluations by attendees report that the quality and, alas, the degree of lavishness of the meals are perceived as having equal weight with program content.

Functions also serve another essential purpose. In Chapter 5, we emphasized timing and pacing. Meals and breaks, as elements of the schedule, define the business and educational sessions and offer a change-of-pace in the program. All too often, they are the only relief for audiences subjected to seemingly endless dry speeches. Successful planners carefully integrate functions into the business and social agendas to create a "gestalt"—a whole that is greater than the sum of its parts.

The reader is undoubtedly familiar with the basics of food and beverage planning for meetings. Most experienced PCOs become knowledgeable about even the more esoteric aspects of this topic, even though they depend on food and beverage professionals for much of the planning and execution. They know how important it is to ascertain, during site inspection, the competence of the staff, the quality of food preparation and presentation, and the adequacy of all food and beverage facilities—banquet, room service, restaurants—to accommodate the needs of the group. (See *The Convention Industry Manual* for basic coverage of food and beverage planning.) This chapter covers some principles and practices developed by successful planners to simplify the process and to solve frequently recurring problems.

BREAKFASTS

Not everyone eats a big breakfast. And breakfast seems to be a bottleneck in the fight for time. A properly organized buffet breakfast accommodates varying tastes and saves time. Here are some suggestions:

- Have bread, rolls, and fresh fruit already at each table, as well as thermoses of coffee, or alert servers to pour as people sit down. A large percentage will eat what is there without going to the buffet tables.

- Set buffet tables to accommodate two lines, and set separate stations for juices, dry cereals, yogurt, and crepes and omelets. This will speed service and separate hot and cold buffets. Have staff members direct people in line to the station of their choice.

- Schedule the program to begin as soon as the tables are cleared. Table topics and case studies are appropriate activities for round-table setups; a room change will not be necessary.

See the section on "Buffet Dinners" for other buffet suggestions.

Some organizers are under the misconception that buffets save money. Not so! In fact, they may be more expensive. At a breakfast buffet, however, the PCO can effect substantial savings by ordering in bulk, rather than by the person. Order coffee and juice by the gallon (20 cups), cut-fruit by the tray, so many pieces of pastry, and so many portions of cereal, eggs, sausages, etc. Not everyone will want everything, and most items can be readily replenished. If you have ordered three fruit trays and the first two are consumed in the first fifteen minutes, there is time to add a fourth.

For smaller groups, it is likely to be more cost-effective to offer breakfast in attendees' rooms. One company invited its attendees to "Breakfast with the Chairman." It was served by room service staff, while guests viewed a video presentation by the Chairman of the Board on the hotel's closed-circuit TV channel. Be sure to advise the hotel well in advance if this is your plan so that they can have enough room service staff.

It is quite appropriate for a four-day program to schedule Continental breakfast for two mornings, or one day with "breakfast at leisure" (on their own). If no group breakfast is scheduled and there is a large group in attendance, the hotel should be advised so that the hotel restaurants and room service can accommodate more guests.

LUNCHES

The same time crunch that seems to accompany breakfast often applies to lunch. Buffet service might be a suitable solution, particularly if the meeting format consists of workshops or other concurrent sessions. Stragglers will not hold up service; in fact, staggered arrival may help. A buffet lunch can be a refreshing change of pace in a program replete with formal meals and can accommodate varying tastes and appetites. A buffet arrangement, in which attendees return to the buffet tables for different courses, permits some movement after a morning of sitting.

PCOs involved in multicultural meetings should be aware of cultural differences in the perception of a buffet. Europeans, for example, tend to return to the buffet table for each course and take smaller servings. This practice calls for multiple stations, and results in shorter lines. As with any buffet, the cost tends to be higher because of the quantity of food and increased service.

One creative compromise between the buffet and a plated lunch is the "Table Deli"—an assortment of sandwich ingredients, breads or rolls, garnishes, and salads arranged on platters for each table. Closely related is the Asian style of serving successive courses on platters. Diners are served some of each course or allowed to help themselves from the platter.

Menu selection for lunches is limited only by imagination, budget, and the cooperation of the chef. Poultry and fish, once considered anathema at group functions, have been appearing frequently on luncheon menus, though it is best to have alternatives for people who still don't like fish. Ethnic dishes are popular and more readily available: In addition to the old favorites Mexican, Polynesian, Italian, and French, chefs have added German, Greek, Japanese, Hungarian, Thai, and North African selections, as well as the varied regional Chinese cuisines.

Organizers should be aware of cultural and religious food restrictions and the growing demand for vegetarian choices, as well as dietary needs related to medical conditions such as low sodium and gluten or lactose intolerance. The low-carbohydrate fad that had a resurgence early in this millennium will likely peter out as all vogue diets do. Nevertheless, menu planning should be sufficiently flexible to accommodate current dietary regimens and trends.

DINNERS AND BANQUETS

Food service professionals generally classify meals according to the style of service:

- *Russian (Butler).* Generally regarded as the highest degree of service. Each course is presented on a platter and the guests serve themselves.

- *French.* Also served from a platter, but placed on the diner's plate by the waiter.

- *Plated.* Each guest receives a plate prepared in the kitchen.

- *Buffet.* Guests serve themselves from tables set according to course: appetizers, salads, main course, dessert. Dinner buffets usually include stations manned by chefs.

Some event planners get so involved in the logistics and details of planning a banquet that they overlook their primary role—that of host. Whether it is a fully sponsored meal included in registration fees or a ticketed event, the guest's expectations and satisfaction must be uppermost. Attendees will accept a Continental breakfast at an ungodly early hour, or a quick, light lunch included in a full program, but when it comes to dinner, they are *guests* and expect to be treated as such. It is a time to relax and socialize with their colleagues, not a time for long-winded speeches or an endless parade of awards that have significance only to the recipients. That is not to say that award ceremonies have no place at such events. On the contrary: They can be an essential element of the meeting objectives and the purpose of the function. They are successful when perceived as entertainment. See Chapter 6 for some guidelines on dynamic recognition programs.

Themed Dinners

Planned evening functions require more attention and creativity than planning breakfasts and lunches. The meeting theme is usually incorporated into the event. For example, the following evening events use sub-themes based on the main meeting theme, such as this nautical one:

Meeting Theme:	"Set Sales for Tomorrow"
First Night:	"On the Beach" (informal beach party)
Second Night:	"Captain's Table"
Third Night:	"Shore Excursion" (dine-around)
Final Night:	"Race for the Cup" (awards banquet)

The theme can be carried out in room and table decorations and in the names of menu selections and drinks.

Convention staffs at hotels often develop excellent motif ideas. Some hotels keep an inventory of decorations and props and offer the event as a stock theme dinner. Basic or elegant, theme parties appeal to participants' desires for escape, fantasy, or nostalgia.

Some organizations repeat a popular theme year after year. One association planner considering Colonial Williamsburg for a convention described their requirement to have their traditional Sunday Night luau. "We don't get too many calls for luaus in Williamsburg," the marketing director remarked cautiously, sensing a sensitive area. "How about a Thanksgiving feast?" The planner bought the idea and billed it as a Colonial Luau, and the audience loved it!

Even the ubiquitous Western Barbecue can be creative, as the Pointe Resort in Phoenix has demonstrated. They make it a glittering black-tie affair: star look-alikes mingle with elegantly attired guests in the Grand Ballroom, which is converted into an authentic Western town for the occasion. At the other end of the spectrum, the independent event planners with International Conference Consultants, seeking a new theme for a client of long standing, came up with an innovative event, which they billed as A Perfectly Outrageous Evening: The room decor was mix-and-match; the buffet menu was an eclectic mélange of fresh seafood, roast turkey, and pizza; and entertainment ranged from Beethoven to Blues to Barbershop. Guests were asked to wear flagrant, mismatched attire, and an award was given for the most outrageous pun. A good time was had by all.

Within budget limitations, each evening can have a different theme. Events can be about international cuisines or variations on popular themes, such as Arabian Nights, Hawaiian Luau, Circus-Circus, Elizabethan Feast, Campus Capers, Roaring Twenties, M.A.S.H, and other nostalgic concepts. One innovative meeting planner inntroduced a "Survivor" theme to the amazement and delight of the guests.

A themed dinner need not be expensive, but the budget should provide for props and decor. A circus or ballpark motif can be very effective with little more than beer, hot dogs, and pizza, especially when more-formal meals are scheduled on alternate nights. A dinner does not have to be a complete five- or seven-course plated event; the popular cocktail reception with "heavy" hors d'oeuvres is a welcome change of pace, especially when it precedes a free evening. Dinner at leisure, with or without vouchers, is particularly apropos at a destination known for the variety and excellence of its dining establishments.

Buffet Dinners

A buffet dinner is usually planned to provide a change of pace, a variety of food, and an opportunity for greater interaction and networking. It is not a budget-control measure. As previously stated, buffets might even be more expensive, because they require more food and more preparation and there is more waste. They do, however, require fewer staff people. Unlike formal dinners, buffet dinners allow for more socializing among people at other tables, which is why they are frequently scheduled for the night the group arrives. Buffets are also time savers if they are properly laid out: Multiple stations and double lines (with carving stations at the ends) can prevent long delays and congestion. Some event planners lessen the time attendees have to stand in line by announcing that the captain will call tables to the buffet. One PCO arranges to have finger food from the buffet served to people in line or seated at tables. Here are a few more buffet-planning suggestions:

- Select dishes that hold their eye appeal, particularly hot dishes. Serve roasts freshly carved, since sliced meats tend to lose flavor and dry out fast. Include the carving fee in the budget and in negotiations.

- Limit the selections in order to reduce waste and time in line.

- Avoid broiled foods, unless they are served directly from the broiler. They tend to lose their flavor if they sit in steam trays.

- Provide a variety of hot and cold dishes and a balance of meats, salads, vegetables, breads, and appetizers.

- Avoid congestion by separating the salad, appetizer, coffee/tea, and dessert stations from the main buffet tables.

- Encourage the catering staff to decorate with food. A fresh fruit or vegetable centerpiece can be as striking as flowers or an ice sculpture and is far more practical and inexpensive.

THE GALA BANQUET

For dinner banquets, the PCO must consider the desired impression, the program, time constraints, and budget. Many professionals, recognizing that people consider dinner banquets to be significant social events, will cut costs on other meals in order to produce one or two lavish dinners during the course of the meeting. But here, too, balance and pacing must be considered. The most elaborate banquet loses some of its luster if it is preceded and followed by others that are equally lavish. The accepted practice is to build toward a gala event on the final night in order to create a lasting impression.

Guests notice the event's importance the moment they enter the banquet room. Room lighting and decor create the first visual impression. Creative use of plants and floral arrangements, combined with low-key lighting and theme decor, are key elements in establishing an ambiance consistent with the degree of formality that each function demands. This is reinforced by table "cosmetics:" choice of linens (possibly portraying the theme colors), centerpieces, candelabras, and the quality, number, and arrangement of flatware, china, and stemware. One should not underrate the impact of cosmetics: The most proletarian menu can be upgraded to a gala meal with silver or gold underliners, bone china, and crystal stemware surrounding an elegant pair of candelabra.

Food presentation, service standards, and entertainment also reflect the importance of the function. The PCO should look for flexibility and creativity from the catering staff when selecting the menu. Banquet menus are only a starting point for pricing and selection; feel free to pick and choose courses from several different menus. Instead of suggesting a fish course, a green vegetable, etc., talk about specific menu items and their method of preparation, and select for proper balance. That balance applies to aesthetics—color, shape, and texture—as well as flavor and nutrition. Visual appeal ranks as high as taste and aroma.

Favorite selections not on the menu can be requested, though a caveat is in order: "Favorite" is from the guests' point of view, not your own. You may think escargot is the greatest dish ever conceived, but some people associate it with garden pests! Avoid gourmet dishes that take time to prepare if the group exceeds one hundred people. Sauté dishes are an elegant complement to any meal, but should not be attempted for more than fifty. Take your time to work out a good menu. It is even customary to arrange a test dinner for major banquets: The chief has an opportunity to demonstrate his or her skills, and you and/or the banquet committee get to sample the proposed meal and make any desired changes.

The number of guests served per waiter determines the level of service. This in turn establishes the desired degree of formality: The most formal is French service, in which each item is served from a tray on to the guest's plate. At formal banquets, one waiter usually serves no more than two rounds of eight (sixteen people at two tables), but more service may be required if wine is poured. The level of service may also vary according to local union regulations. An average level of service is twenty guests per server. Some PCOs upgrade standard service by having waiters serve salad dressings and sauces or pour wine at the table. Such service for buffets is usually computed at one server per four tables.

WINE AND DINE

Wine service with dinners has long been a custom at more-refined evening affairs, but it is mandatory at formal dinners. PCOs and meeting attendees are now fairly knowledgeable about wine, and rely on their own individual tastes rather than on the tastes of wine connoisseurs. White wine is preferred in a three-to-one ratio over red wine, regardless of the accompanying course. (The ratio may be higher at receptions). For planning purposes, that ratio is a reliable guideline, but adjust it to the group's preferences.

Some of the principles that wine connoisseurs espouse are valid: Lighter white wines go well with soups, salads, poultry, and seafood, and robust, full-bodied wines tend to complement game and red meat dishes. It is the *flavor* rather than the color of the wine that should be matched to the dominant flavor of the food, which it accompanies. Some white wines go well with red meat dishes (e.g., Veal Marsala), while a Cabernet might be a good choice for a poultry dish such as Coq au Vin. Solicit the food and beverage manager's advice and keep individual tastes in mind. Other suggestions for wine service:

- Serve no more than one wine per course. A particularly lavish dinner may call for two wines with the main course, but that is an exception.

- Allow one glass of wine (4 ounces) per person for each course except the main course, which averages one to two glasses.

- Instruct serving staff to ask permission before refilling. This can reduce consumption as much as 40 percent, making wine affordable for more events.

- Do not confuse imported wines with quality. Some of the best wines in the world come from California and Washington state.

- If wine is poured, servers should be told to inquire whether the guest prefers red or white. Ask the banquet captain to inform all waiters what kinds of wines are being served, in case guests inquire.

- If wine is to be set at each place, it is best to start with one red and two white glasses per setting at a table of ten, using the proper stemware. Some guests may never touch their claret glass, but it would be a faux pas not to provide it. You'll need to have the glasses replenished about the time the waiters are serving other courses. Therefore, have the captain designate which staff members will replenish the wine and which will serve the meal. To control costs, ask the captain to uncork bottles only as needed.

- Reserve dessert wines and champagnes for only the most festive function. They add a touch of glamour if they are served before or with dessert.

- Order jug wines at receptions, unless it is a wine-tasting or wine-and-cheese function. Base your order on the ratio of three white wines to one red.

- Provide a choice of dry wines and fruity wines.

PLANNING CRITERIA FOR ALL MEALS

During the planning stage, the PCO needs to have a fairly firm idea of what form of food service will be needed, as well as other logistical requirements dictated by the program accompanying the meal. Decisions that will need to be made involve:

- *Type of service.* Reception, buffet, table service, and degree of formality. The latter will also determine the number of people at each table and the number of covers (guests) per server. For example, formal service suggests seating no more than eight at a 90-inch round table because space will be needed for place settings and wine glasses.

- *Decorations and cosmetics.* Floral arrangements, table decor, quality of china and silverware, linens, and centerpieces vary with degree of formality and perceived importance. A simple menu selection can be dressed up and given a gala appearance with the proper cosmetics and ambiance.

- *Room capacity.* The room should hold all attendees without crowding, allow space for proper service, and accommodate the needs of the program. A room that is too large for the group has a negative psychological impact. In such cases, creative placement of plants and subdued lighting can create a warm ambiance.

- *Room setup.* If a head table is planned, the room should be oriented to ensure that there are proper sightlines, so that no one is too far from the focal point of the function.
- *Staging.* If entertainment, audiovisuals, speakers, or award ceremonies are part of the meal, placement of the stage and room setup should be carefully planned.

The PCO must also consider the seating of speakers, dignitaries, and special guests. Speakers should be seated at the head of the table or near the stage. Alert the banquet captain to see that they are served early. If an award ceremony is scheduled, seat recipients near the podium. (See Chapter 16 for details on room setups.)

ROOM AND TABLE DÉCOR

Food and drink costs are increasing, so make the most of every event. Attractive surroundings please attendees and reflect favorably on the meeting sponsor. Plants and flowers (including silk flower arrangements) are not inexpensive, but they are a cost-effective way of enhancing any event. Green plants are usually rented or provided by the hotel at no charge. For a gala event, floral decor may be important not only in the banquet room, but in pre-function areas and hallways. A pamphlet entitled "Flowers for Meetings and Conventions," available from the American Florist Marketing Council, provides some valuable details. One innovative idea is the edible centerpiece: A lavishly decorated cake (possibly bearing the meeting theme) or an arrangement of pastries or petit-fours serve as creative and delicious table décor.

Professional decorators and special-events planners make use of a variety of materials and media: acrylics, fiberoptics, neon, balloons, stretch fabrics, scenic drops and stage dressing, and even light and laser shows to create dramatic settings or establish themes. The possibilities are endless, but one stands out in our memory because of its originality and value after the event: Inter-Continental Hotels hosted a luncheon with a "Babes in Toyland" theme for a December conference of Meeting Professionals International in Miami. Very appropriate for the Christmas season! The room, tables, and pre-function areas were decorated with toys of all kinds. Costumed characters from children's books greeted the guests and circulated during the meal. A children's choir provided entertainment. On being seated, guests learned that the toys were sent from Inter-Continental hotels from all over the world. The final innovative touch was an announcement that the toys were going to be distributed to orphans—in the guests' names—at a Christmas party to be hosted by the hotel!

RECEPTIONS AND HOSPITALITY

There is no denying the value of a reception as an ice-breaker or as a kick-off event for the meeting. Receptions allow attendees to meet on a relaxed social basis before the meeting gets underway. Beverages are served and food can consist of dry snacks, a cheese assortment, a vegetable platter, or a buffet with hot and cold dishes that substitute for a full meal. The menu is determined by the purpose of the reception as well as the budget, theme, and schedule. An opening reception without a dinner has a different purpose than one that serves as an interlude preceding dinner. The meeting planner who schedules a reception buffet with a full range of hors d'oeuvres before an elaborate dinner is doing the guests and the organization a disservice. If people fill up on delicacies, they will not appreciate the dinner.

The purpose of a pre-dinner reception is to allow attendees to assemble prior to the meal and socialize. Convention meals generally start between 7:30 and 8:00 p.m. and most attendees—at least North Americans—are accustomed to eating at home around 6:30 p.m. or so. Hors d'oeuvres are served to bridge the hunger gap. They also serve to ameliorate the effects of alcohol on an empty stomach. Appetizers rich in butter and oils, such as cheeses, nuts, dips, and meat-filled pastries, line the stomach and mitigate alcohol absorption. Pre-banquet receptions should last no more than an hour (experts recommend 45 minutes). This schedule allows for late arrivals and limits consumption, thus reducing food and bar costs.

Receptions that take the place of a meal last longer and require a more-elaborate food presentation (usually a buffet). Event planners control costs at such functions in ways that do not visibly affect the perception of the affair. One method is to have expensive items passed butler-style on trays rather than served on the buffet table. Passing delicacies such as shrimp and crab while people are in conversational groupings reduces consumption.

Another cost-saving method is to order in bulk. Order seafood, cheese, and fruit by the pound, and canapés or hot and cold items by the piece or by the tray. Ascertain the number of portions per tray and spot-check the count at the first event to be sure it is correct. Once the staff knows you're counting, you'll minimize the shrinkage that seems to occur between the kitchen and your guests. Most catering departments estimate five to seven portions per head for a one-hour cocktail reception. If consumption appears to be faster than anticipated, replenish with less-expensive selections and spread the additional servings of premium items such as shrimp throughout the event.

When the event is an elaborate reception that runs into the dinner hour, it is usually best to order by the head. This method is not as economical, but it places on the catering staff the responsibility of providing an adequate supply. The staff's reputation is at stake, and the hotel will take extra pains to see that food is of a good quality, attractively presented and replenished as needed. Such events tend to run two hours or even longer, and food service can tax the budget. It is not necessary to maintain all courses for the entire period. Catering executives suggest holding desserts until the latter part of the evening. Hot dishes would be replaced with cheese and fruit assortments, pastries, and ice cream, or perhaps a coffee-cordial station after the second hour.

Hospitality Suites

Hospitality suites serve many purposes, depending on the nature of the meeting. They are places for fellowship and social contact, or gathering spots during non-scheduled hours, and provide opportunities for buyers and suppliers to socialize. They can fulfill the need to welcome new members of an organization in an informal setting, to have selected people or members of the press meet officers and other VIPs, or to provide an unstructured setting for the exchange of ideas. The sponsor can be the meeting organizer, an allied member such as a manufacturer, or an affiliated association. (Some associations control hospitality room allocations to prevent abuses, especially at trade shows.) Hospitality events are held in ballrooms, meeting rooms, suites, outdoors, and even at remote sites such as marinas, boats, other hotels, or attractions. This section of the chapter will focus on hotel hospitality suites for which the PCO or the meeting sponsor is responsible.

Arrange for a room that accommodates the number of guests you want to be in there at any one time; avoid overcrowding, yet seek rooms that are small enough for fellowship and intimacy. Several smaller connecting rooms are preferable to one large one. The hospitality suite should be away from normal hotel traffic flow, yet convenient to elevators. Soft lighting, good ventilation, background music, comfortable seating in conversational groupings, and a few decorations will create an ambiance conducive to hospitality events. If there are to be audiovisual presentations, they should be unobtrusive and not demand the attention of all the guests. Music and entertainment is best kept low-key; it is not good hospitality if guests have to shout to be heard. The exception is when dance music is part of the entertainment, as in a cabaret setting; at such affairs, incorporate other rooms suited to conversation into the hospitality suite complex.

Determine whether room service or the hotel's catering department is to be responsible for servicing the rooms, and agree on prices well in advance. In many hotels, room service prices are lower than those of catering services, especially for beverages. Otherwise, the planning guidelines for receptions and beverage service also apply to hospitality.

BEVERAGE SERVICE AND CONTROL

Arrangements for mixed drinks, beer, and other beverages will depend on the type of function. The PCO is responsible for negotiating beverage purchases for various functions and for exercising control over bar service through the catering department.

Far too much emphasis is placed on liquor without taking into consideration the changing tastes and practices of meeting attendees. Demand for cocktails and mixed drinks has steadily declined in favor of wine, wine coolers, and beer, particularly micro-brews, which have all achieved respectability for even the most sophisticated tastes. Many people forego alcohol altogether, preferring soft drinks, flavored seltzers, and fresh juices as part of the trend toward a healthier lifestyle.

Another significant trend has to do with the changing personal goals of convention attendees. Objectives are focused more on learning and networking, rather than on partying. Keeping pace with this trend is the attitude of meeting sponsors who are concerned about the image they project and about liability. The PCO must recognize these trends and have a full understanding of beverage pricing and service. Here are some areas to consider as you plan:

- *Number of bartenders.* One per 100 persons is the minimum, diminishing proportionately after 400 persons, but supported by barbacks (busboys).

- *Number of servers and availability of a service bar.* Specify according to group size and type of event.

- *Pour size.* The PCO has the authority to stipulate a 1 ounce or 1½ ounce measured-pour. The price is adjusted accordingly. Insist that shot glasses or Posi-Pours (spouts that pour a predetermined amount of liquor) be used, rather than free-pour.

- *Quality of liquor, wine, beer, and liqueurs.* House brands are the least expensive; call brands and premium brands increase progressively in price. There are two schools of thought regarding quality: Some sponsors believe that even though not everyone drinks, everyone can read a label, so premium brands should be served. Others believe that only serving non-premium or house brands will reduce the demand for mixed drinks, thus trimming expenses.

- *Bottle size and capacity.* The commonly used 1 liter bottle holds 33 ounces.

- Do not announce a last call before closing the bar!

Beverage Plans

Average consumption by type of beverage will vary with each group. However, the per-person, per-hour plan is more costly, unless the group consists of heavy drinkers. The least-expensive way to purchase liquor is by the bottle and most hoteliers will acknowledge this, although their catering policy may not accommodate such plans. The most profitable plan for the hotel is unlimited consumption or per-person and per-hour. This is easy to see when one understands how the hourly rate is computed: A $12 per-head rate is based on consumption of two mixed drinks per person per hour. At the bar, that drink would cost $6. Unfortunately (for the buyer, not for the hotel), this formula overlooks the fact that a large percentage of the guests will prefer wine or beer or non-alcoholic drinks, all less expensive. It also fails to take into account late arrivals, who will presumably drink less.

On the other hand, from an accounting standpoint, this is the simplest method for both the hotel and the PCO. It does make a lot of sense to know up front what the cost will be for budgeting purposes, and, it is always negotiable anyway. This method requires an accurate count agreed to by both parties. There is room for price negotiations if the PCO can satisfy the hotel that liquor consumption is below average. The buyer still has the responsibility for ascertaining service standards and understanding what is included (e.g., dry snacks, hors d'oeuvres, etc.).

Purchasing on the bottle plan offers the PCO the most economy and control, but it demands more supervision. Since charges will be computed on the basis of open or empty bottles, some planners affix a distinctive label to each bottle as bottles leave the storeroom. At the end of the function, only opened bottles bearing the label are paid for; unopened stock is credited and returned. Partially used bottles may be charged proportionately, depending on hotel policy. Alternatively, they can be held for a subsequent function, "married" or combined with other partial bottles of the same brand, or transferred to the hospitality suite—all of which require additional staff supervision. It is advisable to check bartenders periodically to make sure they are using the specified measured pour. A few zealous hoteliers will instruct bartenders on a bottle plan to pour generous measures or overpour, thus selling more bottles. Happily, this is the exception. To avoid any confusion, many hotels utilize Posi-Pours.

When negotiating a bottle plan, be sure you know what the price includes. Usually it includes the room charge, bartenders, ice, mixes, and garnishes. For hospitality suites, the bottle cost is usually lower (but the price includes less). When using multiple bars, knowledgeable planners will close one bar early and "wed" remaining bars (transfer opened stock to the other bars in order to avoid having a surplus of partially used bottles).

Purchasing by the drink offers a happy medium for hosted bar service. The PCO specifies the pour size—usually between 7/8 of an ounce and 1½ ounces—and negotiates a per-drink price for each category of drink. If it is a sophisticated drinking group, a 1¼-ounce pour size or maybe even 1½-ounce pour size would be appropriate. That means a higher cost per drink if the bartender has to pour more liquor into each drink. On the other hand, for a less-sophisticated audience (perhaps younger in age), a one-ounce pour will suffice; if the standard pour is more than that, then negotiate for a lower price-per-person, per hour. In many cases, only the bar manager will really know the exact size of the standard pour.

The price includes all service staff, ice, mixers, and garnishes. Bartenders keep track of the number of drinks served in each category: call brand, well brand, beer, wine, etc. It is possible to check approximate consumption during the event by checking each bartender's tab. If the PCO is concerned that the event is running over budget, you can close the bars early. In another version of the drink plan, the hotel establishes the number of drinks in each bottle based on pour size, and charges according to the number of empties and partials. Here again, some supervision is required. The hotel should provide a copy of the beverage delivery ticket, including any additional stock delivered. This is verified against remaining stock returned at the end of the function.

Cash bars or the use of a ticket system, if appropriate for the event, provide the best control and the least amount of hassle for the PCO and the organization. Under this arrangement, the hotel charges for each drink according to an agreed-upon price structure; the guest pays by cash or tickets purchased in advance. The PCO negotiates a price per ticket, regardless of the type of drink desired—beer, wine, or liquor.

From a budgeting standpoint, only enough tickets are printed to cover the amount budgeted. However, there will be some slippage for nondrinkers or those who only have soft drinks (which should be included without charging or requiring a ticket). For cash bars, the hotel will provide cashiers, unless limited attendance allows the bartender to collect. It is very important that the PCO advise all attendees by announcement, program notation, or both when a no-host bar is planned for an event. It can be a source of embarrassment for sponsor and attendee alike if this is overlooked. For sophisticated, upscale receptions, drink-ticket or cash-bar arrangements are inappropriate.

Whatever the function, it is essential that all elements agreed upon be confirmed in writing, with applicable service charges and taxes spelled out. Taxes are normally computed on meals and beverages, not on the service charge. Conversely, service charges or gratuities are figured as a percentage of the net cost before taxes. The customary 15 percent or 18 percent gratuity on, say, an 8 percent tax can add up!

LIQUOR LIABILITY

Planners and sponsors have become more sensitive in recent years to the matter of liability because of litigation arising out of accidents involving guests at functions where alcohol was served. PCOs who wish to mitigate such risk should heed the advice of attorney Jeffrey King, legal counsel to the Convention Industry Council. "In many cases, because all the attendees are staying in the hotel, planners don't think about liability," says King. "But they can be held liable if an intoxicated guest falls and gets hurt in the hotel on the way to the room." King offers the following suggestions:

- Obtain liquor liability insurance, which is available for single-event coverage and is relatively inexpensive. Sponsor and PCO are the beneficiaries.

- Instruct bartenders. Set limits on size of pour, and specify that obviously intoxicated persons will not be served.

- Instruct meeting staff to refrain from drinking. The staff's responsibility is to supervise. The PCO and staff should observe guests' consumption and act authoritatively, albeit diplomatically, with troublesome guests.

- Control the duration of the event or party. Set a reasonable closing time, stick with it, and do not announce a "last call." Some people—usually the troublesome ones—view a last call as a signal to double up on drinks.

- Arrange an escort and/or transportation for intoxicated guests. If they are staying at the party site, have them escorted to their rooms; if not, provide transportation that has been reserved for in advance.

A REFRESHING LOOK AT REFRESHMENT BREAKS

"Please save me from coffee, tea, and danish," one veteran meeting planner cried. "I have consumed more danish than any mortal should be allowed." In spite of such plaintive comments, the ubiquitous danish pastry (to which Danes fervently deny any claim) appears destined to be as much a standard of meetings as green tablecloths and ice water. That need not be so. Though they have a place and are quite popular, coffee-tea-and-danish is but one choice in a rich cornucopia of refreshment options.

The operative phrase is "refresh." A refreshment break is intended to provide participants with an opportunity to stand, stretch, walk, make phone calls, visit restrooms, and refresh themselves. "Break" has some unfortunate connotations. The last thing organizers want to do is break the continuity of the meeting and the momentum of succeeding sessions.

(Perhaps "interlude" might be more appropriate.) Refreshment breaks also offer opportunities to socialize, discuss session content, visit displays or a resource center, or network in an atmosphere not confined by an agenda. Beverages and snacks are a secondary, though no less important, element. The caffeine in coffee, tea, and soft drinks provides a stimulant, and some foods, as previously mentioned, have a positive effect on mental activity.

The meeting objectives and the budget determine the type of break as well as the menu. Refreshment breaks can range from simple coffee and tea service to lavish culinary extravaganzas limited only by the planners' creativity and budget. Most participants seem to prefer variety. In a three-day meeting with morning and afternoon sessions, plan on three "nuts and bolts" inexpensive breaks with two creative and one themed event. Most PCOs will cut corners the first two days in order to be able to afford an awesome blow-out on the last day.

Here are a few suggestions for low-budget refreshment breaks:

- Avoid per-head charges. Hotels will normally quote $5 to $8 per head for a simple coffee break. Instead, order coffee by the gallon and have tea and decaffeinated coffee included in the price.

- Order other items by the piece, the pound, or by the tray. Average cost: $3 to $4 per head. Keep in mind that 150 people don't need 150 pieces of pastry.

- Request cookies, muffins, or doughnuts and crullers instead of or in addition to pastry. They are less expensive and smaller than most danish (which tend to be larger than most people prefer). That's why some planners ask for the mini-danish.

- If a buffet breakfast is served, specify that leftover fruits, beverages, and pastry are to be set up to serve at the first break and replenished as needed.

- Soft drinks should be served in 12-ounce cans, rather than the larger 16-ounce bottles (which are more expensive and result in waste). On the other hand, if 32-ounce bottles are offered, most people will help themselves to a glassful at a time, thus reducing consumption.

- Augment afternoon breaks with fresh, whole, or cut fruit and granola bars to provide slow-release energy and fight mid-afternoon slump.

- Hold the luncheon dessert and serve it at the afternoon break.

- Understand that the hotel considers budget breaks a convenience to attendees, rather than a profit base. Don't be overly demanding.

The moderate category refreshment breaks call for a bit more variety and creativity, and will not strain the budget. Mini-themes make them more exciting with little added cost. For example:

- *Continental.* Croissants, brioches, French pastries, Viennese coffee. Specially brewed beverages—espresso, latté, cappuccino—are priced by the serving since they are more labor-intensive.
- *Health kick.* Fresh fruit, juices, yogurt, granola, trail mix, veggie dip.
- *Ethnic.* Mini-bagels and cream cheese, pretzels, gelato, Chinese teas, tea-biscuits, scones, dates, baklava, and tropical fruit such as kiwi fruit.
- *Picnic.* Soft drinks, iced tea and coffee, cider, popsicles, popcorn, watermelon, and cookies.

In some organizations, particularly associations, it is appropriate to seek sponsorship for the moderate and gala events. If such sponsorships are available, they can offset expenses considerably. It may be worthwhile to explore the possibility of a complimentary or upgraded themed break for events taking place at the hotel where participants are staying.

Having budgeted carefully, the PCO is now ready for that last-day surprise break. Whether it is scheduled for the morning or the afternoon will depend on other functions. If a gala banquet is scheduled on the last day, schedule the big break for the morning. Involve the chef or F&B manager and seek their advice. Many hotels have successful themes that they can repeat with all the necessary props and panoply. One memorable refreshment break the author was present for some years ago was staged by the Cairo Hilton during the Prime Minister's Tourism Conference. When delegates emerged from the meeting hall, they found that the convention lobby had been transformed into a Middle Eastern bazaar, complete with coffee stalls, exotic fruits, and Middle Eastern pastries. A live camel and two truculent donkeys vied for attention with waiters in *galabiyas* and other native costumes.

New York's Vista International can do a Mardi Gras break with hot beignets, pralines, chicory coffee, and cafe-au-lait.

The Shangri La in Bangkok offers a formal High Tea for groups up to 100, with elegant table settings, a choice of teas and coffees, tarts, finger sandwiches, and mouth-watering scones and jam. A piano, cello, and violin trio plays light classics.

Another novel break for small groups is the Chef's Theme. It is set in the service kitchen, with servers dressed in kitchen whites and chef's hats. Coffee is served directly from urns, and long pastry logs or strudel rolls are cut to serving size at the table for each guest.

The timing of breaks is important. The schedule must permit adequate time for attendees to move to and from the break area and to visit rest rooms. Program needs may require that the break be held in the meeting room where refreshments are served, but this arrangement should be reserved for small groups. The more complex and elaborate the affair, the more time you need to allot.

Are there early risers in the group? Runners? Exercise enthusiasts? They will welcome an eye-opener service of coffee and juice an hour before the scheduled group breakfast. Serve it near the room slated for breakfast, making it part of the same banquet order. Meeting staff, technical staff, rehearsing speakers, and others who have early commitments will also appreciate this consideration.

Plan to have refreshments set up fifteen minutes before the program ends. Minimum service standards are one full refreshment station for every 200 people and one server for every 100 guests. Separate the sugar and cream stations from the beverage and food displays to avoid congestion, and have the hotel provide drip plates under beverage spigots and receptacles for all those messy sugar envelopes, used tea bags, and bottle tops.

GUARANTEES: PLAYING THE NUMBERS

Much of the PCO's reputation as a financial manager depends on his or her skill at negotiating F&B prices and estimating the number of attendees at a hosted event. Neophytes faced with the inevitable request for a guarantee often feel like hapless Christians thrown to the lions. Even veterans experience some malaise at decision time. If they play it safe and overestimate, the sponsor ends up paying for meals not consumed—a potentially expensive practice, considering the cost of food and drinks. If they underestimate, they run the risk of a last-minute scurry for additional tables and the embarrassment of serving some guests an alternative meal. Regrettably, there are no magic formulas and very few guidelines to help planners avoid pitfalls. The best strategy is to do these four things:

1. Keep an accurate record of attendance and guarantees at previous similar events.
2. Establish good rapport with the hotel staff.
3. Provide honest information.
4. Enlist the catering staff's help.

The hotel requires a fairly accurate guarantee far enough in advance so that it can order provisions. Consequently, the usual 48-hour guarantee might not be adequate for functions occurring on Sundays, Mondays, and holidays, since suppliers do not normally deliver on weekends. The more exotic the menu, the more lead-time is needed for deliveries and preparation. If menu selections are foods usually kept on hand, readily supplemented, or served in other hotel food outlets, most hotels can accommodate a relatively short lead-time. Usually hotels prepare 5 percent more than the guaranteed number of meals. If requested, they will prepare for up to 10 percent more guests, thus providing the PCO with a safety margin. But it is not an invitation to "lowball" or give an unreasonably low guarantee. If the attendance is substantially higher than the guarantee and the hotel supplies the requisite number of meals, service will suffer since the larger group must be served by the same number of waiters provided in the planned guarantee.

Some organizations build meal costs into the registration fee. This practice offers a degree of fiscal insurance, but it is still important to estimate the number of meals to be served. Neither the hotel nor the PCO wants to prepare meals for a large number of no-shows. Usually, meal tickets are included in the registration packet or sold at the registration desk. The method for collecting meal tickets must be included on the function control form. One or more staff members should be on hand with extra tickets for guests and for ticket holders who arrive without theirs. A ticket exchange plan is advised for gala functions and events with assigned seating, but tickets are essential for any high-priced meal. Inform attendees in writing and in announcements that they must exchange their tickets for an assigned table card if they wish to attend. Guarantee is based on the actual number of tickets exchanged plus an optional 5 percent.

For first-time events and those for which it is difficult to predict attendance, we recommend the following:

- Reserve a room that will accommodate 100 percent of the group.
- Consider any factors or events that may reduce attendance.
- Include meal costs in the registration fee, and issue tickets.
- Select menu items that are readily available and easily augmented.
- Monitor late check-ins and early departures that might affect guarantees.
- Create a cushion. Alert meeting aides, registrars, AV technician, and other staff who normally join the group for meals to wait until the count is made. If attendance is under the guarantee, call them in. If not, they can use another food outlet. (Be sure to budget for staff meals.)

THE GASTRO-INTELLECTUAL TRACT

Gary Couture, a noted nutritionist and author, described the relationship between food and programming: "The key word in business today is productivity," he advises. "After 2:00 p.m., average people's productivity goes down 63 percent, all because they eat the wrong things and don't exercise. What you eat can have a significant effect on productivity and mental state, whether you're at work or attending a meeting."

PCOs act as planner and host for all functions at meetings. That role demands that they not only plan creative, innovative menus and offer appropriate entertainment, but that they also fulfill an obligation to provide an audience that is alert, aware, and receptive during the business sessions. It cannot be done after a meal consisting of cocktails, Beef Wellington, and two kinds of wine. Red meat entrees, cheeses, wines, mixed drinks, and rich desserts should be saved for dinners, preferably those that are not followed by speakers. For breakfasts, lunches, and breaks, the following guidelines apply:

- If breakfast is served, it should be a high-protein, high-carbohydrate meal that includes whole grains (rolls, cereals, granola) that take time to digest. (This will help prevent mid-morning slump.) A cautionary note: Caffeine is a proven stimulant, but too much of it makes people jittery.

- Avoid foods with high animal-fat content or saturated oils. These include most dairy products, fried foods, beef, pork, and lamb. Substitute poultry or fish for meats.

- Reduce the number of foods you serve that are high in sugar, which produce spurts of energy lasting perhaps forty minutes. A person's energy drops off sharply after that time.

- Provide sources of sustained energy—complex carbohydrates such as those found in breads, whole grains, green vegetables, and fresh fruit. Fruit is a particularly good source of energy and is actually a more effective source of energy than juices because of its pulp content.

- Be aware of the body's time cycle. Blood glucose is usually lowest in the afternoon. Counter that with foods that provide both immediate and sustained energy.

- Take into account the effects of jet lag meetings and the effects of a flight involving three or more time changes. Serve liquids frequently (hot lemon drinks are great), and have plenty of high-fiber foods and fresh fruits to promote regularity. Since travelers tend to retain water, serve diuretic foods such as cucumbers and asparagus. Prevent discomfort from water retention by limiting salt.

- Limit alcoholic beverages at lunchtime or at any function preceding an extended program. One drink or a glass of wine acts as a stimulant and aids digestion, but any more than that dulls the senses.

- At hospitality functions where alcohol is consumed, counter the effects with protein, starch, and high-fat snacks rich in vitamin B.
- Incorporate exercise, even of short duration. This can be as simple as having attendees walk to another part of the conference facility. At refreshment breaks, encourage people to help themselves to to-go snacks such as fresh and dried fruits, nuts, or granola bars. Chewing overcomes boredom, and the foods provide sustained energy.

Some meeting planners supply vitamins that aid the body's metabolism: niacin to open the arteries and vitamins B-6 and C to aid digestion and convert foods to energy. Keep in mind that the PCO's primary concern in catering to a *meeting* audience is not about diet or balanced nutrition, but rather about not serving foods that impede thought processes. Serve foods that enhance mental activity.

Knowing what is needed and getting it is not always easy, however. Try convincing a Cordon Bleu chef to substitute a light vinaigrette sauce for his award-winning, high-cholesterol Sauce Rochambeau-au-foi-de-Volaille. On the other hand, most food executives have become more receptive to the needs and suggestions of meeting organizers. Many have designed menus that specifically accommodate high-energy learning situations. Work with these fellow professionals to make food and beverage functions a complement to the meeting's communication objectives.

Resources:

CIC Manual, Seventh Edition, put out by the Convention Industry Council. www.conventionindustry.org

Flowers for Meetings & Conventions, put out by the American Florist Marketing Council, 1601 Duke St., Alexandria, VA 22314; 1-800-336-4743

Chapter Eleven
Registration and Housing

The process of soliciting, receiving, and processing registrations for an event and for accommodations requires careful planning, monitoring, coordinating, and followup. Computer software and hosted Web sites such as RegOnline and event.com have greatly ameliorated burdensome tasks. (See Appendix B). But all aspects of registration cannot be left to computers. No matter how detailed the promotional information may be, questions arise that demand people-time to answer phones, write responses, give friendly advice, or prevent misunderstanding. Knowledgeable, intelligent people with good communication skills and a fair amount of diplomacy can circumvent potential problems, which can negate even the best promotion and program if they are left unattended.

REGISTRATION PROCEDURES

Meetings in general and the registration process in particular usually involve large numbers of people. Ask any customer service representative what that means and you'll get a one hour lecture on the stupidity, rudeness, and helplessness of presumably intelligent, considerate, and competent people. To keep snafus to a minimum, PCOs prepare clear, concise, and complete registration instructions and meeting information. They design simplified forms and systems that ensure that the data are received, recorded, and processed to yield the desired results. The registration procedure must result in well-informed attendees and provide you with an accurate record of who will attend.

Procedures address two distinct functions: advance registration and on-site registration. Advance registration involves an announcement of the date and place of the meeting (and other details), a detailed form to be returned by the participant, and a system for processing returned registration forms, collecting fees (if appropriate), and providing information needed by the organizers. The forms may also cover membership classification, housing, program selections, social and recreational options, and special needs. On-site registration entails processing of attendees in person at the meeting venue (either online or at work stations). The PCO establishes procedures for verification of credentials and registration status and collection of fees, and related administrative tasks. See Chapters 15 and 16 for additional information regarding on-site registration.

The first step in developing a registration system is to determine what information is needed from the registrant. In its simplest form, this may be no more than name, address, and date of arrival. Is it a corporate meeting for which key executives determine who is to attend where all expenses are to be borne by the company? Is it a sales meeting involving independent dealers who will bear some expense, along with company employees? Or is it an association meeting or a seminar, for which attendees will pay a registration fee and all expenses? Each type of meeting is different, and the information needed differs. In the first example, there may only be an announcement and a rooming list. The information in the next section focuses on registration at events for which fees are charged. Many of the guidelines presented, however, apply to corporate or fully sponsored events as well.

ADVANCE MEETING ANNOUNCEMENT

It is now customary to use all three means to communicate an important message: e-mail, Web site, and postal delivery. Generally, the main meeting announcement will include the following elements:

- An attractive, thematic announcement printed with the name of the meeting, dates, location, the organization's name and logo, and a link to a Web site.
- Site information, map, and hotel brochure or Web page; the meeting's purpose, program information, and tentative daily business agenda (including topics, benefits of attending, etc.); eligibility and requirements for attendance, if any.
- Fees according to category, deadline for early registration, cancellation and refund policies, currency and methods of remittance.
- A list of program elements, materials, and functions that are included in the fee.

- A tentative social agenda, with a notice that guidelines for appropriate attire will follow.

- Exhibition information, including an exhibitor list and hours.

- Registration data and forms.

- Hotel information: rates, deposits or guarantees, billing procedures, pre-registration, early arrival and stay-over, check-in and check-out times.

- Travel arrangements, such as the name of the official airline, special fares, the toll-free number, ground transportation arrangements, car rental information.

Some meeting organizers include detailed program information if the agenda has been determined. In such cases, the registration form may ask the participant to select sessions to which attendance is limited. Details about the social agenda—such as a listing of sponsored and non-sponsored events, optional tours, and leisure activities—ticket purchase information, as well as a list of pre- and post-conference tours can be sent with reservation forms and billing data. In some instances, this is handled by an official travel agency or destination management company.

REGISTRATION FORMS

The design of a registration form has become something of an art, because professionals know that an efficient, trouble-free system is dependent on having proper documents. Forms must be clear, easy to complete, and designed for efficient and accurate processing, whether this is done manually or is automated. The key elements of a comprehensive form are:

- Event name, sponsor, theme, dates, and venue.

- Registrant data. Name, title, affiliation, address to which correspondence is to be sent, daytime telephone number, membership category or credentials, name badge data and preferred form of address (especially important for foreign delegates, who may choose to be called by surname and title). See "Registration" in Chapter 19 for more information.

- Accompanying persons. This is a potentially sticky area, requiring diplomacy. Avoid imposing moral values on attendees. Name and badge data are sufficient.

- Registration fees. Fees will vary, according to the category of attendee (member, non-member, etc.). Note fees for early registration with cut-off date and full or partial registration for accompanying persons; state the cancellation and refund policy and currency and methods of payment, and ask for credit card number and authorization, if applicable.

- Telephone/fax numbers and e-mail address for inquiries.
- Processing data for registration staff.

In addition to these basic elements, the form may include the following:

- Housing information. Name of the conference hotel(s) and rates, system for selection by attendee, arrival/departure dates, special room preferences, credit information or reservation deposit. (See section on "Housing Meeting Attendees" later in this chapter.)
- Ticket policies and prices for special sessions, functions, and other ticketed events, with check-off boxes for designating selected options.
- Listing of special sessions requiring advance reservations. Request that attendees indicate first and second choices.
- Medical or special dietary information. Emergency notification.
- Airline, flight, and arrival time if airport reception is planned.
- On-site registration. Location and hours.

Some organizations use a different form for on-site registration. Whatever the format, certain design criteria apply. The form, printed with the conference logo, should provide the needed information without looking cluttered. A clean typeface is advised, with boldface or color type used only for critical information. Be certain that there is adequate space for the participant to supply the information you need. Nothing is more frustrating for a delegate from West Nachitoches than to have to cram his home town into a line designed for Peoria. To ensure legibility, use boxes instead of lines and try to provide multiple choices in place of write-in spaces. Line and pitch dimensions should be suitable for handwritten, typewriter, or computer responses. Put the fees in table form so that the preparer can add them readily and the staff can verify the total. If registration forms for more than one event are processed together, color-code them for easy identification and sorting. This is where registration software can be most effective.

It's amazing how many presumably intelligent people come across like fifth-grade dropouts when completing a form. Form design calls for the old K.I.S.S. formula: Keep It Simple, Stupid!

AUTOMATING THE REGISTRATION PROCESS

Registration-management software is one of the most frequently used tools among meeting professionals. Only e-mailing and site/vendor research outpace it. According to a *Meeting News* poll, a substantial majority of all meeting planners are using or intend to soon use these multiple-benefit tools.

Use of this resource, however, ranges widely. Most meeting professionals are either unaware of numerous industry-designed applications or have chosen to create their own program. Custom applications come with added maintenance and support costs due to the pace of technology (which is significant and can be costly).

Current approaches used by meeting professionals include:

- Creative use of suite-based applications, such as Microsoft Office
- PC-based registration software
- Online registration systems, ranging from deploying simple forms to highly secured themed event Web sites
- Integrated enterprise-wide applications

As a rule, a blend of the first three methods is required to handle the myriad of details involved in registration management. Relevant technology used for the meeting registration process can be quite cost-efficient; the more registration transactions (including travel and housing), the greater the potential savings.

PC-BASED REGISTRATION SOFTWARE

Throughout the 1980s and early 1990s, meeting technology's gestation period, technosavy meeting planners' hot button was software designed for use on PCs. Registration software led the way, enabling PCOs to automate the burdensome task of processing reams of paper registration forms. Software developers rose to the task; Peopleware and PC Nametag became meetings management icons. Meeting Trak, Plansoft, and Event Solutions entered the fray and also prospered, proving that even with the onset of Web-based programs, there was and is a need for such planning tools. PC solutions tend to be more stable and offer greater security than Web-based registration systems. Consequently, many product vendors have responded by providing front-end Web interfaces in order to compete with dedicated Web-based applications.

PC-based software can handle so many tasks: spreadsheets; budgeting; session tracking; presentation graphics; and badge, ticket, and sign generation. Other applications that benefit from PC software are meeting room scheduling, floor plan design, and attendee evaluation. As in all applications, there is a caveat: Most programs lack the facility for real-time updates of registration and housing data.

WEB-BASED REGISTRATION

Corbin Ball, a leading authority on event technology, foresees growing reliance on technology, ranging from registration software programs to online applications. He points to the following benefits to support his rationale:

- Web-based system providers usually don't require you to install special software, thus saving purchase, installation, and training costs.
- These systems are often very easy to use, requiring no Web-design knowledge to set up Web registration forms.
- Since the administration pages use a standard Web browser interface that is intuitive, substantial training might not be necessary.
- Product upgrades are automatic, requiring little or no action by the meeting planner.
- Some systems allow the user to set up task lists, set deadlines, assign tasks, and track completion status. Planners can coordinate resources with other meeting events using a cross-division event calendar.
- E-mail marketing allows you to reduce costs relating to production, printing, and postage.
- E-mail campaigns, especially with built-in personalization and reminders, can be much more effective than standard mail in increasing attendance and revenue.
- Automatic reminders can reduce no-shows.
- These systems often use a single integrated database that is always up to date, allowing for more accurate forecasting and better management decisions.
- Much of the communication process is automated on the Web, so there will be cost savings in reduced staff time and lower phone charges to manage registrations.
- The total cost of ownership in these systems (paying for registration services on a transaction basis) is often lower than buying, customizing, and maintaining meeting management and registration software.
- Many registration providers offer registration forms that planners can fully customize. Planners should be able to define standard data

fields such as a registrant's name and address, as well as custom fields to collect information specific to the event.

One unique benefit of some Web-based programs is what Ball calls "viral marketing." (No need to be alarmed; this is a friendly virus.) It enables prospective attendees to forward the invitation to others or suggest others who might be interested. "With attendees assisting in the marketing effort, increased attendance can occur," he claims.

As PCOs become adept at bringing online registration functionality to their organizations, they should ultimately work at integrating elements shared by meeting registration data such as travel and housing. This growing trend will leverage the power of computing while providing ease of use for attendees.

A HISTORICAL PERSPECTIVE ON COMPUTERIZED REGISTRATION MANAGEMENT

Meeting planners with access to computer programming in the early 1970s were among the first to recognize the computer's capabilities for storing, processing, and outputting registration data. Some developed mainframe programs, and when microcomputers became available, they were able to access the data when away from the main computer by downloading. The personal computer made technology readily affordable to virtually anyone, and software development followed rapidly: In the late 1970s, there were only a handful of isolated in-house programs; now there is a wide range of software registration, program management, and other meeting functions, as well as membership services. Associations, which routinely process a thousand or more people for a single convention, have benefited tremendously from technology.

Robert Berke of the National Association of Fleet Administrators went through the same trial-and-error process faced by most early computer users as he tried to adapt a packaged software program offered by a service company. It proved to be a disaster, so he retained a consultant and outlined the following task needs:

1. Prepare accurate records of paid and unpaid conference registrations.

2. Produce acknowledgments and invoices.

3. Update registration lists as invoices are paid.

4. Produce an accurate, alphabetical roster of registrants.

5. Produce a summary financial report on the conclusion of the conference.

148 Administration and Logistics

From those initial parameters, Berke was able to develop a program that saved hundreds of man-hours of clerical time. The program was capable of expanding to handle other tasks, such as meal guarantees, meeting room assignments for multiple sessions, speaker information, correspondence, routine membership services, and financial management.

In 1985, the International Dance Exercise Association (IDEA) faced a similar challenge. (The author was personally involved in this effort as a consultant.) This fledgling organization's attendance had skyrocketed, and the number of events offered at their semi-annual conference grew dramatically. The problem the Association needed to solve was to register 1,200 attendees and assign them to some eighty sessions on each of three days! As many as ten sessions were scheduled to run concurrently during most one-hour blocks; potential registrants were asked to select sessions and indicate first, second, and third choices. The manual system used for the first three conventions was not capable of handling large numbers of people. IDEA, like any new association, had cash-flow problems, which ruled out the possibility of modifying existing registration software, most of which was too expensive to buy and reprogram.

After a task-analysis was prepared, I worked with the conference committee and a competent programmer to develop software that performed the following functions:

- Process registrations as they are received and generate acknowledgments.

- Track fee payments and produce cash flow summaries and accounts receivable.

- Assign session registrants a priority code so that early registrants would be given their first choice of sessions.

- Process, by priority, codes in batches of 400, and assign to sessions.

- Alert management as sessions approached 90 percent capacity in order to evaluate room assignments and make room changes.

- On conclusion of room designations, fill sessions, by priority code. As each session fills to 95 percent capacity, assign surplus to second choice, then third choice.

- Flag and hold registrants who did not indicate choices. Make random assignments to fill low attendance sessions.

- Generate confirmation letters and session assignments for all registrants.

- Produce alphabetical master roster with sessions listed. Produce attendance rosters for all sessions.

- Produce color-coded tickets for each session, and assign to registrants.
- Provide a system to accommodate on-site changes and reassignments in case of session cancellations, no-shows, VIP requests, etc.

Most conferences will not involve an unusually large number of sessions. IDEA's software program serves as a model for conference registration software programs.

HOUSING MEETING ATTENDEES

The PCO will be involved with some aspects of housing coordination, unless attendees are totally responsible for their own accommodations. For large, multi-hotel conventions, it is customary to use the services of the local convention bureau. Many of these organizations provide housing coordination at nominal or no cost. Use of these bureaus, however, does not relieve the PCO of the responsibility for supervision. After all, the information is essential for determining room pickups and adjusting room blocks to avoid penalties. Accurate arrival data can likewise be useful in determining guarantees for various functions.

Whether you work directly with the hotel's front office or with a housing bureau, it is important that the form conforms to the system used for processing housing requests. Here are some popular methods:

- Incorporate the housing request in the registration form. The entire form is received by the registration staff, who send the housing data or a copy of the form to the hotel either online or by mail. To avoid excessive handling of funds, request that a separate deposit check payable to the hotel or a credit card guarantee be supplied with the reservation.

- Enclose a hotel reservation card with the registration form. Most hotels can provide self-addressed cards or a stack of reservation forms containing deposit information. The registrant fills out the form, encloses the required deposit or credit card guarantee, and mails it to the hotel. The hotel staff confirms the reservation directly to each guest and submits periodic rooming lists to the organizer. These include room blocks, pickups, cancellations, and related data.

- If a housing bureau is used, the planner may incorporate the bureau's housing information into the registration form and forward housing requests to the bureau, or use the bureau's own form (which is returned, as in the previous example). The bureau then notifies the hotel, confirms the reservation to the guest, and submits periodic reports to the PCO.

The sponsoring organization's policy on suite assignments should be clearly stated on the housing form. Assignments may be made by the hotel, but organizers usually reserve the right to assign suites designated for their use.

Web-based Housing Options

Processing of housing data has made significant strides resulting from Internet access and the open architecture of information systems. With more varied applications designed to manage complex elements, meeting professionals have wider options for contracted room inventories.

Conference housing continues to improve in the scope of services available and in real-time access to inventory. As with all elements involving technology, ease of use, speed, security, and flexibility, along with maintaining a range of data inputs/formats, are essential elements to housing management.

Unfortunately, the comfort level adoption rate in supplying credit card information and other personal data online still requires wider use and acceptance for an online system to be the sole data conduit. Any housing solution then must provide alternative vehicles for processing this type of information, whether serviced through a calling center or through fax or mail processing.

All organizations contemplating online processing need to clearly understand the capabilities and requirements of the medium. There can be substantial cost savings by integrating registration, housing and travel, but without due diligence, an organization can be caught providing technology options well beyond its members' abilities and comfort levels. Unfortunately, not everyone has a personal digital assistant (PDA), a hand-held computer, or easy computing access. Nor do all share the same comfort in using the newer technologies often required in the online transaction process. As a result, meeting professionals need to address a technology solution that meets the core requirements of *their* market.

Corporations have a clear advantage: They can set company-wide policy and provide funding for projects that can clearly show a positive ROI within an 18-month period. Associations are limited to the support of their sponsors and member responsiveness.

The major players in the online housing market have recently made their application protocols available to several online registration companies, providing meeting professionals with the option of making housing and conference registration available to their end-users. The integration of these processes is clearly a benefit to the online user in terms of providing streamlined data-entry and efficiencies in one-stop shopping.

Data privacy within the European community is taken very seriously. Any PCO who captures attendees "home address information" must make certain that the database that contains the information is encrypted at all times. This is also the case for any U.S.-based databases that may be housed in the United States but provide a business service within Europe.

Despite the best of technologies, the three critical components required for the successful acceptance of a housing solution are location, price, and brand identity of the lodging venue, as they are initially offered to an attendee. Simply, if lodging options don't meet user needs, the technology will be bypassed!

PROCESSING ADVANCE REGISTRATIONS

As with all other elements of the meeting, the efficiency with which registrations are handled influences attendees' perception of the organization. A misspelled name on a badge is a small thing, but it is an embarrassment to the person who's stuck with it. A delayed acknowledgment or incomplete registration information, which necessitates a phone call, can leave a negative impression before the registrant arrives at the meeting.

It is important that advance registrations receive prompt acknowledgment. It may be no more than a simple e-mail, letter, or postcard confirming their registration and any sessions to which they have been assigned. A welcome letter from the CEO or conference chairman is always appreciated. Organizations that mail advanced meeting announcements in a higher volume than their anticipated attendance can follow up by sending meeting materials to confirmed registrants. The packet may also contain special airfares, the airline reservation telephone number, information on the destination and hotel, airport reception arrangements, ground transportation fares, and the latest details on business and social programs. Invoices reflecting payment in full or any balance due, if there has been underpayment, may be enclosed or be part of the confirmation notice.

For paper registration, the processing system should be designed so that all data on the registration forms can be readily recorded and retrieved. Some organizations assign a control number or utilize membership numbers; others use names. Control numbers—preferred for computerized registration systems—seem to be better for recording registration and payment, generating receipts or invoices, and maintaining individual account status. They are also useful for recording any changes, cancellations, and subsequent computation of refunds.

A key by-product of the processing system is an attendance roster that can be output in several permutations. Its first function is to provide a master registration list for the PCO and registration staff. Information on the master list will vary according to the input and the various functions the list is to perform. One advantage of an automated registration system is the capability to supply many different reports from the same data. One of these would be an Advance Registration Roster reproduced and distributed to attendees in advance or on arrival. Considered a valuable document, it tells people who else has signed up for the conference. Because final registration can be substantially different, it's customary to produce a supplement during the meeting.

BADGES

Badges are to meetings what kilts are to Scots. They distinguish members of a group. Like the distinctive patterns of the tartan, they provide a sense of belonging. Besides identifying the wearer and his or her affiliation and hometown, badges facilitate greetings and introductions. They help avoid that embarrassing and awkward moment when one recognizes the face but draws a total mental block on the name. Color-coded and under observation of trained personnel, badges are a useful control device for restricting access to certain functions or sessions.

A badge can often reflect the quality of the meeting. A badge bearing the meeting theme in color, with a bold name clearly printed or computer-generated and a durable badge holder does far more for the sponsor's image than the perennial HELLO! MY NAME IS marked up with felt-tip lettering. Not that there is anything wrong with this—when executed by an expert calligrapher! In addition to the attendee's name, title, affiliation, and hometown, badges often display, in larger bold letters, a first name or nickname. Keep in mind that this custom is peculiar to North Americans, Australians, and, increasingly, Britons; many Europeans are reluctant to display such familiarity, and in much of Europe, Latin America, the Middle East, and Asia, the practice is inappropriate.

The badge holder should be the clutch-back type, rather than the pin-back; the pin-back tends to leave holes in clothing, and women are particularly reluctant to wear them. Most people prefer a lanyard. The format may be vertical or horizontal. In the program material or with the badge itself, it is suggested that people wear them on their left side; the eye is naturally drawn to what we see as the right side when shaking hands.

Many computer software programs can be used to generate attractive, distinctive badges using ink jet or laser printers. There are also a number of vendors who specialize in printing badges at a nominal cost. For recognition of officers, directors, the press, and those receiving a special distinction, the ubiquitous colored ribbons are gradually being replaced by color-coded badge holders, with the designation printed on either the badge or the holder.

With the rapid development of meeting technology, badges today can do more than provide name recognition. Thanks to such advances as microchips, bar codes, and infrared and wireless communications, a new generation of "smart badges" have matured into exotic communication devices whose applications are limited only by the PCO's imagination and the sponsor's budget. Some of these phenomena are described in Chapter 13.

Resources:

See Appendix B for a listing of software and Web sities relating to this chapter.

FLASHpoint Technologies maintains a database of over 400 meeting applications. (*www.flashpointtech.com*)

Air/Housing Request Form

PLEASE PRINT

Name _____ Company Name _____
Address _____ Address _____
City _____ State _____ Zip ____ City _____ State _____ Zip ____
Home Phone ( ) _____ Business phone ( ) _____ E-mail _____

Hotel Registration

HOUSING WILL BE ASSIGNED ON A FIRST-COME, FIRST-SERVED BASIS IN THE FOLLOWING ORDER:
HOTELS: 1) Franklin Plaza   2) Plaza Hotel   3) Philadelphia Center   4) Holiday Inn

ARRIVAL DATE: _____ DEPARTURE DATE: _____
ROOM TYPE ( ) Single (1 person)   ( ) Double (2 people)
ADDITIONAL NAME (if sharing) _____
TO RESERVE MY HOTEL ROOM, I AM ( ) **Enclosing my check for deposit ($65)**
                                ( ) **Supplying the needed credit card information below**

Air Travel Request

City/Airport you wish to depart from _____
Class of service   ( ) First Class   ( ) Coach   ( ) Discount
Departure (date) _____ (time) _____ (a.m.) _____ (p.m.) _____
Return (date) _____ (time) _____ (a.m.) _____ (p.m.) _____
FLIGHT/DATE CONFIRMATIONS WILL BE SENT TO YOU BY RETURN MAIL, ALONG WITH YOUR BILLING.

Credit Card Information

I wish to pay for my ( ) Air   ( ) Hotel by credit card
Credit card to be charged to ( ) American Express   ( ) Visa   ( ) MasterCard
My card number is _____ Date of expiration _____
Name on card (exactly as it appears on card) _____
AMI Housing is hereby authorized to charge my air and/or hotel deposit to the above listed credit card.

DATE _____   SIGNATURE _____

Mail your request to:

CONFIRMATIONS ON ALL AIR AND/OR HOTEL REQUESTS WILL BE SENT TO YOU BY RETURN MAIL

For questions on AIR/HOUSING call 1-800-328-0781

FIGURE 11-1 Air/Housing request.

154 *Administration and Logistics*

SAMPLE
CONFERENCE REGISTRATION

Professional Education Conference
DECEMBER 4-7, 1988
OPRYLAND HOTEL
NASHVILLE, TENNESSEE

Please print clearly:
BADGE INFO: This is how badge will read:

First Name or Nickname

Full Name

Company/Affiliation

City   State/Province   Country

Check all that apply:
☐ Executive Committee   ☐ Council of Presidents
☐ International Board Member   ☐ Educational Research
☐ Chapter Board Member   Foundation
☐ Chapter Officer   ☐ Committee Chairman
☐ International Past President
☐ First Time Conference
   Attendee
☐ New Member
   (Joined since June 1, 2005)

PERSONAL GUEST BADGE INFORMATION:

First Name or Nickname

Guest Full Name

City   State

MPI Member # _____
☐ Planner ☐ Supplier ☐ Student ☐ Guest ☐ Press
☐ Speaker ☐ CMP ☐ CM ☐ CAE ☐ CHSE

Title

Mailing Address

Street Address/Box #

City   State/Province   Country   Zip/PC
(____) _____   E-mail: _____
Phone
Chapter Affiliation _____

In case of emergency, contact:

Name
(____) _____   (____) _____
Day Phone   Evening Phone

REGISTRATION FEES
See reverse side for registration policies.

	Early Registrant Discount Before November 18	After November 18	
MPI Member	$350	$400	$_____
Non-Member (Planner Only)	$400	$450	$_____
Student	$175	$175	$_____
One Day (Member Only)	$150	$150	$_____
☐ Monday, December 5			
☐ Tuesday, December 6			
Personal Guest	$175	$175	$_____
	Total Enclosed		$_____

International Funds must be submitted in U.S. Equivalents.

Downtown City Lights, Monday night event. By ticket only.
Tickets will be available in Nashville for those registering on-site. All other tickets will be placed with the registration material.
Please number your choices in order of preference for dinner location.
____ Doubletree Hotel   ____ Hermitage Hotel   ____ Hyatt Regency Nashville
____ Maxwell House   ____ Stouffer Nashville Hotel ____ Vanderbilt Plaza Hotel

Form of Payment
Fees are payable to MPI by check, Visa, or MasterCard. Resgistration **fees must accompany this form** or registration will not be processed.
☐ Check Enclosed   ☐ Visa   ☐ MasterCard

Credit Card #   Expiration Date   Signature

Refund Policy
Full refunds will be granted to requests received in writing at MPL prior to November 4, 2005. A refund of less $30 will be granted to written requests received at MPI between November 4 and November 18, 2005. **No refunds will be granted after November 18, 2005.**

Return completed form and fee to:
CONFERENCE DEPARTMENT
Meeting Planners International
1950 Stemmons Freeway, Suite 5018
Dallas, Texas 75207

For Internal Use only
Received Date: _____   Entered _____
Reg ID # _____   Check # _____
Reg ID # _____   Amt. Rec'd _____

Please complete reverse side of this form for workshop selections prior to mailing.   AB

FIGURE 11-2 Sample conference registration form.

Part Four:

Operations

Chapter Twelve
Communication and the Meeting Environment

A MEDIUM FOR COMMUNICATION

It has been said that anything worth saying is worth saying well, often, and in a variety of ways. This is the principle underlying the need for pacing and balance essential to effective program design. We know that people retain more of what they see than what they hear and an even higher percentage of what they both see and hear. Audiovisuals ensure higher retention. If a meeting is a medium for communication, effective audiovisual software and systems and the proper environment are essential components of that medium. Proper use of appropriate audiovisual techniques aids in the transmission, reception, and retention of the message.

Presumably, one can dispense with speakers altogether and convey the meeting message entirely through exciting multimedia extravaganzas combining video and digital images with a dramatic recorded narrative, augmented with an up-tempo musical track. Right?

Wrong! As resourceful as those techniques are in a support role, they cannot sustain communication without other elements. The audience would be asleep by the end of the first half-hour and the dramatic narrative would fall on deaf ears. That simplistic approach ignores the need for pacing and balance. Audiovisuals are best used in a support role, interspersed with speakers, panels, group discussion, and other program elements. These devices are meant to provide an added dimension to the essential message of the meeting and are not intended to stand alone. Conversely, however serious the meeting, one should not overlook the value of humor and entertainment for attracting attention, dramatizing a critical point, or simply providing relief between two highly technical presentations. Behavioral psychologists, professional speakers, and educators understand the value of humor for increasing attentiveness, conditioning an audience, and enhancing retention. Consider some of the memorable presentations you have witnessed: chances are they have been high in entertainment value.

In the past few decades, the meeting industry has benefited from an accelerated technological development in communication, as well as a clearer understanding of adult learning. Audiences, influenced by television, have come to expect a higher degree of sophistication. Meeting planners and producers have kept pace with more elaborate presentations that incorporate such exotic techniques as total immersion environments, interactive video, multi-visual synthesizers, holographic projection, computer simulation, surround sound, streaming video, and multi-perceptual stimuli. Audiences meeting simultaneously on several continents have been linked via satellite for two-way video conferencing. (It was once anticipated that teleconferencing would replace meetings in the traditional sense. It didn't!) Conference hotels, which once feared the intrusion of video conferencing, are now its greatest beneficiaries and proponents, testimony to the medium's role in meeting support.

The PCO's role in this process is that of the expert communicator who understands the dynamics, as well as the mechanics, of event management, though other experts may be involved in the production and execution. Planning the use of AV support begins with objectives. What is the purpose? Is it to inform? To educate? To convey data? To illustrate? Or is the objective to motivate? To provide recognition? To reinforce an attitude or change it? To instill pride and make the audience feel good about its organization, its community, or its industry? Once the audiovisual objectives have been defined, the appropriate elements must be researched, produced, and integrated into the program.

PRODUCING AUDIOVISUAL ELEMENTS

This chapter is not intended as a text on AV production—that could be an entire series of books. As with other topics covered in this book, a certain level of understanding and competence is attributed to the reader. The author's intent is to review some of the key elements of production and reiterate accepted guidelines.

The PCO, in concert with the program chairman or committee, examines the meeting program outline to determine where and what type of support elements are needed. Some of these elements may be inherent in a speaker's presentation, such as slides (both film and digital), digital animation, video, or prepared transparencies. (A word of caution, however: As explained in the chapter on speakers, the conference organizer is responsible for reviewing all AV media and formats to be used and then advising presenters of the projection format, equipment, and staging for each session.) Other audiovisual elements may already exist among the organization's resources or can come from a variety of audiovisual software and meeting modules, some of which are high-budget productions.

Some AV support elements may need to be produced or customized to meet specific program objectives. They may be produced in-house, given the availability of sophisticated media software (if the organization has that capability.) Professional graphic artists, designers, and audiovisual production services provide, for a fee, the design, creativity, and technical competence that spell the difference between a ho-hum visual aid and a high-impact communication medium. It is possible to produce professional-quality slides, transparencies, and even digital graphics and video at a fraction of the cost charged by outside services. The key criterion is that you must have people who understand graphic design and are able to implement the computer's capabilities to achieve professional quality. This has become particularly true with the dominance of Microsoft's ubiquitous PowerPoint®. Indeed, a large percentage of all individual presentations are currently prepared by the presenter using this popular software.

By the mid-1990s, PowerPoint had largely replaced 35 mm slides and the carousel projector as the presentation technology of choice. Because it is relatively simple to use, with extensive templates, creative transitions, good tutorials, and broad interoperability with other common business and design software, virtually anyone can design his own slide presentations. But there is a downside: You will need someone competent in graphic design, and it will be tempting to use the many visual and audio effects featured in PowerPoint to lard up slide after slide with dramatic swooshes and fancy transitions that serve only to distract and, in the more egregious cases, annoy the audience. Many speakers who are otherwise competent in their subject and articulate in conveying their messages harm their own images with overproduced or poorly designed computer-based presentations.

Given the proliferation of digital presentations, it is contingent on event managers, when providing computers, to ascertain in advance whether presenters will be using Mac- or PC-produced material. Software for such productions should be pre-loaded and tested.

A MEDIA ANALYSIS

The accelerated changes in technology that have characterized audiovisual communication have created opportunities for the meetings industry. Even as this is written, methods and hardware are changing and becoming obsolete, only to be replaced by new systems evoking new techniques for communicating. Review the five primary audiovisual media listed and compared below. (Overhead projection is not included, because it is a visual aid rather than an audiovisual medium.) Before production decisions are made, the meeting organizer should analyze each type relative to the meeting objectives and for its flexibility, impact, and cost.

Medium	Advantages / Limitations	Flexibility	Cost
Slide-sound or multi-image (film and digital)	Short production time. Accepts existing visuals. Multi-track/multi-image projection system bulky, complex, specialized, not universally compatible. Most film replaced by digital media.	Very flexible. Readily updated or modified. 35 mm slides obsolete.	Inexpensive to moderate
Video	Intimate and familiar. Rapid production, especially with digital video. Can combine existing elements. Special effects, computer interface/incompatible formats.	Flexible. Easy to add, change, or update. Readily integrates with other media.	Inexpensive to expensive
Digital animation	Rapid production. Good compromise between limitations of multi-image animation and cost of video production. Limitations: None.	Flexible. Easy to add, change, or update.	Moderate
Film	Compatible with all projectors. Large, good-quality projected image, variety of formats/ Single track except in 70 mm. Long production time. Laboratory required. Projector availability is limited.	Inflexible. Changes require access to pre-print elements. Obsolete.	Expensive
Live theater	Provides immediacy, audience rapport, interaction. Relatively short production. May need complex staging. Travel expense of rehearsal and/or performance.	Most flexible. Spontaneous. Actors can interact with audience.	Moderate if no stars are used

A single medium is seldom used for all the audiovisual support except at some small meetings and seminars. Examples of the use of multi-media would be an event featuring a video meeting opener with laser light show and other special effects or a digital animation with music to introduce a live presentation or PowerPoint slides to support speakers. You could add live actors in a series of staged vignettes or use a series of audiovisual modules or bridges that serve to link presentations, emphasize or illustrate a point, and provide entertainment or comic relief between dry technical presentations. The meeting's objectives and budget dictate the number, quality, and cost of production components. Most meeting managers who are conscious of the limitations on their time and know the value of other professionals with specialized skills will look to a production company, specifically a meeting producer, for most audiovisual production services.

Relatively simple visual aids can be produced in-house, and the aforementioned rental modules can come from libraries. An outside meeting producer is usually contracted for more-complex productions. Some PCOs engage an outside producer to supervise or advise on elements produced in-house in order to ensure continuity of design and uniform quality, and then to direct or "call" the show on-site. Many organizations establish a close working relationship with a production house and use it for all creative support. Others will prepare detailed audiovisual specifications and request creative treatments and bids. Development fees paid to each bidder for preparing a treatment or scenario are allocated in the budget. Another approach is to contract with one production company or a competent writer experienced in the medium to prepare a scenario, which is then put out for bids. The criteria for evaluating bids should be creativity, experience, and kind of service it can provide, rather than price.

WORKING WITH MEETING PRODUCERS

The PCO should meet with one or more producers about four to five months out to discuss the upcoming meeting—its objectives, attendance, agenda, etc. Each producer then submits a creative treatment and proposal that confirms the meeting objectives, establishes a theme, proposes the production elements to integrate the theme, and sets a production budget and schedule. The meeting manager interviews and selects the production company that best meets the aforementioned criteria and demonstrates creativity in its treatment. They develop a production schedule that assigns mutual responsibilities and sets dates for completion of software elements. The schedule that follows (which is typical) provides for periodic reviews. It should be noted, however, that it is the rare production that succeeds in sticking to the schedule, since much depends on the responsiveness of multiple speakers and the decision makers on the client end.

The producer's role as it pertains to entertainment is covered in Chapter 6.

SAMPLE PRODUCTION SCHEDULE

Client	*Producer*
Four to Five Months Ahead	
Review proposal and treatment relative to goals. Approve or request modifications. Accept proposal and confirm elements.	Modify proposal if requested.
Three to Four Months Ahead	
Confirm availability of key meeting rooms for setup, rehearsal, and performance.	Inspect site, survey room. Interview AV rental and staging services.
Provide list of topics and speakers. Research client-supplied elements.	Confirm availability and meeting dates. Research rental of stock AV elements. Begin scripting AV continuity. Finalize production schedule.
Two Months Ahead	
Alert speakers to outline presentations for AV integration.	Interview speakers for content.
Review scripts and storyboards. Provide client-supplied elements. Approve scripts and visual design. Approve talent selection.	Complete and present continuity script and storyboards. Draft and design speaker support AV. Audition professional talent. Revise scripts; submit final draft.
Finalize hotel arrangements for AV staff, cast, rehearsal space, dressing rooms. Arrange staff and cast transportation.	Begin production of continuity elements. Shoot video.
	Record, score, and mix sound tracks. Determine on-site staff, staging, and equipment requirements. Order rental equipment. Finalize and book orchestra, entertainment.
One Month Ahead	
Screen roughcut.	Complete photography. Edit video. Prepare roughcut.
Screen and approve AV production.	Make client changes. Begin fine cut.
Approve answer print.	Produce speaker support visuals. Rent stock films and modules. Begin post-production and programming.
	Fine-tune. Complete multi-image and integrate speaker visuals.
	Confirm on-site rentals. Ship equipment.
On-site	
Pre-conference meeting. Confirm arrangements for setup, rehearsal, house staff. Advise key presenters of rehearsals.	Pre-con meeting. Prepare and distribute rehearsal schedules. Rehearse live cast. Technical rehearsal and setup. Dry-run cues and bridges. Rehearse cast and orchestra.
Dress rehearsal.	Dress rehearsal.
	Fine-tune, test projectors, and align.

PRINCIPLES OF VISUAL DESIGN

There are many circumstances for which simple visual aids will be adequate and when the budget will not permit sophisticated audiovisual production. The ready availability of reliable graphics software greatly expands presentation capabilities. Whether the organization has an in-house graphics capacity or chooses to use a media producer, the PCO needs to have an understanding of what constitutes good visual aids.

"You probably can't read this from where you're sitting, but . . ." Sound familiar? Regrettably, that disclaimer is invoked often by presenters as an excuse for lack of preparation. It reflects the egocentric notion that hearing the speaker's message is more important than seeing the visual. If that is true, why use visual aids at all?

The answer lies in the point that was made in Chapter 5 regarding understanding and retention: we retain 20 percent of what we hear, but 50 percent of what we *hear and see*. Communicators have developed proven criteria for designing visuals that support the spoken word. Visual aids illustrate, clarify, and reinforce the speaker's message. To do so effectively, they must be readily seen and understood by everyone in the audience, including the people in the back row.

Designing Artwork for Projection

Legibility of the image begins with the planning of artwork. Two things need to be determined before the artist can start: the size of the audience and the projection medium. To some extent, the first factor influences the second. Slides and transparencies are appropriate for small audiences; slide projection is good for groups of 200 or more. The following design guidelines apply to PowerPoint and similar projected graphics containing text:

- Limit the amount of copy. Many presenters try to cram a full page of copy on a single slide. The result is a blurred blob. Type slides should merely highlight key points. Follow the "five by five" rule: a maximum of five words per line and five lines per *frame*. If more information is needed, use more frames. The optimum is ten or fewer words per slide.

- Design visuals for a horizontal format. People may not be able to see over the heads of those in front of them because of screen height and ceiling height. Vertical images tend to aggravate this problem and limit audience viewing. (See Figure 12-3.)

- Keep essential information in the upper three-fourths of the slide area. The lower quarter may be hidden by people's heads.

- Specify bold or extra bold, serif or sans serif fonts, and upper and lower case letters. Serif fonts (Times New Roman, Palatino, etc.) are easier to read for large blocks of text, but sans serif fonts (Arial, Helvetica, etc.) are cleaner and make better titles. Avoid busy and stylized fonts except for special effects or visual impact. Do not put long phrases or sentences in all-caps or italics.

- Avoid full sentences. Copy should highlight key points using bullets. Try to use single action words and telegraphic phrases.

- Keep charts simple and uncluttered. Charts should illustrate relationships. Detailed statistical data should be prepared as handouts.

- Use progressive builds (several slides or internal builds) to illustrate successive points in a linear fashion.

Most of these suggestions apply also to overhead transparencies, but vertical formats are fine for overheads.

Legibility of Projected Visuals

In a darkened meeting room, the bright light of a projected image using black text on white background can be harsh on the viewers' eyes. Reverse-text slides (white or colored type on black or dark blue background) offer the greatest legibility. Font colors should contrast sharply with the background—white, yellow, or orange lettering on a black or dark blue field provide the best results. Red lettering is also effective as long as it is *not* combined with a blue background—this combination will make the letters nearly impossible to read. Finally, colors should be bright and vivid; pastels do not project well and result in washed-out visuals. Do remember, however, that some participants might be color blind.

To determine legibility, it is best to view the image on a computer screen from 10 feet away (or, for 35 mm, at arm's length against a strong light). Try to read the copy. If it is legible, the audience will be able to read it when it is projected.

Beyond PowerPoint

Personal computers and user-friendly software packages have revolutionized the production of speaker-support visual aids, and placed professional production methods into the hands of any PC user. Because of the nexus between PCs and large-screen projection, the most sophisticated software applications can be used to generate complex animation in real time. Whether you are giving engineers a live demonstration of Computer Aided Design software or you are playing an animated graphic to illustrate distribution networks for the sales team, computers allow you to provide a visual representation of virtually any information for an audience at a very reasonable cost.

Digital video (DV) has lowered the cost of video production, especially with the introduction of affordable editing software that can be used on desktop and laptop computers. DV, as well as animation software such as Macromedia's Flash®, is increasingly used as a more active, more flexible alternative to slides for presenting visual information. Although these require the services of professional video editors and animators, the relative costs are in many cases comparable to professionally designed PowerPoint presentations.

Even more common is the combination of employing different media within a PowerPoint presentation such as embedding video clips, animated segments, music, narration, and other media within a slide. Continued advances in software designs for graphics applications will offer almost limitless design capabilities.

VIDEO AT MEETINGS

Once limited to the broadcast industry, video usage has evolved and grown in popularity as an essential meeting communication tool. It has been used in training, technical demonstrations, group instruction, and sales presentations. Digital video cameras and simple editing software have lowered production costs and empowered creative communicators to develop innovative and effective applications for this eminently flexible medium. Video is now a common meeting component. In this context, television performs a variety of communication functions:

- *Illustration.* In this most basic form, videotape playback is used to illustrate or explain points in a presentation, much like slides and films.
- *Reportage.* Recording events or information of a timely nature that can be more readily captured on videotape or disk.
- *Image Magnification (IMAG).* Projection of a large video image of a speaker or panel.
- *Overflow.* Providing access to the program for attendees who must meet in a remote location because of limited room capacity.
- *Surrogate address.* Enabling a speaker to address an audience when he or she cannot be physically present at the meeting site.
- *Video conferencing.* Concurrent meetings in several distant locations where people intercommunicate by means of satellite-transmitted video signal.

- *Dramatization.* Use of video for role-playing simulation and similar audience participation activities.
- *Documentation.* Video recording of presentations and meeting highlights for subsequent reference, critique, or dissemination.

The amount, sophistication, and cost of video equipment and technical support will vary with each of these applications. It can run the full gamut, ranging from a simple videocassette player and monitor for showing pre-recorded programs at a seminar for twelve people to a fifteen-city global teleconference encompassing satellite transmission and a full professional broadcast studio and staff. Closed-circuit television (CCTV) can likewise involve video projection or simultaneous display on multiple monitors of a live presentation or pre-recorded tape or disc. All of these applications have three basic elements:

1. A display medium. CRT Plasma or LCD monitor or video projection.
2. Origination source. Video camera or playback deck (DVD or tape).
3. Peripheral systems. Controls, switchers, mixers, and related equipment.

Video's complex technical requirements should not be a bar to its use, as long as the objective justifies it and professionals implement it. In the hands of competent technicians and a creative director, video can provide an added dimension to the meeting and generate among participants a sense of excitement and spontaneity that can materially enhance any event.

VIDEO EQUIPMENT AND SYSTEMS
Monitors and Projectors (LED Screens)

At meetings, the medium employed to display video images will be determined by audience size. The most common are multiple monitors and video projection. Multiple monitors have proven to be a viable means of displaying video information for audiences of limited size, but advances in video projection technology have made the use of multiple monitors virtually obsolete for supplementing or enhancing large screen projected video.

A typical arrangement might include a center screen for speaker support slides and video, flanked by two screens for IMAG, with an assortment of plasma or LCD monitors placed around the stage and around the room that can be switched between speaker support and IMAG or programmed as part of a multi-image show. Additional remote monitors might also be placed in the lobby or in a pressroom to allow viewers to see what's happening in a given session in real time.

Origination Source

The two primary sources of video signals are a camera focused on a "live" or real time object and a video playback device such as a VCR, a DVD player, or a computer. Cameras are available in many configurations and prices. All have essentially the same output: a composite video signal that can be fed to a recorder, a computer, a monitor, or a video projector. Except for video color standard, which is described later, all cameras work the same way and are relatively interchangeable.

Video recording systems suffer from lack of standardization. The various media—cassette tape, disc, computer—require different systems for playback. Furthermore, within each medium, there are different sizes and formats that won't be compatible or interchangeable. A VHS cassette cannot be played back on a Beta VCR, and Beta SP format cannot be used on earlier Beta recorders, for example, DVDs, laser discs, and videotapes require their own specialized machines. Faced with these variables, the frustrated meeting planner may well ask, "How do I know that the equipment I order will play the media I need to use?"

One way is to insist on accurate specifications from speakers and others providing video recordings. Another is to have the material re-recorded or converted by means of a Time Base Corrector. The latter allows materials to be dubbed from one format to another in spite of inherent incompatibility of the media involved.

PCOs managing international meetings need to be aware of the various video color standards in use in different parts of the world. North America and most of Asia have adopted the NTSC color system. Different parts of Europe, Britain, and other regions use either the SECAM or PAL color standard. No video equipment can be mixed from one system to another; they are incompatible. Fortunately, universal videocassette decks are available from many AV rental companies: These decks can play back tapes in any standard and are a less costly alternative to having programs converted to the appropriate standard. DVDs are also encoded in NTSC, PAL, SECAM, and other standards, and have the additional restriction of region codes, a copyright protection measure that prevents DVDs produced for, say, the Japanese market from being played in Europe.

Peripheral Systems

A simple video playback or a single camera recording may require no more than an origination source and a display medium; any more than that will usually call for some peripheral systems. These may consist of nothing more complex than a distribution amplifier to boost the signal to several video monitors or a video switcher to enable transitions from one camera to another. A complex "shoot," however, may call for a video remote unit that is a self-contained TV studio complete with multiplex switchers, several videotape recorders, special effects and character generators, and an editing console. If the signal is relayed live to a broadcast facility or to a satellite, as with teleconferences, microwave relays and other esoteric hardware will be needed. As the amount of equipment is increased, so is the need for qualified technicians to operate it. Even the most experienced PCO is well advised to seek professional help in designing and assembling a system that will achieve the meeting's communication objectives most effectively and economically.

VIDEO APPLICATIONS

Opportunities for incorporating video as a meeting medium are limited only by imagination and budget. In addition to the basic functions of documentation, audiovisual support, and speaker enhancement, various techniques can be used with video to add a vital dimension to the event:

- *TV theme.* The meeting agenda is presented as a day of television programming. Each presentation or agenda element is identified with popular TV formats such as talk shows, game shows, and news breaks. For example, a weather forecaster describes the business climate, and talk shows feature industry experts.
- *Recreation highlights.* An event such as a golf or tennis tournament or a mini-olympics is recorded. The videotapes are edited overnight and shown during one of the social functions, to the amusement of participants and spectators alike.
- *Meeting vignettes.* A number of production companies prepare a videotape of humorous meeting highlights—known as *happy faces*—using a combination of stock footage and live recordings. Some even script and shoot short, funny routines that allow the more-talented participants (or those who presume to be) to demonstrate their acting abilities. Tapes are edited on site and shown on the final day.

These techniques serve to enhance the meeting for the participants and act as valuable promotional tools to motivate those who did not attend.

AUDIOVISUAL EQUIPMENT AND SYSTEMS

Even the rare meeting not using audiovisuals needs *some* equipment, even if it is just a sound system, a lectern, and a flipchart. For most meetings, the media will dictate the equipment. The PCO, the program committee, and the audiovisual producer will determine audiovisual requirements, but sometimes these will be specified by individual presenters. As more sophisticated systems have evolved, professionals who plan and stage meetings and those who service them have had to become more knowledgeable and more technically competent. They have even had to learn a new vocabulary.

This conversation between a PCO and a convention services manager was overheard during a meeting-room inspection:

> "We're shooting RP with a 16-foot throw," the PCO described. "It's a three-screen show with IMAG on the outside and visuals center, along with plasmas on the grid and a couple of Retros flanking the audience. Do you see any problems with that?"
>
> "No problem," the CSM replied. "We had one almost identical last month."

In the past, all that most meetings required were some microphones, a few slide and overhead projectors, an occasional 16 mm projector, and a variety of screens and flipcharts. Multi-image shows with multiple slide projectors were considered complex. Now teleconferencing components, multi-format VCR and DVD players, streaming video, large-screen video projection, PCs, servers, and broadband Internet connections are common communication requirements.

WIRELESS TECHNOLOGY

The impact of wireless technology can materially reduce staging costs while enhancing interaction in a meeting environment. Driven by radio-wave technologies, wireless networks, and miniaturization, audiovisual manufacturers have provided a steady flow of new equipment for business and personal use.

Pioneered by Bluetooth Systems, wireless signal transmission was advanced by the newer, more sophisticated WiFi standard. WiFi itself will undoubtedly be surpassed by standards offering faster and wider transmission distances.

The benefits of wireless systems are numerous for meeting professionals and facility managers:

- Installation is faster than wired environments, resulting in better performance at lower cost.
- Line-of-sight is no longer a limiting factor.
- Transmitting conference information saves attendees from having to fumble through program books, making the meeting more convenient for participants to attend.

- Wireless systems simplify setup and use of audience response systems.
- Exhibitors can beam information to booth traffic and collect data.

The marriage of audiovisual and computer technologies has given presenters and meeting planners a degree of flexibility undreamed of in the 20th century. A wide range of components enhanced by wireless networks, radio wave technology, and miniaturization have been applied by manufacturers to AV equipment and support systems. Small hand-held devices allow a presenter to turn on equipment, advance computer-generated visuals, increase sound volume, and dim or bring up room lighting as simply as using a TV remote. This results in better performance and the welcome abolishment of the awkward "Next slide please."

THE AUDIO IN AUDIOVISUAL

Audio, from the meeting organizer's perspective, encompasses four applications:

1. *Amplification.* Sound reinforcement of, for example, a speaker at a lectern, a panel on the dais, simultaneous interpretation, a microphone in the audience, background music, or the sound track for a film, video, or audio recording.
2. *Playback.* A means of playing pre-recorded materials on film, tape, disc, and other recording media and feeding them into the sound system.
3. *Recording.* A capability for capturing on magnetic tape or computer disk all or parts of the program, including concurrent sessions.
4. *Transmission/Streaming.* A process for sending the audio portion of the meeting over the airwaves or over the Internet in real time.

Sound Systems

All four applications require a dependable sound system with quality components. Unless microphones, amplifiers, and speakers are engineered as a system and are consistent with the acoustical qualities of each room, the best microphones and the highest fidelity recordings will fall short of the mark. Regrettably, many meeting facilities fail to recognize the importance of quality engineered systems; PCOs using such facilities will have to rent professional sound systems.

Amplification is usually not necessary for rooms under 500 square feet in size, unless such a room is a section of a larger room. However, to accommodate a variety of sound applications, such as session recording, audio conferencing, and interpretation, all rooms should be properly equipped.

Custom engineered sound systems become essential when room size or capacity moves beyond that threshold.

Speakers

House systems, in which high efficiency, low distortion speakers are mounted in the ceiling, are adequate for smaller rooms. But for quality playback and amplification, directional speakers and speaker clusters, custom installed for the event, have become the norm. When the room has a specific orientation, the "front" of the room should have no ceiling speakers. If installed, they should be equipped so that they can be switched off to prevent feedback coming from nearby microphones. In larger rooms where the last row of seats is more than 40 feet from the podium, high-efficiency directional speakers are preferred in place of the ceiling type.

Speaker placement is critical. Clustered or directional speakers are placed as high as the room will permit above, or on either side of the front of the stage or podium. These may need to be augmented with additional speakers along the side aisles or overhead. A standard rule is that if the distance from the cluster to the last row is more than three times the distance from the cluster to the first row, additional speakers are needed.

Microphones

A variety of microphones is necessary to support different applications. For voice amplification of presenters and panelists, you should have an inventory of good quality, low-impedance microphones:

- Cardioid, or unidirectional microphones, for use on lecterns and table stands for panelists. The term *cardioid* comes from the heart-shaped pickup pattern that is sound sensitive at the front, while suppressing sound from the rear. These may be used as hand-held or audience microphones.

- Speakers who work with overheads *or data projectors* for freedom of movement prefer lavaliere microphones, particularly wireless. The "PZM" microphones, commonly used by broadcasters, provide unexcelled sensitivity and uniform sound fidelity.

- Headset microphones, popularized by Madonna and other performers, have become commonplace at tradeshows and expos where presenters need to be amplified and have their hands free to demonstrate products. The headset places the microphone very close to the presenter's mouth and thereby reduces interference from high volumes of ambient noise.

172 *Operations*

- Omnidirectional microphones have uniform sensitivity all around and are preferred for roundtable discussions or when two or three panelists share one microphone. One can be placed at the front of the table between two panelists (or in the center of three) and provide uniform pickup. This arrangement avoids the need to move the microphone from speaker to speaker.
- Wireless microphones, whether hand-held, lavalier, or headset, are preferred by speakers and performers, and are commonly used for conference interpretation. New technology and damping systems have reduced their tendency to pick up stray frequencies, but they should be tested beforehand, particularly for exhibitions and other events where multiple wireless microphones are used simultaneously.

Several types of mixers are available to connect microphones and other sound sources and feed their output to the amplifier. Ideally, mixers should be equipped with mic level inputs—one for each microphone—and line level inputs for playback devices such as cassette, CD, and video players. Sound equalizers are used to balance sound frequencies when several different inputs are utilized.

TODAY'S PROJECTION SYSTEMS

A projection system consists of four components: a light source, a lens, a screen, and some type of control mechanism. The four components are the same for an LCD projector in a workshop for thirty people as for a complex multi-media matrix in an auditorium holding a thousand people. Only the size of the screen, the number of projectors, the lens size, and the complexity of the controls change.

What visual legibility is to the design of artwork, image resolution is to the projected medium. Resolution in its traditional sense (as opposed to the resolution rating of a computer screen or projector) is the result of image definition: adequate size and proper focus, and brightness or luminescence. Luminescence, the intensity of light falling on the screen, is measured in *foot-lamberts*. If the projected image is hard to read, is not properly focused, and is not sufficiently bright, it will be like trying to read a telephone directory in a phone booth while wearing grimy sunglasses. It can be extremely frustrating to the audience and can destroy the effectiveness of the best presentation.

Aspect Ratio

Aspect ratio is the term used to describe the ratio of image height to width. It is applied to camera and projector apertures, film frames, video monitors, and projection screens. Each medium—motion picture, video, and 35 mm slides—has its own distinctive aspect ratios; video and 35 mm slides can have several. The PCO must understand these distinctions, because they affect lens sizes and screen shapes, especially in mixed-media presentations. Figure 12-1 illustrates the aspect ratios of commonly used media.

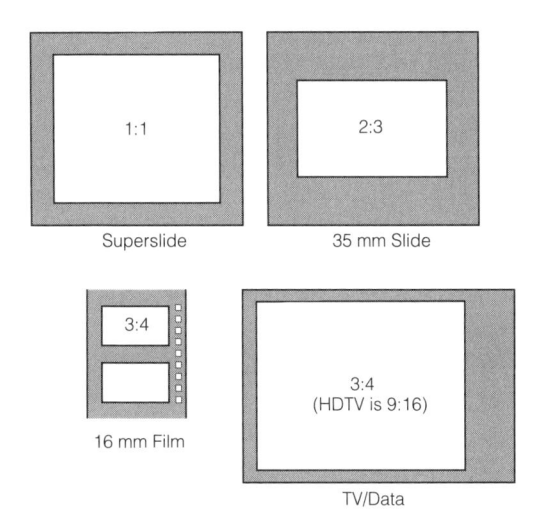

FIGURE 12-1 Aspect ratio.

Projectors

The change in projection technology in the 1990s helped drive the transition from film-based media to video and digital media for speaker support, openers, continuity, and other AV production applications. The ubiquitous 35 mm slide projector, once the workhorse of the audiovisual industry, has given way to data projectors for computer and video projection. Advances in the brightness and clarity of these projectors have accelerated in recent years, keeping pace with parallel advances in the processing power of PCs. And because the technology is so much more complex than the old carousel or 16 mm projector, it is important for PCOs to have a basic understanding of the common projection systems now in use.

Liquid crystal display (LCD) projectors are the most common method for projecting data, and are based on essentially the same stuff used in laptop screens and flat-panel computer monitors. The most common type is the active matrix TFT, which consists of a single panel of LCD glass that modulates all three primary colors. The new generation is the polysilicon LCD projector, which typically consists of three separate layers of LCDs: one each for red, green, and blue. LCD projectors are particularly good at handling computer images such as those used in PowerPoint presentations, but the active matrix TFT projectors have a tendency to shift color slightly toward blue, and do not process video or moving images as smoothly as DLP or the newer polysilicon LCD projectors. Another advanced technology is the Direct-Drive Image Light Amplifier (D-ILA) which greatly increases light intensity and image resolution.

DLP (Digital Light Processor) projectors use a technology known as "micro-mirrors" or DMD (digital micromirror device), which consists of a thumbnail-sized wafer containing a few hundred thousand tiny mirrors, each with its own hinge and motor. The mirrors are tilted to modulate light from the lamp and send it out through the lens. DLP projectors compare well with high-end LCD projectors, and are generally considered to provide superior video projection over LCDs. This is in part due to the fact that LCDs have a very visible "mask" or dark area around each pixel (this can be demonstrated with a close look at a laptop display). However, DLPs have virtually no mask, and therefore can project a nearly seamless image.

Cathode ray tubes (3-gun), the original computer and video projectors, use an RGB (red, green, blue) cable connection, and assign each color its own lens. They typically weigh 80 to 200 pounds and require maintenance, but they offer excellent color accuracy and range of brightness from highlights to shadows, making them very good for video. They also accurately project multiple resolutions, including true 1280 × 1024 and 1600 × 1200.

Regardless of which type of projector is used, resolution is an important variable to keep in mind. In this case, resolution refers to the amount of detail that can be seen in an image. For computers, resolution is expressed in the number of pixels across and down the screen. In video, however, resolution is expressed as the number of lines per inch visible on a test pattern—this is an important distinction that can cause some confusion. The standard resolutions are:

- VGA   (640 × 480)
- SVGA (800 × 600)
- XGA   (1024 × 768)
- SXGA (1280 × 1024)
- UXGA (2048 × 1536)

As a comparison, standard video resolution is 640 × 480, while HDTV goes up to 1920 × 1080.

All DLP and LCD projectors have only one "true" resolution rating, but inputs can be different, particularly when running video and data through a single projector. Most projectors can accept a higher resolution signal and *compress* the data down to fit the projector's native resolution, such as compressing XGA (1024 × 768) for an SVGA projector (800 × 600), but doing so means eliminating about 40 percent of the information. Depending on the compression technology used, the quality of compressed images can vary a great deal—some projectors use simple line dropping schemes, while others achieve higher quality with different "intelligent" algorithms.

A word of warning is in order about simultaneously projecting computer data and video. An example might be a live video feed of a speaker with a picture-in-picture (PiP) box of the speaker's PowerPoint presentation, which might be sent to a remote location such as a pressroom or overflow room. Video signals like those on a television are carried in composite video (if cable) or through the airwaves as radio frequencies; how they are encoded and scanned onto a TV screen is very different from how computer data is displayed on a monitor. Anyone who has ever tried to hook up a computer to a television understands this—the resulting image is a mess. Therefore, a *scan converter* is required to simultaneously project computer data and video signals through a single projector. The scan converter translates the computer data signal into a video signal, but even with high quality scan converters, the result is a much lower resolution image. In our example, this means that while the speaker may look pretty good on screen, the slides in the PiP will be fuzzy and hard to read.

Another variable among projectors is brightness. The amount of light a projector puts out is measured in *ANSI lumens*. There are a number of design elements that will affect a projector's lumen rating, including lamp type, lens quality, and system used to process the light (i.e., LCD or DSP). Projectors can range from tiny microportables with 500 lumens, good for small conference rooms, to industrial-sized projectors putting out 15,000 lumens or more that are used in concert and stadium settings. Choosing the appropriate projector for the event is critical, so here are some general rules of thumb (all descriptions are in ANSI lumens):

- 500 lumens is sufficient on a small screen (60" diagonal) with moderate lighting.
- 1000 lumens will do a good job on almost any small- or medium-sized screen and is sufficient for midsize conference rooms with moderate lighting (able to read notes).
- 2000 lumens is more than sufficient for a 10-foot screen under moderate to bright light, and will be fine on a 25-foot auditorium screen under moderate lighting.
- 3000 lumens will make that 25-foot screen look fine under almost any lighting.

One caveat, however: The brighter the image on screen, the better it will look. One technology company the author has worked with uses 12,000-lumen projectors for its tradeshow theater because they demonstrate their video and graphic design applications where image quality is critical.

Lenses

Lens size (focal length) is dictated by "throw" distance—from projector to screen—and desired image size. The shorter the focal length, the larger the image. All projectors come with standard fixed focal length (*prime*) lenses and many offer limited zoom capabilities (usually a digital process rather than a zoom lens), but third-party specialty lenses are available. These include:

- The Short-Throw Lens, designed to project the largest possible image from the shortest distance. A typical short-throw lens produces an image size of 10 feet diagonal from 7 to 10 feet away. These are commonly required for rear projection, where depth behind the screen is limited.

- The Long-Throw Lens, designed for projection from the back of a long room (often used in projection booths at the back of a theater or conference hall). A typical long-throw lens could project a 10-foot diagonal image from at least 50 to 100 feet away.

- The Zoom Lens, with a variable focal length that can be adjusted to enlarge or reduce the size of the image on a screen without having to move the projector. One drawback, however, is that zoom lenses are not as "fast" as prime lenses, meaning that they do not provide as bright an image.

- Microlenses in any of the preceding configurations enhance projector optics to achieve greater light intensity, thus improving LCD-projected images. This technology has facilitated the production of smaller, lighter-weight projectors.

Ambient Light and the Projection Surface

The optimum projection environment is total darkness, but that is not always achievable, or even desirable. Exit lights, aisle lights, and draped windows generate some ambient light. In classroom situations, you should have enough light level for notetaking. AV professionals compensate by choosing projectors with higher lumens output and by using screens that offer better reflective qualities (or higher gain). The problem with the latter solution is that, with certain exceptions, screen materials that are highly reflective also reflect more ambient light. Add to this the fact that the effective lumens from the light source decrease proportionately with projection distance and image size. Fortunately, the increased availability of high lumen projectors have largely mitigated concerns about screen gain and ambient light.

Screen Types

There are a wide variety of screen types, shapes, sizes, and surfaces available for audiovisual use. The following kinds of screen equipment are commonly used for meetings:

- *Tripod.* The most common type, available in sizes up to 7 × 7 foot.
- *Roller.* The largest size is 12 × 12 feet. It can be ceiling mounted (with manual or motorized controls) or floor mounted ("C-stand"). Because the C-stand screen has a single center support stanchion, there is a tendency for the fabric to distort on the edges.
- *Fast-fold* (originally called "CPE"). Preferred for larger audiences and multi-screen presentations, the system consists of a folding tubular aluminum frame with braced hinges. The screen fabric is stretched over the frame and attached by means of heavy-duty snaps. Adjustable legs are clamped to the frame for height adjustment. Sizes vary from 4 × 6 up to 20 × 30, and the proportion may be square or 2:3 for standard slide projection, 3:4 for motion picture format, or a variety of wide-screen and custom formats.
- *Rigid RP.* Originally produced for big screen TVs, these transparent acrylic or glass RP screens come in standard sizes up to 10 × 20 feet, with even larger custom sizes available. They offer improved viewing compared to flexible RP screens because there is no fabric to wrinkle. However, optimal viewing angle is slightly diminished, compared to flexible screens.
- *Stretch-screen.* A special purpose fabric made of DuPont Lycra, which has been treated on one side to increase reflective quality. Semi-opaque and capable of being stretched in various shapes, these screens are suitable for special front- and back-lighted effects and unique staging designs.
- *Plasma screen.* The manufacturers of laptop computers and digital TVs have given event managers the ultimate in visual display media. The plasma screen does away with slides, films, videotapes, projectors, lenses, and throw distances and offers a 16:9 aspect ratio. Because the image is transmitted digitally—much like a TV or computer screen—a greater viewing angle is possible. Unlike the rear-screen projection's 120 degrees or the LCD data projector's 40 degrees, plasma screens have a 160-degree viewing angle. For PCOs, this means more seating capacity, and for producers, greater staging flexibility and creative variety.

DETERMINING SCREEN AND IMAGE SIZES

AV professionals have developed several formulas to express the interrelationship of screen size, image size, projection distance, lens focal length, and viewing distance. Visuals are designed for "last row viewing"—a sufficient image size to be clearly legible from the last row of seats. Formulas expressing viewing distance and image size use the "H" dimension, indicating the height of the image. Other calculations utilize the "W" dimension that represents the width of the screen, since most projected images tend to be in the horizontal format. For people who don't like formulas, projection calculators are available from Kodak and Da-Lite Screen Co. (see Resources).

To ensure a legible image, the PCO must be able to order the right size screen for each specific meeting room and audience size. One source of frustration is the tendency of some hotel architects to design meeting rooms with inadequate ceiling height. The diagram in Figure 12-2 illustrates the problem.

Since the average seated person sits 4.5 feet high from the floor, the bottom of the screen should be 5.5 feet from the floor to avoid obstruction of the projected image. If the depth of the room and the distance to the last row of seats calls for a 6-foot high screen, a 10-foot ceiling is obviously inadequate. Add to that the problem of chandeliers and other obstructions and you have meeting planners tearing their hair out or compromising their standards.

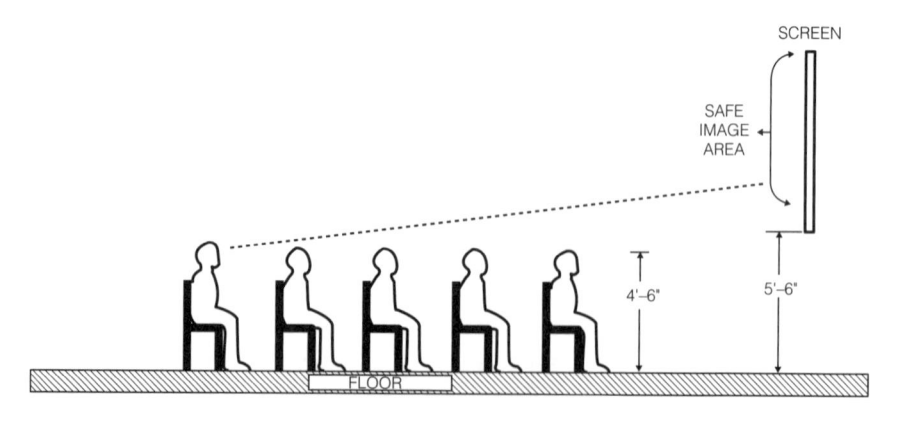

FIGURE 12-2 Screen height.

Screen Materials and Reflective Characteristics

Screen materials vary even more than screen types, and as the preceding list illustrates, the two tend to overlap. Generally, screens can be categorized by three characteristics that influence image brightness and resolution:

1. *Reflective efficiency.* Determined by the type and texture of the screen fabric and its diffusion qualities.
2. *Angle of acceptance.* The angle range at which the screen material accepts the light from the projector and rejects or minimizes ambient light.
3. *Viewing area.* The angle range at which the screen efficiently reflects a quality image to the viewers' eyes.

Some typical screen materials and their advantages and limitation areas follows (courtesy of Eastman Kodak Company).

Matte white screens diffuse light evenly in all directions and appear equally bright from any viewing angle. They tend, however, to reflect ambient light as well. To avoid distortion, viewers should be no more than 30 degrees off the projection axis and no closer to the screen than twice the image height (2H). Matte white and Ideal Matte are best suited to larger audiences.

Beaded screens are white surfaces embedded with glass beads. The beads reflect the light back toward the source, giving this material a somewhat narrow viewing angle. Stray and ambient light are also reflected toward their sources, but the effect is minimized within the optimum viewing area. Reflective efficiency is high.

Lenticular screens are embossed with a very fine pattern of vertical stripes, squares, or diamond shapes too small to be seen at the normal viewing distance. Viewing angle is wide, but it drops off dramatically at the outer edges. Light outside the viewing area is rejected, making such screens ideal in high ambient light environments.

High-gain aluminum screens consist of a grained aluminum foil laminated to a rigid, concave, or paraboloid frame. Projected light is reflected at an intensity almost six times brighter than that of other screens, within a relatively wide viewing area. When properly positioned, the screen rejects ambient light and can be used with normal room lighting.

Rear-projection screens utilize either a diffused, translucent, rubberized mylar fabric or are made of rigid glass or acrylic treated with a variety of coatings. They provide excellent image contrast and color saturation. Image brightness is about the same as matte white. A degree of room lighting can be tolerated without loss of image quality. Projection equipment is positioned behind the screen, providing a neater room appearance. The main disadvantage of rear projection is the additional space required behind the screen for projection. It foreshortens a room considerably and reduces audience capacity by as much as 40 percent.

THE MEETING ENVIRONMENT

Back in the days when the guardians of grand hotels would not dream of exposing their affluent clientele to bourgeois conventioneers, meeting rooms were called ballrooms, an appellation that survives today. They were designed to host grand cotillions and lavish dinners and were lined with mirrors to create a sense of spaciousness. Most were built with columns to support massive ceilings that held rococo chandeliers reminiscent of Versailles. Some of these ballrooms endure to this day, with only token cosmetic changes to attract the meeting trade. Fortunately, many stately old hotels have invested in major renovations and the newer ones have designed public rooms to accommodate meetings. Some innovative hotel chains have formed meeting planner advisory boards to assist architects at the early stages of hotel design.

Whatever the purpose for which people convene, there is a need to communicate. The environment, as well as the software and hardware described above, should be conducive to effective communication. In some meeting facilities, functional and utilitarian considerations are too often subordinate to aesthetics. Conversely, developers seeking maximum utility sometimes overlook the psychological effects of color, space, light, and the acoustical consequences of texture, shape, and density.

The larger the audience, the more stringent the requirements for comfort, safety, acoustics, and staging. Most conference centers and many hotels now offer purpose-built meeting rooms, some with tiered seating and a permanent stage, such as in an auditorium. But no hotel can afford to reserve all of its meeting rooms exclusively for meeting activity, so the multiple function room has evolved. Properly designed, such a room can serve equally well as a meeting environment and as a facility for dining and social activities.

Capacity

The PCO who is planning an audiovisual presentation needs to think about AV seating, rather than the total seating capacity stated in the hotel's literature. A rule of thumb for estimating AV seating is to allow 10 square feet per person theater-style and 15 square feet for classroom seating. The shape of the room needs to be considered when determining capacity because you need good sightlines and screen characteristics previously described. The ideal length to width proportions of a meeting room are 1:1, 3:2, and 2:1, though a 3:1 ratio is acceptable. If the length exceeds three times the width, there will be problems with visual legibility and speaker eye contact.

Meeting professionals often subscribe to a basic capacity formula: the *two-by-eight* principle, which states that the first row of seats should be no closer than two times the image height, and the last row should be no farther than eight times the image height. *Image height* rather than screen height is recommended, since a screen may be used for projection of various media with different aspect ratios.

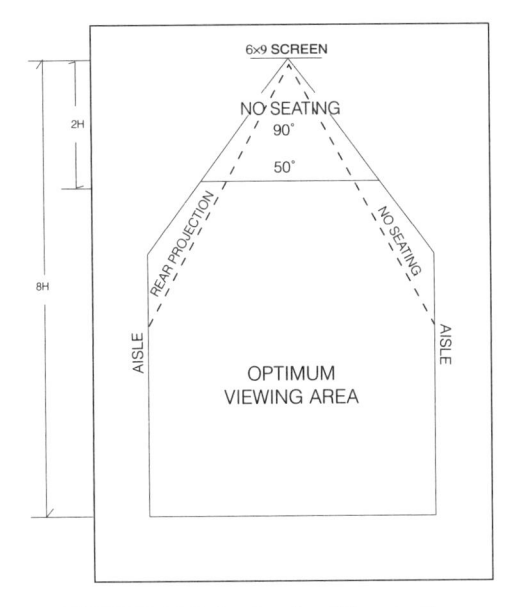

FIGURE 12-3 Seating for AV projection.

Ceiling Height

Ceiling height determines screen size and image height, thus affecting seating capacity. Obstructions such as lighting fixtures and dropped, domed, or sloping ceilings must be considered when calculating net ceiling height. Some creative hotel architects have introduced the retractable chandelier, which can be lowered for intimate ambiance or raised into ceiling recesses for AV requirements. A minimum ceiling height of 10 feet (3 meters) is adequate for conference facilities accommodating up to 100 participants. As rooms increase in size, projection needs suggest a commensurate increase in height.

Acoustics

Ideally floors should be carpeted, ceilings should be acoustically treated, and 40 percent of wall surfaces should be covered with "soft" absorbent materials to avoid sound reverberation. Constructing walls that are not parallel and use of acoustical baffles also tend to reduce reverberation. To ensure sound isolation, construct movable partitions out of dense materials and extend them from the floor to a rigid ceiling member. Acoustical engineers rate such structures by Noise Isolation Class (NIC). An NIC rating of 44 or better is suggested for dividers. Silent opening doors are a must. Nothing disrupts a meeting more than squeaky doors.

Décor

Soft, muted colors are more conducive to learning activity and communication than vivid colors and dramatic designs. Solid-color wall treatments in beige, grays, and gold tend to blend well with graphics and other decorations used for meetings. Wood surfaces, if they are well maintained, add character to the room, but mirrors, ornate sconces, stainless steel, and other reflective surfaces can be a hindrance to effective projection.

Doors

Service doors must be equipped with signs on the corridor side to indicate that a meeting is in progress. Some hotels will place a room divider in front of the door, improving appearance and reducing noise from the service area. Fire exits, clearly marked, should be sufficient in number for the room's capacity. Too often these exits are located on walls that are logical areas for staging.

Lighting and Electrical Needs

Overhead lighting that is recessed into the ceiling is preferable to chandeliers. Incandescent lights that can be dimmed should augment fluorescent lighting. These should be wired in banks from front to rear, each bank controlled by a dimmer inside the room. It is especially helpful for a presenter utilizing slide or film projection to keep room lights off the screen, yet still have adequate lighting in the rest of the room so that people can take notes. If fluorescent lights are the only lighting in the room, these should be equipped with dimming ballasts. Certain fluorescent frequencies cause fatigue and irritability. The safest are the so called "dual spectrum" lamps.

Power strips capable of accommodating a variety of hanging fixtures are flexible and desirable. Larger rooms, which may be used for stage productions, should have provisions for hanging lighting trusses or grids with theatrical instruments from the ceiling. These are preferable and safer than portable light trees. Circuitry should be located in a control room or a panel opposite the probable stage location. One service outlet should be available for every 10 feet (3 meters) of wall space in rooms not used for exhibits. Rooms with windows must be equipped with drapes of adequate density to reduce ambient light for projection.

VOICE AND DATA COMMUNICATION

Telephone and networking outlets should be located at regular points around the room. Standard dial-up phone jacks are adequate for data transmission and Internet access in smaller rooms. However, facilities used for complex graphic presentations (streaming video, net conferencing, or Web casting) need to be equipped with greater bandwidth capacity. (Bandwidth is the range of frequencies a transmitted signal occupies.)

The more complex the transmission, the more bandwidth needed for reception or transmission. Complex data signals can be "squeezed" into narrow bandwidths, but that will slow down the transmission. For instance, a two-minute video clip transmitted on an ISDN line would take six to eight minutes to receive. Video requires high speed connection.

How high is "high speed"? The chart below is a comparison of the most common high bandwidth transmission systems in kilobytes (Kbps) or megabytes (Mbps) per second:

System	*Bandwidth*
Telephone	56 Kbps
ISDN	64–128 Kbps
T1	1.5 Mbps
DSL	6.1 Mbps
T3	44.7 Mbps

ISDN is adequate for text and most graphic presentations (such as PowerPoint). Anything more complex requires higher bandwidth.

Ed Goodman, general manager of Dallas-based AVW network, has some good recommendations:

> A convenience offered by technology-oriented venues is the use of a central server system in distribution of data. Both AVW and AVHQ offer this service on-line before and during the presentation. We recommend a standard general-use computer in each breakout room connected to a central server to send presenters' files to that location in order to minimize presenters using individual laptops. This takes too much time and many laptops look fine when embedded videos run on PowerPoint but can't perform with a second screen to a projector.

High-Tech Meeting Environments

Recognizing the increasing role of technology, owners of hotel companies, convention facilities, and conference centers are vying with each other to provide tomorrow's communication environment today. Conference centers, long the innovators in advanced learning facilities, have even come up with a handle for it. International Conference Resorts calls it "architechnology." Such state-of-the-art venues reflect the interaction among presentation technologies, human perception factors, and the environment. How effectively the message is conveyed from the presenter to the audience is influenced by the environment wherein that communication takes place.

Recognizing the need for such advanced architechnology, Marriott Corporation—already a leader in meeting venues—developed an inventory of conference centers in the 1990s. The concept grew from a recognition that corporate America is placing more emphasis on learning through technology.

Perhaps the most dramatic examples of high-tech meeting environments are the briefing centers that corporations proudly display to their clients, associates, and the few middle-management individuals who are privileged to attend. These remarkable facilities incorporate the very latest in communication technology to ensure that the company's message is imparted in the most effective manner possible. At Hewlett Packard's generous 40,000 square-foot briefing center, a presentation is more than communication—it's an experience! Such a complex is to a typical meeting room what an Imax theater is to the neighborhood moviehouse.

These centers have also added a new title to the ranks of conference professionals. The specialists who manage briefing centers and their technical staff are called "briefing program managers." And yes, they have their own professional society: the Association of Briefing Program Managers (www.abpm.com).

STAGING WITH AV

Staging at meetings encompasses not only the placement of the stage and audiovisual equipment, but the total room layout. Instructional objectives and format determine audiovisuals and staging for certain types of sessions, such as educational seminars. Audiovisuals are incidental to the tutorial style employed at such sessions. In other types of sessions where motivation and entertainment are key ingredients of the message, AV becomes the focal point and staging reflects its importance. (Room setups and table arrangements are presumed to be basic fare for the PCO and are not covered in depth. Readers wishing to learn more about them are referred to the *Convention Industry Manual*, which treats the subject in-depth.)

Educational Sessions

Seating for educational sessions differs according to audience size and session format. Classroom style and the various configurations of conference seating (U-shape, T-shape, round tables, board of directors, etc.) are the most common. Generally the focal point is a platform, lectern, or dais prepared for one or more presenters or a panel and moderator. Visual aids include chalkboards, flipcharts, copy-boards, whiteboards, overhead and data projectors, and video playback. Lighting is mostly at room level, but being able to dim the lights is important: participants should be able to see the audiovisuals but still have adequate light for note-taking.

Ideal screen placement is on one side of the lectern, at a 45-degree angle to the audience. Optimally, data projectors are mounted to the ceiling; otherwise they can be equipped with long-throw lenses and placed on high projection stands at the opposite corner in back of the room. This arrangement permits the speaker to see the projected materials peripherally without having to turn away from the audience. In rooms where there is a fixed screen or that require the screen to be in the center, the same results can be achieved by reversing the placement of the presenter or panel so that their relative angle is maintained. The overhead or data projector may be on a stand next to the lectern or on a table at the front of the room. To avoid the keystoning commonly associated with overhead projectors, some presenters will specify a screen with a keystone compensator that positions the screen so that it is at a right angle to the horizontal projection axis. Data projectors typically have built-in keystone compensators.

Staging for Entertainment

Staging for motivational sessions and events that include elaborate audiovisual and theatrical productions is influenced by the media and the needs of the performers. As described in Chapter 6, some entertainers have very detailed staging specifications. Some audiovisual presentations, particularly multimedia productions, require unique and complex staging. Unless the event is part of a banquet, theater-style seating is the preferred configuration. A room with a high ceiling (16 to 22 feet or 5 to 7 meters) is essential to allow for adequate screen height and to accommodate theatrical lighting where required. Floor lecterns, angled in relation to the screen, are placed to the sides of the stage so as not to interfere with sight lines. Lighting will range from dim to total blackout; it should be controlled by AV or stage technicians from one location.

If the room does not have strip lighting or theatrical lights, the organizer may want to rent them. Since the room will be dim or dark much of the time, the lecterns should be spotlighted. Cross-lighting is preferred in order to avoid light spill and shadows on the screen. Projection equipment is placed on platforms or scaffolding so that lenses are as close to perpendicular to the screen as possible, particularly for rear projection. If front projection is employed, it is necessary to position it on risers in order to clear the heads of people seated or moving in aisles. The projection platform should be dressed with themed decor or draped for a presentable appearance.

Staging for banquets with AV or entertainment involves a different set of problems. Since people are seated at round tables, some of the guests will have to turn their seats in order to see the screen or stage. Because of the complexity of staging for entertainment, the PCO must request the room for advance setup and rehearsals, and must require written confirmation of dates and exact access times. It can be frustrating to arrive with two tons of equipment at the stipulated ballroom on the stipulated date only to find that setup can't begin until the self-help seminar is cleared out.

RENTING AND SHIPPING EQUIPMENT

Ship or rent? That is the question. Some PCOs will not consider taking an AV presentation on the road without shipping all their own equipment. Others may ship key pieces like computers and rent projectors, sound systems, and bulkier equipment on-site. Yet others will take only their software and rent everything locally. The choice depends on the availability of suitable equipment and the presence of a reliable AV rental firm at the meeting site. If the venue is a foreign destination, the expense and complexities of shipment and possible variances in electrical current or media formats may dictate on-site rental. (See Chapter 18 for additional audiovisual guidelines for meetings abroad.)

Renting Audiovisual Equipment

Many meeting facilities will maintain a basic inventory of microphones, screens, flipcharts, projectors, projection stands, and related accessories. Some are provided at no cost to the meeting organizer. Conference centers, for instance, include the use of all audiovisual equipment and the services of technicians in their flat daily rate. In the larger conference hotels and most convention centers, the in-house AV contractor has become a standard, though salespeople will explain that the client is not required to utilize those firms. Some hotel contracts specify that a service fee is customary for equipment brought in or rented from another source. A firm objection during negotiations will usually eliminate the fee, since most ethical suppliers support the customer's freedom of choice.

Whether depending on the in-house AV supplier or selecting an outside company, the PCO should base decisions on the following criteria:

- Extent of AV inventory and availability of current models. Inquire whether needed equipment will come from local inventory or be sub-contracted.

- Reputation for maintaining equipment. Proper maintenance is critical.

- Experience, training, and technical competence of AV staff.
- Recommendation by other meeting professionals who have met at the same venue.
- Competitive pricing structure; reduced rates for back-up equipment.
- Ready availability of substitute or back-up equipment.

The last item may favor use of in-house audiovisual services since their proximity will usually guarantee availability of back-up equipment (often at no added cost). Furthermore, the staff will be familiar with the facility and accustomed to working with the convention service staff. Some PCOs prefer to work with firms with whom they have had experience and a good working relationship, which ensure that critical extra effort.

Audiovisual Orders

Determine the AV requirements for each session in consultation with the producer, if one is employed. Equipment generally falls into two categories: that which is required for continuity (theme, overture, bridges, breaks), and those items specifically requested by presenters. When AV presentations are part of the general session, be sure to inform all speakers of the type of equipment available and the projection format. Suggest that they adjust their needs to available equipment in order to avoid duplication. A diagram of the screen configuration is informative.

If ordering from an AV contractor or contracting with the facility itself, inquire about rate structure. Most rental companies charge three times the daily rate for a full week. Others will charge a reduced rate for the second- and third-day's rental. Establish at the outset what delivery charges, if any, will be billed. *If charges are billed to the master account, a service fee is customary* (but it is negotiable).

SURVEYING FACILITIES FOR AV

During site inspection, note the general qualities of the meeting rooms at each venue visited. Then, once the venue is chosen, return for a detailed survey of the rooms to be allocated using a Meeting Room Survey form (a sample is included in Figure 12-4 at the end of this chapter). Be sure that the survey trip is scheduled far enough in advance of the meeting to allow for a change in venue if glaring deficiencies are discovered.

To be certain that specific rooms will work, try to be at the facility when its meeting rooms are in use. That is the advice of audiovisual professionals who have spent enough time in the trenches to have encountered just about every problem. During the survey trip, you will find it extremely helpful to

188 *Operations*

talk to the meeting planner for the group currently using the facilities; get permission to observe him or her using the equipment without disrupting the session.

When that is not feasible, meeting pros conduct a survey when the rooms are not in use and ask the AV supervisor or house engineer to accompany them. They request floor plans of key meeting rooms and use a survey form to record observations. The convention service manager is asked about union regulations for projectionists, spot operators, stage hands, and other crafts. Other questions include: hourly rates, working rules regarding hours, breaks, overtime, and penalty times.

Barry Taylor, a veteran UK conference organizer, has the following suggestions:

- Identify obstructions, such as pillars and chandeliers.
- Make sure that ceiling height is adequate for projection.
- Check clear sightlines from all seat positions.
- Observe the room lighting and the accessibility of controls for dimming lights.
- Ensure that the sound system is of high quality and fidelity for AV presentations.
- Check for noise distractions, such as proximity to the kitchen.
- If the room has dividers, see if there is adequate sound isolation.
- Verify that there is a sufficient number of electrical, audio, and data outlets.
- If the room has windows, make sure there is a way to get full blackout.
- Check the ventilation and air-conditioning.

The accelerated change in technology for audiovisual communication has created incredible opportunities for the meeting industry. Even as this book is written, methods and hardware are changing and becoming obsolete, only to be replaced by new systems evoking new techniques for communicating.

Audiovisual Resources for PCOs:

Kodak Projection Calculator, Eastman Kodak Co., Rochester, NY 14650
   The Arranger (Meeting room capacity calculator) MPI, www.mpinet.org

MEETING ROOM SURVEY

FACILITY: CITY: ROOM:

Dimensions E-W: N-S: Ceiling height: Chandeliers?

Capacity: Banquet: Reception: Classroom: Conference:

Theater: Theater w/RP*:

Dividers: Section dimensions: Sound isolation: Room acoustics:

Obstructions: Windows: Blackout drapes:

Wall color: Wall surface: Sconces/mirrors: Carpet:

Tiered seating: Balcony: Projection booth: Stage: Dimensions:

BUILT-INS: Screen: Size: Type: Blackboard/whiteboard: Flipchart:

ELECTRICAL: Outlets: 110V/a.c.:   220V/a.c.:   Amps: Phase: Thermostat:

     Number of circuits: Total capacity: AC Extensions provided: Cost:

LIGHTING: Type: Track lights: Spots: Dimmers:

     Dimmer location: Remote dimmer control: Stage lighting:

PA SYSTEM: Amplifier: Location: Watts: Inputs - High Z: LowZ:

     Mixer: Inputs: Cost: Speakers: Type:

     Mies: Provided: Cost of Additional   Lavalier: Cost: Wireless: Cost:

TELEPHONE: Phone jacks: House phone: Data ports: Type:

Suitability for Exhibits: Table top: Booths:

ACCESS: Door locks?   Service area: Exterior: Handicapped:

REMARKS:

DIAGRAM:

*RP: Rear Projection. Reduces capacity by 20 to 30%

FIGURE 12-4 Meeting room survey.

Chapter Thirteen
Meetings and Event Technology

MEETINGS IN CYBERSPACE

As in all other professions, technology has revolutionized the PCOs way of doing business. Meeting organizers who once had trouble programming their home VCRs are venturing into the realms of cyber-meetings, streaming video, satellite downlinks, and fiber-optics. Today's technology requires the event professional to have at least a general understanding of wireless communication, archival technologies, and document preparation even for the burgeoning handheld-computing format. While technology has certainly helped automate processes, today there are many more document formatting options available. Each of these call for careful consideration based on user needs and abilities.

Paper forms ruled the registration process throughout the 20th century: paper tickets were the only way to book travel, and paper literature was the sole resource for researching venues. Although these elements still have a place in event management, they are largely supplanted by online registration, e-tickets, and venue Web sites. Meeting organizers today work with a variety of data formats that are used to gather site, registration, and ticketing information. Due to the varying range of technology access and know-how, organizers now need to plan for phone call-in, fax backed forms, electronic processing via the Internet, and wireless transfers of registrant information.

Similarly, the way content is presented has undergone a metamorphosis. The 35 mm slide presentation of decades past—which required weeks of lead time for production—has yielded to the ubiquitous and far more flexible PowerPoint presentation. Digital media—videography, digital photography, complex animation—and real-time point-to-point transmission have all helped make communication more engaging, and therefore more effective. And because presentation content is largely digital to begin with, it can be easily distributed over the Internet or on CDs, reaching much wider audiences than ever before. Digital media also provides meeting organizers with opportunities for creating ways to generate greater revenue for their organizations. Archival technology allows for the reuse of meeting presentations for either resale to delegates not able to attend or for post-meeting reference.

Even the meeting venue itself is reflecting that transmutation. Videoconferencing technology surpassed early predictions that it would take the place of face-to-face meeting and plays an important and practical role in the industry, but the real revolution is in the digital realm of Web conferencing and Web casts. From the comfort of their own desks, in the office or at home, "virtual attendees" can observe and even participate in gatherings taking place half-way around the world. A virtual meeting can be either an active or a passive experience. Depending on the level of technology deployed, participants can monitor or engage in real-time interaction via electronic messaging or white boarding functions. In addition, real-time surveying and polling can be incorporated.

In 2001, IBM hosted an experimental cyber event it called "WorldJam," in which all 320,000 of its employees around the globe were invited to participate. More than 52,000 people took part in the three-day online event dedicated to brainstorming and sharing ideas for best practices. Using interactive elements like electronic bulletin boards, moderated chats, and online polls, WorldJam generated over 6,000 proposals and comments. Although the cost is thought to have been in the millions of dollars (IBM didn't release that information), it was certainly a less-expensive option than transporting all 52,600 participants to a single site for three days.

This chapter will look at the technology that is revolutionizing the meetings industry.

PC/CMP: COMPUTERS AND MEETING PROFESSIONALS

During the late 1990s and early 2000s, the need for improved computerization in the meeting industry brought about by the explosion of the Internet attracted numerous outside investors. Millions of dollars were invested in the hopes of defining an electronic standard for the meeting industry. New vendors and newly merged technology companies flooded the market with new applications for meeting professionals. However, technology investments became carefully scrutinized in 2001 by application developers and potential purchasers of improved technologies as the economy slowed. The dollar tightened for the developer as well as the purchaser. Those who rushed through financing and ultimately to market learned several valuable lessons: They learned that managing meetings is a complex undertaking and they learned that in order to develop meeting management technologies, they needed a very deep and thorough knowledge of the business methods surrounding the meeting process. They also learned that this had to be then translated into flexible, robust applications. Not an easy task, by any means! Even today, many application developers think online registration, for example, is easy to do, so they build less-than-ideal programs. In the rush to market, many technology companies opted to purchase established software, hoping to grab a bigger market share overnight as a way to leverage newly developed Web-based tools.

Newly funded companies rolled out national sales forces and launched massive marketing campaigns aimed at selling to meeting professionals. Developers found that a product designed for a mass audience was not accepted by the market. As there was no established standard for managing meeting processes or for data handling, the technology just couldn't address an individual organization's unique needs. They discovered that more robust reporting, enhanced financial management, and the ability to produce customized forms were required in order to be successful.

In the end, many dot com companies learned painful lessons; many were forced out of business or had to merge. The outcome has been a very slow stabilization of some major application providers. Thankfully, there are ROI gains for meeting professionals willing to invest in the newer Web-based technologies. However, challenges still lie ahead.

The fact is that the personal computer as we know it today will radically change even in this decade. PCs will continue to shrink in size and grow in computing power. It is forecast that PCs will ultimately be phased out as even newer hardware and communication technologies are introduced. We have already seen a fast entry of handheld computers, powerful personal digital assistants (PDAs), and other similar devices that impact market sales of traditional laptop and desktop computers. Continued change in the marketplace will result as hardware evolves, and meeting professionals had better broaden their awareness of new technologies and learn how to take advantage of continued increases in computing power.

Since the early 1990s, routine tasks like site selection, registration, travel, housing, and meeting management have been automated (thanks to the development of event-specific software). With the proliferation of Internet services, some of these support functions were taken over by third-party application service providers (ASPs). Many of these Internet-based tools are now being combined by ASPs offering end-to-end meeting management services.

Independent meeting professionals have especially benefited from computer technology and the Internet. Terri Breining, a credentialed meeting planner who started her meeting-management firm in the 1980s, believes that the Internet in particular played an important role: "Development made it possible for entrepreneurs with limited resources to reach a broader client base and provide them with the full range of event management technology."

AUTOMATING THE MEETING PROCESS: "A Typical Technical Day"

A conference planner might well take three months, a year, or several years organizing and staging a given event with its thousands of details. If you think of the entire planning process in terms of one "day," no matter how long it is in real time, the task order will go something like this:

In the "morning," the PCOs must first develop a conference timetable. Software can help generate a critical-path diagram, tracing key planning phases on a timeline, identifying tasks and deadlines for each phase, and tracking progress, thus alerting the user to upcoming tasks in order of priority. A planner who is comfortable with the technology can use software such as MS Project to do overall project management with little effort.

The second task is to do site selection. Many hotel and destination databases are directly accessible by computer or distributed on CDs. Some software as well as event Web sites allow users to view and evaluate meeting rooms and exhibit halls, and diagram ideal seating arrangements, staging, projection, and exhibit-floor plans as part of the venue assessment. More sophisticated programs allow visitors to take a virtual tour of the facility. Applications developed for popular convention cities can help the planner research local attractions and their proximity to recreational venues, and even book tee times or make restaurant reservations. A great time-saving advantage of some Web sites is their ability to create a report that helps you compare venues.

Once a site is selected, the administrative burden shifts to procedures and financial management. At a minimum, therefore, a good conference management program should help you with:

- Event and session registration
- Accommodations and itinerary tracking
- Speaker and exhibitor assignment
- Confirmation letters and mailing labels
- Name badges and signs
- Delegate lists, session/event counts, and other reports
- Budget and financial summaries, including room-block management
- Integration with Web-based registration systems

Around "noon," a document begins to take shape, which we refer to as the Meeting Plan or Staging Guide. When completed, it will take up most of a three-ring notebook. While many planners prefer the familiar printed text consisting of checklists, function forms, budget reports, roster, contracts, correspondence, etc., this guide really should be done on computer. (Today's electronic palmtop organizers, power books, and notebook-size think-pads are equal to the task, and offer voice and fax communication as well.) Thanks to the APEX Initiative (more later), standardized forms have been developed for use in documenting a meeting's plan.

This is also the time to generate business, educational, and social agendas. Software can schedule all such program elements—particularly concurrent sessions—and the physical and logistical requirements of each, such as room assignments, speaker designations, and audiovisual support. Sophisticated applications can warn you when sessions are over-subscribed, and help you manage waiting lists.

The data is entered into a registration databank as soon as a response is received. The actual process for data entry varies among organizations. With Web-based integration, much of the data is being generated by the attendee and is electronically passed to the organization's database upon validation. Recording this information gives organizers what they need to create attendance analyses, alphabetical rosters by category (delegate, spouse, speaker, exhibitor, etc.), payment and registration cost analyses, income and expense projections, and session attendance. These menus should also generate confirmation letters, payment receipts, selected seminar schedules, name badges, and seminar rosters. The same program allows users to assess their mailing list. Many applications will also offer delegates an itinerary to be used as a personal time schedule for a conference.

With appropriate technology, an event organizer can incorporate marketing efforts with the registration process. By integrating promotional efforts, an organization can significantly lower marketing overhead costs.

In the "afternoon" of our planning timetable, we must track and confirm accommodations, function space, and travel arrangements. Unless hotel reservations are made directly with the hotel or via a housing bureau, the database should be able to generate rooming lists and confirmations. If travel arrangements are made through an official airline, their data can be imported to provide arrival and departure times and flights. These are especially helpful in confirming hotel reservations and meal guarantees, and for organizing airport greetings.

A flexible meeting-management program takes much of the effort out of function controls. All meeting elements, from the conference headquarters and registration area through the final banquet and departure, are assigned a function number. From this master résumé, planners can generate conference programs, banquet orders, and support requirements.

The "evening" of our metaphorical day is devoted to on-site operations, beginning with an agenda for pre-conference meetings with facility staff and ending with post-conference evaluations and accounts settlement. During this period, it is also possible to gauge attendee satisfaction: Polling stations or kiosks can survey attendees' attitudes throughout a conference, allowing organizers to identify opportunities to further improve their meetings.

In between, the system helps the conference manager and staff anticipate and manage the many details involved in even a small conference. Serving as a master checklist, it schedules tasks related to all staff functions and events, highlights uncompleted tasks, and checks for conflicting activities.

The PCO and the Technology Team

Introducing newer technology takes advance work and organization. Without careful planning, new technology will simply automate a poor or an inefficient process. There are six steps involved:

1. Define what constitutes a Return on Investment (ROI).
2. Document the process.
3. Identify process costs.
4. Develop a list of prioritized needs.
5. Implement the technology plan.
6. Measure and further improve the process.

The return on investment is determined primarily by an organization's Chief Financial Officer. Expectation of a return can be very simple or exceedingly complex, depending on the organization's culture and financial reporting structure.

After identifying a process, schedule a meeting with the Finance Office or Budget Manager to document so that a review of the process and associated costs can be documented and mutually agreed upon. It is important to remember that the hardware or software is not *the* process; it is only a component of a process (such as registration management). Thus, for an application to better manage registration, ROI is more than the cost of the registration system.

The ROI team establishes goals and definitions early in the documentation effort. Mapping out the process using software that can map, document, and measure processes within one application comes later. Another option is to make a thorough and sequential outline of the steps taken and the forms used when you are working on a process. Take registration, for instance: What does a potential attendee have to do to register for an event? Record the steps and media required for the registrant—fax, e-mail, mail, etc. The same applies to staff in processing the registration.

As the steps are identified, the number of transactions and the timeframe for processing are measured. Reducing the processing time will give you the greatest return on your investment in technology.

Equipped with a process map listing sequential steps, costing information, and other measurements, the team can move forward with improving the process.

PRESENTATION TECHNOLOGY

Never before in the history of meeting management has the delivery of content been more important. Time has simply become too valuable a commodity to waste. Today, event organizers not only need to provide a strong program, but they must consider the diverse methods available for delivering it. How will speakers interact with the audience? Will video be used? Will a speaker need real-time access to the Internet? If they do, will the connection be fast enough for use in a live presentation? Do all speakers present on-site, or will some connect from a remote location? Are any of the presentations to be archived and used after the session? These and a thousand other questions need to be considered in today's electronic age.

Perhaps the most readily visible development has been in presentation technology. New tools ranging from high resolution screens, electronic whiteboards, and numerous add-ons for use with PowerPoint and related graphic applications are developed each year. Stay abreast of the breakthroughs.

The electronic whiteboard is one invention that has become almost indispensible. It adds a whole new dimension to communication within meetings: Write on an electronic whiteboard, and your images can be stored to computer, printed out, e-mailed, faxed, or edited later. In addition, many electronic surfaces will work with projectors, allowing annotating of presentations, controlling the computer, entering data, and much more. They can be integrated with Web and video conferencing systems, as well as enterprise software packages such as Lotus Notes.

Message Boards and Chat Rooms

These Internet-based resources can also function as presentation media, though not in the conventional meeting environment.

The message board is used to post details of a particular topic of interest to a specific audience. Participation is non-synchronous and is especially suited to participants in differing time zones. The medium enables the target audience to access a presentation at their leisure and study it, respond to it, or download it for further action. Task forces and working committees find message boards an effective way to communicate, solicit feedback, and share information. Guidelines for the participant, prepared by the organizer, should provide the following information:

- Internet Web browser, address, and connection method
- Software requirements
- Scope of topic
- Protocol for posting messages
- Method of archiving and accessing archives

Chat Rooms

This popular Internet medium enables two or more participants to communicate by means of the computer keyboard, or by telephone attachment or voice-recognition text. Where several users participate, the designation of a moderator permits a smooth-flowing discussion. Because participation is synchronous, chat room meetings are limited to a reasonable time-zone spread. As with message boards, specific protocol should be established and posted.

Both media offer the capability of directing participants to other Web sites that may be relevant to the topic under discussion.

A HARD LOOK AT SOFTWARE

The most widely used event management technology is that which relates to registration. Selecting the right medium involves a core understanding of the internal registration process, its cost, and how prospective attendees will interact with the application. This assessment is essential because you will need to know whether or not the system will be able to deliver the results you want.

Technology-based options can be segmented into four general categories:

Off-the-Shelf Suite

An off-the-shelf system, a widely used approach within the meetings industry, will often include word processing, a database, a spreadsheet program, and e-mail management utility, along with calendar and task management. Integration among individual components enables the entire suite to be easily applied to general event management. While this strategy provides a low-cost and user-friendly option, it does not necessarily achieve cost savings.

PC-based Event Management Software

Numerous software systems are in use throughout the meetings industry. In general, PC-based systems are well advanced and more stable than most Web-based solutions. They often provide a database structure, with core interfaces for registration, session tracking, speaker management, budgeting, and financial management. Most software systems offer pre-defined reporting, custom report capability, and badge and ticketing options. These systems require a degree of customization in order to optimize housing, travel, and e-marketing functions. Their strength is in the logistical aspects of managing registration and meeting details.

With this class of product, applications can reside on a network and be shared throughout an organization.

Web-based Registration Applications

These resources provide a variety of management functions, including strong e-marketing capabilities. Most offer event-based Web site integration for online registration, e-market tracking and analysis, and real-time reporting, resulting in cost and time savings. They offer electronic marketing content and an event-related themed Web site seen by prospective attendees. All have a maintenance interface and a registrant interface, and can be readily implemented within days. Strong in their marketing aspects, these solutions often fall short in addressing general meeting management functions such as room setup, AV specifications, food and beverage planning, budgeting, and speaker management that can be handled by PC-based systems. While some products are stronger than others in providing similar performance, most are not as proficient as PC-based programs.

Enterprise-wide Applications

This product category is often managed from a centralized department and distributed at an organization-wide level. As a result, incorporated planning tools such as site selection, registration, travel, and housing are readily available to all who need access to the application.

From a management perspective, enterprise-wide deployment allows an organization to truly assess spending levels. For the largest corporations and associations, these systems can provide the greatest return on investment.

EVALUATING EVENT MANAGEMENT SOFTWARE

The key to any computer program's value is the output—the information and by-products that will simplify registration and carry out management procedures during the planning phase as well as on-site. There are a wealth of new software programs in a wide range of prices that can accomplish those goals. The PCO who will assess such software should look for these capabilities:

- Store, process, and display registrants who have been sorted by membership category, chapter, nationality, and demographics (e.g., sales volume or other factors).
- Integrate Web-based registration into database.
- Display status of fees paid or due, credentials, room reservations, sessions assigned, arrival/departure, and social and recreation options.
- Generate customized letters and mailing labels.
- Generate name badges, tickets for functions and sessions, and graphics.
- Display status of room blocks, room pickup, rooming lists, and availability of rooms and suites by types for each hotel.
- Manage waiting lists.
- Copy meeting set-up information to a new date pattern.
- Provide lists of no-shows and cancellations, noting status of refunds (if applicable).
- Monitor meal guarantees and correlate with attendees' arrivals.
- Generate alphabetical master lists and attendance rosters for each session.
- Generate advance and supplemental registration lists by membership category or status (press, guest, exhibitor, etc.), and cross-reference by affiliation.
- Manipulate financial data to provide budget projections, an income and expense summary, accounts payable and receivable, billing statements, deposits, daily journals, operating statements, and budget reconciliation.
- Monitor function room assignments and generate function control forms and change orders as needed.
- Provide program management functions (speaker assignments, session chairmen, correspondence, confirmations, handouts, suspense lists, fees and expenses, travel arrangements, and speaker support needs).
- Monitor and display exhibitor lists, booth sales, registrations, and exhibitor profiles. Generate an exhibit master list, correspondence,

and control forms. Track exhibition attendance and prepare statistical reports.
- Provide capability for on-site checklist, e-mail, tickler file, and message center.

Other desirable options are attendance forecasting, evaluation of promotion effectiveness, incentive program qualification tracking, event newsletter publishing, continuing education (CEU) administration, credit card and bank deposit records—in short, any repetitive administrative tasks that might be automated. Considering the vast number of variables involved in even a relatively small meeting, the computer can maximize the PCO's effectiveness and that of the meeting staff, freeing them up to devote their attention to the essentials of planning and event management.

MEASURING SOFTWARE EFFECTIVENESS

Earlier guidelines alluded to ROI as it pertained to technology in general. The same methodical evaluation needs to be applied to specific software. Effective event management software must provide benefits to the user. When properly designed, the system should reduce time and labor for the organization and the registrant. A proposed software investment should address these questions:

- How will operations be improved?
- Will the number of applications currently used in the process be reduced?
- Will it facilitate registration confirmations?
- Does it reduce the frequency of attendee Web site visits?
- Is target marketing enhanced, thus effecting savings in list processing or postage?
- Does the time saved result in fewer temporary staff?
- Is there a substantial saving in management time?

Other measurements or metrics that are useful in evaluating process components are:

- Time spent on researching a new meeting site
- Time devoted to writing meeting contracts
- Number of travel tickets processed per month
- Number of room reservations processed per month
- Frequency of itinerary changes

- Time spent processing contracts
- Monthly volume of meetings
- Number of registrations processed for each event
- Handling cost to process registrations
- Production and mailing cost per marketing piece
- Number of meeting cancellations and costs
- Volume of attrition charges
- Average cost per attendee, including pro-rated indirect charges
- Volume of e-mail addresses stored on present system

These measurements can help gauge system requirements and provide benchmark data for making ongoing assessments of how well the system and the overall process is operating.

The software needs of the meetings industry are quite specialized; you can't go to your local office supply or computer store and pick up a conference registration software program. Hotel companies and convention bureaus have recognized the benefits and wide-spread dependence on technology, and have adapted their systems to the wide range of software available to their meeting clients.

THE INTERNET AS A PLANNING TOOL

Cruising the Infobahn

The Internet has truly become the gateway to the world. PCOs can work with partners or clients on virtually any continent. The ability to communicate through e-mail or search the Internet has become a daily task.

As we move through this decade, one of the most significant enhancements we will see is in how the Internet is searched. Currently, when we need information, we either enter the specific Web site address or we search for information using a search engine (such as Google). The next innovation is to place the power into the search function. The emphasis will be placed on finding the exact information, as opposed to searching or scrolling through many possible options. The result will allow for faster and more accurate informational retrieval.

Voice recognition will become more prevalent, as well, allowing further refinement in speech-to-text or text-to-speech between one or multiple languages. This technology will in time be integrated with surfing the Internet.

Research at the End of a Mouse

Meeting venue Web sites provide users with free access to online information upon providing a username and password and organization demographics. Some third-party providers offer functions beyond site selection. These may include request for proposal (RFP) planning, online auctions of available space, meeting specifications for third-party processing, chat rooms for counterpart discussions, industry news, and more.

Site Selection

Search engines can locate a property after a user has clicked on a map or region of the world or provides a facility name and city. On some sites, secondary filters allow the selection of a facility based on variables such as the number of sleeping rooms, size and amount of meeting space, and location within a venue (such as airport, downtown, or resort location). PCOs can quickly identify potential space, drill down into a facility, and review room diagrams and view menus, site and venue amenities, and local attractions. Advanced sites even provide virtual tours of select property space and 3-D views of function space. Reporting options allow users to develop comparison reports in order to quickly align properties that meet primary needs.

One of the most valuable features is the ability to generate and submit an RFP, a cost- and time-saving function available on some sites. By using an online RFP utility, the PCO can effortlessly present RFPs to a single venue, a national sales office, or to all venues identified.

Elements of a Site Selection RFP Utility

- Ease of selection
- Detailed search criteria, including location, brand, price, capacity, meeting space
- Number of venues/properties listed on the site, which will vary from site to site, depending on premiums charged to the facility
- Amenities and services available at the venue
- Active link to a facility's Web site
- Access to floor plans, menus, meeting space capacities, meeting space calculator
- Reporting options, including capabilities to export select data and comparison reports
- Virtual tours and multimedia presentations

- Ability to download brochure or fact sheet on selected properties
- Storing and saving capabilities of specific search queries; save, modify, or update RFP
- Meeting pattern options: preferred and alternative date options

Site selection utilities and RFP modules will dramatically save time and money. Once planners adopt these effective features, they can focus their time on marketing, content development, and other core meeting/event demands.

Registration

There are several registration options available for the PCO. E-marketing systems have become very popular among professionals who need a registration system. Text for electronic invitations can be created directly in the system or pasted from a word processing application into a pre-defined template. Depending on the system, templates can be customized to match specific needs. E-mail addresses are required for processing electronic invitations.

For larger meetings with multiple sessions, a Web-based or integrated PC-based system is appropriate.

There are many advantages to using an electronic registration process. Delivery and response time are considerably shortened from weeks and days to hours and minutes.

Dedicated Web Sites

For larger meetings, organizers should consider creating a dedicated event Web site. These themed sites provide many benefits, including an event portal that attendees can visit to communicate with the event sponsor, network with fellow attendees, register for sessions, and download specific documents. More elaborate sites allow registrants to book housing and travel, register for special events, or view archived events.

The aim of any dedicated Web site is to provide ease of use and a portal that encourages users to regularly browse the site for updated information. E-newsletters linked to the event Web site are a perfect added feature to convey updates to registrants.

Badges and Ticketing

In this planning function, a computer can save the event sponsor money and time. Most off-the-shelf software (with word processing functions) and industry-written, PC-based solutions can generate badges and tickets. They use laser print badge stock or thermal stock for printing badges, tent cards, and tickets. Web-based solutions offer the ability to export files to a word processing program for badges and tickets. The print quality, size, design requirements, and type of data shown on these items vary greatly within the industry.

Factors to consider when using computer-generated badges:

- How will attendees wear their badges? This will determine stock and size specifications.

- What is the badge's purpose? The purpose served will influence both stock type and size, as well as the type of printer. A 1-up badge template wastes no paper, while 6-up to 8-up templates can waste stock. Thermal-printed badges often used in 1-up designs require both specialized printer and stock.

- What logo and theme graphics will be on the badge? Print vendors can pre-print and perforate badge stock, as needed.

- Will the badge help provide lead or contact information? Bar coding technology can make this possible by passing on basic data to vendors.

- How will last-minute or on-site badge requests be processed? This process may be different than the one used prior to going on-site.

- How should data for merging into a badge be exported?

Smart Cards

Badge design for networking requires much less pre-planning than identification for security control. Security calls for use of smart-card technology. A smart card does much more than a badge:

- It serves as a unique ID for photographic recognition.
- It can be used as a credit or debit card.
- It facilitates lead retrieval.
- It allows you to track the wearer through an exhibit hall.

Thanks to the microchip and embedded math coprocessors, smart cards not only speed up on-site registration, but manage session attendance, payment processing, CEU tracking, lead retrieval and processing, and data transfer from a "name badge" to a vendor or an organization's affinity program.

An innovative device named "nTag" was introduced as a state-of-the-art communication device in 2003. Using infrared sensors and an LCD screen, this remarkable apparatus is to the name badge what a calculator is to an adding machine. Planning for Smart Card usage involves these tasks:

- Outline your objectives. Determine what you want to achieve by using this technology. Be specific.

- Set a budget. Include cost of research and investigation, technical support, and infrastructure requirements. The technology can be very expensive.

- Set a realistic timeline. Lower-tech, smart card applications technology, such as magnetic strips, have been available for years. However, embedded chip technology using contact (reader) and contact-less (wireless protocols) are constantly evolving.

- Hire a consultant early. Find an expert to help you in gathering industry-appropriate information, since no two implementations are exactly the same.

Smart Cards and nTag applications designed primarily for exhibition attendees are further described in Chapter 14.

Housing

With room attrition penalties becoming the norm, PCOs need to carefully monitor room blocks to avoid being assessed fees. In Chapter 11, we talked about the three critical components required for the successful implementation of a housing solution: location, price, and brand identity. These lodging parameters can be found on the various Web sites.

Major players in the online site-selection market have made their application protocols available to several online registration companies, providing PCOs with the option of offering housing and/or conference registration.

With online housing solutions, the PCO needs to clearly understand the requirements of their attendees. While there can be substantial cost savings in integrating registration, housing, and travel, organizers must look out for features their clients won't find useful. They need to provide technology solutions that meet core requirements.

Elements of online housing systems include:

- Search capability (by property, by location, by brand, and by price) and flexibility in choosing arrival and departure dates
- Access to real-time inventory
- Capability of confirmed registrants to edit their records after the initial registration is made
- Verification of e-mail address

- Ability to showcase conference/destination themes and attractions and show photographs and illustrations of the site
- Processing capability for multiple credit cards (personal/corporate)

To avoid penalties, PCOs should manage room-block attrition. One way to prevent "booking around the block" is to offer registrants a low-cost housing option. Continual tracking of room pickup is mandatory for any contracted room blocks.

Marketing

Never before have meeting professionals had so many opportunities to strategically increase event attendance. Blended marketing (taking advantage of both electronic and traditional methods) can itself provide efficient returns. As in all marketing efforts, a few basics are required: when you do your marketing assessment, do the following:

- Develop an attendee profile. Why is the registrant attending the meeting? Are expectations communicated?
- Survey the client base in order to identify an updated profile.
- Find out how many potential attendees have e-mail access.
- Determine what publications they read.
- Determine if the attendee matches the exhibitors' profile.

Creating an Integrated Marketing Plan

Your marketing plan needs to be integrated well in advance of the event. Consider a combination of traditional marketing channels (Internet-based strategies, optimized e-marketing through personalization, and list segmentation) messaged for focused audiences.

Consider how market communications will be coordinated among meeting management, marketing, Web development, and graphic design. When creating marketing elements, consider formats and message updates that could include formatting for the Internet, e-fax, e-mail, traditional fax, wireless devices, and printed communications.

Communication: From Snail-mail to E-mail

Meeting professionals must build professional networks. Prior to the Internet, traditional networking activities included corresponding with colleagues, membership in professional organizations, writing articles, and attending seminars and industry events.

Computers give the PCO broader options for networking, such as participating in industry chat rooms (real-time communication and bulletin boards where messages can be posted for colleagues). These options are useful for researching venues and/or suppliers within an area or seeking help from a sub-contractor. Instant messaging, an overnight success, provides a way to communicate in real-time and between devices such as a PDA and a PC or pager.

Instant Replay: Archiving the Event

Archiving technologies provide content for those interested in filing away notes from a meeting or session that was of particular interest. Being able to listen to and share a presentation from a previous conference while providing added value is also possible through archiving technology—an ideal format for training and education.

With conversion to a digital format, electronic broadcasting and distribution not only save on paper use, but also can reduce shipping, storage, and handling costs.

PCOs need to consider widening generation gaps. Younger, savvy computer users thirst for digitized material, which archiving technologies allow you to provide. They also serve as potential revenue channels.

Available options include media such as tape and CD, or the Web, including features such as:

- Audio with synchronized elements (e.g., slide images, transcription, video)
- Navigational features, such as an index menu or transcription search capability
- Availability of presentation materials in universal formats, such as Adobe Acrobat
- 24/7/365 guaranteed uptime on Web components

The options are limited by budget and the capabilities of an audience.

When working with a service provider, the PCO should consider these criteria:

- Will the archive work on both the MAC and Windows? In what format is the audio?
- Can the audio-only version be played in a standard CD player (car or home stereo)?
- Can Internet links and sponsorships be included?

- How is technical support provided?
- Will the content be available on constant demand times via the Web?

Event archiving is a technology that will continue to grow in popularity. The PCO should always consider this technology as an added value option that can provide added revenue, extended learning, and marketing exposure.

MEETINGS WITHOUT WALLS

Teleconferencing

Teleconferencing in its most basic form is communication between two or more distant points at which groups or individuals have gathered for a meeting. The method by which that communication is facilitated is the essence of teleconferencing as a technology. The methodology encompasses message content, delivery, and the technical systems for capturing, transmitting, and disseminating the message.

When a few limited videoconferences were successfully produced back in the mid-1970s, many hotel executives were worried that this new technology would make meetings a thing of the past. Apparently their fears were unfounded, because today hotels are some of the most active proponents of video and Web conferencing. Major chains such as Hilton, Marriott, and Sheraton have equipped many of their larger hotels with dedicated teleconference capabilities, and are actively marketing them. As the technology has improved to allow transmission of full-motion video and audio across phone lines, meeting planners and hoteliers alike have discovered that video can be an added dimension to a traditional meeting, a means of conveying a concentrated message or dialogue across great distances with a sense of urgency and immediacy, but without the high cost of satellite uplinks. Web conferencing extends the life and reach of conferences, allowing non-attendees to participate during the conference or to catch up after the fact.

Truths and Myths About Teleconferencing

It has been suggested that teleconferencing came into its own during the energy crunch of 1978 to minimize travel. It can be argued that it is less expensive to gather 500 people in five cities at satellite meetings averaging 100 each than to bring them all together in one place. But it may still be necessary to transport, house, and feed those same people at five locations. Any savings in travel time may be offset by the loss of leverage imposed by the reduced volume. Add to that the cost of videoconferencing and it might be even more expensive. The issue is not a teleconference versus a meeting; teleconferencing is merely one means and one process among many for holding the meeting. The point is that teleconferencing is not a tool for reducing meeting expenses; it should be viewed as an added dimension for enhancing some aspects of a conference, much as an audiovisual presentation enhances elements of a program.

Andrew Wright, principal and producer for California-based Premier Images, is even more adamant about the medium's purpose: "The idea behind video-conferencing is the immediate delivery of critical, time-sensitive information to a global audience."

Cost savings, according to Wright, can accrue from teleconferencing. "Some applications result in substantial savings while with others, the benefits may supersede consideration of costs. Because of escalating meeting costs, higher prices for accommodations and meals, creeping air fare increases, and the true value of executive time, it may be possible to affect economies with teleconferencing."

The following are some of the benefits, financial and otherwise, that teleconferencing can provide:

- Link meetings on a global scale, reducing the need for participants to travel great distances.

- Enable executives and authorities to simultaneously address multiple audiences in widely separated locations.

- Increase attendance. For example, association members who are unable or unwilling to devote travel time and expense to a national or international convention may be willing to attend a regional meeting linked to other meetings by video, or to log on to a Web conference at their office.

There is a distinction between dedicated networks for business communications and ad hoc teleconferencing as an element of meetings. Business networks connect branch offices of a company in order to facilitate training and continuing education. They also involve more people in the decision-making process, shorten the length and frequency of meetings, and produce savings in travel costs and time.

Ad hoc or special event teleconferencing differs from these networks in the same manner that off-premises meetings differ from those held at the participant's primary place of employment.

An Overview of Teleconferencing

The concept of teleconferencing once evoked images of television cameras, microwave antennas, and satellites. While the more elaborate event does indeed involve all those elements, there are certainly other options. (The prefix "tele" came from *telecommunications*, not *television*, as some believe). Audio teleconferencing, which permits people at a meeting to communicate with other groups by means of telephone lines, had been in use before the Internet and video entered the picture. (No pun intended.) It did not enjoy great success because its applications were limited. More illustrative of the medium are the teleconference configurations displayed on the chart that follows, which notes key characteristics:

Technology	*Type of event*	*Resources*
Videoconference-Satellite Signals transmitted and received via satellite dish.	Appropriate for events where picture quality is important, such as a CEO's presentation to worldwide sales force. Works for single or multiple locations, but cost is significant for multiple interactive uplinks (vs. a single origination site).	Professional crews, extensive mobile control studio, satellite uplink. Requires set-up and rehearsal time for production elements and satellite uplink.
Video teleconference Compressed video and audio signals carried over telephone system. Image quality depends on available bandwidth. May be some delay between sound and image, some pixilation may occur	Appropriate for small to moderate-sized events or when budget constraints trump picture quality. Excellent for interaction between multiple locations.	Professional crews, video and audio equipment, specialized control units, computers. Each location must have connections to T1 lines, TV monitors, microphones, and speakers.
Web conference Web sites, prerecorded streaming video, animated and graphic presentations, chat rooms.	Excellent for knowledge transfer (such as distance learning), with growing use when the goal is interactivity between and among a variety of participants and presenters.	Significant support from in-house IT staff or ASP. Preproduction of presentations, Web sites, etc. Internet servers and broadband connections.
Web cast Compressed video and audio streamed over the Internet. Image quality depends on bandwidth available to viewer.	Great for extending the reach of any event to viewers unable to attend. Because it is also asynchronous, a Web cast allows viewers access to events after the fact.	Professional crew or in-house computer techs, digital video cameras, microphones, server and software, broadband Internet connection.

A further explanation of characteristics relevant to these applications follows:

- *Graphic.* Transmission of graphic data and images in support of a presentation, demonstration, or discussion. Input may be a video camera recording a procedure; a computer generating visual data such as a simulation; electronic whiteboard images of lecture notes; or any visual image other than a talking head. This medium may be transmitted on telephone lines or via broadband Internet connections. (See Compressed Video, below.)

- *Video (point-to-multipoint)* with two-way audio. A means of delivering a message or demonstrating a process from one central point to several locations where members of the audience ask questions or make comments.

- *Video (point-to-point)* with audio. Same as above, but with the added capability of enabling all participants to be seen and heard. "Live" images and audiovisual or graphic data may be transmitted from all points.

- *Compressed video.* A technique that transmits only those parts of a picture that change, using digital technology to distinguish between static and changing images. Compressed video is substantially less expensive than satellite transmission and continues to improve as broadband and fiber-optic networks expand.

Videoconferencing

Videoconferencing is the original teleconference, but what once was a rare, high-priced, complex event requiring mobile TV studios and satellite uplinks is now relatively commonplace. Advances in telecommunications have allowed video signals to be carried over telephone wires, which has dramatically decreased costs. Video technology has also improved, reducing the need for studio lighting and large control suites.

Planning Considerations for Videoconferencing

The cost of satellite time has become more affordable because more satellites are now orbiting the earth. In fact, it may be a small part of the teleconference budget.

Planning, including budget preparation, begins with these questions:

- Is a videoconference the most effective way to achieve meeting objectives?

- Where will the telecast originate? (The *uplink*)

Meetings and Event Technology   213

- Is two-way video necessary or desirable? Each point will be an uplink.
- To how many locations (*downlinks*) will the signal be broadcast?
- What production will be required prior to and during the conference? What production capability exists in-house? What is to be contracted?
- What program elements will be televised?

Once you have answers to these questions, get a cost quotation from a professional video producer, an audiovisual production company with television experience, or a firm that specializes in videoconferencing. Upon acceptance of the bid, the PCO and the producer work together according to the guidelines presented in the preceding chapter. You will need several things if you are planning a videoconference. Put these needs on the PCO's checklist:

- Meeting rooms with adequate space and ceiling height for positioning of cameras and overhead lighting
- Availability of room for setup and rehearsal
- Provisions for briefing speakers on TV technique (e.g., proper clothing colors, eye contact with audience *and* camera lens, etc.)
- Redundancy of equipment and control to ensure backup in the event of failure
- Open telephone lines for coordination, control, and two-way audio
- Display medium appropriate to the audience (monitors or video projection)
- An experienced videoconference coordinator at each downlink

When is teleconferencing justified?

Some years ago, the author was responsible for coordinating and producing a series of meetings celebrating Zenith Corporation's 50th anniversary. The project involved over one hundred presentations in sixty cities, ten audiovisual crews, and thirty corporate executives who traveled across the United States over a six-week period. The message was delivered on film by Zenith's spokesman, Arthur Godfrey. Had videoconferencing been available at the time, the savings could have been substantial, and Arthur Godfrey could have delivered his message live to all Zenith dealers and salesmen at the same time.

In recent years, it has become common for the chairman or CEO of a multinational corporation to address employees at concurrent meetings all over the world through videoconferencing. For example, Sheraton Hotels celebrated its golden anniversary with a teleconference that linked 6,000 of its employees at eleven locations around the world. Even Sheraton would have been hard put to transport and house that many people in one location!

There is high consensus in the meetings industry regarding the viability of teleconferencing when the logistical demands of numbers and distances make a single meeting impractical, or when the objective is merely to convey information. But where interaction between speaker and participant or among participants is essential, a teleconference should be viewed as an additional dimension rather than a substitute for the meeting.

VIRTUAL MEETINGS

Teleconferencing and videoconferencing are generally enhancements of conventional site-based events. Virtual meetings, however, use the resources of the Internet as the broadcast medium.

Meetings are no longer required to be site-based. Virtual meetings are growing in acceptance and can be conducted from the desktop or even from the palm of one's hand. From product announcements, trade shows, and sales meetings to press briefings or product demonstrations, alternative delivery options can meet the need.

Web Conferencing

Not all meetings must be site-based. Web conferences—though not considered a substitute to conventional face-to-face meetings—offer yet another dimension for content delivery and communication.

Web conferences typically involve a live teleconference that consists of participant interaction. They can also include documents, video, and other graphics. These events fulfill a specific need to communicate with participants at distant locations—usually when an in-person meeting is not justified or practical.

With this scenario accessible through any PC, a user will connect to a pre-determined Web site or a virtual meeting room from which the session will be hosted.

In this case, audio is best achieved through a conference call "bridge." The flexibility of these desktop systems varies widely: Some require a high degree of testing and at least a 56K connection speed. Advanced systems allow for multiple leaders to share in presentation responsibilities, and may feature chat rooms, whiteboarding, multimedia presentations, Web surfing, and application-sharing and collaboration. Readily available group collaboration software, such as Microsoft's NetMeeting, provides many of the same features as higher-end applications. However, these have to be operated without a third-party service provider, so participants need to be adept at the technology being used.

Given this type of connectivity, a group of computers can be temporarily networked using the PC's unique IP addresses. Once connected, properly authorized participants can share and exchange files, programs, and documents.

Appropriate bandwidth, hardware availability, and internal PC settings, plus a degree of testing, are required for these applications. However, the primary criterion for a successful session is pre-notification of participants so that appropriate settings on each PC can be made in advance. Once call groups are established and settings are defined, future calls can be readily facilitated.

Collaborative applications are best suited to proposal reviews and edits, small task-force meetings where documents need to be reviewed, and for general system maintenance. The price range for this class of product varies from no cost to a few hundred dollars.

Web Casts

Web casts are broadcasts on the Internet that augment a live meeting in progress or to archive an event that took place in the past.

The Web cast presentation can be live or taped. Taping the session allows time for editing and the inclusion of value-added material. It then can be broadcast via the Internet, satellite, or a CD. Remember, broadcast quality sound and lighting are highly recommended, as are speaker rehearsal and coaching. Consider hiring a production manager whenever you need to communicate something that is mission-critical.

Interactive Web Casts

This medium involves two-way communication and high-end media.

An interactive Web cast requires serious advanced production and coordination. Will it entail point-to-point or point-to-multipoint? Is the broadcast directed to service centers where an audience can gather, or is it directed to other corporate locations? Will the broadcast be by satellite, or via the Internet?

These sessions call for broadcast-quality lighting, sound, and production.

Third-party Services

Third parties offer technical services for participants and leaders, and can provide moderating and scheduling services. Third parties provide competent control and quality assurance, but all participants will be required to pre-load either a client application or a leader application. This is made available by the service provider, and can be downloaded and set up in short time.

Even when using a third party, encourage all participants to test their connectivity. Service providers can make sure that the hardware and connectivity are appropriate. All links and phone numbers should be pre-tested by event staff or the service provider.

The chief advantages of contracting with service providers are that they can provide online technical assistance and the ability to utilize multiple leaders. The latter is very useful. Should one designated leader have a temporary computer problem, the lead can be silently passed to a secondary head and the presentation can continue. No one in the audience even needs to know. Of course, leadership control and presentation coordination need to be reviewed and rehearsed by leaders in advance in order to ensure seamless performance.

The threat of terrorism and the availability of technology have generated a dramatic growth in virtual meetings. They continue to gain greater acceptance as an effective way to meet and train distributed groups. The ease of use and sophistication of these virtual technologies continue to improve. Virtual trade shows will also become more popular for select industry sectors. What are now pioneering technologies will finally enter the acceptance stage of product life, resulting in a growth of market share. While the virtual space of technology has limitations, it also holds many promises as the worldwide marketplace evolves.

SIMULTANEOUS INTERPRETATION

To PCOs whose activities routinely encompass multicultural events, it may seem odd to refer to simultaneous interpretation (SI) as advanced communication, because SI is part and parcel of most of their meetings. This section of the chapter is intended for meeting organizers who have had little exposure to this technique and need to gain a better understanding.

International conferences that include dialogue in multiple languages make use of sophisticated SI systems to convey the speaker's words to the interpreters, who then convert the remarks into the languages of the attendees. A typical SI system consists of the speaker's console, the interpreter's console, a distribution transmitter, and the requisite number of receivers and headsets. In a panel or conference configuration, each speaker and the chairman will have a microphone. An operator's console may be added to enable a technician to activate one microphone at a time to ensure an orderly flow of discussion and avoid audio feedback. When the principal speaker is at a lectern, the sound is fed to the interpreters' headsets, as well as to the house amplifier.

The interpreters are housed in sound-isolated or soundproof booths situated so that they can observe the speaker, usually through a window. (Some installations make use of closed-circuit television.) They have a headset and a microphone through which they transmit their translation, each in a particular language. In permanent installations, the interpreters' voices are transmitted to the attendees by means of a hard-wired system that distributes the signal to the switchable headset jack built into each auditorium seat. The listener selects the preferred language by switching channels on the console. Some more-sophisticated congress centers also incorporate a microphone at every two or three seats, in order to accommodate comments from the audience.

A more-flexible system evolved with the development of wireless radio frequency (RF) receivers operating within an inductive loop antenna that transmits up to eight channels of sound to lightweight, portable receivers equipped with headsets. Many of the newer conference facilities have substituted this type of system for the hard-wired configuration. A caveat for PCOs involved with meetings of a confidential nature: RF-based wireless systems can be invaded by sophisticated listening devices outside the meeting room. If security is a concern, stay with a hard-wired system or one based on infrared (IR). IR systems utilize infrared radiators that transmit the signals from the amplifier to the person's headset. They are readily portable and relatively secure from eavesdropping.

Most North American conference centers do not, as a matter of course, incorporate dedicated SI facilities into their design. Portable sound booths and a variety of portable SI systems are available, however. Shipping costs for these systems tend to be high, but not as high as interpretation services. (See Chapter 19 for additional details on the use of interpreters.)

What Lies Ahead?

The APEX Initiative, an exciting five-year industry-wide effort conducted and managed by the Convention Industry Council, has had a profound effect on improving the ability to communicate electronically between facilities, solution providers, meeting professionals, and attendees.

Here is the Convention Industry Council's mission statement:

> ... To spearhead an industry-wide initiative that brings together all stakeholders in the development and implementation of industry-wide accepted practices which create and enhance efficiencies throughout the meeting, convention, and exhibition industry.

Collectively, volunteers working on behalf of the APEX Initiative have developed and identified best practices in the areas of terminology, history/post-event reports, requests for proposals, résumés, work orders, meeting and site profiles, registration and housing, and contracts. With the assistance of the Technology Advisory Council, led by co-author E.J. Siwek, comprehensive data definitions and guidelines will be prepared to help industry technology providers develop commonly defined data structures. In time, the effort should help applications share electronic data more efficiently than is possible under the current framework. While there is much to be done, the hope is that by educating the meeting industry in the adoption of best practices, greater levels of efficiency will be possible, saving organizations and meeting professionals time and cost.

The APEX Initiative has coordinated efforts on the seven focused areas noted above. In November of 2003, the APEX Commissioners officially released the final Terminology Report and the History Post Event Report to the industry.

The future of technology within this industry holds much promise, but there are clearly new obstacles and challenges ahead.

Chapter Fourteen
Planning and Managing Exhibitions

Many PCOs with years of meeting management experience have only a cursory knowledge of exhibit planning and operations. This chapter is intended to give the novice some valuable pointers and to reinforce the knowledge of the expert.

It is important at this point to distinguish between two substantially different kinds of events (though they share some characteristics): Exhibition and Trade Show. Here are our working definitions:

Exhibition or exposition: An event at which products or services are displayed. It can be an event held in conjunction with a meeting, or an event that stands alone and to which the public may be invited.

Trade show: A stand-alone exhibition of products and services to which the public is *not* invited.

In the context of this book, the prime focus is on exhibitions as events that are held in conjunction with a meeting or convention that are restricted to attendees and exhibitors. However, some pointers on independent exhibitions are included where appropriate.

DECISION FACTORS

The decision to organize an exhibition hinges on a variety of factors. The first of these is the objective. For associations, it is a primary source of non-dues revenue, a learning resource for their general membership, and a key marketing vehicle for their supplier members. At scientific or technology events, exhibits can introduce new products or services, demonstrate procedures, and provide attendees with opportunities for hands-on experience.

Return on investment is important from the exhibitors' perspective. Organizations bearing the costs related to designing, shipping, and staffing an exhibit, exhibitor fees, and contracting services seek assurance that the event sponsors will provide adequate "traffic"—the volume of visitors to their booths. Organizers can maximize that traffic with strategic marketing so that registration is adequate and by allocating sufficient time in the program for exhibit visitation.

Coordinating exhibit hours with the meeting's program schedule often produces conflict: Exhibitors need to be assured that time and attendance will justify their expenses. The program committee, on the other hand, is reluctant to surrender program time. Organizers know that exhibitions can be as much an educational resource as presentations and workshops, and thus try to mediate in order to arrive at a fair balance.

VENUE SELECTION

Criteria for selecting exhibit sites (convention center, exhibition hall, or hotel) vary according to the event's size, scope, and audience. When seeking off-site convention and exhibition facilities, planners tend to select sites that meet the following selection criteria:

- Center that is convenient to headquarters' hotel
- Facilities that are adequate in terms of capacity, dimensions, floor load, head room, number of meeting rooms, docking space, and appointments
- Resident staff that is properly trained, permanently employed, and multilingual
- Adequate provisions for utilities, lighting, sound, and technical support
- Provisions for traffic flow (people and vehicles), loading docks, and parking
- Reasonable pricing for exhibit space, meeting rooms, services, and extras
- Flexibility in selection and use of outside contractors of client's or exhibitor's choice
- If trade unions are involved, rules that provide for manageable costs, reasonable policies, and accommodation for special situations
- Staff offices that have proper communication channels for secretariat, show management, program participants, media, and special staff

- On-site catering, quality food preparation, and negotiable prices and policies
- Staging facilities, equipment, and technical staff to fit program needs
- Simultaneous interpretation facilities and equipment for key meeting rooms (if applicable)
- Medical and emergency care facilities and qualified personnel readily available
- Security/surveillance systems and trained security staff

The event organizer will also need to ascertain what other events are scheduled at the site, whether they will conflict, and what provisions are planned for isolating them. During the site inspection, the PCO will ask detailed questions on policies and operating procedures regarding surcharges on products sold at the show, union regulations and work rules, status of labor contracts and potential disputes, restrictions on exhibitor booth setup, and materials carried in or out. Loading, docking, crate storage, and truck holding areas must be checked to determine time allocations for loading in, setup, dismantling, and loading out.

Depending on the scope of the exhibition, the sponsoring organization may retain a show management firm or an exhibit service company. These entities act as a prime agent, subcontracting with other suppliers for a variety of support services. Whether the exhibition sponsor utilizes one of these agents or acts as the prime contractor, it is important to understand the relationship of various services to the convention center, as well as the degree of discretion the organizer can exercise when selecting suppliers. The table that follows lists services normally provided by an exclusive contractor, services usually selected from an approved list of contractors, and services that are discretionary. Keep in mind that "normally" and "usually" denote general policy; circumstances will vary.

Since most convention centers are managed by municipal authorities, the PCO should be aware of the bureaucratic influence and mind-set that often acts as a barrier to reciprocal negotiations. Fortunately, the proliferation of convention centers has created a more-competitive marketplace; when the organizer's needs cannot be adequately met at one site, there are others that will be more accommodating.

EXPOSITION HOTELS

The construction of mega-hotels with extensive exhibit space has created a viable alternative to convention centers for exhibitions of limited size. Planners

Service	Exclusive	Approved or in-house	Discretionary
Audiovisual rental		X	
Cleaning			X*
Crowd control		X	
Decorator			X
Drayage and Freight			X
Electrical		X	
Catering	X		
Security		X*	

* tending toward in-house contractor

and exhibitors cite convenience for attendees and exhibitors and lower costs as the key benefits of having meetings and exhibits in the same facility. Because exhibit space also increases the hotel's revenue, the sponsor enjoys increased leverage in negotiating other meeting elements. Restrictive municipal ordinances and union regulations that characterize many convention centers tend to be of less concern at hotels. Attendee attrition during exhibit hours is an ongoing concern of show managers; once people leave for meetings or meals, there is a chance that they will not return. At a hotel, people can go to their rooms or to a meal function and conveniently return to the exhibits.

The determining factors for considering an exposition hotel are show size and whether or not it is open to the public. Most hotels are not equipped to handle several thousand visitors. Parking, hallways, and food service outlets are not adequate for large numbers. Other drawbacks common to hotels are the fact that few have a single room that is large enough in floor space for all the booths required, thus necessitating multiple rooms. Docking facilities, freight elevators, floor loads, and ceiling heights are restrictive; and most in-house services common to exhibit halls must be sub-contracted. Nevertheless, for a 50- to 100-booth show, such a hotel bears valid consideration.

Yet another configuration, the in-room exhibit or display, may be appropriate for certain kinds of exhibitions. Under these conditions, each exhibitor occupies a break-out room or converted guest room, preferably on one floor or on contiguous floors. For small, specialty shows, this concept offers advantages to the organizer and the exhibitors. For the former, it simplifies planning, reduces the number of subcontractors, and increases room block. For exhibitors, there are the benefits of security, privacy, generally more space, freight savings, individual identity, and the convenience and cost savings of using a furnished room—complete with telephone and amenities—for display space. Naturally, this configuration is feasible only for services or products that are small, lightweight, and portable, and that do not have unusual power requirements.

To help prevent attendees from getting lost, detailed maps and floor information desks are essential. For the hotel, in-room exhibits have some drawbacks in disruption of services to other guests, use of service elevators during setup and dismantling, and potential damage to furnishings. However, these are offset by premium room rates (normally 1.5 times the double-occupancy rate), higher occupancy, and increased food and beverage sales.

OTHER PLANNING CONSIDERATIONS

After the venue has been selected, certain decisions will have to be based on the nature of the event. If it is a closed exhibition (limited to meeting registrants), the process is relatively simple. If it is a public show held in conjunction with a convention or conference, the planning becomes more complex. Consider these things:

- Are the program and exhibits held at the same facility, or in close proximity? If not, how much transit time should be allowed? Will transportation be needed? What are the costs and turnaround times?
- Can the exhibit hall accommodate all the anticipated booths, or will overflow space be required? A safe rule for computing required gross space is to total the net square footage required for booths, and then double it.
- If overflow areas are utilized, what type of traffic pattern is needed to ensure balance and proper flow? Will exhibitors who cannot be accommodated in the main hall be offered reduced booth rental rates?

MARKETING THE EVENT

From a marketing perspective, organizers of shows that are not affiliated with a specific event must pay attention to two interrelated functions: exhibit space marketing and attendance promotion. If attendance is ensured, the prime marketing focus will be to attract exhibitors.

If the event is a repeat of previous exhibitions held in conjunction with the meeting, the main challenge for the organizers is to get past exhibitors to return and to attract new ones. If it is a first-time event, a broader effort is required. In either case, the main draw is the demographic nature of the meeting attendees. Data on the organizations whose members attend, their interests, and their buying habits are the key elements in attracting exhibitors. Also of importance is accurate previous event data on floor traffic, lead-generation, and—if available—sales volume resulting from those leads. A database displaying these elements is essential for collecting and disseminating the decision-making factors exhibitors need to justify the cost of participation.

One tactic that show organizers use to promote exhibitor participation is to offer to exhibitors at a show a reduced rate if they sign up for subsequent shows. Such a backlog of "charter" exhibitors provides some reduction in marketing expenses.

PROMOTING ATTENDANCE

In addition to marketing the exhibition to potential exhibitors, there will be costs involved in attendance promotion, even where exhibits are part of a convention. Sometimes there is a need to attract additional traffic to the exhibits. Marketing costs might cover design of printed materials, printing, postage, Web hosting, sales commissions, and staff and clerical time. Attendance promotion will likely require funds for advertising, publicity, graphics, printing, and postage. The exhibitors are not only the focus of the marketing effort, but an adjunct as well. They support the organizers' efforts by promoting their exhibit to registered attendees and inviting them to visit their Web sites and come by their booths (and often offering incentives to do so). The show organizer encourages such promotions and facilitates it by providing exhibitors with registration data, mailing information, and Web site participation.

The attraction and efficiency of Internet marketing notwithstanding, most show organizers view it as an adjunct to—rather than a substitute for—print and mail.

THE EXHIBIT PROSPECTUS

When details about the exhibit venue, hours, rates, etc., are determined, various media channels are used to invite exhibitors to contract for booth space. In the case of associations, trade groups, and professional societies, the organization's journal is the obvious first choice for advertising the event. Concurrently, the association's Web site should post information about the coming event and direct potential exhibitors to a Web page displaying the exhibit prospectus and appropriate forms for responding.

While new technologies are fascinating to play with, the question the exhibit organizer must always ask is, *"Is it easy to use?"* Software delivered over the Internet that requires lengthy download time is inadvisable. Offering colorful brochures that must be downloaded from the Internet is inconsiderate if they are not accompanied by a printer-friendly version with minimal color and graphics. The focus must be on how to give enough information to exhibitors to make them want to register via the Internet. Try to focus on changing user-habits and eliminating the mailing of print catalogs and print-versions of exhibitor manuals—the cost savings can be significant.

Exhibitions are traditionally promoted through a series of mailings that includes the exhibit prospectus, culminating in the complete information kit for interested exhibitors. Contracts are executed and space is assigned during the months following the initial promotion. The exhibitor's prospectus and kit include:

- Information about the date, location, and nature of the show; anticipated attendance; and market demographics
- Exhibitor eligibility requirements if there are restrictions imposed by sponsors
- The marketing plan, which includes publicity, advertising schedule, event Web site, attendee demographics, and other attendance-promotion measures
- Exhibit hours and a floor plan showing booth dimensions, booth number, utility access, obstructions, and variations
- Data on available utilities, floor loads, ceiling height, door sizes, freight elevators, docking, crate removal, storage, and return
- Shipping and drayage information; pre-printed labels and assigned PRO numbers for each exhibitor
- A contract for space that specifies fees, deposits, discounts, payment schedules, and conditions governing cancellations and refunds
- Information, price lists, and order forms from the exhibit service contractor regarding labor, signage, booth furnishings, rentals, cleaning, and decorator services
- Hours for installation, rigging, and dismantling (most contracts stipulate date and time when dismantling may begin)
- Registration database and procedures for exhibitor personnel and attendees
- Restrictions imposed by the facility or municipality that govern exclusive contracts, booth sales, union rules, and safety ordinances (such as limiting the use of toxic or flammable materials in booth construction or display materials)
- Specifications on exhibit booths that cover items such as carpeting, drapes, lighting, etc. (provided by the sponsor)

- Restrictions on signs and sound-amplification limits for demonstrations and/or entertainment
- Security procedures governing ingress and egress for exhibitors and the public; badge control and package-removal policy
- Insurance coverage addressing limits of liability, bonding requirements, and disclaimers
- Form for exhibitor-listing in the exhibition directory, including directory advertising rates
- Exhibit Contractor's Web site, with information and order forms for special services: pager and PDA rentals, telephones, photography, computers, data transmission, video and audiovisual rental, floral and plant decorations, and temporary help (such as demonstrators and models)

BUDGET AND FISCAL PLANNING

Exhibitions are part of the learning environment at corporate meetings. They provide attendees with a first-hand look at products and services related to their careers. They also offer the same benefits for associations, but are also a major source of revenue, often exceeding income from delegate registrations. The basic premise is that the show organizer rents the hall at a gross rate, determines total booth capacity based on net salable space, and arrives at a per-booth price that includes rental cost, certain services, and a profit margin. Organizations that hold annual exhibitions as part of their meeting activity can project exhibit booth sales based on past history and should expect an increase as the event grows in popularity.

Organizers of a first-time event do not have that luxury. They must project participation based on industry characteristics and the perception, on the part of potential exhibitors, of the exhibition's value as a marketing medium. Under such circumstances, planning must include a decision to cancel if booth sales do not meet expectations. The exception would be a meeting at which the exhibits' educational value justifies their inclusion, regardless of economic consequences.

Exhibit Booth Pricing

The booth rental fee is normally set at a fixed amount that ensures at least a break-even if only the minimum number of exhibitors participate. It must also reflect industry standards in pricing, the stature of the meeting, available exhibit hours, and attendee profile. Steady traffic comprising highly qualified potential buyers is preferred over a large mob of people (many of

Planning and Managing Exhibitions 227

whom are just looking or collecting literature). Smaller exhibitions that are part of a meeting are often held at a hotel, instead of at an exhibition center/hall. As pointed out earlier, this usually translates into lower labor costs and consequently a more reasonable booth fee.

PRODUCTION AND OPERATIONS

The cost of producing the exhibition includes the hall or room rental and fees for the services and equipment required to stage and manage the event. Exhibition production will include some or all of these items:

- Utilities, unless included in the rental fees
- Management, supervisory, and clerical staff
- Labor and materials for decoration of booths and public areas
- Security and emergency medical services
- Communications (Internet access, telephone, fax, mobile radio)
- Web site design and operation
- Signage, including special signs required during the show
- Pressroom, equipment, and staff
- Refreshments and catering
- Audiovisual equipment and staff (other than those ordered by exhibitors)
- Registration (booths, badges, forms, computer services, office equipment)
- Parking for staff, trucks, contractors, VIPs
- Truck routing, drayage, and related shipping services
- Entertainment, exhibitor hospitality, prizes
- Insurance, bonds, and licenses
- Custodial services
- Off-site holding and storage areas

It is customary to engage an exhibition service contractor (sometimes called the decorator). If this will be the case, many of these budget items will be included in the fee. Careful review and periodic monitoring of the exhibition budget is still required.

EXHIBIT TECHNOLOGY

Registration

If the exhibition is part of a convention, there is no need for separate registration of audience or exhibitors. If it is a discrete event, even held in conjunction with a meeting, registration procedures are necessary. Fortunately, most meeting registration software can handle that function as well.

Software should be evaluated in terms of functions specific to exhibitions. At a minimum, the program should have the following capabilities:

- Monitor and display exhibitor list, booth sales, registrations, and exhibitor profiles.
- Generate exhibit master list, correspondence, and control forms.
- Track exhibition attendance and prepare statistical reports.

Exhibitor Registration

The exhibitor registration desk is set up during the installation phase. It should be manned by representatives of the sponsoring organization or show management firm, if one is employed. While most exhibitors will have registered in advance, their registration materials and badges might need to be issued on-site. Other people will wait to register on-site, so there will usually be a few substitutions and additions. These may be covered by the rental fee, but if the exhibition rules set a limit on complimentary registrations, provisions must be made for collecting added fees. In many meetings, exhibitors also participate in all or select business and social programs. Thus, the registration procedure may include distribution of meeting materials, tickets, programs, and other elements in addition to badges. An updated list of attendees is a valuable tool for exhibitors. To avoid congestion at the exhibitor registration desk, several additional positions might need to be staffed. A senior staff member should supervise the registrars and act as a troubleshooter. Exhibitions are an important revenue source for associations, and exhibitors should be afforded the courtesy to which they are entitled.

Visitor Registration

In a closed exhibition, admission is limited to meeting attendees and, perhaps, media and guests. Their badges serve as identification, and no special registration is required to attend. A variation of this is where the organizers issue "Exhibits Only" badges or passes to people who are not registered for the conference. Unless these are mailed in advance or issued by exhibitors to their clients, a registration desk is established. For large shows to which the public or a significant number of people are invited, extensive registration facilities are needed. If badges are the means of admission, it is customary to set up desktop computers at counters or tables separate from the registration desk, where visitors can fill out the proper form. At the desk itself, a registrar mans each position. Some organizations have a separate area, organized by alphabetical groupings, for pre-registered visitors. It is also a good idea to have a "long line contingency" that enables off-duty registrars to man additional positions. Most registration software systems allow the organizers to audit daily attendance figures and generate follow-up mailing lists—data that is also important to exhibitors.

Smart Cards

"Smart Cards" are rapidly replacing paper badges. These cards make use of bar codes (or use more-advanced technology in the form of embedded chips) to store a variety of essential data about the visitor. So-called smart badges can hold demographic information and information regarding buying interests, contact data, a company, or a product. Once it is read by an on-site reader, information can be automatically sent via e-mail or attachment page. A thank-you note or product information can be electronically sent to the attendee.

Smart-card technology also can be used to maintain high-level security. Holographic images and embedded chips can store a wealth of information, while also used for emitting radio signals for tracking the whereabouts of an individual or for transmitting data to PDAs and handheld computers.

Wearable Technology—nTag

Introduced in 2003, nTag functions as both an identification device and a communication medium. Using infrared technology and an LCD screen the size of a conventional name tag, nTag records, displays, and communicates data entered by the wearer. Like a smart card, it can receive data from the show sponsor—event changes, messages, etc.—or it can display wearer-generated communications such as "Need affordable venue in subtropical site." Its built-in radio facilitates use as a communication or feedback device at program sessions. Far more than a name badge, nTag is available for rental. For details, contact *info@nTag.com*.

ON-SITE OPERATIONS

Where exhibits are part of a conference, the exhibit manager attends the pre-conference meeting in order to review arrangements and logistical requirements with the facility staff and support companies (the key one is the exhibit service contractor). The exhibit operations manual serves as the master plan, since it contains elements of the Staging Guide pertaining to this activity. It should be provided to key personnel two months before the event. It is a day-by-day listing of activities in preparation for and during the exhibition. The manual details specific functions, completion times, and responsibilities of the organizers, exhibitors, the service contractor, the facility staff, and any subcontractors involved in a support role.

Prior to any activity, the PCO and the service contractor review the operations manual and floor diagram. They physically walk the exhibit area, designating aisles, service areas, lounges, and food and beverage areas to identify any possible problems with traffic flow, security, or material handling. Locations for the registration area, show office, and service desk are determined. The service desk will be the focal point for all exhibit functions during setup and operations; it is manned by the service contractor's staff, who supervise drayage, decoration, rentals, and related exhibit support activities.

Installation Phase

After the floor plan has been reviewed and adjustments have been made, the service staff marks off the floor and begins installation. Though pipe and drape are the standard in the United States, Canada, Europe, and most of Asia tend to favor rigid wall booths ("stands" in Asia and Europe). In some countries, local labor laws require that they be constructed on-site, though modular components have all but replaced such labor-intensive methods. Utilities, computer, and telephone lines are hooked up and run to the booths as ordered, and rental furnishings are put in place while decorators complete the booth areas. Scheduling is critical: As the booths are laid out and decorated, exhibit freight that has been warehoused or held in a marshaling area is delivered by the drayage company so that no down time is incurred. Exhibit components are unloaded, placed, and assembled by the service contractor, and empty crates are labeled and moved to a storage area until required for load-out.

Once the heavy freight has been placed and the crates have been removed, aisles are carpeted and theme decoration is installed. At the same time, special booths for the sponsoring organization, affiliates, and trade press are set up and decorated. As installation is completed, the meeting executive, exhibit manager, and service contractor conduct a final walk-through inspection to observe proper placement of signage, lighting, decorations, cleaning, and observance of exhibition rules. Common infractions to look for during the initial and daily inspections include:

- Booth elements that protrude beyond specified height dimensions. The object is to avoid looking at the back of a booth. Island and perimeter wall height restrictions are more flexible.

- Booth decorations or components that block sightlines. To avoid partitions that block adjacent booths, organizers may specify that all components over a certain height must be confined to the rear part of the booth.

- Distracting or irritating lighting effects (e.g., strobelights).

- Sound amplification in excess of specified volume. Amplifiers should not be apparent until actual operation, and should be carefully monitored.

- Demonstrations that would cause people to assemble outside booth limits. Use of unauthorized or unsafe equipment or materials.

- Offensive or unethical conduct by booth personnel: sideshow tactics, merchandise sales (if prohibited), raffles, and giveaways bearing objectionable or distasteful graphics.

Exhibitor Briefing

A briefing session is conducted for exhibitors by the exhibit manager or exhibit committee one or two days before the show opens. This is when rules and regulations are reviewed; exhibit hours, security arrangements, and any changes are announced; and questions or disputes are resolved. If booth sales are permitted, information on procedures, taxation, and parcel passes (for removing merchandise from the exhibit floor) need to be disseminated and clarified. In some facilities, merchandise sales are the exclusive right of specified concessionaires and a substantial surcharge is added for any items sold in the building by exhibitors.

Security

Around-the-clock security is necessary to safeguard products in the exhibit area. A precise pass system must be worked out with the security supervisor to cover exhibitors, show labor, and staff. This is particularly critical during setup and dismantling, when the area is most vulnerable to theft. During exhibit hours, the security force may need to be augmented for badge and pass control: Professional criminals often target exhibitions involving high tech and expensive consumer products, and are quite adept at forging credentials. For this reason, exhibitions displaying such products should also include armed plainclothes patrols, manned by trained officers authorized to make arrests. Policies and forms controlling removal of items from the exhibit area must be clarified to exhibitors and security guards.

If there is a heightened threat level (as issued by the U.S. Department of Homeland Security), public assembly facilities will be potential terrorist targets, so additional defensive measures will be in order. The International Association of Assembly Managers (IAAM) Safety and Security Task Force developed the following guidelines:

- *Public Access Areas/Lobbies.* All points of ingress and interior are to be manned. There is no passage allowed without photo identification and proper event credentials. Spot checks should be made of packages, delegates, and couriers.
- *Coat Check/Baggage Check.* These are restricted to event badge holders only. There should be spot checks of coats and baggage.
- *Driveway/Roadway Access.* Private vehicles are allowed on access roads only if on event business. Driveway access is limited to event-authorized, placarded shuttle transportation.
- *Leased Spaces/Meeting Rooms/Exhibit Halls.* A pre-convention meeting is required with show management. Clients should limit credentials to essential show personnel. Designated locations will function as emergency aid stations, should the need arise.

Exhibit Operations

In every exhibition there is that magic moment when the doors open to admit visitors. Booth personnel, dressed in their best attire (many in costume denoting the character of their product, region, or service) eagerly await potential clients. It is county fair, circus, and theme park combined. Exhibitors, having spent megabucks to design, ship, assemble, and man their booths, invest additional funds to attract traffic to their location. They use a wide variety of visual stimulation and entertainment to do this—live and recorded: The ubiquitous sexy models are still to be found, but they have been augmented if not replaced by a wide range of creative mixed-media productions and innovative gimmicks.

Interactive performances—live or on video—attract visitors and captivate them with comedy, music, juggling, and creative dialogue featuring the exhibitor's product or service. Media theaters present the sponsor's message in exciting multimedia formats. Candy, drinks, and palate-tempting foods attract visitors and hold them there long enough to hear the exhibitor's message or see its product.

Technology has impacted the exhibition in many ways. IBM brought the popular PDA into its PartnerWorld show. The company discarded the bulky information binder and replaced it with a hand-held PDA containing all the graphics and data, and then provided one to each of their 4,000-plus attendees. Shows that don't have IBM's budget can rent PDAs to their visitors and download the entire show schedule and exhibitor information. Hotsynch cradles in the registration area or spotted around the exhibit floors allow attendees to insert their PDAs and download updated information or messages. One innovative approach might be to sell PDA banners to exhibitors, thus defraying system costs and offering visitors yet another medium for their message.

Operational Checks

During setup, show operations, and dismantling, the organizers, the exhibit manager, and his or her staff make continuous inspections of the exhibit floor and adjacent areas. They should be equipped with two-way radios that net with the organizer's office and key support services. At larger shows, electric carts or scooters are provided to minimize fatigue. Specifics to check include:

- See that registration area, lounges, and aisles are kept clean and free of debris.

- Ensure proper and timely operation of food-service outlet.

- Guard posts to ensure that security people are performing to standards, and are courteous but firm, and that they are alert for violations.

- Monitor exhibits for noise violations and infractions such as demonstrations that cause congested aisles; illegal sales; and dismantling or abandonment of booths before the published closing hour.

The exhibit manager has the authority to enforce compliance. He or she may remove an exhibit if it is in violation of contractual regulations. Conversely, these inspection trips afford the manager and officers of the sponsoring organization opportunities to interface with exhibitors and to solve or mediate problems, inquire as to their satisfaction with the show, and build goodwill for subsequent events.

Exhibiting Abroad

Exhibitions held in Asia, Europe, or Latin America have their own characteristics—many of which are quite different from domestic events. Some valuable pointers on exhibiting abroad are covered in Chapter 18.

What of the exhibitions of the future?

Doug Fox, a veteran meeting professional and acknowledged technology sage, envisions a time when virtual trade shows are "morphed into personalized one-to-one marketing opportunities that are integrated with powerful databases of customer information."

Fox's crystal ball reveals the following scenario: Buyers will access a virtual trade show on the Web. The Web site will automatically identify the buyer and make recommendations based on the buyer's previous activities (which booths were visited at last year's show).

The program will then offer the buyer an opportunity to see virtual booths in those categories.

"These virtual booths will be much more sophisticated than those we are accustomed to today," explains Fox. He envisions animated product demonstrations, with streaming video and audio augmentation. "If a buyer wants more information, he or she will be able to click on a button to speak by Internet telephone with a sales representative."

Illustrating how prophecy can rapidly become reality, one of Software Management Inc.'s subsidiaries is ConventionNet.com. This company provides a template-driven virtual booth product used to supplement trade shows and exhibitions. It is provided at wholesale cost to show managers, who can re-sell the product to exhibitors.

As with any technological development, such options do not replace "live" exhibitions; they simply bring yet another dimension to this vital and essential medium.

Chapter Fifteen
Pre-Meeting Coordination

This phase of meeting management begins prior to arrival at the meeting site, during the two or three weeks preceding travel. It continues through the first days before the main group arrives. It is a time for checking, verifying, and finalizing the elaborate arrangements and multitude of details set into motion during the months of planning that precede most meetings. It is a time when the PCO needs a competent staff, detailed checklists, and frequent communication with other executives, committee members, and suppliers.

Effective meeting management during this critical phase requires efficient time management. With so many details to be addressed, problems to be solved, and last-minute changes to be implemented, the PCO's day can slip away unless he or she follows the key principles of time management:

1. *Delegate.* Choose not only what to do, but what not to do. Rely on other professionals or staff for arrangements not requiring personal attention.

2. *Communicate.* The accurate transmission and reception of information is essential at all levels of meeting management. Important considerations are what to communicate, when to communicate, and how to do it effectively.

3. *Organize.* Information must be at the PCO's fingertips when it is needed. Organize, all elements for the meeting, from planning stage to completion, in a Staging Guide or similar workbook, or enter them on a laptop or PDA.

4. *Summarize.* Every discussion involving transmission of information, person-to-person or over the phone, should be recapped.

This helps avoid mistakes and time-consuming notices that must be sent to correct misinformation.

5. *Ask questions.* If not sure, ask for clarification. If you are not sure others understand, ask for confirmation.

6. *Get a gopher.* Having the help of an eager, bright student or intern staff member greatly reduces the demands on the PCO's time. He or she can deliver messages and run errands, find supplies or equipment, and fill in as needed. A competent "aide-de-camp" can be invaluable.

As the conference looms closer, pay exacting attention to detail. This will save time on site. It will also prevent many of the surprises that can consume so much of a PCO's time once the meeting is underway.

PRE-DEPARTURE CHECKLIST

Pre-departure coordination is the final important stage in conference organization prior to arrival on-site. Make a list of all the components and details of the meeting and review it prior to departure to the site to ensure that nothing has fallen through the cracks. This checklist is an essential planning document; appropriate elements can and should be sent on to suppliers and site managers as confirmation of existing arrangements. The greater the detail, the lesser the chance that an item will be overlooked.

Throughout the last weeks prior to departure, send meeting materials to the site for distribution to registered attendees, speakers, and other participants. The checklist covers the shipping and arrival confirmation of materials from all sources. Particular care should be given to the labeling of such material, especially those goods going to a hotel (which may be receiving many shipments). An example of label copy for a convention is as follows:

```
Annual Conference
Association for the Chronically Cool

Hotel Fiesta Tortilla

110 Avenida de la Contrarevolución

Boca Lave, Mexico

ATTN: Jorge McGillicudy, CSM          1 of 14
```

Major considerations in the development of the checklist are what to do and when to do it. Some elements will take precedence over others; some will need to be handled earlier than others. Starting at a period of three weeks before a typical conference, the following preparations should be completed:

Pre-Meeting Coordination 237

- Registration folder inserts printed, on hand, and ready for shipping.
- Verification letter sent to hotel with the pre-conference memorandum (agenda for pre-conference meeting, staff and speaker room blocks, rooming lists, menus, guarantees, master account instructions, etc.).
- Required AV equipment ordered and technical personnel confirmed.
- Instructions for session chairmen prepared and reproduced.
- Speaker introductions received and on hand.
- Attendee and speaker badges checked for accuracy and corrected as needed.
- Confirmation letters mailed or e-mailed to attendees.
- Final speaker confirmation packets mailed.
- Signs, banners, and award plaques received and checked for accuracy.
- Advance registration list prepared and printed.
- All conference handouts on hand, collated by session, and ready to be shipped.
- Special menus or services (e.g., provisions for people with disabilities) arranged.

Once part of the checklist has been completed, it is time to deal with any problems or changes. Updating the checklist, dating completed items, and having staff members initial them will ensure control and isolate those details needing attention.

One week prior to the conference, these final preparations must be completed:

- Speakers' briefing/rehearsal announcements (date, time, and location)
- Supply boxes against supply checklist
- All travel arrangements
- Final attendee list and mail or fax to hotel
- Speakers' name badges on hand and accurate
- Time, place, and attendance for pre-conference meeting
- Appointments for meetings with support personnel and suppliers not attending pre-conference meeting

- All speaker support elements in order; missing components listed
- Shipped materials confirmed with hotel shipping/receiving department

(For shipments abroad, see the section titled "Shipping Materials and Equipment" in Chapter 18.)

A final, pre-departure staff meeting is held to determine the status of each element on the checklist; time is allocated for follow-up, if necessary.

Arrival on-site brings together the full "cast and crew" of the complex production—the meeting. It is the time to put faces with names and to finalize all plans in person with the individuals responsible for their execution. You have communicated by mail and by phone; the person-to-person interaction and communication is the final step in confirming details.

PRE-CONFERENCE MEETING

The final briefing session between the meeting staff, convention service manager, and facility department heads is arranged during the last weeks of the planning stage. It is the first on-site meeting, held just prior to the conference opening, and it is crucial to the management and control of the event. The pre-conference meeting is when all conference elements are reviewed and reconfirmed, problems are addressed, and gray areas are clarified. Emphasis here is on confirmation of facts—not on issuance of new information (although changes are inevitable). Allow ample time in the planning stages for all meeting details to be established. An outline of the Staging Guide and the Pre-Conference Memorandum mailed prior to arrival can serve as the agenda for the meeting, which the PCO chairs. Some or all of the following participants attend the meeting:

- PCO and select meeting staff
- Sponsor-organization representative (if other than the PCO)
- Hotel sales representative
- Convention services manager
- Department heads, including accounting, front office, reservations, catering, engineering, and security
- Audiovisual supervisor
- Exhibit manager, if appropriate
- General or resident manager (courtesy visit only)

Consider other participants carefully. Suppliers and contractors need not be included if their roles are minor, though individual meetings should have been prearranged with these people as well.

Pre-Meeting Coordination **239**

At this meeting, introduce the facility staff and the meeting staff to one another, and clarify the chain of command and procedures for communication. Dialogue should be encouraged among all participants to help establish easy working relationships. Accordingly, the meeting agenda should allow for full discussion on all elements of the conference. The following is a sample agenda outline:

- Make introductions.
- Provide a conference overview (by organizer).
- Review principal activities.
- Discuss registration and conference office requirements. Reservations and Front Office: Review room block, early arrivals, cancellations, VIP and suite assignments, check-in and check-out procedures, telephone operator instructions.
- Accounting: Confirm credit arrangements, billing, master account instructions, and authorized signatories.
- Catering: Verify food and beverage needs, guarantees, charges, staff meals, special menus; review refreshment breaks and times. Discuss special billing for event sponsors, if any.
- Convention Services: Review all events with attention to room setups, set-up times, start and end times, special equipment, special requests.
- Discuss arrangements for clerical, fax, and photocopying services (and costs, if required) during meeting.
- Shipping and Receiving: Verify arrival of materials shipped; arrange delivery to appropriate locations by house staff.
- Security: Review all security and emergency procedures. Identify VIPs and security-sensitive participants.
- Room Service, Housekeeping, Concierge, etc.: Cover appropriate areas of meeting (special in-room deliveries, amenities, etc.).
- Verify equipment and personnel needs with AV supplier.
- Confirm entertainment functions and requirements.
- Review VIP reception and special arrangements.
- Review parking fees and passes and transportation pickup and drop-off areas for tours and off-site events.
- Verify placement areas for signs and banners, easels, reader boards, and/or in-house video notices. Discuss procedures for changes.
- Review responsibilities and communication channels. Confirm phone and pager numbers for key personnel (see Figure 15-1).

When scheduling the pre-conference meeting, be sure you avoid hotel "rush hours," such as noon and late-afternoon check-in and check-out times. Hotel managers are at their busiest at these times, and often cannot devote the necessary time and attention to the meeting. Early-morning meetings will allow night managers to attend as well as their daytime counterparts; weekday meetings are good because more facility personnel will be on the property and thus available. The meeting should also be held one to two days in advance of the conference opening date to allow time for problems to be ironed out.

A few helpful hints for the pre-conference meeting: Don't try to make major or contractual changes. Should there be such a need, schedule a separate meeting. Don't grind an axe. If a problem cannot be solved, come back to it later, at a separate meeting if need be. And keep the agenda moving; don't get bogged down over issues that may entail personal involvement and negotiation. Remember, those participants attending the briefing have other responsibilities. They appreciate a succinct, well-run meeting.

```
Dear Convention Planner:

We would like you to have this list of our personnel involved in your meet-
ing. Should you need a specific question answered, these people are at your
service:
```

		Extension	Pager
GENERAL MANAGER	Dietrich Von Schramm	212-215	
RESIDENT MANAGER	Janos Toth	218	
VICE PRESIDENT OF SALES	Richard Prechtl	270	
DIRECTOR OF SALES	Amy Cheng	229	27
CONVENTION SERVICES MGR.	Niko Kavasaki	238	35
ASSISTANT TO CSM	Andrea Bushong	227,228	36
MAITRE D' HOTEL	Henri Le Blanc	340	
CATERING DIRECTOR	Gino	221,223	
HOUSEKEEPING	Edith Braun	261,262	44
ENGINEERING	Roman Pransky	271,272	49
COMPTROLLER	Ahmed Ben Amig	209	
CONCIERGE	Razi Ramatkan	381,384	
AUDIO-VISUAL SERVICES	Dimitri Brezhnev	245	32
FRONT DESK MANAGER	Jose Bustamante	380	
HEAD HOUSEMAN	John Kenyata	226	37
DIRECTOR OF SECURITY	Wolfgang Gehlen	211	11
SHIPPING SUPERVISOR	Anton Romonescue	275	

FIGURE 15-1 Sample roster for key personnel.

STAGING GUIDE

The format of the conference has come into focus; final touches are being added, and the program has been fine-tuned. Answers and solutions have replaced questions and problems, and a great many decisions have been made. Those decisions are organized in such a way as to allow fast reference to all elements of information by all those involved in the meeting's management. Though e-mails, letters, and memoranda have documented all these details, it is necessary to have available a precise, step-by-step guide to every event and every component of each event.

The staging guide is the final compilation of all the elements of the meeting. It includes schedules, and staffing and communication information. It is the ultimate source of information about the conference, the outcome of communication with the various management participants. It is the culmination of the prospectus sent to the hotel in the months prior to arrival and has been fleshed out since then as more details were solidified. The hotel's event résumé or set of event orders, based on the prospectus and used internally within the different departments, is also incorporated into the guide. A copy of all event orders will be provided to the PCO, who will check them to ensure that nothing has been lost or left out in the translation. If revision is necessary, the PCO communicates the changes immediately to the CSM and requests a revised draft or change order as confirmation.

The staging guide is compiled chronologically. It includes elements such as supplier information and arrangements, staff assignments, sports and leisure activities, etc. In short, it is the meeting "bible," containing every piece of information that will be required throughout the course of the conference.

Organizing the Staging Guide

In its traditional format, the guide makes use of pre-designed loose-leaf forms containing the required information. Each event is detailed on a separate form and arranged chronologically in a binder. Dividers can include: Master Schedule, Meeting Prospectus (MESG), Pre-Departure Checklist, Pre-Conference Memorandum, Program and Presenters, Room Diagrams, Transportation, Rooming List, Day 1, Day 2, Ground Operations, Event Orders, Audio Visual, Budget and Accounting, etc. The loose-leaf format facilitates changes and allows you to use fresh sheets for every revision. (Some meeting planners color-code changes for high visibility.) No erasures or white-out are needed, and information remains clear and accessible.

Personal Digital Assistants are popular with organizers. While some PCOs prefer the familiar three-ring notebook, many have gravitated to laptop computers or the multi-functional PDAs for their ready-reference and compact design. (Most of those still have the loose-leaf binder as a backup.) These convenient palm devices can hold and display much of the data generated on personal computers and serve as scheduler, to-do reminder, notepad, and address book. They go beyond notebooks, giving the user wireless access to e-mail, the Internet, and other staff members' PDAs or cell phones. The PDA-based guide merely requires the addition of a scanner for entering information submitted on paper.

Diagrams are used in conjunction with the staging guide forms, particularly those involving room setups and floor plans. When drafting these diagrams, PCOs use stage directions (stage right is audience left) and compass directions (north wall, east door, etc.). These are the standards within the facility and will clarify directions to the set-up crew. Each diagram is numbered and indexed for easy reference. The accuracy of any internal translations used by the hotel staff is double-checked against the original documents.

Another important part of the staging guide is communication. The guide should contain the names of all meeting staff members, with titles, responsibilities, room numbers, and telephone/cell phone or pager numbers. It also contains the same information on the facility staff, as well as their night-duty counterparts. The guide includes supplier contact names, numbers, and emergency service information. Any information on special attendee requirements, names, and specific needs are annotated.

Maintaining the Guide

This database is only as good as the information it contains. If the information being used is no longer current, there will be headaches and miscommunication. Therefore, it is critical that you note all changes, no matter how minor and update the staging guide during staff meetings to make sure that the changes are made known to all meeting personnel. Each change should be dated and initialed, and out-dated elements must be removed and filed. This record of changes, including original and revised forms, will be helpful during the post-conference meeting and future conference planning.

Whether a heavy, bulky notebook, a laptop, or a hand-held device, a well-organized and properly maintained staging guide is invaluable to the PCO and meeting staff as immediate reference and in resolving questions or problems.

HEADQUARTERS AND STAFF ORGANIZATION

The conference headquarters is the communication and operations nerve center of the meeting, and its smooth functioning is essential to the proper management of the many meeting elements. Through this office, all participants, staff, suppliers, and speakers are coordinated. It is the crisis management center and the complaint management center. As such, it must be staffed by knowledgeable personnel who can immediately deal with any and all problems that might arise.

An effective headquarters operation depends on these elements:

- Good communication by and through telephone, cell phone, radio, pager, bulletin board, and computer

- Staffing during meeting hours, with clearly posted hours of operations and staff phone or pager numbers when closed
- Close proximity to conference area and speaker's lounge
- Clearly marked (signs) and capable of being secured

Staff Planning

A competent, highly dependable staff is not only invaluable to the meeting planner, but its degree of professionalism will reflect directly on the planner. A reliable staff can help ensure smooth operations by constantly attending to the details, relieving the PCO of the need to micro-manage the meeting and encouraging him or her to delegate more authority. The PCO will also gain an enhanced perspective and will be able to "see the forest through the trees."

Beginning with arrival on-site, the staff is introduced to one another and to their various counterparts during the pre-conference meeting. Daily staff meetings will aid communication: They can keep everyone abreast of new developments or alterations, as well as provide opportunities for people to air concerns. Job functions should be clearly delineated so that staff members know where to turn when questions arise. A staff organization table will help clarify responsibilities. The table in Figure 15-2 would pertain to a staff for a conference of 400 to 1,000 attendees:

Headquarters Planning

TITLE	FUNCTIONS
Meeting Manager	Overall supervision, business program, VIP coordination
Senior Meeting Planner	Registration, functions and hospitality, transportation
Registration Supervisor	Registration, badges, tickets, room assignments
Program Supervisor	Business (educational) program, speakers, audiovisual, exhibits (may be assigned to Exhibit Manager)
Comptroller**	Budgeting, master account, disbursements, fiscal controls
Meeting Producer	AV and staging, entertainment
DMC Representative	Transportation, theme events, social program, pre-/post-conference tours
Aides (As required)	

** May be handled by Meeting Manager

FIGURE 15-2 Staff organization and functions.

Headquarters Planning

Several factors are involved in the location and physical setup of the meeting headquarters. Cramped quarters, poor traffic patterns, or an ill-conceived floor plan can all adversely affect the operations of the headquarters and its staff. When inspecting potential HQ locations during site inspection and when designing the operational features, consider the following details:

- Location of phone jacks, electrical outlets, windows, doors
- Quality of lighting, ventilation, noise insulation
- Storage space needs for meeting materials, supplies, signs, etc.
- Furniture: chairs, tables, desks, phones, wastebaskets, easels
- Office equipment specifications: word processors, printers, modems, calculators (handheld or desktop, printout or display)
- Security and access to keys to headquarters
- Staffing requirements, breaks, and schedules

A floor plan drawn to scale will help organize the storage and work spaces and establish manageable traffic patterns that will minimize distraction or interference.

COMMUNICATIONS AND TRANSPORTATION

As in any enterprise, the ability to communicate, to transmit data and information, and to provide mobility are essential to efficient on-site operations. Proper planning and organization of these elements are each important to the meeting outcome, and must be accomplished in the planning stages to ensure positive results. Based on the resources required, the size of the meeting and support staff, budgetary constraints, and other factors, arrangements for communication and staff transportation are made well in advance of the conference date. During the pre-meeting phase, those arrangements are confirmed and adapted as necessary for trouble-free headquarters control and supervision.

Communications

Advances in communications technology have given PCOs a varied mixture of systems and media to meet their complex needs. The marriage of the telephone and the computer has opened up a wide range of electronic communication methods such as facsimile transmission, e-mail, and the electronic message center. These developments are at the PCO's disposal not only as conference media, but as a means of communicating the volume of data and information demanded by the logistical and administrative aspects of meeting management.

During site selection, some attention should have been given to the in-house communications system. If either the PCO's organization or the hotel or convention center do not have advanced systems, contact can be established through independent communication services at nominal cost. The advantages of fast, accurate message and document transmission far outweigh their relatively low costs. Communication components a meeting manager might need include telephone systems (internal and external), electronic pagers, two-way radios, PDAs, and message centers. Here are some considerations applying to each:

- *Telephones.* Will the house system be adequate? The headquarters phones are especially important. Are the numbers assignable to other extensions? Is there direct outside access, or must all outgoing calls go through the switchboard? Is there direct access for incoming calls? What features are available for messages? All requirements must be pre-ordered, especially if an outside line is being installed by the phone company. Numbers should be requested in advance, but can sometimes change without notice; check all pre-assigned numbers on arrival. Specify all requirements when ordering from the hotel and include a ring floor plan for multiple extensions. The ubiquitous cellular telephone has brought technology and convenience to business systems and found a place in on-site communications as well, often replacing pagers.

- *Pagers.* In somewhat limited use, these small, one-way radio receivers are assigned phone numbers. They beep when the number is called (signaling that a message has been left), and the message can be retrieved from a pre-assigned number. There are several types of pagers: Many go beyond the basics. The *dual beeper* has different beeps, corresponding to one of two numbers called. The *voice pager* acts as a one-way radio, allowing the message to be heard directly. *Digital pagers*, which receive up to 15 discreet impulses, display messages on the pager's liquid crystal screen. Pagers are available from either the facility or from local AV companies. Pagers are usually less expensive to rent than two-way radios and have ranges of 15 to 45 miles.

- *Radios.* A step above pagers and cell phones, two-way radios offer an immediate communication link between any number of people. However, for all the convenience of instantaneous contact, there are a number of drawbacks to their use. They generally have short ranges (one or two blocks, unless used with a booster station) and are open to interference from structural components inside buildings. They are also bulky and more expensive to buy or rent, due to licensing requirements.

Thought should also be given to the planning and function of a headquarters message center. Some advanced phone systems have electronic message center features. However, if these are not available, a bulletin board in the headquarters office can serve that purpose, though someone must make a habit of checking it periodically, noting time and reception of messages. Some meeting software also provides that capability, enabling messages to be viewed on satellite displays as well.

Transportation

Regardless of the size or scope of a meeting, ground transportation is a necessity for efficient staff operations; cost and availabilities necessitate early research and arrangements. Routine local transportation to pick up supplies, check out local attractions, or transport arriving speakers calls for one or more staff cars that are readily available. Vans and station wagons are best because of their greater capacity for passengers and cargo.

If arrangements have been made to appoint an official car rental company, one or more complimentary staff cars may be furnished. If not, rental fees should be part of the headquarters operations budget. If the hotel has a courtesy car or van, occasional staff use may be negotiated. Ground operators (DMCs) who have a substantial meeting support role will often place a car and driver at the PCO's disposal, particularly in foreign countries.

REGISTRATION STAFF AND FACILITIES

Registration is the attendee's first impression of the conference and sometimes is the most lasting. If the registration process is slow or disorganized, it will make a negative impact on the overall success of the meeting. Therefore, a smooth, efficient operation staffed by experienced personnel is a must. When planning the operation, the PCO must consider the number and qualifications of staff members, location and set-up of the area, and operating procedures and systems. Planning begins well in advance of the conference opening.

Staff

Professional registration personnel are worth the added expense because they have experience handling large numbers of people. Attempts to save in this area by using inexperienced or volunteer help may create problems and delays. If volunteers are being used, train them well and provide detailed written instructions; these things, plus expert supervision, are absolutely necessary. Training or dealing with volunteers tends to take up valuable on-site time, possibly offsetting any cost savings. Registration staff services can be obtained through the convention bureau, on written request specifying the number and type of personnel required and the hours they are needed. (Industry standards suggest approximately one registration clerk per 100 attendees for peak periods.) That ratio may be reduced if automated registration work stations are provided. If monetary transactions are to occur, you might need bonded personnel. Arrange for meals and rest periods, and attend to details such as transportation or parking expenses, and gratuities.

The registration staff must be well briefed in all facets of the registration process, and must also be acquainted with meeting staff personnel they will be working with. The briefing and the registration manual should cover:

- Information needed on forms, who fills them out, what to do with copies
- Information to appear on badges, various styles, and who gets which one
- Method of accreditation for attendees, exhibitors, press, contractors, and others
- Registration fees, ticket prices, publication prices, etc
- Orientation on registration software and online systems where applicable
- VIP names, badge designations, special VIP care and handling
- Key staff members and their phone and/or pager numbers
- Handling conflicts and registration problems

Responsibilities should be outlined, and clear, step-by-step written instructions on procedures should be provided. These cover other registration area services as well (e.g., ticket sales, tour registration, information desk). Procedures should also be established for handling any problems registration personnel may encounter. Rare is the meeting that doesn't encounter lost badges, refunds required, misplaced registration forms, or misdirected billing. Therefore, contingency plans and responsibility for problem solving should be worked out. The registration supervisor must be available to advise and to mediate conflicts.

Facilities

In Chapter 4, site inspection topics such as the location of the registration area and factors concerning size, lighting, traffic flow, signage, and communication were discussed. There must be adequate room for an easy traffic flow during peak periods without lines interfering with each other. Sufficient lighting must be available, and phone and power sources must be accessible. Easels, signs, and bulletin boards or video/computer displays should be readily visible and information must be clearly and simply displayed. The location of the registration area should be properly posted and publicized in the final mailing and through the hotel front-office staff. A diagram of convention facilities may be posted in the main lobby and should remain available throughout the meeting. The registration area should be in close proximity to the meeting headquarters, or at least linked to direct communication channels.

Determine the support services and equipment that will be required for the area. Display companies frequently supply registration equipment and are usually listed with the convention bureau and hotel CSM. Be specific when ordering number and type of materials such as computers, printers, tables, cash boxes, etc. Plan on separate desks for pre-registered attendees and on-site registration. Expedite the process for advance registration as a benefit and incentive. Service desks should be arranged according to their function; information and message centers should be in close proximity or at the same desk. Other designated desks or areas may include:

- Ticket sales and exchange
- Hospitality
- Materials distribution
- Pressroom
- Resource center (publications, etc.)
- Emergency housing
- Member services
- International visitors' lounge
- Tour desk
- Business center

An analysis of past registration experiences, good and bad, can lead to valuable insight into the dynamics of the group attending. Knowing previous peak periods will aid in organizing staff personnel and facility schedules more effectively.

COMMUNITY RESOURCES

A wide variety of resources are available through the host community. Some of these can add a special touch, making the meeting all the more memorable. From airport reception to program planning to recreation and entertainment, the community is able and often eager to help make the venue fun and exciting for the conference attendees. Some resources are obvious, while others are well-kept secrets revealed to the PCO only after an atmosphere of mutual trust and rapport has been achieved. Often they are the most memorable. Some customary examples are:

1. Local dignitaries or personalities often make a proclamation or welcome speech. A mayor's welcome or an "XYZ Company Day" proclamation is a pleasing refinement to any conference opener.

2. Police and traffic departments are usually eager to ensure the security of VIPs, and provide protection and escort if called upon. But beyond that, some cities (especially those anxious to host more conventions) supply either police or traffic officers as escorts for special group excursions. This can be particularly helpful in cities with high traffic density.

3. Local arts groups can be contacted through municipalities, especially if they are representative of the local culture. Vocal ensembles, dance and folkloric groups and bands are always a pleasing addition to a banquet, or even used for special airport reception. Hawaii is famous for handing out leis at the airport. Most cities in Canada will readily provide a piper (bagpipe) band.

4. Museums, historical points of interest, and tourist areas are all listed with the local visitors' bureau, and are very useful for planning tours and spouse activities.

5. Public buildings ranging from waterworks and schools to City Hall itself are often made available to an organization for special events if its membership and financial impact on the local economy justify it.

6. Public transportation can be used for airport transit as well as charter services. Special transport, such as trolleys, trams, or ferryboats, may also be available.

7. Local business organizations and special events companies can assist in many endeavors, from arranging an off-site reception in a corporate headquarters to hosting a board of directors dinner in a private residence or mansion.

8. Parks and recreation departments will help fulfill requirements for sports facilities or parklands for sporting events, picnics, and group functions.

Safety, health, and medical services can be provided, and special services can be arranged for at little or no cost (fire and rescue teams, life guards, ski patrols, etc.).

One note of caution, however: For all the willingness of the host community to help a PCO organize a meeting, there will still be some red tape and bureaucracy. Therefore, detailed preparation, patience, and an influential local contact are essential in planning for and use of public resources.

RECEPTION PLAN

How you receive and welcome conference arrivals—on-site or at the airport—is an important factor in attendees' first impressions. Well-organized, smooth-running transport and registration arrangements go a long way to easing the stress caused by travel, and a few creative touches can create feelings of excitement and anticipation toward the coming event.

If attendees are responsible for getting themselves to the site, the whole welcoming or reception process actually begins when you post detailed information on the Web site and/or mail the final information packet. Appropriate data on location and cost of car rentals, shuttle buses, and public transportation from the airport should be provided, along with detailed directions to the site for those who drive. The plan covers hotel reception, starting with parking facilities, and continues with reception at the registration area. Smooth, personalized service will reassure attendees that they are in capable, professional hands and help them relax and enjoy themselves. Some form of entertainment, display, or special welcoming ceremony in the lobby will help make participants feel at ease and even enliven the registration process.

For airport reception where the sponsoring organization is responsible for transfers, ground operators can often provide comprehensive reception and transit service. If reception service is arranged, the following guidelines are customary:

- Have reception personnel wear a distinctive, pre-arranged "uniform" that is recognizable to attendees.
- Select the area where greeters will meet incoming passengers, whether at the arrival lounge or baggage area, and clear it with airport management.
- Design and display appropriate signs or banners acceptable to airport authorities.

- Have a clearly marked desk or booth at the arrival area to direct passengers to transportation. This is an option that can help smooth peak arrival periods.

- Be sure the ground operator is flexible on the scheduling of vehicles: You might need a fleet during peak arrival times or shuttle buses or vans for early or late arrivals, for example.

- Provide VIP prestige service if appropriate.

- Clarify provisions for baggage handling with the airlines and DMC.

All pertinent information regarding reception (airport or otherwise) should be included in the attendees' final packet, along with distinctive luggage tags for ease of identification by baggage handlers.

Once the basics have been attended to, use your creative flair to add that one touch that will make for lively conversation at the cocktail reception later on. On arrival at the airport, have the attendees look for "the Hula girls giving out white hyacinths" or "the gospel choir singing old favorites," or even "the reception desk beneath the giant laptop screen." You and your staff will come up with several ideas based on site location and conference theme. And entertainment need not stop at the airport: If the bus trip to the site takes more than thirty minutes, have a tour guide, a costumed greeter, or music on the bus. Some companies have buses equipped with video monitors; use them to highlight local attractions or show a video of last year's conference. Depending on local laws and company policy, serve soft drinks, beer and wine, and "munchies" on board.

Upon arrival at the hotel, the less time spent registering and getting to rooms, the happier attendees will be. The ground operator's airport representative could contact the registration staff to notify them as buses depart and report the number of people on board and anticipated arrival time.

HANDLING VIPs

VIPs can include organization officers and management, guests, and program participants such as speakers and celebrities. Their treatment can reflect on the PCO's performance. They must be handled in a manner befitting their position or status. Treatment of speakers will reflect in the quality of their presentations; a speaker who is satisfied and well-cared-for is more relaxed during the program than someone who was forced to wait in registration lines or a long taxi queue at the airport. It is the PCO's responsibility to guarantee a worry-free atmosphere throughout the VIP's stay. To provide quality service, brief meeting staff and facility personnel (from Front Desk and Concierge to Housekeeping), assign hosts from the meeting staff or organization personnel, and provide personal attention from the meeting executive. Proper emphasis should be given to the following details in the pre-conference stage:

- Confirm all travel plans, including ticketing, seat assignment, departure and arrival times, airport baggage handling, and customs clearance (for international travel).
- Confirm meet-and-greet arrangements: who, where, and when.
- Arrange the use of airport VIP lounge if more than one flight is to be met.
- Confirm ground transportation to site, with attention to route, travel time, and parking availability at the airport.
- Pre-arrange registration so that each VIP can be given their room key upon arrival and escorted to their room.
- Have the PCO, an officer, or an assigned host greet the VIP in person or through a personal note of greeting upon arrival at the site.
- If a VIP is arriving by personal car, make parking arrangements and alert the registration desk to notify staff upon arrival.
- Arrange for special amenities (fruit basket, wine and cheese, flowers, etc.) and perhaps a welcome letter from the hotel general manager and organization CEO to be waiting in the room.
- Attend to the health and well-being of the VIP by inquiring after any special personal needs.

Check-out and departure procedures should be of the same high standards as were arrival and registration. Double check transportation to the airport, ticketing, and flight information. Some PCOs call to make certain that the VIPs have arrived home or at their destination safely.

Speakers

Chapter 6 covered the PCO's responsibilities to speakers, but a few additional remarks may be in order regarding VIPs and their sensitive egos. Payment, for instance: Prepayment of the fee can express confidence and encourage the speaker to deliver superior performance. If expense details are clarified in advance, little discussion is required upon arrival. Early reimbursement and settlement of accounts after the conference signals appreciation.

Plan to have program participants meet the audience they will be addressing. This allows the speaker to better "read" the audience and customize the program. A special dinner with the sponsoring organization's officers underscores the message that this person is held in high esteem. At all group functions, assign someone to escort presenters, provide personal attention, and make introductions.

Nothing concerns speakers more, once on-site, than the handling of their presentation materials. Pay special care and attention to these elements, and provide adequate opportunity for rehearsal (if called for). The session chairman is responsible for familiarizing presenters with the mechanics of the microphone and lights, stage setup, and room layout. The PCO should confirm responsibility for stage management of the program (light controls, projection and sound equipment, etc.) and introduce support personnel. Presenters need to know that someone is backing them up during their session. After the program ends, speakers should not be allowed to feel that they are being dismissed; they will truly appreciate being recognized for their contribution through a gift or award, even when compensation is made. Offer to mail materials or gifts that they may not care to carry home. When the whole conference is over, send a token of thanks from the conference chairman. This will add a final touch of personal and professional appreciation for their participation in the event.

MASTER ACCOUNT PROCEDURES

The importance of good master account organization and communication cannot be overstated. The master account must document facility charges accrued just prior to and during the meeting while it is compiled and recorded by the facility's accounting staff, the PCO is ultimately responsible for detailing instructions before the event, overseeing the account, and approving charges. Familiarity with hotel accounting staff and procedures is essential. Meet with the accounting department during the planning stages and inquire about their policies.

During the pre-conference meeting, review previously provided master account instructions with the front office staff. Charges will be applied accordingly, based on the following folio configurations:

1. Master account folio: paid in full by the sponsor organization.
2. Individual folio: paid by the individual attendees, and including rooms, room charges, etc.
3. Split folio: some charges paid by the organization, others paid by individual attendees, as specified in advance.

Clear instructions will ensure the proper billing of charges to the correct folios. Designate charges authorized to the master account (versus those to be posted to guest folios), and clarify billing and financial management authority. Also define the maximum financial responsibility of the sponsor organization. Provide a list of names and sample signatures of those individuals authorized to sign for master account charges. Request that all banquet checks be submitted upon conclusion of the function. See Figure 15-3 for sample master account instructions.

Governor's Tourism Conference
October 18–20, Denver

Master Account Authorization

HOTEL: Double Tree Hotel, Denver

Please post charges * as indicated below.

Master account (MA):
Staff rooms
Conference guest rooms (as designated)
HQ telephone charges (local and long distance)
Business services
Cash pay-outs
Audiovisual services
Banquet charges (except as otherwise noted)

Individual accounts:
Room charges
Incidentals
Restaurant charges

* to include taxes and gratuities, where applicable

CONDITIONS:
The University of Colorado Center for Sustainable Tourism:
- is not responsible for delinquent charges posted to individual accounts
- will not guarantee payment of attendee bills
- will not guarantee personal checks

Select speakers and guests (names to follow) should be pre-registered. Their room and incidental charges will be posted to the master account and reviewed by a representative of meeting sponsor.

Billing information: Business Research Division (Tax exempt)
                             Campus Box 420, University of Colorado
                             Boulder, CO 80309-049

Persons authorized to accept Master Account charges:
NAME: Prof. Charles R. Goeldner   Rudy R. Wright

SIGNATURE: _____   _____

Authorized by:

Rudy R. Wright, CMP
Conference Manager

FIGURE 15-3 Sample master account instructions.

Using the staging guide, review with the convention services manager or the food and beverage manager the guaranteed menus and unit costs for each event. The CSM will normally provide event orders well in advance of the meeting on a standard form (see Resources). Review these carefully, and compare details with the master schedule and function controls.

A banquet check or event order showing actual charges, details, and changes must be presented to the PCO upon conclusion of each event. This document should include:

- Group name
- Date, type, time, and location of function
- Detailed charges, applicable taxes, and gratuities or service charges
- Guarantee or actual verified head count if higher than guarantee
- If a banquet check, name of individual in charge of event

Fiscal Timetable

Several months prior to the conference, send the hotel all billing and master account information. Stipulate your preferred system for confirming and reporting attendee housing reservations and room pickups.

Two months out, arrange a meeting with the hotel representative to review billing instructions, individual and master account folio requirements, and reservation deposits or guarantees.

One month before the conference, review rates and miscellaneous charges and credit and billing procedures for attendees. Include a specimen rates and charges bulletin in the registration confirmation packet and/or Web page (see Figure 15-4).

XIV ANNUAL CONFERENCE - San Diego - September 14-18

Dear Conference Attendee,

The following rates and charges have been negotiated by our organization for the Conference and will be in effect during your stay at the hotel. Rates listed are the maximum you should be charged during the inclusive dates of the conference.

ROOM RATES: (Continental Plan, continental breakfast included)
    Double Occupancy - $ 115.00 per day (Twin, double, or king-size)
    Single Occupancy - $ 105.00 per day
                            plus 8% transient occupancy tax

These rates are in effect for two days preceeding and three days following the conference dates. Rates include complimentary use of the Health Club. They do not include Health Club services (massage, etc.), gratuities for maids or bellmen, minibar consumption, or any incidental charges.

TRANSPORTATION:
    Airport to hotel:
                    Airport bus - $ 11.50 per person, each way.
                    Taxi - Approximately $18.00
    Taxi rates: $ 1.40 for first 1/4 mile; $ 0.45 each 1/4 mile.
    Car rental: Hertz is offering a special convention rate.
        See enclosed flyer for details.

                                    The Conference Committee

FIGURE 15-4 Sample specimen rates and charges bulletin.

A copy of the bulletin should be sent to the hotel for their acknowledgment, with the following stipulation added:

The group rates listed on the above bulletin are correct and will apply during the conference, including early arrivals and late departures up to the number of days indicated.

Include signature blocks for the PCO, the reservations manager, and the hotel comptroller. One week prior to arrival on site, confirm the master account requirements with the CSM or the front office (auditor, accounting supervisor, or front office manager). The hotel may assign a group billing coordinator to oversee the organization's particular master account, or the convention service manager may assume that function.

Arrange for inspection of early arrivals' folios for set-up accuracy. Arrange for daily review sessions of the master account to be held throughout the conference (specify time and place), and plan for post-conference review of all accounts, as stated in Chapter 7.

Resources:

EVENT ORDER

Page__of__

| Event Day/Date: | | Event Order #: | |

| Group Name: |
| Post as: |
| Address: City: State: |

	Function	Time (Set/Ready)	Location
On-Site Contact:			
Phone:			
Fax:			
E-mail:			

| Room Rental | Guarantee: _____ |
| Plus ____ % Tax | Set: _____ |

This final guaranteed attendance must be submitted _____ working days prior to your event, or the number of guests expected will be considered as the GUARANTEE.

THIS NUMBER IS NOT SUBJECT TO REDUCTION.

FOOD AND BEVERAGE	ROOM SET
SPECIAL INSTRUCTIONS:	AV:
	BILLING:

Please refer to reverse side for Catering / Banquet Policies

© Copyright 2001 by Convention Industry Council (CIC). All rights reserved. This form may be duplicated or reproduced without expressed permission of CIC for use by the purchaser only, provided that the copyright notice identifying CIC as the copyright owner appears on the face of the form that is duplicated or reproduced.

Chapter Sixteen
On-Site Operations

The operations phase of event management begins after all the pre-conference details have been attended to and continues through the meeting until everyone departs. It is the culmination of the vast myriad of planning details and efforts that preceded the meeting. For most events, this phase starts one or two days before the meeting with preparations for the arrival of the main group. During this time, further meetings are held with various outside suppliers and facility staff. Review, disseminate, and confirm the details for the following meeting elements:

- Morning and/or evening staff meeting schedule
- Assignments and areas of responsibility, especially with volunteers
- AV materials, programs, equipment setup, rehearsals, and personnel
- Accounts (including master account)
- Headquarters operation schedule and duty roster
- Emergency, contingency, and security plans and procedures
- Evaluation of meeting by session and overall evaluation
- Food and beverage functions, menus, and guarantees
- Housing, reception, and registration
- Information for switchboard and reader boards or video displays
- Conference materials and handouts
- Message center operations and staff
- Pressroom facilities, staff, and accreditation of media representatives
- Conference registration, badges, packets, tickets, etc.

- Room setups and turnovers
- Program support: Signage, speakers, room chairmen, collateral, evaluation forms
- Exhibit setup and operations
- VIP reception and policies
- Transportation and tours

SECTION A: SETUP AND DAILY TASKS

RECEPTION

Hotel Registration

One of the most frequent complaints on evaluation forms concerns the inconvenience of having to stand in a long line at the guest registration desk—especially when large numbers of registrants arrive at the same time. To ameliorate the situation, experienced meeting managers arrange in advance to have additional staff man the reception counter.

Other strategies to avoid congestion or speed up the procedure include putting pre-registration on the hotel's Web site and combining hotel and event registration in the same area. In both methods, key cards are given out on arrival (thus confirming occupancy).

Taking their cue from the airlines, Hilton Hotels introduced a welcome feature at many of their hotels, and other venues are following suit: They have installed self-service kiosks, developed by IBM, to help guests avoid long lines, complete the registration procedure, and receive their key cards. The same system can accommodate check-out and airline check-in.

Event Registration

The registration area should already have been planned according to requirements of space and use. A floor plan prepared prior to arrival and reviewed at the pre-conference meeting will allow rapid setup of equipment and furnishings, and leave time to complete decorations such as banners, floral arrangements, and displays. Consider music, either live or recorded, to help relieve the monotony of standing in lines. Place signs in designated locations throughout the area, but they must be clear: Signs printed rather than handmade, color-coordinated to attract, with liberal use of conference theme graphics will enhance the appearance of the registration area.

Once the physical setup is complete, be sure registration personnel are briefed and rehearsed on the following:

- Registration requirements on eligibility, classification, fees, and charges
- Materials to be distributed and their location
- Reports and documents
- Cash/collection procedures

If cash is to be collected, we recommend a nominal opening fund, setting up with policies established for the occasional removal and deposit of large sums.

When planning staffing and physical arrangements, consider incorporating a "trouble desk" to take care of any problems that arise during registration. This keeps the normal lines flowing, and allows one staff member to concentrate on problem solving. This person should have immediate access to key managers such as the meeting executive and the front office manager.

The hospitality desk may include local representatives or convention bureau personnel to provide information on area attractions, as well as maps and brochures. Some planners arrange for demonstrations by local artists or craftsmen, always a popular addition. This desk can also provide restaurant and tour reservations, transportation, and personal and business service recommendations. If a ground operator is retained to handle tours and special events, this is the logical location for their staff.

Message Center

The message center is an integral part of the conference communication system, serving both the meeting staff and participants. It allows attendees to keep in touch with colleagues and their families and offices, and serves as a communications focal point. There are a variety of systems available: The basic message center incorporates a staff member, equipped with all the necessary meeting and area information, who takes messages and posts them on an electronic message system using video monitors or work stations, or on a bulletin board divided into alphabetical groupings. Messages are taken over the phone by arrangement with the switchboard, or left by individuals. Each posted message is flagged for the attention of the intended recipient and posted in the appropriate alphabetical section of the display. If the facility does not provide messaging systems, monitors and electronic message boards can be rented from suppliers listed with the convention bureau. Other systems range from simple overhead projector message displays to sophisticated computerized message retrieval. Each system requires that the recipient check in either by phone or by stopping by the center. Policies and/or procedures need to be established for expedited messages such as emergency telephone calls and for locating or paging recipients. A new generation of "smart" badges (described in Chapters 14 and 17) facilitate instantaneous notification of wearers.

Be sure the message center is centrally located in the meeting area and publicize and post its location. Adequate space is needed for equipment layout. Telephones may be equipped with visual light ring indicators if you think audible rings will be disturbing. Preprinted message forms (either stock pads or specially designed forms incorporating the organization logo or conference theme) will provide uniformity of information. Have a good supply of pens (in public areas, they tend to grow legs and walk away). Telephone directories or disks are helpful to have on hand, and envelopes should be supplied to allow for sealed messages.

DAILY DUTIES

Once the conference is underway, the PCO must stay on top of the many details already planned and confirm and reconfirm them, as well as monitor events from start to finish. A ship just launched doesn't run on its own, but requires a crew and a competent captain to make sure it goes where it's supposed to. The meeting manager's day-to-day activities during the conference encompass participants, the meeting staff, facility staff, and suppliers. To ensure that responsibilities are met, even though they may be delegated to other staff members, use a checklist such as this one:

- ☐ Review each day's schedule of events at morning or evening staff meeting, and brief the staff for the following day.
- ☐ Monitor master account.
- ☐ Review current and following day's events with CSM.
- ☐ Verify registration and room pickups.
- ☐ Review list of hotel no-shows before releasing rooms.
- ☐ Require front desk to advise you if they are oversold.
- ☐ Inspect meeting room setups.
- ☐ Meet major speakers at session location.
- ☐ Monitor events for participant reactions.
- ☐ Observe restaurants, lounges, and facilities for service and attendee use.
- ☐ Be prepared for on-the-spot press interviews, if applicable.
- ☐ Work closely with media for proper meeting coverage.

☐ Take the opportunity to rest whenever possible. Don't over-eat or drink.

TROUBLESHOOTING

> Nothing is as easy as it looks. Everything takes longer than anticipated. Anything that can go wrong, will go wrong—and at the worst possible moment!

Every meeting veteran is aware of Murphy's infamous Law. It seems that Murphy himself must have been a meeting planner; his law fits the industry so well. For that reason, PCOs tend to become professional troubleshooters, or quickly leave the industry. With so many plans, people, and variables coming together at one time in one place, the margin for error is substantial, no matter how well planned the meeting may be. But a professional who prepares for the worst and anticipates the unforeseen will at least avoid being surprised, and can better cope with problems that inevitably arise.

George Bernard Shaw hit it right on the head when he wrote, "The greatest problem with communication is the illusion that it has been achieved." Lack of communication and miscommunication are the most frequent causes of mistakes and problems. When arranging for services from facilities or vendors, satisfactory results depend on the quality and timeliness of the information communicated. Often, when it comes to obtaining essential information, PCOs are at the mercy of the sponsoring organization and its management. Conversely, they must ensure that management and participants understand the importance of timely, accurate input. "Guestimates" from an ill-informed meeting planner are invitations to disaster.

The PCO can expect some problems to occur in the field. Contingency plans are established to handle them. Typical problems that can arise include:

- Guests "walking" to another property
- A speaker who is late or doesn't show up at all
- A meeting or banquet setup that is wrong or late
- Materials that were lost in shipment
- Strikes at hotel, airlines, ground transportation, restaurants
- Remodeling or construction at the hotel
- Medical emergencies
- Changes or disruptions to transportation schedule
- Slow or poor food service

- Slow check-in or check-out, causing congestion and missed flights
- Non-availability of key meeting personnel
- Inclement weather and storms
- Civil disturbances and strikes

Prevent conflict, miscalculations, and problems by anticipating them. Review the Staging Guide and ask "What if. . .?" For example:

- What if AV or hotel equipment breaks down, or electricity fails?
- What if services are delayed or not provided according to contract?
- What if an attendee becomes unruly?
- What if a VIP is mistreated or feels mistreated?
- What if meeting rooms are unavailable at contracted times?
- What if meeting rooms are noisy or overcrowded?

Considering such questions well ahead of time prepares the meeting professional for contingencies. Should problems arise, be willing to accept the recommendations of the facility staff: They are professionals too, and have a wide range of experiences from past meetings. To ensure their support, ask to meet with the general manager to verify the CSM's limits of authority in troublesome situations. Should problems occur that are not being solved satisfactorily, go to the top! Other helpful hints:

- Keep an ear out for scuttlebutt at the meeting. Rumors, whether they involve staff, attendees, or facility personnel, should not be ignored. Analyze them and make contingency plans (and hope they won't be needed).
- Knowledge of local laws, customs, and holidays, off-shore as well as domestic, will also reduce surprises.
- Inquire about unions and their importance in the various service categories, and find out if contract negotiations are pending.
- Obtain AV requirements and specifications well in advance. See that equipment is tested with the actual program elements (especially critical with videos and DVDs).

When errors occur, as they invariably will, keep a record of the problem, the cause, and the solution. These can be invaluable tools in planning the next meeting. But don't agonize over what fell through the cracks. This time; learn from it! The only mistake to regret is the mistake repeated.

MEDIA RELATIONS AND THE PRESSROOM

Conference coverage by local and trade media is an important aspect of the meeting that is too often ignored. Good coverage not only showcases the event, the organization, and its issues, it also builds anticipation for future meetings. Inviting media representatives to the conference and expediting their registration and housing are just the beginning. Throughout the conference, these people need special attention and service to encourage their interest and support so that the organization gets the coverage it desires.

Experienced event managers use the communication or media relations committee or designate an experienced staff member to serve as media liaison—not the public relations executive, but a member of the meeting staff charged with logistical support of media activities. This person must be knowledgeable about the organization, the issues of the conference, and customary press operations. In some organizations where there is no permanent public relations staff, this individual (or a publicist retained for the occasion) can initiate contact with the trade press and local assignment editors. This advance planning will help ensure that a spokesman is designated and appropriate media representatives are notified, invited, and accredited.

Before contacting local media, astute event professionals familiarize themselves with local newspapers and business publications, as well as the television and radio stations serving the host city. Find out the kinds of stories local editors and news directors run on their slow days, especially weekends. And provide a schedule of possible noteworthy events, including a press conference with the meeting's newsmakers. Supply the news media with story ideas and background on the conference and its participants. This will stimulate interest, especially with the local media (who will want to know how the conference affects their audience or readers).

Prepare and distribute press kits, containing news releases about the conference and the organization. If the press packets are complete and properly compiled, even media companies that are not represented will have material to use for fillers and spot-news items. The packets should consist of:

- An attractive folder imprinted with the conference name and logo and perhaps the name of the sponsoring organization
- Releases covering provocative issues or newsworthy activities or people
- Event information and a printed program, names and biographical information on noteworthy speakers or guests, with a synopsis of each speakers' text (particularly that of the keynote speaker)
- Organization history, background, and statistics

- Photographs and biographical information on the officers and speakers
- Demographic data on attendees

Make sure that the press packet reads well; it must hold the attention of a busy editor or news director, informing without swamping them with detail.

During the meeting, the duties of the staff representative will include supplying all required information to the media people; arranging interviews with executives, exhibitors, and VIPs; and answering questions ranging from program content to the location of restrooms. This person should be given the authority to manage media activities and act independently.

Media Center

When contacting media representatives, let them know that a fully staffed and equipped media center will be available. This will provide further inducement to cover the event. A well-equipped center helps correspondents by supplying needed equipment and serving as a clearinghouse for all announcements and appointments. The center should be managed by the staff media liaison and clerical personnel who can staff registration and message centers. Reporters greatly appreciate perks such as complimentary coffee and tea, snack items, and soft drinks (contrary to the stereotype of hard-drinking reporters). Provide sandwiches and fruit for the reporters who often miss meals while covering a story—an occupational hazard in their field. Pressroom setup requirements include the following:

- Sufficient electrical outlets to accommodate equipment needs
- Good lighting, preferably with access to windows
- Adequate desk space and chairs
- Several multi-line telephones, preferably with outside lines and data ports
- High-speed Internet access
- Computers with word processing software; a network printer
- Copier and an adequate supply of copy paper
- Paper and other clerical supplies
- Amenities: refreshments, message board, wall clock, coat rack, etc
- Information resources: Organization background and data, annual reports, industry statistics, biographies, histories, photographs, copies of speakers' texts, and contact names and phone numbers on all forms

- If exhibits are part of the conference, provide exhibitor/product literature

A space should also be set aside as a news conference area. This can be an extension of the pressroom or a separate room. This area can also serve as interview space; equip it with comfortable furniture in conversational groupings. A poster or banner bearing the conference theme can serve as a logical photographic background. When arranging appointments, establish ground rules covering topic and duration. Find out the purpose of the interview and who will be conducting it, and prepare those who will be interviewed with ground rules and subjects to be covered.

It is customary for the pressroom to be set up and open before the beginning of the conference and to remain open each day during conference hours. During off-hours, security staff should be instructed to open the room for designated media representatives, should they require access.

STAFF MEETINGS

A football team huddles before each play, even though the plays have been designated long before the game. The staff meeting fulfills the same role. Though all facets of the conference have been reviewed during the preconference meeting, daily staff meetings provide a forum for continued communication and clarification. They are also used to discuss last-minute changes or refinements. Some meeting planners schedule their staff meetings in the evening to go over the next day, and to critique the one just ending. Others prefer a morning breakfast meeting, when the staff is well rested and people are ready to face the day afresh. Whenever the meeting is scheduled, it should be stressed that the staff is encouraged to communicate their problems and concerns openly, though confrontation should be avoided. It is a time for pep-talks and encouragement of teamwork and for mutual support.

The meetings need to be held in an area free of distractions, allowing sufficient time to cover all elements of the day's schedule and any questions that may arise. Function control forms and other meeting documents are reviewed, and time is allowed for any alterations to be implemented smoothly and without haste.

TICKETS AND BADGE CONTROL

Many organizers give only minimal attention to these elements in the planning stages of the conference, but proper planning will save you a great deal of time. Tickets for program sessions and functions should be numbered consecutively, color coded for each event, and properly accounted for. Print the time and location of the event on each ticket for which it is issued to avoid confusion and simplify record keeping. This also helps attendees who do not always have their program schedules handy.

For ease of accounting and cash handling, keep ticket prices in whole amounts, and provide preprinted receipts for tax and expense purposes that can be filled out quickly. If a major function is included in the registration fee, provide coupons to be exchanged for tickets in advance by those planning to attend. This adds a step to the process, but you'll reap substantial savings because meal counts will be more accurate. A count of tickets sold, unsold, complimentary, and any unaccounted for, will provide a record of the function. This can be extremely valuable during post-conference accounting.

Badges

The exotic high-tech, multi-function badges previously described serve a wide variety of specialized functions. However, for most events, printed paper badges are still the norm.

Badges come in a variety of designs, generally falling into three categories: self-adhesive, plastic-encased, and laminated. Adhesive badges might work for small, one-day events, but they do not last long and are not aesthetically pleasing. The plastic-encased and laminated badges are more versatile and durable. They utilize various fastening devices, including:

- Pin fasteners. These are often avoided because they damage fine fabrics.
- Pocket inserts. These require breast pockets, which are not always found on formal or casual apparel.
- Clip fasteners (clutch-back or "bulldog"). These are the most popular kinds of badges. The clip rotates and allows for a variety of fastening positions.
- Lavalier. Vertical badge holders with a die-cut slot at the top can be used with a ribbon or snap-in and swiveling clip fasteners.

Inserts for badge holders are ordered in perforated strips of six to eight for ease of printing. They should be sized to fit snugly into the holders. Printing the badges with the name of the conference and the logo ahead of time has become an almost universal practice; attendee names and affiliations can be added later. Minimize the information you put on the badge to avoid crowding the badge. Bold type should be used, standardized for all badges. Use different colored borders to denote special status or position rather than the ubiquitous ribbons. (Many organizations still prefer ribbons that are attached to the badge holder, denoting the attendee's status or office.)

A variety of computer graphics programs, peripherals, and services specializing in badge preparation enable PCOs to offer attractive, pre-printed badges in bold typefaces. This can simplify on-site badge preparation and offer many other creative options not available with the old "wood-burning" bulletin typewriters that were once standard fixtures at conference registration desks.

Knowledgeable registration supervisors keep an extra supply of blank badges and holders on hand to replace lost or incorrect badges or for unplanned walk-in registrants, guests, or personnel. Stress to attendees that their badges are the identification needed for access to the meeting events, and that they must be worn at all times.

MONITORING MASTER ACCOUNTS

A daily review of master account charges will help minimize surprises during the post-meeting review session. Daily statements should be required, with detailed backups of all charges available for inspection. This policy encourages the hotel to exercise care in identifying and documenting all master account charges. At each session, approve correct charges, and identify any disputed charges and delayed or missing items. A periodic check with the front office will help clear up discrepancies, as they often receive charges not covered by the master account billing instructions. Many PCOs contact the night auditor just prior to retiring each night to find out if there were any billing questions that came up since the last review session.

SECTION B: PROGRAM MANAGEMENT

Program management refers to the activities and procedures related to the support and proper conduct of the meeting program: the business agenda, functions, exhibits (if they are part of the event), and social activities. These are probably the most critical meeting elements, since they have the greatest influence on attendees' perception of the event.

MEETING ROOM SETUPS

Perhaps the greatest test of the PCO's competence is whether or not he or she can estimate the number of people attending a session or function, accommodate those who arrive, and adapt to variations between estimates and reality. Proper planning and controls certainly help to minimize surprises, but meeting professionals still anticipate changes and incorporate contingencies in their planning. For theater-style seating, for instance, it is customary to leave rear and side aisles for standing room if an overflow crowd is anticipated. In classroom setups, it is good planning to add a few rows of theater-style seating in case of overflow; this also encourages early arrivals to sit forward in the room.

This is probably the only book on event management that does not contain detailed diagrams on the various room setups available to the meeting manager. The topic is well documented in the *Convention Industry Manual* and other texts, but you can study the most common seating configurations and the area required for each in Figure 16-1. The reader is no doubt familiar with this information, but it may be valuable to briefly touch on the major setups and their advantages and limitations:

- *Theater-Style.* This format permits maximum-capacity seating and rapid setup or reset, and directs attention to a speaker or single focal point. Because of the row seating, this setup restricts interaction, limits note-taking, and is not conducive to extended sessions. (NOTE: Unless otherwise directed, the house staff will set chairs directly behind one another and butting side-to-side. For better sight lines, ask that seating be staggered. If capacity permits, specify that there be a minimum of four inches between chairs.)
- *Classroom/Schoolroom.* This style is considerably more comfortable for extended periods. It directs attention to the speaker, offers better sightlines, and is suitable for writing and positioning of program materials and beverage service at tables. Interaction is possible, but it will require rearranging of chairs. Limitations: reduces capacity; requires additional set-up time.

A more recent insight by Paul O. Radde proposes a format for breakout sessions where the dynamics of networking and interaction among attendees is desirable. Radde suggests using a modified classroom setup in which participants can make eye contact with one another. This can be achieved by arranging the tables and chairs in an arc or semi-circle.

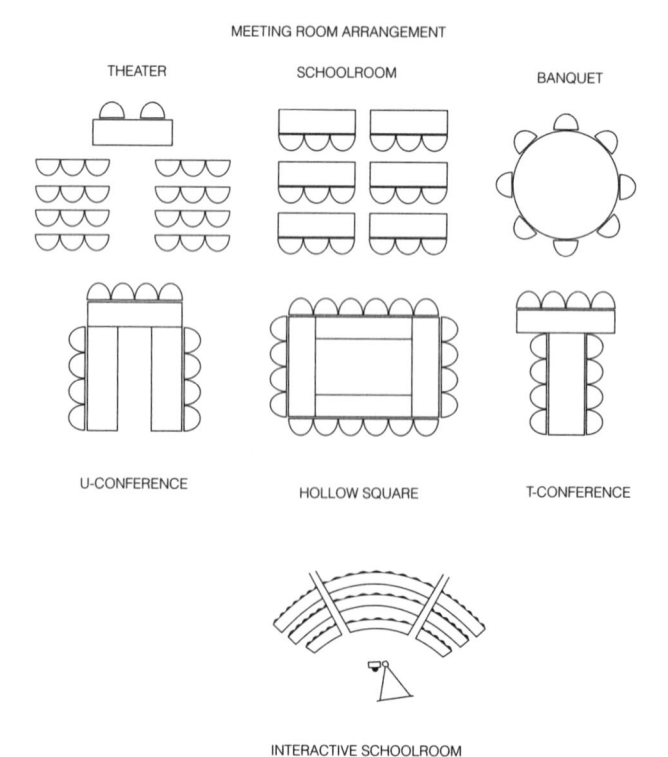

FIGURE 16-1 Room setups.

- *Conference.* Conference styles include U-Shape, T-Shape, Hollow Square, and variations of the same. Appropriate for smaller groups, they characteristically allow participants to face one another, thus facilitating interaction. Attention is still directed to the speaker or panel, and contact is more intimate. The styles are effective for use with a data projector or whiteboard. The limitations are the same as for the classroom style.

- *Rounds.* Tables of 5 to 6 feet in diameter, while standard for meals, can also be designated for educational sessions. They offer maximum intimacy and interaction among participants, and accommodate note-taking and beverage service. They are ideal for case-studies and nominal group technique. Limitations: There is no clear focal point, thus limiting speaker contact. Round tables restrict use of visual aids, reduce capacity, and require additional set-up time. (Some hotels might impose a labor charge if no food is served.)

Having communicated the setup for each session by means of the staging guide, cautious PCOs will try to be present when setup begins. If that is not practical, it is essential that the setup be observed by a staff member far enough before the session begins to make minor changes. Check for these things during setup:

Room Entrance:

- Signs identifying the session have been properly posted.
- There is a table for literature (if called for).
- The door can be propped open for attendees' entrance and egress.
- If weather is inclement and attendees are arriving from outdoors, have provisions been made for coat-check or coat racks?

Seating Area:

- Chairs and tables have been set to specifications, with adequate space between chairs, adequate distance between rows, and adequate aisles.
- There are good sightlines for audiovisual projection. The front row is no closer than 2H; the last row is no farther than 8H (where H = image height).
- Lighting and climate controls have been set to comfortable levels. The room should be cooler than normal, since body heat tends to increase room temperature.

- Water pitchers or bottled water and glasses have been properly placed.
- The telephone and the public-address system have been turned off. (Any music played during entrance should be turned off before the session starts.)
- Projectors have been properly set up, connected, and focused. The right-sized screen has been placed for optimum height and viewing angle.
- The projector stands have been positioned so as not to interfere with traffic flow. All exposed cables have been taped.
- Handouts are ready for distribution, if called for.
- Floor or wireless microphones are set and are live, adjusted for sound level.

Presentation Area:

- Lectern has been set according to plan. The reading light is working. The ceiling or stage light is focused on the lectern. Water carafe and glasses are available.
- The screen is positioned away from the lectern so that the speaker can see visuals. Front overhead lights have been turned off to prevent light bleed on screen.
- The lectern and/or lavaliere microphone is working and set at the proper level. The wired lavaliere microphone cord should be long enough for freedom of movement.
- The table for a laptop computer is in place, with AC extension cords and cable run to the data projector.
- There is a draped table for a panel discussion. If set for panel, check table microphones (minimum one for every two panelists). Speaker materials are set close to the lectern.
- The podium or platform has been correctly placed to height and size specifications. Draping and stairs are as called for.
- Flags, banners, and other stage decorations have been properly placed, according to protocol.
- If a rear-projection format is used, the screen should be draped to the full width of the stage. The lectern is positioned to prevent light from spilling on the screen.

- The projector has been connected and focused. The screen is properly positioned for optimum viewing. Other visual aids are placed as requested (flipchart, whiteboard, eraser, laser pointer, marking pens, etc.).

SPEAKER SUPPORT

Chapter 6 outlined in detail the booking and treatment of speakers. During the operation phase, the PCO's primary concerns are to see that speakers are properly briefed, given an opportunity to rehearse, and provided such support as they may require for an effective presentation. You must also make sure that any principal speaker arrives at the site and is present for his or her session.

Reception and Housing

Once you have established travel arrangements in advance and confirmed arrival time prior to the meeting, plan for certain speakers to be met at the airport and transported to the meeting site. Some organizations assign this responsibility to a speaker host (usually a member of the program committee). Others delegate that function to a receptive operator or convention bureau "greeter." For celebrities, high government officials, and security-sensitive individuals, learn the protocol and security considerations that govern the extent of the reception and escort. The general rule is that VIPs are met by officers of equal rank. Occasionally, government officials may need to be involved in reception planning. Police escorts or other honorable recognition may be appropriate.

Sometimes a conflict arises between speakers and hotel staff regarding room accounts. The hotel will typically insist on a credit card imprint to cover incidentals when the room is charged to the master account; some speakers claim that this leads to double billing. If the room charges are on the master account, a separate folio should be established for incidentals and then cross-referenced on the room folio. If the room and the meals are charged to the master account, note "Room and Meals only to master account" on the folio. In such cases, a credit imprint will not need to be requested. In the rare instance that a speaker abuses the privilege, it is the PCO's responsibility to settle accounts tactfully. Since final fees are not paid until after the performance, the PCO has considerable leverage for settling disputed charges. Regardless of the policy, clear instructions must be given to the hotel to avoid embarrassing the speaker.

Not all presenters need to be housed in suites, but they should be given upgraded rooms. Accommodations must reflect the speakers' rank or stature. They are also entitled to VIP status on the rooming list. The concierge, the telephone supervisor, and the duty manager (and in select cases, the head of security) need to be aware of their presence. In some instances, the general manager should be on hand to greet the prominent guest. Even for non-VIP speakers, gestures such as meeting them on arrival at the hotel and escorting them through registration procedures are nice touches. Professional speakers often have delicate egos and having to stand in long lines lowers their self-esteem. Courteous touches, expedited registration, an upgraded room, and a bowl of fruit, are all appreciated and this will be manifested in the subsequent performance.

Speakers are routinely invited to attend all hospitality and social functions. They are seated with the organization's leadership—not merely for prestige, but also to give them an opportunity to discuss and understand the nature of their hosts, their objectives, and their special needs. Receptions and less-formal gatherings are opportunities for the speaker to mingle with the audience, gauge their private agendas, and gain valuable insights into the nature of the group they will be addressing. Some speakers take this opportunity to build a camaraderie, which permits them to address some remarks to specific individuals during the presentation, thus achieving greater rapport with the audience.

Speakers' Lounge

It is customary to set up a speakers' lounge in the vicinity of the conference area so that speakers can rehearse their presentations, view and cue audiovisuals, or just relax before and between sessions. If staff allocations permit or volunteers are available, the lounge should be manned during conference hours by individuals who have been properly briefed. They should be introduced to the audiovisual supplier in case last-minute equipment is needed by speakers. The room should at minimum be equipped with an overhead and LCD projector and screens; add other audio and video equipment as needed. Refreshments are optional, although ice water, soft drinks, coffee, and tea are basic for most meetings. A sewing kit, steam iron, and ironing board are helpful for those last-minute wardrobe adjustments, and most presenters will appreciate a full-length mirror.

Speaker Briefing

However detailed the speaker information kit may be, most PCOs consider it essential to hold a briefing, particularly when a number of presenters and session leaders are involved. It should be held the day before, though some program managers find that a breakfast meeting on the day of the presentations works quite well. One executive who frequently serves his association as conference chairman invites speakers to dinner the night before. At this meeting, the program chairman reviews the meeting's objective and conducts a verbal walk-through of the agenda, emphasizing points that involve or affect speakers. Special announcements, introductions, session formats, and AV support are detailed. If session chairmen or room captains have been designated, they are introduced to their presenters at this time. Encourage them to check their meeting rooms before the sessions begin, if they have not done so.

Session Chairmen

Proper program planning calls for a chairman for each session. Some organizations also designate a room chairman; others use only a room captain, whose function is expanded to include some of the duties of the chairman (speaker introductions, time monitoring, etc.). Generally, the room chairman serves in a logistical support capacity, whereas a session chairman is part of the program. The session chair may also act as moderator when a panel discussion is involved. The role of the chairman is similar to that of a master of ceremonies, guiding the audience and presenters through the program, keeping presenters on time, acting as a continuity link between several presenters in a session. If the discussion gets heated, the chairman may have to become a referee or master-at-arms who controls the more outspoken participants, keeps the program on track, and makes sure that the participants' behavior is consistent with decorum.

Where chairmen act as a moderator, they have additional responsibilities: They must make sure that speakers' comments are understood by the audience and ask for elaboration if necessary. The moderator guides the discussion, oversees or poses questions from the audience, and monitors responses to make sure that they are clear, concise, and relevant. As timekeeper, the chairman has the difficult task of getting verbose speakers to limit their presentations to the prescribed time frame and making sure that the session begins and ends on time.

A chairman's brief or the room captain's written instructions should contain the following elements:

- Session title and outline or text of presentations
- Speaker introduction(s)
- Copies of papers, handouts, and instructions for dissemination
- Attendee roster
- Badge or ticket control instructions if attendance is restricted
- Copy of function form designating room setup, staging, AV, etc.
- Diagram of prompter signals for communicating with speaker (see Figure 16-2)
- Instructions on timer controls or lights if available
- General instructions on duties, timing, and announcements

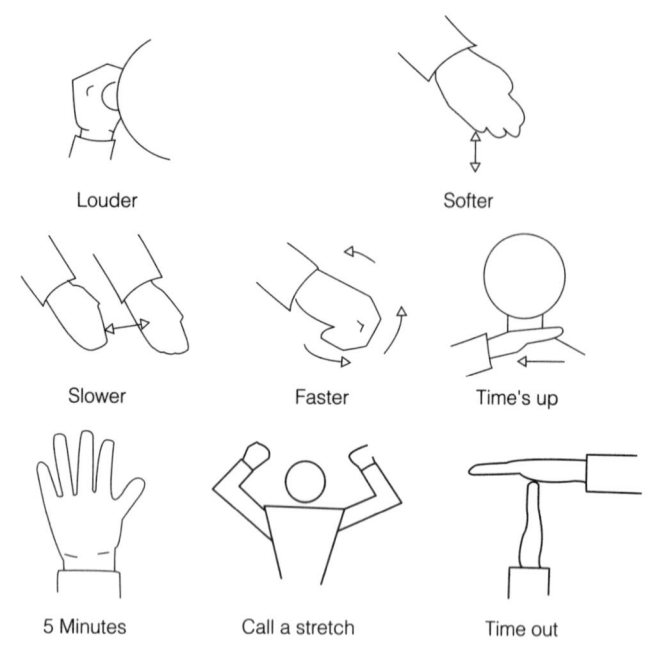

FIGURE 16-2 Prompter signals.

THE BUSINESS AGENDA

Sometimes called the educational program ("scientific program" at scientific congresses), this element of the meeting is its focal point. It is the vehicle by which the meeting's objectives are achieved. Everything else, though important, is subordinate to it. Because of the emphasis and high visibility of the educational program, PCOs generally supervise all program elements personally, delegating other activities and logistics to staff members. The business agenda is also of primary concern to the organization's leaders, though its planning and conduct may be delegated to a program chairman or committee, with the PCO acting as implementer, communications expert, and a major contributor.

During the execution phase, the PCO meets frequently with the program committee and session chairmen to review each forthcoming session. Presenters can meet with their session chairmen and the PCO. The program chairman can meet individually with principal speakers sometime before the sessions begin in order to orchestrate key elements. The purpose is to discuss changes, scheduling, content, presenters, or logistics; to solve any problems that have come up; to anticipate others that may arise; and generally, to ensure a smooth-running program.

Rehearsals

Major presentations, particularly those involving complex productions, are usually rehearsed in the room where they are to take place. Live cast productions, special effects, and programmed AV elements such as multimedia and multi-image presentations may require one or more technical rehearsals, as well as a final dress rehearsal. If computer-supported sessions are part of the program—as they usually are—check the bandwidth capacity of data ports (see the "Voice and Data Communication" section in Chapter 12) and encourage presenters to rehearse that aspect of their program.

To ensure availability of the site for staging, setup, and rehearsal, it is best to reserve the room in advance and to list that activity on a function control form. PCOs and convention service managers practice space economy; space that is not needed should be released for other functions. If the stage, let us say, is in section "C" of a divided ballroom that will be used in its entirety for a general session, it is usually possible to close off just that section for the rehearsals, releasing "A" and "B" for other functions.

The actual conduct of speaker rehearsals is a matter of individual or management choice. Some presenters will want to rehearse their materials verbatim, some will require the services of a speech coach. Others will merely rehearse cue lines or "jump cue" their line (a technique of going rapidly through the script and reading only the cue lines for the benefit of the technical crew and to verify the correct sequence of visuals). If timing is critical, however, it is best to rehearse all audiovisuals, presentations, bridges, and continuity in real time.

Abstracts

Technical and scientific congresses utilize abstracts of current research as the key element of their technical program. A "call for papers" is sent out as much as a year ahead to the members, to professional journals, and to ancillary associations in related disciplines providing information on the conference. The call for papers stipulates the specifications for abstracts, including format, acceptable length, and deadline for submission. Abstracts are reviewed by the program committee for relevance as they are received and either rejected or accepted. The authors of accepted abstracts are then contacted and advised as to the date, time, and place of their presentation, the time allotted for presentation and audience participation, the name of their session chairman, and various administrative details. The program committee can choose to have the author deliver a lecture or serve as member of a panel, according to their concept of programming.

Abstracts are posted on the conference Web site, reproduced, and either handed out at each session or bound into the proceedings and distributed to attendees. Aside from providing detailed information, the abstract system is intended to encourage presenters to concentrate on highlights, key points, and conclusions—thus avoiding the dry, tedious speeches that seem to plague scientific meetings. Unfortunately, some speakers insist on reading their papers word for precious word, unaware and unconcerned that half the audience is off in dreamland.

GUEST PROGRAMS

Back in the old days, "conventioneers" were mostly men, and a good time took precedence over learning. Some even brought along their wives. The sponsors, feeling guilty about leaving the women at loose ends, started doing "wives programs" to keep the women occupied. (Also to keep them from troubling their pretty little heads about the organization's business, which everyone recognized was man-talk.) The programs were those considered of interest to women: gourmet cooking, fashion shows, beauty tips, interior design, and homemaking.

Then came the 1960s. Enlightened women wanted programs with more substance: investments, estate planning, financial management, world affairs. The organizers of sales meetings looked around the audience and found that many of their "salesmen" were women! And those husbands or companions who accompanied them also wanted topics with substance. What's more, as women joined their husbands in entrepreneurial activities or left the house and embarked upon their own careers, they became active partners and wanted to sit in on the business sessions. So "spouse programs" came into being. Soon afterward, meeting attendees discovered the financial benefits of combining conferences with family vacations, and kids' programs were added to the meeting manager's responsibilities.

In the 1970s, the big ethical question facing corporations was how to handle the growing number of meeting attendees who came to the meeting with partners other than wives and husbands. "Significant-other programs" sounded a bit too unwieldy, and the Census Bureau's POSSLQ (Person of Opposite Sex Sharing Living Quarters) was even worse. You simply *could not* have a "POSSLQ" program! The terms "Companion Programs" or "Guest Programs" evolved and survive today—at least until the next social revolution, whatever that might be.

How did all this affect the PCO? For one thing, this phenomenon placed greater emphasis on topics for men and women: topics about career and family life, and topics on interpersonal relations, communication, and personal development. Today, these are as much a part of the educational program as Product Liability, Outsourcing, and Aneurysms of the Subclavian Aorta. Corporations have come to the realization that company objectives get short shrift when they conflict with personal and family goals.

Conference organizers must plan innovative guest programs, budget for them, and arrange for speakers and logistical support, but there is an added element of uncertainty when it comes to planning meal functions, providing guarantees, and estimating seating capacities for business sessions. Many companies and most associations find it beneficial to have the attendee's guest attend the business sessions. Thus, in estimating room setups, most corporate planners will factor in a percentage of guests to ensure adequate seating. Associations generally restrict guest attendance—except at general sessions—unless the guest pays the full registration fee.

During the operations phase, one of the PCO's concerns is how to balance the guest programs with the business agenda. Some have let their enthusiasm for innovative guest agendas carry them away, to the detriment of the educational sessions. It is important to understand that participants who bring their spouses or friends to a meeting site want to share in sightseeing excursions and recreational events. A fine balance must be maintained in designing a program that is interesting yet won't interfere with the business agenda. Nothing is more corrosive to a PCO's reputation than to have a $10,000 speaker address only half of the registered delegates, while the rest are shooting the rapids on the Hootchie Kootchie River with their Significant Others. A competent DMC can be a tremendous help in planning and managing guest and joint programs. They are familiar with local speakers and resources and can relieve PCOs of much of the burden of supervising and administering the program, allowing them to devote full attention to the business agenda.

AUDIOVISUAL AND STAGING NEEDS

It is customary for the meeting producer or a representative of the AV service company to attend the daily staff meeting to review audiovisual and staging requirements for the following day, order additional equipment if needed, and confirm call times for cast and support staff. If speaker and/or presentation rehearsals are scheduled, that information is covered and then disseminated to the appropriate participants.

If rehearsals require the use of the stage and audiovisual equipment designed for the general session, they should be scheduled and incorporated in the Staging Guide, just like any other event. That is necessary to avoid conflict with other scheduled events. On occasion, it may be necessary to conduct rehearsals late at night if the room is being used for evening functions.

Staging for Entertainment

If entertainment is planned for either business sessions or social functions, certain types of performers will need to rehearse, usually the same day if it is an evening performance. Vocalists and musical groups may require rehearsal with an orchestra, though a piano accompanist is sufficient for most. Some acts will require spotlight operators to be present in order to rehearse light cues. Others may need a full stage, lights, and sound and stage crews. Under such circumstances, it is essential that no meetings be scheduled in the room set for entertainment; reserve and set it up early enough to permit several rehearsals.

If the facility has a fixed stage, many of the technical support elements are incorporated, though they may need to be augmented. As with audiovisuals, it is best to have the services of professional theatrical technicians when complex staging is employed. This is particularly true when a stage must be erected and theatrical lighting and sound systems are installed. It is not a job to be left to amateurs or even hotel engineers. A simple staging setup may require no more than a platform, a spotlight, and microphones. On the other hand, some of the high-impact theatrical productions seen at today's meetings may involve some or all of the following elements. And even if a producer or stage manager is employed, it behooves the PCO to have at least a cursory understanding of stage terminology.

- *Follow-spot.* A movable spotlight manned by a spot operator. Usually set on platforms opposite the stage or in a projection/light booth (if available), this light source may be incandescent (good up to 40 feet), quartz-halogen (100 feet), or carbon-arc for longer throw distances (auditoriums, etc.).

- *Fresnell.* A flood light utilizing a condenser lens capable of soft edge illumination of relatively wide areas.

- *Ellipsoidal* (commonly called a leko). A spot light with a compound lens and a framing device that produces a hard-edged, flat field of light. It is used for highlighting areas and objects on a stage, such as a lectern.

- *Chase light* (rope light). Low-voltage lighting used to frame or call attention to signs or stage features.

- *Par Cam.* Broad floodlighting that lights large areas, such as a stage apron or backdrop.

- *Pin Spot.* Usually a halogen light for illuminating a small area or object.

- *Strobe Light.* A bright, rapid-flashing light used to achieve special effects, this device should be used in moderation. It might cause discomfort to some audience members who have disabilities.

- *Fiber Optics.* Microscopic fibers that transmit light from a central source and distribute it as pinpoints to create dramatic visual effects.

On-Site Operations   281

- *Laser.* Multicolored beams of condensed light for producing dramatic effects.
- *Dimmer.* A control device that allows the operator to adjust the intensity of theatrical lights. They normally come in a bank on a dimmer board that controls all of the lights, individually or the entire bank of lights in the master setting. For complex productions, lighting plots and cues can be preset and controlled by a computer.
- *Sound Console* (mixer). The audio control system consisting of amplifiers and a bank of attenuators ("pots") that controls the degree of sound gain coming from each sound source (tape, microphone, video) and going through the amplifier to the speakers. This may be as small as a four-input mixer or as complex as a 40-channel studio console, complete with graphic equalizer, reverb, echo, and other audio effects.
- *Intercom.* Essential for complex AV, video, or theatrical productions, these two-way communication devices permit the director to relay cues to the stage manager, spot operators, cameramen, projectionists, orchestra leader, and anyone else on the production staff.
- *Special Effects.* Today's meeting spectacular might involve a wide range of visual effects: theatrical fog generators, strobe lights, laser projectors, chaser lights, blacklight, color organs, etc.

In addition to commonly used theatrical terms, the PCO should also be familiar with stage directions. Figure 6-2 in Chapter 6 illustrates some of the more common ones.

Preventing Technology Glitches

Nothing is more disruptive to a meeting than visuals that are out of focus, out of sequence, backwards, or upside down—unless it is an equipment malfunction. It may be a computer failure, a jammed slide, torn film, a projector lamp that blows out in the midst of a presentation, or that omnipresent gremlin: feedback. No one anticipates that a piece of equipment will go bad when it has been working fine during rehearsal, but the PCO can take certain precautions to reduce malfunctions and mishaps. Here are a few precautions you can take:

- If slides are used (some presenters still use them), verify that they have been checked for proper sequence and positioning.
- Run videos and any motion picture films to check cueing, focus, and sound level. If several segments are used, have them assembled in sequence to avoid cassette, disk, or reel changes. Re-cue to the start position after rehearsal.

- Check all sound equipment and microphones at working level to make sure there is no feedback, hum, or electrical interference. Turn off telephones, music, and the paging system.
- Run microphone tests, and walk around the room to check for dead spots. Sound level in an empty room should be fairly "hot," since people will absorb sound. Test wireless microphones for interference. Be sure batteries are fresh.
- Locate circuit breakers and light controls for each room being used. Label switches and dimmers, and be sure someone in the room knows how they work.
- Set projection stands high enough to clear audience heads and standing visitors who enter after the program starts. If rear-projection is used, caution speakers and stage personnel not to walk in front of the projection beam backstage.
- Tape down all sound, video, electrical, and projection cables.
- Have emergency work-lights and flashlights on hand in case of power failure.
- For multimedia and other complex projection formats, have projector lamps changed before the session begins. Refocus and align projectors, and do a run-through of the presentation. (If a new lamp is going to blow, it will usually do so in the first half-hour of operation.)
- For single projectors, check availability of spare bulbs and accessories. Have a backup projector or someone able to change bulbs in case of burnout. Test remote control if speaker is running projector. Otherwise, be sure projectionist has a current cued script.
- Check video players with programs to be shown to be certain of compatibility.
- Examine screens for proper alignment, height, and angle. Look for rips and defects.
- Check overhead projectors for proper focus and alignment. Have spare acetates and marking pens available.
- If chalkboards, whiteboards, or flipcharts are called for, verify that they are equipped with chalk, eraser, marking pens, chemical eraser, etc.
- Test the laser pointer. Replace batteries if they are weak.
- Check script lights on lecterns.

- Darken the room and put a picture on the screen to check image quality and viewing angles, especially at the sides of the room.

- If the session is to be recorded, see that you have equipment and enough blank tapes on hand. Remind presenters to repeat the audience's questions for the recording.

- Brief presenters about the microphones and controls.

- Go over special cues with the session chairmen, room captains, and tech staff.

- Arrange for security of audiovisual equipment during breaks. Expensive items have a tendency to disappear.

- Make sure rental equipment is promptly returned to avoid late fees.

Not all of these recommendations will apply to all sessions, nor are they equal in importance. In the normal order of priorities, it makes sense to concentrate primarily on general sessions. These tend to be more complex and have the highest vulnerability and visibility. That is not to say that smaller sessions shouldn't be thoroughly checked—they should—but glitches and goofs at these gatherings are more readily forgiven and accepted. Mistakes and malfunctions at sessions attended by the organization's management, its membership, and guests are magnified for all to see and comment upon.

THE SOCIAL AGENDA

When Anthea Fortescue was affiliated with Conference Associates in London, she received an inquiry about spouse programs. She responded to her caller that the company does not conduct "spouse programs," but provides social agendas for delegates and guests. This next section addresses those elements that are not part of the business agenda, but that involve meeting attendees and those who accompany them—the so-called "social agenda."

Previous chapters have stressed the *communication* aspect of meetings, but communication does not end with the close of the business sessions. It also applies equally to social and recreational programs. It is essential that participants understand why they are being entertained and rewarded—particularly at incentive meetings. Associations and corporations invest substantial time and funds to accomplish an end for which the meeting is the means. Attendees are subjected to emotional and motivational cues intended to convey the sponsor's objectives and its image as a gracious host.

It has also been proven that social and recreational events contribute to fellowship, esprit de corps, and well-being, and that those afforded the opportunity to participate are more alert and receptive to the sponsor's message. A proper balance and diversity of hospitality, recreation, and learning experiences that are based on attendee demographics, preferences, and past history are the elements that ensure a meeting's success.

Attire

An Army officer found running nude down a hotel corridor while on R&R in Hong Kong offered the following defense at his court martial: "The regulations state: . . . officer, when not in uniform, shall be in attire appropriate to the sport or other activity in which he is engaged." In that anecdote is a germ of truth for conference organizers. Attendees and their guests appreciate knowing, in advance, the attire appropriate for various social functions. This is particularly true if the meeting is in a foreign country where dress codes and even designations vary. In the Philippines, for instance, the cool, lightweight "barang" shirt is quite appropriate for evening wear. At the other extreme, dressing for dinner in the United Kingdom means a dinner jacket or tuxedo for men and long gowns or cocktail dresses for women. In most parts of the world, "black tie" or "semi-formal" are the designations for black or midnight blue dinner jackets, except in the tropics or warm weather, where white or off-white is acceptable. "Formal" means white tie and tails for men and long gowns for women.

"Business attire" can be requested for business sessions, except at resorts where a more-casual atmosphere is desired. It may also be called for at evening functions. The interpretation of business attire is subject to local custom, however: In the Eastern United States and Canada, all of Europe, and much of Asia, business attire is a suit; in the Southern and Western United States and parts of the Pacific region, sport jackets are acceptable. To avoid confusion, the program should indicate "suits" or "jacket and tie." It is not chauvinistic to designate men's business attire; women understand and readily interpret according to their wardrobes.

For sports and leisure activities, dress codes are less stringent. Tennis whites are only enforced in tournament play. Golfers have come a long way from the days of tweed knickers and sweaters; multi-colored slacks and shorts are common sights on the links today. However, find out if there are any restrictions: Some country clubs, while they accommodate visiting golfers, have very stringent dress codes. In Muslim countries and monasteries and religious shrines in Christian or Buddhist areas, shorts, sleeveless shirts, and short skirts are considered to be in poor taste—possibly even forbidden. In Greece, for instance, people think nothing of going topless or bathing nude, but anyone visiting a religious shrine had better be fully clothed, with a minimum of skin showing. Let attendees know what is appropriate so that they can plan their wardrobes and avoid embarrassment.

Receptions, Meals, and Breaks

During the operation phase, the PCO constantly monitors activities and conditions that may influence planned events. Guarantees are reviewed and revised according to registration data and history—right up to the last-minute deadline set by the catering staff, in order to avoid paying for meals not consumed. Guarantees are an inexact science, but meeting professionals consider it a matter of pride and a measure of competence to achieve a close match between guarantee and actual count.

For most breaks, some receptions, and very simple meals (e.g., Continental breakfasts), it is possible to revise guarantees up to an hour or two before the function. Alternate plans such as "on consumption" or bulk orders ameliorate the problems of exact guarantees. For those meals that require extensive preparation or special order, 24 or 48 hours is the customary cut-off point. A staff member should be designated to verify the count for every function; at seated meals, this can be done quickly just by counting the empty place settings. The count is then verified with the banquet captain and any discrepancies resolved. Some meeting planners, when faced with an over-guarantee situation, will suggest that the surplus meals be donated to an orphanage or a homeless shelter. Most hotels will readily cooperate in such community support solutions.

After guarantees, room set, menu, and other details have been confirmed at the staff meeting, a staff member checks each function room or area during setup to ensure that it is proceeding on time and in the manner designated by the Staging Guide. Any changes (there are always a few) should be communicated to the head houseman or the CSM at this time. Some PCOs will specify "round eights" or "round tens" for a banquet setup and

Diameter	Square Footage	Capacity
72"	122	9, 10, or 11*
66"	110	8, 9, or 10*
60"	100	6, 7, or 8*

* Depending on room fit and presentation method.

conclude after setup that the tables are too crowded. To avoid such misunderstandings, it is important to know that round tables come in three diameters: 60, 66, and 72 inches. Many hotels have only one size, though they may set it for 8, 9, or 10 people. Verify table sizes and the number of place settings during the pre-meeting coordination visit. The chart that follows shows seating capacities for various table sizes.

Dance floors can also cause problems. The PCO is expected to know or at least estimate what percentage of attendees will dance, and should use the formula in Chapter 10 to specify the dance floor size in the Staging Guide. The general rule is to select a room with adequate capacity to accommodate all the diners and the largest percentage of dancers. Then estimate the *average* number of dancers and specify a dance floor 10 to 20 percent larger. Certainly, some musical selections will attract more than the average number, but those enthusiasts who cannot fit on the floor will find other places to boogie.

Bars should be closely observed to ensure that guests are served promptly, that no long lines develop, and that bartenders are using the specified pour size. As the event draws to a close and demand slackens, some bars can be closed and their stock wedded with that of the open bars if the bottle plan is in use. Look for accumulations of empty glasses, bottles, and plates, full ashtrays, and other bussing oversights; call them to the captain's attention if they are not promptly attended to.

Monitor buffet and hors d'oeuvre displays to see that items are replenished or substituted, and that the tables are continuously bussed. An adequate number of bus stations will keep people from leaving their empties on the buffet table, the piano, and on or near expensive theme decorations. As trays are emptied and no replenishment is planned, have the decorations and remaining food spread out, or have some of the tables removed. An empty buffet table looks bad. Check the coffee stations at buffets and breaks to be sure that receptacles have been provided for those nice little sugar and tea bags that look so unsightly when strewn around. It's amazing how often such a simple thing is overlooked. Make sure that empty cups and saucers are removed.

At all functions, the PCO or designated staff member should call for the checks shortly after the function ends. This is the best time to ascertain what is owed and resolve disputed charges, while the facts are fresh in everyone's minds. Some event managers use a rubber stamp to approve banquet checks and verify counts.

Off-Site Functions

With all the logistical responsibilities facing the meeting organizer on-site, it has become common practice to retain the services of a DMC or ground operator to coordinate off-site events and even some of the more-demanding on-site themed functions. Such contractors will usually quote a per-person rate that includes planning, supervision, staff, transportation, admission fees (if required), food and beverage services, entertainment, and theme decor. Some meeting planners prefer to do it all themselves or contract for certain services, use volunteer hosts, or hire a ground operator or other specialists to attend to specific details. They view the function itself as an extension of their planning and supervisory duties. Whatever method is used, the PCO has ultimate responsibility for the event and its success. He or she must pay close attention to the following recommendations regarding program elements and logistical details:

- Tour the site a day before the event and review details with management. Observe the physical condition of the facilities and pay special attention to food service areas, reception, and entertainment.

- If it is a ticketed event (such as a theme park, a concert hall, or a theater), review costs, ticket distribution procedures, admission, and block seating. Have management ensure that adequate ticket takers and ushers are on hand so that there are no long lines or bottlenecks. If it is an exclusive performance and the organization has bought out the facility, you can be far more demanding.

- Review transportation arrangements, especially the number and type of vehicles, spot times, boarding and debarking points, guides, shuttle frequency, and on-board and inter-vehicular communications.

- If time permits, drive the route during the same hours to ascertain traffic conditions, identify possible obstacles, and verify turn-around times.

- Review weather contingencies and method of implementation.

- Have a staff member check to see that vehicles and guides are on hand at specified spot times and stay to observe loading and dispatch. Another staff supervisor should go to the facility to observe preparation, guest arrivals, and reception.

- Meeting staff representatives should remain at the site to settle billing, distribute gratuities, oversee departures, and round up strays.

Recreational Events

Some meeting managers delegate recreational events to a DMC or to a member of the recreational staff (such as a golf or tennis professional). The latter will very often organize tournaments and oversee many of the logistical details for a nominal fee, thus relieving the PCO and conference staff of much of the burden. The volunteer staff can be organized to handle specific duties under the supervision of the pro; they can act as judges, scorekeepers, refreshment vendors, and prize committees. Elaborate group recreational events such as treasure hunts or the ever-popular mini-Olympics justify the use of special-events coordinators, who use their own trained staff, special equipment, props, and experience to ensure a successful event and maximum participation. The PCO can elect to retain control over elements such as transport, prizes, and refreshments, leaving the actual conduct of the program to the event manager.

The key to any recreational event should be enjoyment rather than competition, though the latter can add excitement and camaraderie in multidivisional companies or organizations with a chapter structure. However, it is essential that all attendees and guests be given an opportunity to participate and be part of the team. They should all receive recognition, regardless of their level of skill.

Any event that involves sports or physical activity carries a potential for injury. Safety regulations should be reviewed and made known to the participants, and provisions should be made for emergency medical services. Even in more sedentary pursuits, anticipate the possibility of sunstroke, a serious fall, or the occasional heart attack, and plan for quick response.

As we stated in Chapter 4, many meeting-goers now combine a convention with a family vacation; a growing number bring children to the event. Responding to this trend, some organizations provide child-care services and children's programs. If a significant number of children are expected, the PCO should make arrangements for special programming through a ground operator who offers such programs or through special and volunteer staff assembled for that purpose, if the numbers justify it. The cost of such a program may be subsidized in full or in part by the organization. The program can also be self-sustaining if you charge special registration fees. Otherwise, parents can be provided with options through local firms (in advance, or as part of the leisure activity information available at the hospitality desk).

Daily Procedures

The daily review of master account charges will forestall surprises during the post-meeting review session. Require daily statements and detailed backups of all charges listed chronologically and attached to the document. Daily statements encourage the hotel to carefully collect, identify, and document all charges made to the master account. At each session, approve all correct charges and earmark any disputed ones or delayed or missing items. A daily check with the front desk will help clear up discrepancies, as they often receive charges not covered by the master account billing instructions. Many PCOs contact the night auditor prior to retiring or early in the morning to see if there were any billing problems or questions that came up since the last review session.

During the post-conference meeting, attempt to settle any disputes still outstanding and establish dates for payment of undisputed portions of the bill. Schedule payment of delayed items and final resolution of disputed charges. Also, resolve any vendor or supplier charges identified as "paid out" on the master account statement.

SECTION C: POST-MEETING PROCEDURES

For the PCO, the meeting doesn't end with the wrap-up speech. There are a number of details that must be attended to if you want the following: attendees to depart the meeting site in the same good order that they arrived, your accounts reconciled, to recognize special efforts, and the meeting to be critiqued and documented in such a way as to provide important data for future planning. The natural tendency is to heave a sigh of relief and relax when the hectic pace of post-meeting activities is slowing down, but there are critical tasks to be accomplished at this phase.

THE DEPARTURE PLAN

Some meeting planners expend considerable effort to formulate a good reception plan, yet neglect to apply the same principles to their guests' departure. The last impression is perhaps as important as the first impression; the memory of a perfect meeting can be tarnished by a bad experience at check-out or a hassle getting to the airport. Knowledgeable PCOs devote the same meticulous effort to these final elements as they do to any other part of the program.

Departure planning is included in the program structure. If the meeting is in the West and a large number of attendees must cross several time zones traveling east, the final day's program should end early enough to permit early afternoon departures (or arrangements made to stay over until the following morning). The latter is a particularly good strategy for international meetings that necessarily entail long-haul travel itineraries.

To avoid congestion, encourage attendees to either check out during the morning break or use automated check-out if the service is available. Arrange to have additional cashiers on hand if large numbers are involved. Whether the organization provides transportation or each attendee makes his or her own arrangements, supply all needed information. If buses or vans are furnished, provide attendees with times and frequency of departures, departure points, luggage handling provisions, and any special arrangements at the airport (e.g., group departure lounge, early boarding, etc.). Inform international passengers of any departure taxes, currency exchange regulations, and special documentation that may be required. Be sure that staff members are on hand to supervise, answer questions, and lend special assistance to those who need help.

MEETING EVALUATION

Attendee evaluation is one of the PCO's most valuable tools, offering insights into the event just concluded and preferences for meetings to come. It serves as a documented record of the meeting—an objective measure of staff performance that reveals where improvement is needed. The evaluation then becomes a guide for future events and a source of data to be used for the organization's future negotiations. If the PCO is concerned with management credibility, the evaluation acts as a report card—a reliable yardstick for performance assessment, and a key support document for career advancement. It has been proven that people who consistently achieve management expectations tend to be considered managers in their organizations.

Veteran meeting professional Jim Daggett offers these pointers:

> Various stakeholders will be interested in different information. Directors may require an overall summary of all evaluation data. Attendees may want to know how their objectives were met. The sponsoring organization will certainly be interested in financial data, and exhibitors want to know the number of attendees and their demographics.

Areas that should be evaluated include:

- Conference program
- Site and venue
- Services
- Costs
- Exhibitions (if applicable)
- Social and guest programs, recreation, entertainment

Every organization that evaluates its meetings has developed forms suitable for its purposes. There is no uniform format, yet they are similar in content (if not design). Evaluations are intended to perform four important functions:

1. Indicate whether the meeting met its objectives.
2. Identify problems and areas needing improvement.
3. Ascertain which features were popular and should be continued.
4. Rate the program, facilities, and services and provide valuable feedback for future planning.

Program Evaluation

Some planners provide a critique form for every educational session and an overall evaluation form for the entire event. This is a good way to assess individual speaker performance and session content and collect valuable data for the program committee. The program evaluation should, at a minimum:

- Rate each presenter's performance in terms of subject knowledge, communication effectiveness, rapport, and use of handouts and visual aids (if applicable).
- Rate session content on relevance to participant needs, usefulness of information, and how well the content met expectations.
- Identify best features, as well as those needing improvement.
- Provide space for attendees to offer comments and suggestions.

Written evaluation forms distributed and collected at each session are the most common method, although the use of electronic devices continues to gain popularity. Computerized audience-response systems are effective tools in gathering evaluation data. This technology makes use of compact transmitters, which are distributed to the audience at a final general session. A moderator guides audience response, posing questions that would normally appear on an evaluation form. The questions are projected on a screen and audience responses are instantly tabulated and displayed. They are then stored in memory for future retrieval. (Evaluation Technology is covered in detail in Chapter 13.)

Session critique forms may be placed in the conference notebook or handed out at each session. Presenters and room chairmen can remind attendees at the beginning and the end of the session to complete and hand in their critiques before departing the room. The forms are tabulated sometime after the meeting and used as part of the program evaluation. Key comments are highlighted and supplied to the program committee, with copies delivered to the conference chairman and each speaker.

It is also useful to survey presenters and members of the program committee to ascertain the adequacy of speaker information, the validity of the program, the planning timetable and deadlines, suitability of meeting rooms, and the quality and adequacy of the support services and staff. The survey should gauge the effectiveness of the overall program structure and focus on concurrent session conflicts, session lengths, attendance distribution, and breaks. These observations are valuable to subsequent program planning.

Post-Conference Evaluation

The overall conference evaluation is more detailed, designed to elicit feedback on all aspects of the meeting. Electronic means are widely used here also, although written evaluations tend to allow for greater detail, and are preferred for seminars and small group sessions. A written evaluation would normally include:

- Demographic data on the individual who is responding
- Effectiveness and adequacy of pre-meeting information
- Ratings for educational program format, content, duration, and presenters
- Evaluation of guest social programs and recreational and hospitality events
- Ratings for destination, attitude and efficiency of hotel staff, meeting facilities, food service and quality, transportation, and travel planning
- Mode of transportation and ticketing, if arranged by respondent
- Assessment of registration procedures, administration, meeting staff, message center, communication, and support services such as the DMC
- Comments on the most- and least-favorable meeting features
- Suggestions for subsequent meeting duration, location, time of year, range of room rates, and arrival/departure pattern
- Comments on probable attendance of spouse, guest, or children
- Recommendations for program content, structure, and allotted time

Documentation and Tabulation

There are several techniques for eliciting the desired information. One that is frequently overlooked is random personal interviews. Though interviews are somewhat subjective, they remain a valuable barometer for gauging the meeting's success on the spot, and often produce beneficial insights. The most common method is the evaluation questionnaire distributed to the participants at the end of the meeting or mailed or e-mailed shortly after they return home. Some PCOs use interviews and questionnaires, thus receiving spontaneous reactions on-site and retrospective ones after the respondent has had an opportunity to reflect on the event. Response rates are higher when surveys include a cover letter from the CEO or conference chairman, a deadline, and a Web site response address or a self-addressed, business reply envelope.

Web-based evaluations are normally solicited after the event. A home page banner and/or individual e-mail reminders encourage attendees to complete the assessment.

Making the questionnaires anonymous achieves high objectivity. For ease of tabulation, a substantial number of questions should be multiple choice and qualitative, though the respondent should be given every opportunity to offer suggestions and comments. Questions must be perceived as non-threatening and be couched in short, declarative sentences, written in clear, simple language.

Responses are tabulated and recurring comments and valuable suggestions are extracted, reproduced, and disseminated to all concerned parties.

STAFF CRITIQUE AND DOCUMENTATION

It is customary for organizers to hold a debriefing session at the close of the conference to critique the meeting, document data, and identify problem areas. Meeting staff members, hotel representatives, and key support staff members should attend. A number of conference hotels also request that the PCO provide a detailed evaluation of the various departments that were involved with the event. Some invite the meeting executive to attend the hotel's own debriefing session and comment on the performance of various departments.

The staff critique should look at all the functions, services, and activities over which the staff exercised supervision or coordination. These areas include some or all of the following:

- *Promotion.* Costs and media utilized, response statistics, cost per attendee, response evaluation by media, cost per paid registrant
- *Registration.* Attendance by category (delegates, guests, press, etc.), cancellations and refunds, registration revenues, percentage pre-paid, number of accompanying persons, arrival-departure pattern, no-shows; advance and on-site registration procedures, problems encountered
- *Hotel sales staff.* Negotiating flexibility, contract fulfillment, response to changes, timely communication, regional sales office assistance

- *Convention services.* Pre-meeting communication, liaison with other departments, response to requests and changes, room setups as specified, coordinator visibility and availability

- *Meeting facilities.* Condition and/or effectiveness of furnishings, lighting and sound system, state-of-the-art technology; seating adequacy, issues relating to room capacity and traffic flow; meeting-room utilization report received for review

The staff critique should determine whether or not the conference met the objectives and standards set by the organizers. The following can be put in checklist form for review or phrased in question-form for evaluation:

- *Front Office.* Proper handling of registrations and changes; timely reports on reservations and cancellations; efficient check-in and check-out procedures; expedited handling of VIPs; efficient, courteous telephone and message center services; fast and helpful concierge and bell desk service. Also data on total room pick-up, no-shows, and cancellations by category.

- *Accommodations.* Room conditions satisfactory and equipment in working order; housekeeping services timely and thorough; room change requests honored when feasible.

- *Functions.* High quality of food and service at group functions and breaks; food replenished promptly where required; serving staff efficient and courteous; attendance within range of guarantees. Complete data on tickets sold and collected and number of tickets pre-paid. Discrepancies on pricing and guarantees resolved; bar service and brands as specified; controls and pour specifications adhered to; prompt room service; group utilization and quality of hotel outlets.

- *Accounting.* Master account status provided as called for; charges accurate and signed by authorized staff members; pricing discrepancies resolved; final billing and backup ready or available prior to departure.

- *Audiovisual services.* Equipment properly maintained and in good working order; backup and additional equipment promptly delivered; AV equipment delivered and set up on time; accessories included and functioning; AV technicians competent, knowledgeable, and helpful; rental billing correct.

- *Business agenda.* Presenters arrived on time; presenters available for orientation and rehearsals; presenters in place prior to session start; presentations consistent with content outline; presentations effectively delivered; presentations met audience expectations;

presentations supported with handouts and visual aids; audiovisual segments properly rehearsed and executed; overflow problems promptly resolved; evaluations turned in. Attendance data complete for each session.

- *Social and recreational.* Response consistent with projections; attractions and recreational facilities met expectations; good participation by attendees and guests; courteous, efficient staff services. Attendance data complete.

- *Ground operations.* DMC staff prompt and competent; vehicles spotted on time; signage and information on boarding points adequate; delivery, turnaround, and return timing as projected; equipment clean and in good, safe mechanical condition; crowd controls unobtrusive and efficient; food and beverage quality and service as presented; entertainment effective and well received by audience. Cost/revenue analysis completed.

- *Convention bureau.* Prompt response to information requests; assistance with site visits; requested services and support staff provided; personnel competent; personnel helpful and made visitors feel welcome; pamphlets and other supplies provided as promised; housing bureau efficient and accurate.

- *Exhibits.* Number of booths utilized; exhibit revenues and expenses met projections; daily visitor census taken. Exhibit service contractor efficient, prompt, and responsive to exhibitors; contractor complied with contract; sub-contractor performed to standard; equipment and/or services delivered on time and in good working order; floor layout conducive to good traffic flow; shipping and drayage service timely and satisfactory. Problems encountered recorded and reviewed.

- *Shipping.* Total shipping costs recorded; timely arrival and accounting; storage or retrieval problems resolved; lost or delayed shipments handled.

- *Media relations.* Trade press attendance as expected; event covered by local media; pressroom operations and utilization satisfactory; publicity costs vs. results evaluated.

- *Special recognition.* Staff members surveyed to identify individuals whose superior performance deserves to be rewarded.

Obviously, not all of these areas can be covered at every meeting. Some events, such as international and scientific congresses or incentive meetings, will involve specialized operations and services that need to be reviewed and critiqued. Not all of the data needed for an accurate statistical analysis of the event will be available until some time after the conference. Nevertheless, the critique and the statistics give the PCO and the sponsoring organization an accurate overview of the success of the event in terms of organizational objectives, attendee satisfaction, cost, and performance. The resulting financial data provide a valuable budgeting guide and an accurate assessment of the value of the organization's business to the hotel and other suppliers.

Community Impact

Convention and visitors' bureaus and associations routinely analyze meetings in terms of financial impact on the host community. This is useful in determining the value of the organization's business, and it is a key factor in negotiating rates and services. Data for such purposes can be obtained by tracking and analyzing several kinds of information:

- Average length of stay by out-of-town visitors
- Room occupancy, rates, and number of room-nights
- Total room revenue and taxes collected
- Group food and beverage revenues
- Individual room charges for telephone, food, laundry, and incidentals
- Estimated visitor spending on gifts, shopping, parking, car rental, tips, entertainment, attractions, personal services, etc.

The compiled statistics provide a picture of average delegate spending. In addition, organizational expenditures are factored in. These include contract services such as transportation, facility and equipment rentals, temporary help, AV and exhibition services, off-site catering, attractions and tours, group recreation activity, and local purchases and other event-related community revenues. Extrapolating average delegate spending and organizational expenditures enables the PCO to gauge the financial impact of the meeting on the host community.

AUDITING AND FINANCIAL ANALYSIS

During the post-meeting phase, all financial transactions, hotel and/or convention center master accounts, invoices from vendors, contractual obligations, and revenues from a variety of sources are reviewed and audited. Some PCOs prefer to do this on-site so that any disputes can be resolved on the spot; others allow a time lapse to ensure that all charges are in and adjustments have been entered. Those who manage large meetings will normally assign the tasks to an accountant or comptroller. At the same time, all other fiscal transactions are tabulated, analyzed, and reconciled against the meeting budget. Meeting professionals pride themselves on how closely the final accounting follows budget projections, and consider this as a measure of their proficiency. Needless to say, corporate and association management are also concerned with the bottom line. Therefore, a thorough and accurate financial analysis is an essential meeting management tool.

At the post-conference meeting, master account disputes are settled and payment terms agreed upon before the final invoice is prepared. Other open account invoices from vendors should be reviewed prior to leaving the site. They should be corrected if there are discrepancies and must be paid promptly to protect the organization's credit rating. Disputed charges that are discovered need to be discussed with the vendor, but do not delay payment of the undisputed portion of the bill.

Reimbursement of staff and speaker expenses can usually be handled after return to the home office. Some PCOs routinely mail speaker expense checks with a cover letter thanking each speaker individually for their participation and commenting on their performance. If the speaker has not submitted an expense statement, include a reminder with the letter. Once expenses are received and verified, reimbursement should be prompt. Any speaker fees due are also paid upon receipt of the invoice.

Chapter 7 identified the meeting budget as a viable document subject to revision as requirements and statistics change. In reconciling the budget, both the original and last revised figures are shown for each line item.

Unanticipated and non-budget expenses that invariably arise are assigned to contingency. Even with skilled budgeting and conscientious cost controls, some line items will reflect budget overruns, while others will come in under budget. This is quite acceptable, as long as the bottom line is within predetermined tolerances. Figure 16-3 illustrates a typical budget reconciliation for a corporate event.

GRATUITIES AND SPECIAL RECOGNITION

Gratuities are dispensed in recognition of extraordinary service. Repeat: *extraordinary* service! Regrettably, in the hospitality industry the custom of giving a gratuity is no longer considered discretionary—it is commonplace, and often results in commonplace service. When exemplary effort is encountered, meeting planners feel compelled to reward it above and beyond the "normal" gratuities.

298 Operations

INCOME		PROJECTED		REVISED	NOTES	ACTUAL	
REGISTRANTS	FEE	#	TOTAL	#		#	
Full conference	$ 150	50	$ 7,500				$ 24,030
After cut-off	$ 180	100	$ 18,000				
Wednesday reception	$ 50						
After cut-off	$ 50						$ 350
Thursday only	$ 100	25	$ 2,500				
After cut-off	$ 120	50	$ 6,000				$ 6,540
Friday only	$ 50	20	$ 1,000				
After cut-off	$ 60	20	$ 1,200				$ 380
Scholarships			$ -				
Subtotal		265	$ 36,200				$ 31,300
EXHIBITORS	$ 350	30	$ 10,500				$ 7,600
SPONSORSHIPS			$ 12,000				$ 21,000
SILENT AUCTION			$ 3,000				$ 7,600
MISCELLANEOUS							
TOTAL			$ 61,700				$ 67,500

FIXED EXPENSES						
PROGRAM/Speaker exp.		$ 1,000				$ 3,275
AV support		$ 2,000				$ 1,850
Program materials		$ 600				$ 540
Promotion expense		$ 1,200				$ 1,446
Registration expense		$ 600			supplies *	$ 435
Staff support (Staff rooms)		$ 700				$ 571
Decoration, signage		$ 300				$ 248
Awards		$ 200				$ 210
Extra gratuities		$ 150				$ 180
Misc. & Contingency		$ 1,000				$ 468
TOTAL		$ 7,750				$ 9,223

VARIABLE EXPENSES	ESTIMATED			REVISED		ACTUAL	
	@	#		#		#	
Wed. Reception - food **	$ 18.50	150	$ 3,883				$ 3,883
beverage **			$ 1,000				$ 760
Thurs. Breakfast &- Exec pkg	$ 16.95	150	$ 3,026				$ 3,026
Lunch **	$ 15.95	150	$ 2,847	230	$ 4,365		$ 4,365
Reception		150	$ 1,900				$ 1,840
Friday Breakfast **	$ 8.95	125	$ 1,332				$ 1,516
Friday Break			$ 400				$ 317
SUBTOTAL Food & Beverage			$ 14,388				$ 15,707
Program materials			$ 500				$ 412
Badges			$ 100				$ 122
Misc. & Contingency			$ 1,500				$ 1,344
TOTAL			$ 16,488				$ 17,585

SUMMARY	ESTIMATED		REVISED		ACTUAL
TOTAL INCOME		$ 61,700			$ 67,500
FIXED EXPENSES		$ 7,750			$ 9,223
VARIABLE EXPENSES		$ 16,488			$ 17,585
SURPLUS		$ 37,462		$ -	$ 40,692

FIGURE 16-3 Budget reconciliation.

The question of whom to tip and how much has plagued meeting managers for decades. Numerous panels of experts, columnists, and industry committees have addressed this sensitive subject without formulating any but the vaguest catalog of industry practices. One of the more positive benefits is that a definition of tips and gratuities has emerged: A "tip" is a form of reward or incentive for superior service, given by the meeting executive in the form of cash or gifts. A "gratuity" is a percentage routinely added to the food and beverage costs of group functions and distributed to eligible employees as a bonus. (However, some hotels make it a practice to add this to their total revenue and give employees only a percentage.) Since gratuities are not discretionary, this segment will deal with tipping practices and other ways of rewarding superior service.

Tips are given for more than simply quality service. When considering rewards, many PCOs look at overall attitude, cooperation, deportment, courtesy, response time, and high visibility, as well as extraordinary effort. The value will vary with the length of the meeting and the degree of performance. Some meeting planners will tip select staff members such as housemen and bell staff in advance, with a promise of more to come. It is intended to be an incentive, though most professionals disapprove of the practice, contending that it sets precedent and will eventually come to be expected (thus losing its motivational influence).

There is a wide range of opinion as to who should receive tips. Most PCOs agree that the following positions are eligible for cash awards:

Head Houseman	Set-up Crew
Bell Captain	Bell Staff
Concierge	Banquet Captain
Convention Coordinators	

As for other positions, here are some useful guidelines, subject to the meeting manager's discretion:

- Waiters, waitresses, busboys, and bartenders should be included in the standard gratuity. Tip individuals whose service and attitude are outstanding.

- Managers (sales, catering, F&B, convention services, front office) are not given cash rewards, though a nice gift is definitely in order. A letter of commendation and/or appreciation is also in order; send a copy to the general manager.

- Other employees, such as doormen, parking and pool attendants, and golf or tennis professionals should be tipped at the time service is rendered.

Many resorts and most foreign hotels add a service charge to the room charges to cover staff gratuities. In such cases, a nominal tip for truly superior service may be in order. In all cases, consult with your staff to decide who should be rewarded. To avoid taking large sums of cash on-site, arrange for cash payouts charged to the master account. Distribute them in envelopes with a handwritten thank-you note on a letterhead. If a consolidated tip is given to a supervisor for distribution to others, list those who are to receive the cash, and ask that the supervisor obtain recipients' signatures on the list. This a perfectly acceptable practice that protects both the PCO and the recipient in the event of an audit. A similar list should be prepared for non-cash gifts, showing the cost of the gift and to whom it was given.

The letter of commendation is a form of recognition that costs the grantor nothing, but is appreciated by all who receive one. Be generous and punctual in expressing appreciation to all who supported the event, and be sure to copy their superiors. Some meeting managers award plaques and trophies to hotel executives and other suppliers. These mementos are proudly displayed by their fellow PCOs, those who service the meeting and contribute to its success.

COURSE EVALUATION FORM

PROFESSIONAL EDUCATION CONFERENCE

COURSE TITLE: _____

COURSE SPEAKER: _____

Please rate this activity on the following items: (circle one number)

	LOW			HIGH	
Knowledge of subject	1	2	3	4	5
Ability to present ideas clearly	1	2	3	4	5
Ability to adapt to audience needs	1	2	3	4	5
Ability to provide usable ideas	1	2	3	4	5
Ability to utilize audiovisuals	1	2	3	4	5
Ability to actively involve audience	1	2	3	4	5
Ability to use humor	1	2	3	4	5
Ability to handle questions from audience	1	2	3	4	5
Ability to pace speed of delivery	1	2	3	4	5
Ability to choose proper vocabulary or level	1	2	3	4	5
Confidence as speaker/trainer	1	2	3	4	5

Was the presentation relevant to your job? _____

Was the content what you expected from reading the program? _____

Would you ask the speaker to present again? _____

What could be done to improve the course? _____

Other comments? _____

(Please complete and return your evaluation at the conclusion of this course. Thank you.)

FIGURE 16-4 Evaluation form.

Chapter Seventeen
Emergencies, Safety, and Security

Meeting management, some industry professionals have suggested, is akin to crisis management. Each event at which several hundred people are gathered carries a potential for catastrophic incidents, medical emergencies, fire and bomb scans, corporate espionage, protests, and other threats to the security and well-being of those in attendance.

In addition to all their other responsibilities, the PCO must be a professional crisis manager throughout the conference. The possibility of disruption from protestors, catastrophic accidents, or terrorist acts or threats hangs like a Damocletian sword over every large gathering at a public facility. Under these circumstances, the PCO has to be able to summon the forces of James Bond and Dirty Harry if the occasion calls for it. Regardless of how thoroughly you plan and how meticulously it is managed, the potential for conflict is omnipresent. Knowledgeable meeting executives carefully tend to the *known* elements of the meeting and take precautions against the *unknown*. The safety and security of the conference attendees is uppermost in their minds.

Contingency planning is an integral responsibility of any event organizer, and solid preparation is needed to guard against any unforeseen emergencies developing into crises. The contingency plan addresses various scenarios and anticipates that even the most routine meeting can be disrupted by a medical emergency, a fire, or a labor conflict. For events that have a high risk potential, a "Plan B" or contingency plan is invaluable. The plan details exact procedures to be followed and defines responsibilities. The simplest guideline for contingency planning is to expect the unexpected.

Medical Emergencies

Of all crises that could occur at the gathering of a large number of people, a medical emergency is the most common, but it is also the easiest to prepare for. Accidents, sports injuries, and illness attributable to changes in diet and surroundings, alcohol consumption, and fatigue are the most likely medical emergencies, but other life-threatening emergencies such as a stroke or heart attack can also occur where several hundred people gather.

The convention bureau and facility representative can help the meeting organizer develop an effective medical emergency system using their knowledge of such available resources as hospitals and emergency medical services. Consider having medical services available on-site or on short notice. Your planning should also include dental emergencies. Most organizations ask each attendee to supply advance information on special medical needs, potential health risks, or provisions for those with disabilities.

It's best to have on-site medical services if the conference site is far from medical facilities or the meeting attendance is particularly large. There are private companies that supply Emergency Medical Technicians (EMTs) on location. EMT teams are highly trained paramedical professionals who can administer immediate medical attention for anything from cuts and sprains to childbirth and heart attack. Each team is equipped with an EKG heart monitor-defibrillator, emergency medical supplies, portable oxygen, and radio communications linkage to local medical facilities.

Demonstrations

Some emergencies are more foreseeable than others. Anticipate the possibility of demonstrations against a sponsor organization, a celebrity speaker, or guest dignitary, especially if some element of the conference is controversial. It is the PCO's responsibility to create a secure environment during the conference, and attention to security details is essential. The hotel or convention center will be able to supply information and trained security personnel, but other factors must be considered if demonstrations are expected.

Generally, demonstrators voice opposition to some policy or activity of the sponsor organization or program participant. They are trying to make a statement or disrupt the meeting, and in so doing, hope to gain media attention for their cause. Perhaps they simply want to air their views before an assembly to which they are not invited. A peaceful demonstration must be handled delicately, lest it turn into angry confrontation between demonstrators and irritated organization leaders. Demonstrators cannot be allowed to overshadow the conference, but they should not be ignored. Involvement of local police agencies may be necessary if a demonstration is expected; advise them and seek their support. However, primary responsibility for security lies with the organization. Consult with the hotel's chief of security on the use of private services for crowd and access control.

In addition to such passive measures, there are a number of active ones to be considered. There are ways of defusing a demonstration, but they will demand extraordinary communications skills. Consider offering the demonstrators a forum for airing their concerns, such as, for example, a booth for displaying literature, or a meeting in a controlled environment with organization officials, participants, and attendees. These are things the sponsor has some control over, and they might placate demonstrators whose likely purpose is to air issues before the assembly. Appoint a competent spokesman to speak on behalf of the sponsor to the demonstrators and to the media. This delicate task calls for a person with good communication skills and a level head—someone who can maintain control under trying conditions and provocative questioning. If you anticipate a demonstration, notify all participants immediately. This will aid in the management of the protest because if people know what to expect, they can come prepared.

Protests have grown violent in recent years as radical groups infiltrate peaceful demonstrations and infect them with mob psychology. Typical of these attacks is the aggression that greets any conference whose topic is global economic activity. Such events and their predictable mob attacks call for more stringent protective measures:

- An area remote from the site for demonstrators that is "close enough to protest but not to disrupt"; cordons manned by police riot squads
- Security staff at all meeting venue entrance and exit areas
- Ingress limited to registered guests who will be subject to bag-checks
- Distinct photo IDs for participants, their guests, and all members of the media
- Photo IDs for all facility staff members and contractors
- Round-the-clock on-site police and fire presence
- Background checks on all recent staff hires
- No unscheduled deliveries
- Loading dock policed by armed security officers
- No vehicles allowed to approach without passing through a remote inspection site
- On-site guest and staff parking restricted to previously cleared automobiles

Security and Risk Management

At one time, meeting planners were concerned with security only as it related to sensitive government officials, celebrities, and the safeguarding of exhibit areas. Retired police officers and guard services filled most of the need. All that changed dramatically in the wake of 9/11 as terrorist acts, kidnappings, and corporate espionage have become viable threats to everyday life. The hotel "dick" in the blue serge suit has been replaced by trained professionals, many of them former military or law-enforcement officers. In today's sensitive environment, security is a critical component of the planning procedure beginning with site inspection.

Former FBI agent Richard Hudak, Loews Hotels' director of security, has these pointers:

- Ask for and review the facility's security plan.
- Check type of IDs worn by the staff.
- Are radios provided for direct contact to security staff?
- Are all entrance and exit points and employee entrances monitored?
- How many security staff are on duty between midnight and 7:00 a.m.?
- Are fire stairwells well marked, lighted, and clutter-free?
- Is an emergency response team organized and trained?
- Is an evacuation plan in place? At what point is it implemented?
- Are parking areas well lighted and patrolled?
- Are guest floors regularly patrolled?
- Can meeting room and/or exhibit hall locks be re-keyed or changed?
- Is access through meeting room service entrances restricted?
- Is lobby security visible at all times?

Private security services offer an exotic mix of electronic bug detectors, metal detectors, counter-terrorism counseling, armed guards, and drivers trained in evasive techniques. Several conduct resident courses in executive protection, unarmed combat, and weapons training. Key meeting venues have marshaled community response assets into task forces that train for scenarios from the unmanageable to the unthinkable.

The PCO needs to be a part of the threat-assessment team, acting as liaison between facility security staff, contracted services, and any security personnel who are part of a guest's personal entourage. When heads of state, governors, ministers, cabinet-rank officials, and high-ranking military officers are part of the program or are in attendance, your staff should be prepared to defer to their security staff's demands. For example, when a head of state or former U.S. president is invited, a Secret Service advance party will arrive several days before the event. They will have very specific instructions on room assignments, program scheduling, protocol, the placement of the lectern, and type of microphones (they usually bring their own), and the individuals who will be permitted on stage during the program. PCOs will be asked to provide information for clearance of meeting staff, stage crew, hotel staff, and program participants. Faced with such demands, event managers may feel like they're losing control of the meeting, and in a sense they are. Nevertheless, they should respect the professional competence of government security personnel and demonstrate their own by being knowledgeable, flexible, and prepared.

High-security meetings in which the participants, the subject matter, or both are of a sensitive nature require extensive security provisions. In such cases, it is best to hire a professional security advisor (see Resources). Such consultants will conduct a security assessment of the facility, check staff employment records, and sweep the premises for explosives and surveillance devices if necessary. They designate "frozen" areas where hotel staff must be accompanied by guards in the conduct of their duties. A list of registrants is provided, and each one may be required to submit positive identification in order to obtain a name badge. Badges are likely to have photographic IDs. Entry points are guarded by uniformed and plainclothes security staff. Purses, briefcases, and packages may be subject to visual or electronic inspection, and metal detectors may be employed.

Advance publicity, commonplace for most meetings and an essential part of marketing, is normally curtailed where security is a concern. A total news blackout could be imposed during the event (though that may be difficult to accomplish, given media intrusion and instinctive attraction to secret proceedings and newsworthy people). If possible, hold back publicity and news releases until after the event.

Safety

No meeting professional can eliminate all risks to conference attendees, but steps can be taken to remove some of the more obvious risks. Fire emergency plans should be reviewed during early site inspection of the facility. Transport operators should likewise be examined for vehicular safety devices, procedures, and insurance coverage. But some things—Mother Nature in particular—cannot be controlled.

Natural disasters and unexpected harsh weather even hundreds of miles away can create problems for the event. A blizzard in Chicago can influence an exhibition in New Orleans. A hurricane in Florida can affect a meeting in Dallas. Weather can influence shipping schedules and airline flights, delaying meeting and exhibit components, attendees, and speakers. Should problems occur, the PCO and sponsor may have to alter or modify the meeting or its various events to compensate for no-shows, late arrivals, and delayed speakers or entertainers. Careful research into locally available program participants and entertainers during the coordination phase will identify potential backup resources should inclement weather force program changes.

Weather sometimes interferes with departure plans. You might have to do some fast negotiating with hotel management; they might be having as much trouble with delayed arrivals as with delayed departures. Use a bit of creative improvisation and you might just turn a potential disaster into a memorable event. A number of meeting planners are members of the Marriott Lincolnshire "Snow Shovel Club," initiated during an impromptu party for stranded conference attendees at the height of a Midwestern blizzard.

Weather contingencies on-site need not be totally disruptive. Research and imagination are all you need. One Western barbecue at Scottsdale's Pinnacle Peak might have been washed out by an unexpected rain storm, but the PCO in charge had a quickly assembled staff of volunteer couturiers whip up cowboy hats and vinyl ponchos made up out of plastic trash bags. The upshot: a good time, albeit a damp one, was had by all. Golf outing rained out? Book racquetball courts and indoor skating rinks, and offer those as an option. Or ask the golf pro to conduct a clinic in the ballroom. If it is an outdoor function, reserve backup facilities in any climate that is subject to sudden weather changes.

Labor Disputes

Strikes, work stoppages, and slowdowns can also affect a planned event. Transportation strikes occur all too often, causing havoc with a conference schedule. There is little that can be done, but make the best of whatever is available. If there is an airline strike, contact alternative carriers (though special fares may not be honored). With ground operators, substitute suppliers or modes of transportation can be investigated. But should a strike occur at the hotel or convention center hosting the event, patience, ingenuity, and a willingness to improvise are the organizer's best strategies. Staff and facility management can be expected to fill some roles and some attendees might volunteer to help, but events may have to be altered, exhibits pared down, and banquet arrangements revised. Union contracts should be covered during site selection, with special attention to contract renewal dates. (Research the history of labor relations at the facility you are considering.)

General Precautions

Professional hospitality security consultant Rick de Treville believes that best practices should be followed at all times.

"Proper pre-conference security planning can protect attendees. It can also buffer meeting planners and their employers from some civil liability. De Treville offers these five pre-conference recommendations:

1. *Insist on "intelligence information" about criminal activity in the area around the hotel.* If the hotel claims no knowledge about local crime, contact the local law enforcement agency and ask them for tourist safety tips or advice for your attendees.

2. *Ask for customized hotel assistance with any intoxicated or disruptive attendees.* Personalize a response plan that includes early notification of conference staff before law enforcement is contacted.

3. *Request information about the anticipated medical emergency response time and typical travel time to the nearest trauma center.* Find out the storage location of the closest oxygen cylinder. Determine whether or not the hotel has defibrillator machines.

4. *Ask about the hotel's recent history with labor disputes or civil protests.* Make sure none are expected. If protestors are a concern for the conference, ask about the hotel's response plan.

5. *Discuss the hotel's lost and found policies, and request customized response to items found in conference meeting rooms.* Coordinate the return of items that are found in attendee rooms after checkout.

Community Resources

In most key meeting destinations, the PCO can call on local and federal agencies for intelligence and threat assessment. In high-attendance events, highly specialized, trained responders can assist organizers in planning for and preventing threats, ranging from domestic violence to weapons of mass destruction.

A prime example is the Tourism Oriented Policing and Security (TOPS) program organized and coordinated by FBI Special Agent John Sylvester in San Diego, California. Sylvester has been involved in security planning and coordination for high-profile events such as the 1996 Republican National Convention, as well as Super Bowl XXXII and XXXVII.

In San Diego and most major event destinations, a typical TOPS task force can call on the following response assets in case of a perceived threat or emergency:

- Law enforcement
- Fire and Rescue
- Hazardous Materials (HAZMAT) response teams
- Bomb squads: Explosive Ordnance Disposal (EOD)
- Emergency Medical Services (EMS)
- Hospital trauma centers and clinics
- Diagnostic laboratories
- Military commands
- Public venue security personnel
- Private industry and academia

GOING ABROAD

At any large gathering of people, there is a risk that some ill-timed incident will take place, usually at the least-opportune moment. Although the chances of a crisis happening at an international event are no greater than at a domestic meeting, the situation may be more chaotic in a foreign country or where attendees are from several cultures.

In addition to having to concern themselves with the myriad of details surrounding any event, meeting professionals must anticipate and prepare for numerous potential hazards. They need to make security a fundamental part of the planning process. In other words, they must become as knowledgeable about safety and security as they need to be about menus and venues. Faced with such high-stress conditions, meeting organizers cannot be blamed for developing a sense of paranoia.

In order to prevent incidents and emergencies from developing into catastrophes, careful, intelligent preparation and development of possible scenarios offer the best defense. The PCO should thoroughly research conditions in the destination under consideration. Aside from contracting a professional security consultant to do a threat assessment, try to get up-to-date reports from government agencies. The U.S. State Department's hot line and Web site are 202-647-5235 or www.state.gov.

A comprehensive emergency plan should anticipate all potential hazards, detail emergency responses, and assign responsibilities. The guideline for contingency planning previously stated bears repeating: expect the unexpected.

Medical Emergencies

As with domestic events, medical emergencies are the most frequent hazards encountered abroad. In most destinations, tourist bureau and hotel staff can assist in preparing a medical emergency response system by advising on the availability of emergency services, hospitals, doctors and other resources. Paramedics should be assigned to the meeting site or available on rapid response if it is a large event. On-site medical teams are recommended if the meeting is at a remote location. Dental emergencies should also be part of the planning.

Knowledgeable organizers preparing for a meeting abroad will include in their participant communications a questionnaire regarding special diets, medical conditions, and disabilities. Information on travel insurance that covers medical emergencies should be made available to attendees (see Chapter 4 Resources for providers).

Weather and Safety

Natural disasters, theft, and criminal assault pose threats to meeting participants, even in countries perceived as "safe," and must be considered in contingency planning. Once on-site, attendees and key staff members should be briefed on fire precautions and procedures.

At international events where delegate travel may originate anywhere in the world, severe weather conditions can result in unanticipated delays. At the destination, inclement or severe weather can have a disruptive effect on even the most meticulously planned program, potentially endangering attendees. The PCO needs to keep abreast of weather conditions, at the meeting venue and at departure points where a large number of delegates originate, and then plan accordingly.

With the exception of protection at the meeting or exhibition site, there is not much the organizers can do to protect participants from criminal or terrorist acts. But they can and should be advised to take certain precautions to protect themselves when abroad. Some of these are:

- Keep hotel room numbers confidential.
- Verify deliveries before opening the door. If in doubt, call the front desk.
- Make use of hotel safe deposit boxes for valuables and important documents such as passports.
- Avoid dark streets and bad areas, especially at night. Take taxis or travel in groups.
- Dress inconspicuously when leaving the hotel. Don't stand out, and avoid wearing jewelry.

SECURITY

In the wake of terrorist attacks and other forms of violence and disruption, security service personnel who are experienced in dealing with meetings and exhibitions have become strategic assets. Starting with the hotel security director, PCOs should review contingency provisions for staff, VIPs, attendees, and facilities.

Private security services offer an exotic mix of counter-surveillance devices, metal and explosive detectors, sniffer dogs, armed guards, and drivers trained in evasive driving techniques. Attendance of security-sensitive people such as key executives, high-ranking government officials, and controversial speakers, and events where either the venue or the organization has a history of problems call for security assessments. This is the function of professional security consultants; they conduct an assessment of the city and facility, check employment records, and coordinate with local law-enforcement agencies.

On site, the consultants will form a threat assessment team that also includes the meeting planner. They will contract for guards, designate "frozen" or restricted areas, enforce badge access, and, if warranted, sweep the premises for surveillance devices and explosives. Other precautions in security-sensitive meetings include pre-screening of registrants and staff; the use of photo ID badges; use of uniformed and plain-clothes guards; visual or electronic inspection of parcels, purses, and briefcases; and press blackouts.

Travel Security

During periods when the terrorist threat is high, look to the media for a wealth of travel advice (remember that not all travelers will have the same risk profile). You must guard against other threats, such as theft and muggings; consider giving special training to high-risk people. Low-risk travelers need only to take certain common-sense precautions that should be passed on to all attendees:

- Go through your wallet or purse and weed out items not needed abroad, such as excess credit cards, voter registration, military ID, business cards identifying the bearer as a highly placed executive, etc.
- Avoid traveling with expensive luggage or using distinctive luggage tags that pinpoint you as an executive or a wealthy traveler.
- Dress to project a low profile and blend in. Leave business suits in your luggage, and wear casual clothing. Avoid designer fashions and clothing with cartoon characters, printed messages, or slogans.
- Do not wear expensive jewelry. If you need it abroad, check it with your luggage (insured and inventoried) or conceal it on your person.
- If you must travel during elevated threat conditions, don't fly first class. Those travelers are presumed to be wealthy and are therefore targets for hostage-taking.

- Try to avoid peak travel times. If possible, stay away from crowded areas at the airport. Get boarding passes in advance, and check your luggage at the curb, if permissible.

- Take a minimum of carry-on luggage; it can restrict movement in case of trouble.

- Stay out of cocktail lounges, and avoid drinking too much alcohol. You need to remain alert.

- Be aware of cultural taboos, behaviors, and modes of dress that are considered offensive in some areas. Do your research ahead of time.

DISRUPTIONS

Labor disputes that occur during an event can be extremely disruptive and will demand flexibility and some ingenuity. Transportation strikes can cause havoc with a meeting schedule. Alternative transport providers should be researched in advance.

If some element of the meeting is controversial, organizers can anticipate demonstrations and make provisions to ensure that they do not disrupt the event. You don't want a peaceful protest to turn into an angry confrontation, so take passive measures and get the cooperation of security and law enforcement officials (and perhaps publicity blackouts). The strategies described for domestic events earlier in this chapter also apply to meetings abroad.

Contingency planning is an integral responsibility of the meeting organizer. It is intended to ensure that unanticipated emergencies do not become disruptive crises.

Resources:

Rick de Treville, Hospitality Security Consultant: *rdetreville@hotmail.com*
American Society for Industrial Security in Alexandria, Virginia: www.asisonline.org
Bureau for Diplomatic Security, Department of State, Washington, D.C.: www.state.gov
Kroll International in New York, New York: www.krollworldwide.com

Part Five:

International Conferences and Multicultural Audiences

Chapter Eighteen
Managing International Events

In a 1989 interview with editors of *Meeting News*, John Naisbitt, author and futurist, made this prediction:

> Within the meeting business, my own guess is that in the next decade the most spectacular growth will be in international meetings.[1]

One of the major megatrends predicted by Naisbitt was that national and regional economics would give way to an integrated *global* economy. We have seen this developing trend in the proliferation of multinational corporations, international associations, and world-wide business services and networks. This broader perspective is generating a concomitant increase in global interaction (commercial, scientific, social, and cultural). For the meetings industry, this translates into more *international* meetings, as Naisbitt pointed out.

Elements of this trend manifested themselves during the last decade of the millennium. The Union of International Associations revealed that international congresses increased in frequency, though they declined in attendance and have become more specialized. The number of congresses increased from 3,100 in 1980 to well over 5,000 in 1995. UIA predicted that by the end of the decade, that figure would double again—and it did. And UIA's data do not include transnational association events or corporate meetings held abroad!

Though the influence of the corporate segment has stimulated this expansion, the most reliable yardstick for tomorrow's meetings (and, indeed, the future of the industry) is the proliferation of international

---

[1] Naisbitt ibid

associations. Associations, after all, develop out of the recognition of a common need to share information in specialized fields. They serve as bellwethers for the meeting industry's future direction.

The development of international associations reflects the greater emphasis now placed on this global perspective. Several important industry organizations came to be as a result of the need for information and education in the meetings field and especially for international conferences. Here are a few:

- American Society of Association Executives
- Association for Conferences and Exhibitions
- Foundation for International Meetings
- International Convention and Congress Association*
- International Association of Professional Congress Organizers*
- International Association of Convention and Visitors Bureaus*
- Meeting Professionals International*
- Professional Convention Management Association

Those designated by asterisks are members of the Joint Industry Council, a prestigious organization of international associations that serves as a forum on issues impacting the meetings industry worldwide. See Appendix A for a complete list.

TRANSNATIONAL AND INTERNATIONAL EVENTS

Before proceeding, it may be helpful to clear up some semantic confusion. *Transnational* events are those in which participants of one country travel off-shore or outside their borders to another country. *International* meetings, conferences, and congresses are those in which participants from two or more countries travel to a specific destination. For example, a conference held in Seattle, attended by Canadians and Americans, is an international meeting. In generic use, however, "international" refers to both.

While this book is intended for the professional meeting manager who is likely to be somewhat involved in international meetings, there is also a great deal of value to those planning a transnational meeting for the first time. Some readers might ask, "What has this to do with me? My company or association doesn't hold foreign meetings." Perhaps not *today*. What of tomorrow? And what of the organization you may be serving sometime in the future, if not your current employer?

Event organizers need to be knowledgeable about international meetings as well as domestic ones. This chapter will explore some of the facets of foreign travel and international event management.

Managing International Events

The good news is that most planning criteria for international meetings is identical to criteria for domestic events. The bad news is that one cannot go it alone without expert help. But more good news: help is readily available.

The Global PCO

Meeting and incentive organizers new to international events often approach the matter of protocol with apprehension, or they leave it to others. Even experienced planners who pay meticulous attention to matters of protocol and cultural diversity sometimes neglect to ensure that their delegates and participants are equally well-oriented in the finer points of international etiquette and customs.

Asked to distinguish between event planners who operate on a global scale and those whose responsibilities are confined to domestic meetings, McGettigan Partners CEO Christine Duffy offered these observations:

> It has to do with mindset. Most of the planners who work internationally maintain an open attitude and a curiosity about places and cultures that communicates itself to the people with whom they deal.
>
> Many are adventurous and prepared to take risks in search of the new unusual and exotic. They do not try to replicate the Chicago/ Orlando/ Las Vegas conference experiences in Rome, Cape Town or Hong Kong. The most successful global planners anticipate the learning process. Beforehand they learn how the locals operate and how their culture differs, then adapt accordingly. Afterwards they regard the event as a useful learning experience—whatever happened!

Finding Help

The planner who is considering a foreign destination for a meeting has access to a veritable cornucopia of data and information from a variety of resources. Consult resources for domestic meetings, as well as these helpful assets:

- National tourist offices (NTOs), which represent foreign countries in major cities; visit www.inquisitivetraveler.com

- Multinational marketing organizations such as the European Federation of Conference Towns (EFCT), the Asian Association of Convention and Visitor Bureaus (AACVB), and the International Association of Convention and Visitor Bureaus (IACVB), as well as their individual convention bureau members (see Appendix B for Web sites)

- The Bedouk International Directory, which is the leading reference for worldwide meeting facilities, convention bureaus, and support services in Europe, North and South America, Africa, Middle East, and Asia-Pacific; Incentives & Meetings International's Workbook, which is also a helpful source (see Resources)

- Destination management companies (DMCs), often organized into consortiums such as Euromic, Networld, Duyff International, etc.
- National and international airlines
- International offices of major hotel chains
- Professional congress organizers (also referred to as *PCOs*)

DESTINATION CRITERIA

Before selecting a destination, formulate a meeting profile the same way you do for a domestic event. Consider the meeting objectives, participant profile, time and distance allowances, tax impact, social and business agendas, time of year, and organizational policy. Then apply the following criteria to each proposed venue:

- Choice of airlines, flights, and lift capacities from key gateways
- Number, quality, and price ranges of hotels and meeting facilities
- Political stability and security considerations
- Favorable climate and seasonal factors
- Conformity with the objectives of the meeting
- Area's appeal to attendees
- Availability of adequate, competent ground and support services
- Variety of cultural and recreational attractions
- Presence of a host organization in a related field, if appropriate
- Relative ease of customs and immigration procedures
- Accessibility of city and/or hotels from international airport
- Access to tourist offices in major cities

Start with the National Tourist Office

First, contact the National Tourist Office (NTO) of the country under consideration. If there is no NTO, get in touch with the consulate. Most countries interested in attracting meetings business maintain offices in major metropolitan centers. These offices are staffed with competent professional people who understand the meeting planner's needs and are able to advise on the many facets of international meeting and incentive management.

NTOs can help arrange site inspection visits. Indeed, many of them schedule periodic destination study tours for qualified meeting planners. NTOs also work closely with airlines, hotels, and DMCs to assist with special site inspections where there is a potential for meeting business.

The NTO staff is a valuable information resource and subsequent liaison with suppliers in their country. They will advise on availability of hotels, meeting facilities, and discount seasons, and arrange contact with professionals who can best handle the event, such as reliable DMCs and Professional Congress Organizers (though they will seldom recommend a specific firm).

The NTO can provide site literature and information on social customs, attractions, and other valuable data. In some countries, the NTO or its convention bureau subsidizes or helps finance associations as an incentive for holding their meetings in those venues. NTOs and convention and visitor bureaus (CVBs), like their domestic counterparts, provide housing bureau services and support activities such as:

- Promotional assistance: Shells, brochures, maps, videos, mailings, etc.
- Letters of invitation from dignitaries
- Liaison with counterpart organizations and government offices
- Advice and assistance with pre- and post-conference tours
- Assistance with legal, tax, health, and security procedures
- Liaison with Customs and Immigration to expedite entry of attendees, exhibits, and meeting materials

National Tourist Offices can be a valuable resource if these guidelines are followed:

- Contact the tourist office well in advance of the meeting, even if only for information.
- Provide all available data on attendee profile, proposed time-frame, number of rooms required, meeting room needs, support services, and social and recreational programs.
- Information and recommendations regarding equipment, exhibits, and materials that must be shipped.

Many NTOs and convention bureaus have formed regional federations such as EFCT, AACBV, and their individual convention bureau members. These associations are valuable resources for regional information. (See Appendix A.)

BASIC PLANNING FOR OTHER CULTURES

PCOs experienced in international event management accept the fact that doing business in another country is different. Not necessarily more difficult—just different. There are cultural anomalies, for one thing. Christine Duffy makes these observations:

> Patience is a useful trait when dealing with some cultures. Most of us have to put aside our natural inclination "to get down to business" immediately. The smart planner takes time to get culturally acclimated and spends time getting to know the hosts and local suppliers. Establishing good relations at the outset can reap later benefits. As a corollary to that, savvy meeting professionals are slow to take offense and understand the meaning of "sympatico." It goes without saying that global event professionals are good networkers, who take great care to develop and maintain their international relationships.

Some experienced planners who pay meticulous attention to matters of protocol and cultural diversity sometimes neglect to ensure that their delegates and participants are equally well oriented in the finer points of international etiquette and customs.

Protocol is the lubricant that permits people of disparate cultural backgrounds to interact in an atmosphere of understanding and mutual respect. At any gathering of people from more than one culture and nationality, proper etiquette and decorum is essential to avoid embarrassment or affront. The customs governing such behavior vary according to culture and usage, but certain rules of protocol apply to most international events. For those responsible for organizing such gatherings, understanding those rules and acquiring cultural competence are essential.

Global PCOs avoid developing a geographical mindset. They understand that there is no European or Asian culture as such; each country has its own customs, culture, and taboos. And very often, within a country, there can be substantial regional differences.

"People from other countries tend to stereotype Germany as the land of lederhosen, Oktoberfest, and oom-pah-pah music," says Dieter Von Lehnsten of the Hamburg Convention Bureau. "That's not Germany," he claims. "It's Bavaria!"

Even North Americans, who tend to be informal, outgoing, and impatient with social niceties in business settings, have regional differences. French Canadians are also culturally different from their countrymen in Vancouver. Chicagoans have a social and cultural style that is distinct from that of people in Atlanta. But in spite of cultural differences, there are also similarities. The essential key to cross-cultural competence is to focus on the similarities while being sensitive to the differences.

A casual, first-name business style so common in Australia, Canada, and the United States is inappropriate in more-formal countries, particularly those in Asia, in the Middle East, and to a lesser extent in Europe. Study the cultural characteristics and business protocol of the destinations being considered, and keep in mind that even in English-speaking countries there are shades of meaning and nuances that can result in misunderstandings. Miscommunication is more likely to occur where other languages are involved, so put all communication in writing and confirm agreements reached in conversation with a memorandum.

In the planning stage, consider the following recommendations, which are specifically germane to international events.

Currency and Fiscal Management

Rates for accommodations, transportation, services, and other elements to be purchased on-site will vary from time of planning to time of the event because of currency fluctuations on the international exchanges. It is possible to plan for and lock in rates by means of a "hedge" or "future transaction." Check with the international department of a commercial bank or with a currency broker. (Details are covered later in this chapter.) It is also advisable to open a bank account at the destination well in advance of the event. This provides check-writing privileges on the account to settle bills. A letter of credit will likewise afford that flexibility. It is not a good idea to pay bills or send deposits in domestic currency (dollars in the case of North American organizations); always pay in the local currency. Otherwise, the vendor determines the exchange rate, which can be 5 percent to 15 percent higher than the bank's rate.

Administration

For international meetings involving delegates from many countries, it is advisable to establish an administrative office or secretariat in the host country to receive registrations and respond to inquiries.

Government Regulations

Check with the convention bureau or NTO for passport and visa requirements, as well as customs regulations regarding:

- Restrictions on items that can be brought in as personal baggage.
- What must be declared when entering or departing.
- Airport departure taxes and export restrictions.
- Bonding and other controls for equipment, products, and program materials (if extensive, use a customs broker and freight forwarder).
- Special taxes: Many countries charge a value-added tax (VAT) on all purchases. While this can run as high as 14 to 33 percent, some or all of it may be refundable upon departure.

Staff and Support Services

Organizers will probably call on outside sources and people to assume many of the functions normally performed by staff. It may not be cost-effective to take staff members to help with out-of-country events; if you hire locally, you can put together a staff that is collectively familiar with the area, language, resources, and local customs. In most cases, support staff and other services can be retained through a local Professional Congress Organization or a destination management company.

Program Support

When the meeting requires audiovisual support, it is advisable to rent equipment locally if a suitable rental service is available. Shipping is costly; equipment rented on-site will be compatible with electric current specifications. Video formats in Europe vary from one country to another and from most of Asia and North America; convert videotapes to the required format, and show them on equipment rented locally. Better yet, convert videotapes to DVD format, which is universal.

HOTELS AND FACILITIES

The criteria for selecting a hotel are much the same abroad as anywhere else, though the hotels themselves may not be the same. Older hotels in capital cities such as London, Rome, and Vienna may not have the extensive meeting facilities one is accustomed to finding in Australia, North America, and in later-developed cities. It has been customary in the traditional capitals to have a room block at a hotel and hold the meetings at a nearby conference center. Hotels built during the late 1900s and since have substantially increased meeting space.

When negotiating with hotels in general, negotiate for *service*, rather than price. If the selected hotel is part of a chain having international offices, involve the local representative from the beginning. As always, be sure to put all details agreed upon (including the specifics on meeting rooms) *in writing*. Unlike their North American counterparts, most hotels abroad charge for meeting space, though the rate is subject to negotiation. Include specific meeting rooms, dates, and hours in the contract and provide a sketch of each room setup to avoid misunderstanding. Acquire a working knowledge of the metric system and use it when designating distances and dimensions.

PROGRAM PLANNING

When proposing meeting programs at distant venues, consider the effects of lengthy flights and time zone changes. For instance:

- Do not plan business sessions on the first day, and keep social functions to a minimum so that participants have a chance to rest up.
- Avoid "over-programming" attendees. Allow adequate free time for sight-seeing and shopping.
- Offer pre- or post-conference tour options, to break up the trip.
- Arrange to have program materials printed on-site by sending graphic CDs or camera-ready art to save shipping costs, duty, and possible delay.
- Select awards and gifts locally. Products native to the country will be less expensive and more meaningful to recipients.
- Make use of local dignitaries and celebrity speakers. The NTO staff can assist with speaker selection and advise on protocol.

Addressing Multicultural Audiences

If the meeting is international rather than merely transnational or will include a substantial number of foreign guests, alert speakers that it is going to be a multinational audience. Presenters addressing an audience whose native tongue is other than their own need to follow certain guidelines to ensure rapport and effective communication of their message. Even though listeners are fluent in the speaker's language, certain nuances may elude them, resulting in misunderstanding or non-comprehension. Pass along the following pointers to program participants speaking before multinational groups:

1. Avoid the use of colloquialism and idiomatic or slang expressions.
2. Resist the temptation to demonstrate your vocabulary prowess with arcane and esoteric words such as "arcane" and "esoteric."
3. When giving examples or using analogies, don't be provincial. Instead, adopt a global perspective. Illustrate your comments with references to international cities such as Copenhagen, Tokyo, or Cairo, rather than Chicago or Los Angeles. Don't assume that the audience is familiar with North American geography (though most will be).
4. In referring to yourself, your government, or your industry, try not to use the term "United States"; say "North America," unless you are giving data specific to Canada or the United States.
5. Survey the audience to find out where they customarily travel and do business. If the talk is a technical one, ascertain their level of understanding and familiarity with the subject. But never talk down to them or appear condescending.

6. If the subject is a technical one, provide an outline or abstract containing as much detail as possible. It aids understanding and retention. If simultaneous interpretation (S/I) is used, supply copies of the presentation text to the interpreters to help with accuracy.

7. Recognize that even among English-speaking people (British, Australian, Canadian), some words, nuances, and connotations will carry different meanings.

8. If the speech is a ceremonial one, be sure you research, understand, and abide by the rules of protocol for the host country, particularly if dignitaries are in attendance.

9. Make use of visual aids if possible. Pictures are universal, and greatly aid in comprehension.

10. Develop a working knowledge of metrics, at least with respect to distance (kilometers), dimensions (meters), area (square meters), and temperature (Celsius). (See Resources for a list of easy conversion formulas.)

11. Conclude the presentation with a summary of the key points. To achieve rapport, end with a quote from a source known and respected by the audience: a poet, a philosopher, a statesman, or a religious leader.

12. If a question-and-answer session is scheduled, be sure the speaker repeats all the questions before responding.

GOING THE DISTANCE: INTERNATIONAL AIRLINES

The choice of an airline for a foreign destination served by more than one carrier is contingent on the airline's reputation for service and safety, frequency of flights, scheduling, and lift capacity—much as with domestic travel. Security considerations can also influence the choice. PCOs experienced in foreign travel will contact several carriers that meet their criteria and compare the eligible ones, weighing their advantages and limitations. The objective is to select one official airline, thus exploiting negotiating position.

Organizers now have more options in the choice of airlines. International carriers have expanded their routes while increasing lift capacity and frequency. The choice is further enhanced by alliances and code-sharing between regional and major carriers. Code sharing is an ad hoc "free sale" partnership among two or more airlines by which each partner carrier has full access to the other airlines' flight inventory. This explains why passengers booked on one carrier find a notation on their boarding passes advising them that the flight is operated by another airline. To the PCO, code-sharing translates into possible fare concessions and a greater choice of flights.

The latter is especially helpful when traveling to and from remote destinations that do not offer daily flights (which is true in many parts of the world.)

The prime consideration must be service rather than price. This is particularly important for international carriers that are somewhat restricted in fare pricing because of bilateral agreements. That is not to say that there is no room for negotiating price—there is. Domestic and international carriers apply revenue management analysis to compute fares. This allows carriers to calculate how many seats on a given flight can be sold at various price categories. The system also determines the number and percentage of discounted seats.

It is more critical that the PCO understand how international airlines operate and how concessions can often outweigh reduced fares. Do pay attention to fare discounts; many foreign carriers that are subsidized by their governments can be very competitive in fare pricing. But in the final analysis, foreign carriers, like their domestic counterparts, are dependent on revenue passenger miles for their profitability. One major difference, which works to the advantage of the organizer, is that national airlines, especially those that are government owned, have a vested interest in promoting their destination. As a planning strategy, negotiate air travel before the final decision is made on the destination.

Aside from the fare structure, there are a number of benefits and planning services an international air carrier can offer for group travel to and from a global event. In Chapter 8, we mentioned a few of these benefits. Here are several more:

- Assistance with customs clearances for passengers and freight
- First Class amenities, including beverages, for passengers in coach
- Advance group seat selection (which might include blocking off one or more cabins), with the organizer given the option of seat assignment
- Subsidies or special rates on accommodations at stopover cities during long-haul flights (these rates may be applied to overnight or day rooms)
- Off-airport check-in and baggage check (now rare, because of security concerns)
- On-site assistance with "post" trips, ticketing, and flight changes
- Reduced fares on cruises if they are booked in conjunction with the meeting
- For larger conventions, troupes of entertainers and folkloric performers that might be available to help promote the destination at the kickoff announcement

Within their prescribed limitations, airlines have some degree of flexibility in quoting guaranteed fares, usually with an advance deposit. This can be particularly helpful in the face of long lead times and currency fluctuations. Cancellation penalties and cut-off dates are also subject to negotiations.

Prior to designating an official airline for an off-shore event, the PCO conducts a distribution analysis to determine points of origin for all delegates planning to attend. Online research will indicate which carriers have the requisite gateways to serve those points and adequate lift capacity to the destination. At this stage, airlines can provide valuable counsel to meeting organizers. Some have full meeting departments staffed by personnel trained in accommodating conferences and incentive travel.

Last but not least, international airlines with their widespread networks are valuable sources of site information and planning assistance.

USING A DESTINATION MANAGEMENT COMPANY (DMC)

Destination Management Companies are usually full-service companies that can provide ground transportation, theme events, audiovisual support, temporary help, entertainment, and interpreters. They may act as prime contractor, subcontracting for any services required. In some venues, the convention bureau performs that function.

Generally, the overseas destination management company plays a more extensive role than its North American counterpart. It may negotiate for hotel rooms, function as a travel agency, and act as a facilitator in whatever role is required. During the planning phase, the DMC maintains frequent contact and uses creativity and intimate knowledge of the area to design a memorable program. It continues advising the PCO on all facets of the business and social agendas, local changes, and events that may impact the meeting positively or negatively.

Patti Roscoe, whose widespread destination management company specializes in global events says that DMCs can shepherd clients through the host country's cultural, religious, linguistic, monetary, and time-zone differences and can suggest ways to take advantage of local festivals and holidays.

Roscoe advises event managers who are planning incentive travel or post-conference options to include several cities in their programs. DMCs have relationships with local air, motorcoach, and rail transportation companies as well as relationships with affiliated destination managers. This facilitates their client's transport needs and often adds personalized service or entertainment en route.

The DMC generally looks after the client's interests. Because of their extensive involvement and the seriousness of their responsibility to their clients, DMCs are judged by higher standards of competence and performance than companies supplying solely ground services.

During operations, a full-service DMC can provide the following support services:

- Meet and greet attendees on arrival; assist with Customs expediting.
- Brief the group upon arrival at their hotel about currency exchange, banking hours, postage, shopping tips, protocol, and program overview.
- Staff a hospitality/information desk with multilingual personnel.
- Provide licensed, professional, multilingual guides for group excursions.
- Arrange with local restaurants for group meal functions or dine-around programs.
- Coordinate car rental reservations, as well as motorcoach supervision for group movement.
- Coordinate and supervise recreational and leisure events, off-site theme parties, and functions.
- Administer pre- or post-conference tours. Assist with travel itinerary changes, reservations, ticketing, and VIP coordination.
- Act as liaison with government agencies and arrange special services.
- Supervise media relations and publicity.
- Recommend, contract, and supervise entertainers, technical staff, conference aides, and administrative personnel.

WORKING WITH PROFESSIONAL CONFERENCE ORGANIZERS

In most countries, it may be advisable to retain the services of an independent meeting professional who specializes in international event management. As professional congress organizers, these PCOs are usually highly skilled, very professional, scrupulously ethical, and intimately familiar with the destination, including its attractions, customs, and resources.

The Professional Congress Organizer becomes the liaison between the meeting organization and the local convention bureau, hotel, and support service providers (which may include a destination management company.) Unlike DMCs that usually charge on a per-person basis, congress organizers receive a fee for their services. The PCO relieves the organizing committee or meeting executive of the many logistical and administrative details involved in a meeting of international scope, thus freeing them up to concentrate on the program and to participate fully. These functions include but are not limited to:

- Advice on accommodations and facilities; assistance in negotiations
- Assistance with Customs, taxation, and related government compliance
- Consultation on the program relative to local influences, customs, and peculiarities
- Budgeting advice based on the congress organizer's experience with similar events
- Arranging foreign bank accounts and letters of credit; collecting fees, disbursing funds to vendors; administering and auditing accounts
- Establishing a secretariat and arranging for staff and administrative services
- Supervision, receipt, and processing of registrations
- Contracting, organizing, and supervising exhibit services; collection of exhibitor fees and other exposition management functions
- Providing interpreters and multi-lingual staff members; arranging for translation, reproduction, and dissemination of proceedings and other meeting documents
- Advice on protocol, cultural differences, VIP handling, and security
- Supervision and coordination of support services and logistical or operational details
- Coordination of post-conference tasks, closing out of accounts, preparation and supervision of return shipments
- Post-conference critique and reconciliation of budget and expenditures

AUDIOVISUAL SUPPORT

Conference centers and the newer conference hotels in major meeting venues tend to have extensive audiovisual equipment that often rivals that found in North American cities. Multi-image presentations are as widely used abroad as they are is in this country. While comparable in sophistication and quality, AV media are, however, different. Computer-generated media follow a universal standard, and 16 mm film, overhead and slide projectors, microphones, and sound equipment are pretty much the same the world over. However, there are some disparities in electrical current: Multi-image productions, for instance, should be programmed on equipment capable of switching from 110 volt/60 cycle to 220 volt/50 cycle.

This is also true of video standards. As mentioned before, NTSC, the Japanese and North American standard for video, is not compatible with PAL formats found in most of Europe, Australia, Africa, and Southeast Asia nor compatible with the SECAM system used in France, Russia, and the Middle East. To show a video program produced in NTSC, it must first be converted to the appropriate format. If video is to be used, determine the standard in the host country and then locate a production company that can make the conversion.

Some might ask why it isn't better to simply convert the videotape to DVD, and avoid the standards problem altogether. Unfortunately, it's not that simple. In fact, DVDs can add another element of confusion. Here is a quick summary:

A DVD can be played in any computer anywhere in the world. As long as an LCD projector is connected, the DVD can be played for an audience. Though it will work, full screen playback on a computer will not look as good as regular playback through a DVD player. On the other hand, if the playback medium is a regular DVD player and not a computer, the same NTSC/PAL/ SECAM rules will apply, since the player is producing a video signal in the country's standard.

Professional standards and levels of expertise vary widely from one country to another, just as they do from site to site in domestic venues. The in-house AV contractor so common in North America is relatively rare in other parts of the world. In most foreign venues, expect to be dealing with an audiovisual rental firm, or the house AV staff. Supervisory staff will be bilingual, but don't expect bilingual stage hands, cameramen, or projectionists.

These technical considerations should not deter organizations from incorporating audiovisuals in their events abroad. On the contrary! The impact of music and visuals can be powerful aids in communicating, motivating, and ensuring comprehension. Translation of narrative and playback in multiple languages is the best solution. Discriminate sound tracks on DVD, audio, and videotape make this option quite feasible at the presentation phase. Before arriving at that stage, however, these principles should be part of the planning during production:

- Have the script translated by professionals who are native to each country. Verify the translation with people familiar with the vernacular.
- Keep words to a minimum on data projection type slides or callouts.
- Use generic visuals that focus on pictures, numbers, or universal symbols.
- If English is the conference language, caution the narrator to avoid slang and idiomatic language. This is also recommended for narratives that must be translated.

EXHIBITING ABROAD

The decision to exhibit at a foreign trade show, or to incorporate exhibits in a meeting abroad should be approached with a full appreciation of the marketing value of such a strategy and an understanding of what it entails. The sponsor must weigh the benefits against the expenditure of time and funds and the additional logistics. The task is somewhat lessened for organizations that have branch offices, affiliates, or effective counterparts in the host country. Nevertheless, for such organizations, and certainly for those lacking such convenient resources, a thorough analysis of market reach, competing shows and their venues, and availability of services is mandatory.

Diane Silberstein, an authority on international exhibitions, offers this illuminating comparison:

> According to the Union of International Fairs, the first time people got together to exchange their wares was the **Foire de Saint Denis** near Paris, founded in 629 A.D. Europe still accounts for the majority of the world's largest fairs and its practices have influenced how much of the rest of the world conducts exhibitions. When we exhibit elsewhere in the world we play by their rules. And those rules can be substantially different.
>
> Unlike the United States, where shows take place every six months to one year, major international trade fairs may be held bi- or tri-annually. Geneva Telecom, the prime event for the telecommunications industry, is held every four years. The infrequency of these fairs and the distance people travel to get to them leads to longer show schedules. Also in contrast to the customary five-day or less North American show, the major international fairs are a minimum of seven days and can last as much as one month or more.
>
> This adds a new dimension to "booth duty." Staffing the show and setting staff schedules must be carefully planned.
>
> Furthermore, major North American cities like Chicago, New York, Las Vegas, Toronto, Vancouver, and Atlanta have convention complexes in their urban centers. The fairgrounds of Europe can be large tracts of land considerable distances from their host cities. Hannover Fairs, the world's largest fairground, has over 5 million square feet of indoor space in 27 separate halls, for a total footprint of almost 11 million square feet. Compare this to Chicago's McCormick Place with 2.2 million square feet of meeting and exhibit space in two halls, the largest facility in North America. The distance and size of the fairground will affect your transportation mode and budget, as well as the length of time at the show.
>
> Attendees of all levels come to international shows, including senior business executives, government officials and heads of state. Many of the international shows boost revenue by inviting the public to attend on certain days.

Attendee Assessment

Analyze the potential audience: Are they primarily domestic in scope, or international? For existing shows, ask the organizers for attendance history, demographics, and audit reports, if available. Seek out exhibitors and solicit their views.

Logistics

Ascertain fixed and variable costs, the language used in display and promotional materials, show hours, and booth sizes. (In most countries, booths are called "stands" and size is expressed in meters.) Read the regulations thoroughly and pay particular attention to special government regulations, union rules, and tax laws. If the show organizers have an office in your country, work directly with them. The commercial attaché at the embassy or consulate can be a valuable resource, as are international airlines, Customs brokers, and forwarding agents.

The U.S. Department of Commerce and the Canadian Ministry of Trade can offer valuable information and assistance with promotion, market data, expedited shipments, export licenses, and related services. Other useful strategies for exhibiting abroad include:

- Increase your lead time. Two years for planning is not unreasonable.
- Supplement your promotion budget to allow for translation, multilingual printing, and increased mailing costs.
- Allow additional time for mailing and responses.
- Investigate having the translation and printing done abroad.
- Increase the operating budget by 100 percent to 200 percent over domestic shows. Then add a budget line item for contingencies.
- Check with the convention bureau for competitive events, national holidays, and other factors that may interfere.
- Make provisions for collection and disbursement of funds and for the filing and payment of local taxes.
- Select a freight forwarder who is experienced with overseas shipments.
- Ascertain legal distinctions between exhibit materials to be re-exported and promotional and advertising materials or souvenirs left behind. Learn which materials, including prizes and trophies, are subject to duty fees.
- Have the customs broker advise on booth equipment, audiovisual needs, and office equipment (including requirements for bonds and permission for goods and services to enter the country).
- Be aware that some countries draw a distinction between visas granted to meeting attendees and those intended for business activity (which may include exhibitions).
- If bringing entertainers, ask about waivers on work permits and union jurisdictions. Consider hiring local entertainers.

Design Dilemmas

One can never begin the design and construction process early enough. A minimum of 12 to 18 months lead time is preferable; this allows flexibility to deal with communication issues, time differences, and financial requirements such as currency conversions and wire transfers. You should also consider such a long-range timetable for availability, exhibit-space planning, hotel accommodations, and hospitality venues.

Construction techniques, materials, and codes also vary from U.S. standards. On the very basic level, "pipe and drape" is replaced by what is referred to as hard wall "shell scheme." It is common to custom build exhibits on-site, especially when there are long set-up times available (months, in some cases). Setup on the floor of a European exhibition hall looks more like your exhibit builder's shop: table saws, drill presses, sawdust, even pneumatic paint sprayers—everything needed to create an exhibit. The high demand for exhibits results in smaller hall footprints that translate into multi-storied exhibits.

Given the size of trade fairs and the distance from services, "stands" or booths often do much more than simply showcase graphics and hardware. They must be functionally designed to accommodate information centers, conference seating, increased storage requirements, and refreshments, if possible. On-site, it is the builder and not the general contractor who will be the best resource for labor, cleaning, plants, etc.

Protocol

In North America, an admission badge contains a volume of data about a visitor. The rest of the world guards this information very closely. Badges and reader cards almost do not exist. Capturing lead information is back to the basics—engaging in conversation, asking thoughtful questions, and taking the time to communicate to a non-native speaker. An absolute must is to have a comfortable place within the booth to sit and talk.

The casual, informal behavior that is commonplace at North American shows may not be appropriate at European or Latin American events, and it is definitely frowned upon in Asia. At such exhibitions, be sure to follow these rules:

- Adapt a more reserved demeanor.
- Set and keep punctual time/date appointments with prospects.
- Exchange business cards.
- Refer to people by their family names and titles, unless invited to do otherwise (Mr. Smith, Chairman Riley, etc.).
- Dress appropriately and avoid casual attire (unless it is appropriate for your product or service).

Incidentally, think metric—the rest of the world does! The metric system is decimal-based, so it's actually much easier than inches and feet.

PREPARING PARTICIPANTS

Experienced meeting and incentive executives recognize that preparing participants for an international journey is much different than preparing for domestic travel because it involves a whole new body of knowledge for planners and attendees. Even sophisticated, experienced travelers are inclined to overlook some details. This can prove embarrassing and cause inconvenience upon arrival.

At the minimum, prepare a packet of information for each attendee that includes the following:

1. *Destination brochure.* The brochure you send out should contain a good map and complete information on the host country and city. Brochures are usually available at convention bureaus and national tourist offices.

2. *Passport and visa requirements.* Provide policies regarding visas, fees, and the address of the consulate or embassy. Recommend that attendees make a photocopy of their passport in case of loss and bring extra passport-size photographs with them on the trip.

3. *Currency information.* Suggest that attendees prepare small-denomination currency packets for each country to be visited or transited. Recommend that they use travelers' checks in foreign currency, and provide the name, address, and service hours of a bank near the hotel.

4. *Automobiles.* Supply driving and highway regulations and auto rental rates and agencies. International driver's licenses, once mandatory for driving abroad, are no longer required; most countries accept domestic licenses.

5. *Insurance.* Suggest that attendees purchase special coverage or a floater policy for personal property and a casualty floater for auto rental (if a traveler's policy has exclusions). Give attendees a list of sources for travelers' medical insurance coverage.

6. *Medical situations.* Suggest that people bring a refill prescription for all medications and an extra pair of eyeglasses. Request a medical profile for each of your elderly attendees, attendees with disabilities, and those requiring restricted diets or special attention.

7. *Ground arrangements.* Provide full information on transfers, vouchers (if used), courtesy transportation, taxi fares, and mass transit.

8. *Baggage handling.* Give attendees information on baggage (weight limitations, special tags, "hot" tags, Customs clearance points, group expediting procedures, etc.).

9. *Hotel information.* Include a hotel brochure with full address, telephone number, e-mail address, fax number, and locator map. Provide the direct-dialing country code and city code for relatives and business associates. Give telephone rates and surcharges for calls from the hotel.

10. *Electrical, phone, and data transmission outlets.* Ascertain and inform attendees of the types of outlets available at their hotel, and suggest that they bring adaptors.

11. *Secretariat.* If there is one, provide the full name, address, e-mail, phone/fax, name of contact, and event name.

12. *Cultural information.* Provide "good-to-know" details about cultural differences, local customs, taboos, dress code, dining, social customs, festivals, holidays, and ethnic foods.

13. *Protocol for business and social activities.* Explain the proper formal and familiar forms of address and any appropriate protocol for dignitaries and guests. State the appropriate attire for all functions.

14. *Clothing.* Provide other clothing and dress requirements for men and women for social, business, and recreational activities. Include information on the effect of climate on attire.

15. *Security.* If you will meet in a potential-risk area, offer advice on precautions, conduct, profile, and emergency information.

16. *Government policies.* Supply information regarding restrictions on local travel, funds, alcoholic beverages, pets, drugs, firearms, and other controlled items. Include tax information such as VAT, refunds, and departure taxes.

17. *Legal.* Provide the address and phone number of the consulate and any other useful information on law enforcement policies and procedures that will be followed if an attendee is detained or arrested. Include the name of a host-government official who is familiar with your event.

18. *Services.* Provide information on international business centers and services, and the address of the nearest American Express office.

19. *Phrase book.* Include a pocket-sized card or booklet of phrases in the host language, such as helpful phrases and social niceties.

For first-timers and inexperienced travelers, provide:

- U.S. Customs regulations
- Airport diagrams and transit procedures for passengers

- A recommended packing list, such as a flashlight, umbrella, electrical adaptors, travel alarm, and similar travel aids
- Steps to take before leaving home (e.g., advise neighbors or relatives, leave itinerary, advise police, hold mail, stop newspapers, etc.)

MANAGING FOREIGN CURRENCY AND FINANCES

Competent meeting and incentive executives who are otherwise undaunted by what is needed for international events have been known to succumb to chronic anxiety syndrome when facing relatively common decisions relating to foreign currency and exchange. Some seem to ride boldly through the gauntlet of language, customs, cultural differences, protocol, and long-haul travel, yet hoist the white flag when the monetary monster rears its crenellated head. But have no fear! This beast can turn into a pussycat when properly handled.

Managing fiscal matters takes no more than common sense and expert advice available at a bank offering international exchange. First, acquire a basic understanding of fiscal and monetary exchange principles and a passing familiarity with the terms. For expert advice, first go to the bank's international department, which deals routinely with such matters as currency futures, forward transactions, and letters of credit. It also has the resources, through correspondent banks and overseas branches, to meet the event's financial needs in most countries. If the sponsor's bank does not have an international department, it may be best to consult one of the prominent multinational banking concerns (Barclay's, Citibank, Credit Suisse, or Sumitomo), depending on the site.

There are also a number of international currency brokers and accounting firms that provide advisory as well as actual monetary services. Of the former, American Express, GCI Financial, and OzForex are the best known and most widespread. In the second category, consult KPMG International or Price-Waterhouse-Coopers. A helpful, guidebook, "Foreign Exchange Information—A Worldwide Summary" is available from Price-Waterhouse. In addition, the local offices of national tourist organizations can provide valuable data on currency, as well as a wealth of information on taxes, government regulations, and related matters.

The wise manager seeks expert advice in areas outside his or her expertise. But a basic familiarity with foreign currency matters is valuable, if only to formulate one's questions. Here are some useful definitions the meeting manager needs to be familiar with these areas, defined below:

- *Bank draft.* A check drawn on a domestic bank with a face value expressed in foreign currency is the most economical means of paying foreign vendors.

- *Currency options.* Negotiating options to purchase foreign currency at a predetermined price during a specified period, as a hedge against currency fluctuations. A premium is charged for the privilege.
- *Forward contract.* A more binding transaction that locks in a guaranteed rate for sale or purchase of a stipulated amount of currency on a specified future date.
- *Eurodollars* (Euro). The medium of exchange established by the European Council of Ministers. Each country's currency is fixed daily in terms of European Currency Units or ECUs. Permits planners to contract at ECU rates.
- *Spot price.* Current price at which a currency trades, expressed in dollars or Euros. Fluctuates daily and hourly.
- *Cross rates.* Price levels established between two other world currencies, expressed in the domestic currency (e.g., Egyptian Pounds vs. Yen in dollars). Applies when visiting several countries and you wish to convert excess foreign currency to another foreign currency, rather than exchanging it for your own.
- *Letter of credit.* A monetary instrument issued by a bank that permits the holder to draw, up to the specified amount on that account at correspondent banks abroad. It may be drawn in dollars or in foreign currency at the spot price in effect at the time it is issued.
- *Value-added tax.* VAT taxes are national government taxes added to goods and services purchased abroad. The tax varies for each country and may be refundable to foreign nationals.
- *Carnet.* Essentially a visa for goods and equipment to enter a country, with a bond posted to guarantee that it will be exported (thus avoiding duty charges).

A Scenario

The Long Life Insurance Company is planning an incentive meeting for its Hot Shot Club producers. The venue is the Moon Palace Resort, a lovely resort complex on the lush Costa Maya beaches of Mexico's Mayan Peninsula. The proposed date is a year away. Now, anyone who has been reading the newspaper knows that the Mexican peso is subject to inflationary pressures. On the other hand, the dollar isn't always consistent either.

"Nervous" Olsen, Long Life's meeting manager, has been given a ground cost budget of $1,400 per head. At an exchange rate of 10 pesos to the dollar, that translates to 14,000 pesos.

The incentive house has come up with a proposed ground package of 12,000 pesos per head. It submitted a nine-month schedule of deposits in order to hold the dates at the popular resort and to ensure availability of support services. That's lower than budgeted, but the peso has been fluctuating as much as 12 percent against the dollar. Who knows where it will be in twelve months? What to do?

Long Life could buy pesos at the current rate to cover the deposit and subsequent payments, thus protecting their budget. But that means loss of working capital over an extended period of time—hardly sound fiscal management for an insurance company. They could always wait and continue to monitor the currency market, buying pesos when rates are favorable. But who can predict the vagaries of *that* volatile market? Not even the company's visionary actuaries! Being naturally a nervous type—hence his nickname—Olsen consults their bank's international manager.

This astute individual points out that Long Life could buy a forward contract for the full amount of the needed funds. This is a 100 percent hedge. It requires a 10 percent deposit to lock in the rate. That solution is easier on working capital, but since the number of qualifiers may fall below the budget estimates, Long Life may end up having to sell some of the contracted pesos at an unknown rate of exchange. Instead, this knowledgeable banker suggests a forward contract for 50 percent of the needed funds at the current rate, purchasing the balance as required by the schedule of payments. Thus, even if the dollar weakens as much as 15 percent against the pesos—an unlikely possibility—the budget is protected. If the dollar strengthens, Olsen can purchase the remaining funds at a better rate, which is a win-win solution.

VALUE-ADDED TAX RECOVERY

The Sixth EEC VAT Directive, implemented in 1988, allowed organizations from countries outside the EEC to recover much of the value-added tax on purchases and hotel, restaurant, and service charges in Europe. For organizations to do so, however, they needed patience, tenacity, and the services of a local tax attorney. Original invoices and extensive documentation was required, and each of the member countries set its own rules. (That deplorable situation was somewhat relieved in 1992 by Council Directive.) Still, the process can be time-consuming and expensive. However, considering tax rates of 14 to 33 percent, the tax refund on major expenditures may be well worth the effort, but organizations must factor in the cost of a local tax expert, who will charge a commission of 7.5 to 11 percent for this service.

To learn more:
http://europa.eu.int/comm/taxation_customs/taxation/vatindex_en.htm

AVOIDING CUSTOMS AND IMMIGRATION BOTTLENECKS

All countries tend to guard their frontiers to ensure that goods and materials imported meet customs regulations. It is the responsibility of customs officials to levy the appropriate duty fees for those products that are imported. Within the meetings industry, there are frequent exceptions to the rule involving importation of materials, equipment, and supplies that will be consumed or transported to another country or point of origin. Yet another set of rules apply to passenger baggage, gifts, and goods for personal consumption. How these are treated varies according to category, use, and country. Organizers planning an event abroad should contact that country's consulate for specific information regarding passports, visas, and customs documents. The thumbnail guide that follows should be helpful.

Personal Baggage

Arrange for all group luggage to be unloaded and cleared through Customs together. The use of distinctive luggage tags and arrangements with the airline can ensure the former; airline representatives or a DMC can arrange the latter and also overcome language difficulties. Be sure that everyone understands the limitations on funds and controlled substances, such as liquor and cigarettes (and in some countries, reading materials). Magazines such as *Penthouse* and *Playboy* are frowned on in most Muslim destinations. Narcotics, of course, are anathema in almost all countries, and many of them use sophisticated sensing equipment and sniffer dogs to prevent their entry. In Malaysia and Thailand, possession of drugs carries the death penalty! Such exceptions aside, grouping all personal baggage tends to result in favorable treatment, aside from the customary security inspections.

One knowledgeable PCO, having faced many times the frustration of ambiguous Customs practices in a certain Latin country, now has all materials, including even audiovisual equipment, carried by his staff as personal baggage. He swears that he never has a problem, though this practice is not for the faint of heart. A reasonable quantity of gifts can also be brought into the meeting country with personal baggage. A particularly trouble-free gift idea always appreciated by people in the host country is to bring pictorial books from your own country or region. Sound judgment must be exercised, however. Don't expect to breeze through Customs with five cases of *Springtime in Fairbanks* for giveaways at the booth.

The other side of the coin is the process for clearing Customs on the return home. Obtain and disseminate to your team the current regulations governing:

- The amount of gifts and purchases that can be brought home duty-free.
- Which items should be declared and listed individually.
- Which items carry a quantity limit or are prohibited altogether.
- The amount of duty payable on goods exceeding the exemption.
- The currency or form of payment that will be acceptable to the Customs bureau.

When it comes to expensive items taken abroad (cameras, jewelry, furs, foreign-label clothing), those in relatively new condition should be accompanied by proof of purchase or a dated appraisal and photograph. Otherwise, they should be registered before departure. In most countries, only serial-numbered items can be registered, but once that is done, the same document will suffice for subsequent trips.

Passports, Visas, and Health Records

Attendees must be advised well in advance of departure to apply for a passport, or to make sure that theirs is current. Some travel organizers include passport applications with their initial mailing. It is a good idea to have travelers make a photocopy of the inside cover and first page of the passport. This speeds replacement in case of loss, and serves as identification.

Visa regulations vary from one country to another. The PCO is responsible for researching visa requirements and assisting attendees in making applications, usually through the organization's travel representative. For groups traveling together, it is possible to arrange for group visas. Be aware that countries may require visas of certain nationals and not others. Even if all passengers originate from one country, determine whether or not the group includes resident foreign nationals, as they may be subject to different visa regulations. Government passport offices and sub-agencies can usually provide a booklet entitled *Visa Requirements of Foreign Governments*. If a travel agency assists with the planning, it will normally process visa applications. Keep in mind that even countries that do not require visas for individual travelers or convention delegates may demand that paid staff and speakers apply for business visas. Clarify these points with the travel counselor or the NTO representative.

There are some countries for which inoculations are required or advised. Some areas are known to have a high incidence of malaria, amoebic dysentery, hemorrhagic fever, SARS, or other exotic disease. Travelers to those regions should obtain the necessary inoculations or be prepared to show a proof of current immunization. Caution attendees on this point. Health authorities can detain, inoculate, and isolate travelers who are not properly immunized—not a very happy prospect for one's overseas adventure. For diseases such as malaria, a daily preventive prescription is advised. Contact the World Health Organization or the NTO for information on required and recommended immunizations.

Shipping Materials and Equipment

With the tremendous expansion of air cargo service over the past few decades, air freight is now an economical option and is thought to reduce the possibilty of damage or theft. Generally, ocean freight is not much cheaper for shipments under ten tons than air cargo, though delivery time is vastly different and container-construction costs are higher. For surface shipments of intra-continental freight between points in Europe or within North America, truck and rail freight may be a suitable option, time permitting.

Even the most astute PCOs contract for the services of a transportation coordinator, Customs broker, or forwarding agent. These professionals can handle all of the documentation and transportation required to get materials from point of origin to meeting site and back. And their nominal fees are well worth the savings in problems, delays, and unforeseen expenses. The shipper can arrange all documentation, including carnets, bonds, and manifests, but can also help ensure trouble-free transportation. Here is a list of important tasks:

- Prepare accurate lists of contents, by container, with particular attention to correct serial numbers, where applicable. Number and label all cases, and include the case number on the manifest.

- Enter the weight. Some countries calculate duty by weight.

- Prepare invoices listing the value of all items. Separate materials will need to be distributed, such as product literature, giveaways, etc.

- Containers should be readily opened and resealed (but not too readily).

- Avoid having a shipment arrive on a holiday, on a weekend, or the day before a holiday or weekend so that there will be adequate clearance time.

- If transiting countries, have the carnet stamped at each frontier. (This is no longer applicable in EU-member nations.)

- Use a local freight forwarder who is familiar with the regulations and knows local customs officials.

If truck transport is utilized in Europe or the United Kingdom or between North American countries, the key to smooth transit is experienced transport drivers. They tend to have cordial relationships with customs officials and know how to avoid some of the problems that face less-knowledgeable drivers. They also take pride in their work, and exhibit a protective attitude toward the freight they carry. Consult a freight forwarder about this point.

No treatise on shipping practices would be complete without at least a passing reference to a rather sensitive subject. Call it *baksheesh, grease, gratuity, mordera,* or whatever euphemism applies to that "little something extra" that seems to be an inescapable fact of life in international shipping. In many countries, it is an accepted practice that carries no opprobrium, though its legal status may be questionable. Nevertheless, it is the lubricant that allows goods to move smoothly across national borders. It may be as blatant and obvious as a medium-denomination bill inside the document envelope or a pack or a carton of cigarettes (or something more subtle). One conference organizer includes extra "take-out" gifts when he ships give-away calculators, coffee mugs, or T-shirts (always a popular item).

Special precautions are in order for audiovisual, video, and computer software. Customs officials seem to take great delight in hassling speakers who carry DVDs, VCR tapes, or the distinctive Kodak Carousel tray boxes. Speakers have recounted tales of usurious bonds on a tray of slides to be used in their presentation. For the few who still use the standard American Carousel trays, be aware that they do not readily fit the Kodak SAV projectors used in the rest of the world. It is best to transfer the slides to DVDs or video (although they may also be suspect). This obsession with these types of software apparently stems from Customs officials' inherent mistrust of anything that cannot be readily examined. To avoid problems and potential delay of program materials, either have them shipped in bond or shipped as personal baggage.

There is also some ambiguity surrounding consumable goods (i.e., prizes, gifts, literature, and supplies). Very few countries have specific rules such as those governing durable goods. They are not listed on a carnet, since they are not re-exported. The safest tactic is to supply proof of purchase and a statement of the purpose for which the goods are being brought in, with a copy sent ahead to the ministry responsible for tourism or to the convention bureau.

Understanding Customs Documentation

The *Convention Industry Council Manual* suggests that the following documents be prepared to accompany shipments:

- *Commercial invoice.* An inventory of goods shipped, listing the value of each class of item.
- *Carnet.** A document that permits duty-free entry of goods into foreign country and free transit or re-entry into the country of origin.
- *Export license.* A document authorizing export of sensitive technical or military materials.
- *Certificate of origin.* A formal statement from a government agency stipulating that the goods originated from a specific country.
- *Export declaration.* Required by some governments on shipments exceeding a stated value, export declaration is used by the U.S. government to monitor the dollar volume of export shipments. Check with the customs broker.
- *Limited power of attorney.* Authorizes the customs broker to complete customs documents on return of your shipment to the point of origin.

SUMMARY OF KEY PLANNING POINTERS:

- Check for a counterpart organization in the country or, for corporate events, branch offices and affiliates. If feasible, involve them in the planning as well as the program.
- Appoint an official airline. Aside from some fare concessions, the carrier will offer other valuable services such as early group boarding, in-flight welcome, and baggage and freight expediting.
- A site-inspection trip is essential; even more than for domestic meetings. Ask the congress organizer, the destination meeting coordinator, or the convention bureau liaison to make arrangements and to accompany you. Try to schedule the trip for the same time of year as the meeting in order to observe climate, tourism volume, and other conditions.
- Prepare detailed contingency plans that cover medical emergencies, security provisions, lost passports, and other crises. Keep in mind that procedures and laws are different in other parts of the world.

---

* ATA Carnets eliminate the need to pay value-added taxes (VAT) and duties, as well as the posting of security normally required at the time of importation. Call the Carnet Helpline at 1-800-ATA-2900 or e-mail carnets @ atacarnet.com.

- Provide participants with detailed advance information on the country, the venue, social customs, appropriate dress, and other pertinent details described earlier in this chapter.

Without a doubt, planning and executing a meeting in another country place greater demands and responsibilities on the meeting executive. However, the anticipation and rewards of an offshore destination far outweigh the added planning burden. Global travel broadens the delegates' perception and gives them a heightened perspective of the world at large. It opens opportunities for new business contacts and access to other viewpoints. It contributes to an environment that can dramatically enhance the meeting and ensure achievement of its objectives.

Resources:

> OFF-THE-CUFF METRICS
> Here are some easy-to-remember formulas—not exact, but functional enough for everyday use:
>
> A meter is about 3 inches longer than a yard.
>
> An inch is roughly 2.5 centimeters. A foot is about 30 centimeters.
>
> 100 kilometers is 60+ miles.
>
> Divide square feet by 10 to get approximate square meters.
>
> Multiply square meters by 11 to get approximate square feet.
>
> A liter is about a quart (liquid).
>
> A kilo is just over two pounds.
>
> 100 grams is 3+ ounces.
>
> A hectare is 2.5 acres.
>
> Metric/Imperial tables on the Net: *www.metric.fsworld.co.uk*
> *www.allmeasures.com*
>
> To convert from Celcius to Fahrenheit, double the number and add 32. To reverse it, subtract 32 and then divide by two. That's close enough! And once you understand that everything in the metric system is divisible by ten or 100, you realize how convenient metrics can be.

Professional Meeting Management, by Tony Carey. MPI Publications (www.mpinet.org)
Planning International Meetings, put out by ASAE Publications (www.asaenet.org)
Bedouk Worldwide Directory (www.bedouk.com)
The Workbook, put out by Incentives and Meetings International (www.i-mi.com)

HEALTH INFORMATION:
Foreign Travel Immunization Guide available from the U.S. Centers for Disease Control (www.cdc.gov)
International Association for Medical Aid to Travelers (advisory service; www.iamat.org)
Travel Assistance International (Medical emergency insurance; www.travelassistance.com)
International SOS (Travelers' Medical Insurance; www.internationalsos.com)

CUSTOMS AND IMMIGRATION:

Visa Requirements of Foreign Governments, put out by the U.S. Bureau of Consular Affairs, State Department, Washington D.C. (www.travel.state.gov/)

Know Before You Go, put out by the U.S. Customs Office, Washington D.C. (www.customs.ustreas.gov/)

Guide to Canada Customs, available through Canada Customs (canadaonline.about.com/cs/customs)

Some of these resources are also available from regional Customs offices and consulates.

EXHIBITING ABROAD:

International Exhibitors Association (www.cix.co.uk)

International Trade Administration, Department of Commerce, Washington, D.C. (www.ita.doc.gov)

More information is available through Department of Commerce offices in most cities.

348 *International Conferences and Multicultural Audiences*

(issuing Association)
(Association émettrice)

UNITED STATES COUNCIL FOR INTERNATIONAL BUSINESS, INC.

ATA/US/

INTERNATIONAL GUARANTEE CHAIN............ .... A.T.A. CARNET No. ▓▓▓▓
CHAINE DE GARANTIE INTERNATIONALE   CARNET A.T.A. No.

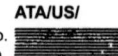

CARNET DE PASSAGE EN DOUANE FOR TEMPORARY ADMISSION
CARNET DE PASSAGE EN DOUANE POUR L'ADMISSION TEMPORAIRE

CUSTOMS CONVENTION ON THE A.T.A. CARNET FOR THE TEMPORARY ADMISSION OF GOODS
CONVENTION DOUANIERE SUR LE CARNET A.T.A. POUR L'ADMISSION TEMPORAIRE DE MARCHANDISES

(Before completing the carnet, please read notes on page 3 of the cover)
(*Avant de remplir le carnet, lire la notice page 3 de la couverture*)

CARNET VALID UNTIL..INCLUSIVE
CARNET VALABLE JUSQU'AU   *INCLUS*

ISSUED BY.......... **UNITED STATES COUNCIL FOR INTERNATIONAL BUSINESS, INC.**
DELIVRE PAR

HOLDER...
TITULAIRE

REPRESENTED BY*...
*REPRESENTE PAR**

Intended use of goods/*Utillisation prevue des marchandises*.......................................
....

EXPORTATION COUNTERFOIL No. ....   A.T.A. CARNET No. ▓▓▓▓
SOUCHE DE SORTIE No.   *CARNET A.T.A. No.*

---

1. The goods described in the General List under item No(s). ....
   Les marchandises énumérées à la liste générale sous le(s) no(s).

.... have been exported.
                                                                                  ont été exportées.

2. Final date for duty-free re-importation* / *Date limite pour la réimportation en franchise*.........

3. Other remarks* / *Autres mentions*...
....

| (Customs office) | (Place / *Lieu*) | (Date / *Date*) | (Signature and stamp) |
| *(Bureau de douane)* | | | *(Signature et Timbre)* |

* Delete if inapplicable. / *Biffer s'il y a lieu.*

EXPORTATION VOUCHER No. ....   A.I.A. CARNET No. ▓▓▓▓
VOLET DE SORTIE No.   *CARNET A.T.A. No.*
A) This carnet is valid until / *Le carnet est valable jusqu'au* .... inclusive. / *inclus.*
   Issued by / *Délivré par* **UNITED STATES COUNCIL FOR INTERNATIONAL BUSINESS, INC.**
   Holder / *Titulaire* ....
   Represented by* / *Représenté par**..

FIGURE 18-1 Carnet form.

Chapter Nineteen
Organizing and Hosting Multicultural Events

Many of the same elements involved in out-of-country international meetings apply to events held at domestic venues that include delegates from other countries. The task is simplified somewhat because the organizers are working on familiar ground, adhering to well-rehearsed practices. Unlike to exclusively "domestic" meetings, there will be additional considerations prompted by the many cultures represented by participants coming from several different countries. The host organization represents the host country (as well as the meeting sponsors) to the foreign guests. This expanded role calls for a global perspective and imposes certain demands that are not characteristic of national meetings.

Most large meetings involving a multinational audience are what we call "congresses," a term that will be used throughout this chapter. The purpose of an international congress is to provide a forum for the exchange of information among counterparts worldwide; to learn of recent advances in specific fields of knowledge or practice; to address problems common to other nations and seek solutions; and to establish dialogue with colleagues on a global scale. The sponsoring organization hopes that attendees will depart feeling enriched by newly gained knowledge that will benefit them and others in their industry or field of endeavor.

CONGRESS ORGANIZATION

As a rule, congresses fall into one of two categories. In the first category are events sponsored by an international society and held at least annually according to charter. These societies have permanent secretariats responsible for administration. The secretariat may also be responsible for planning and managing the congress in conjunction with the governing body and its appointed committees, or in concert with an organizing committee in the host country. The second category includes what are sometimes called ad hoc congresses. This type has no permanent patron, and the function of planning and hosting the event is rotated among member countries. Also in this category are congresses convened by members of an industry or discipline on a one-time or first-time basis. The patron may be a government, a university, a corporation, an interdisciplinary group, or a group organized just for that congress.

Committees

The organization and function of congress committees differ somewhat from domestic meetings where committees sometimes have an honorary role and most of the tasks are performed by paid staff. The secretariat of an international congress might be located halfway around the globe; committees manage much of the planning and operations. They are structured along functional lines under an overall organizing committee. A typical structure is shown in Figure 19-1.

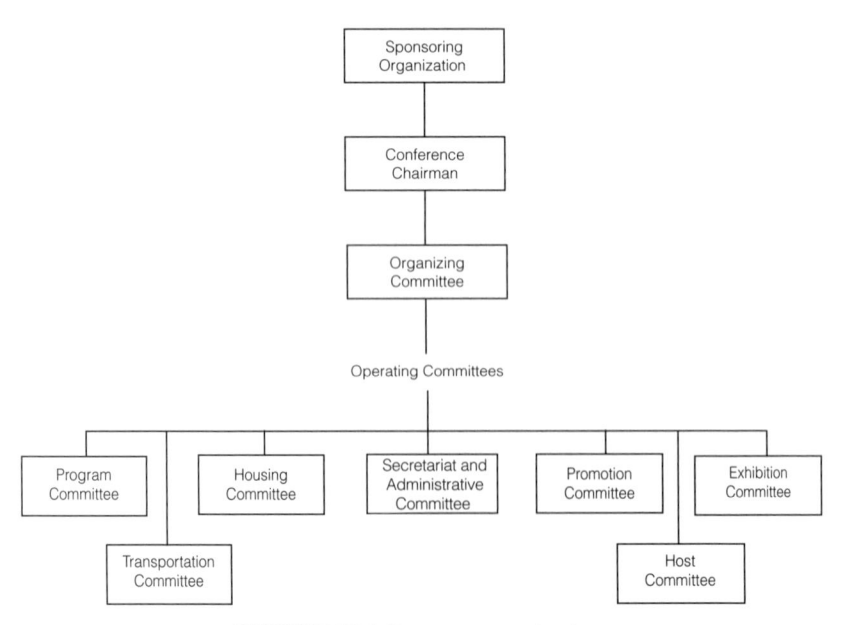

```
                    Sponsoring
                    Organization
                         |
                    Conference
                     Chairman
                         |
                    Organizing
                    Committee
                         |
                Operating Committees
                         |
  ┌──────────┬──────────┼──────────┬──────────┐
Program    Housing   Secretariat  Promotion  Exhibition
Committee  Committee     and      Committee  Committee
                    Administrative
                     Committee
     |                                  |
Transportation                       Host
Committee                          Committee
```

FIGURE 19-1 Congress organization.

The general chairman can be honorary. When that individual has the actual responsibility for the event, however, he or she usually chairs the organizing committee and the executive committee. The organizing committee has overall responsibility for planning the congress and supervising the tasks of the operating committees. It is usually composed of officers of the association, permanent staff members, and host country members representing the industry or discipline. Because committee members are often geographically dispersed, this body meets infrequently to establish guidelines and policy, and to review actions of the executive committee. The smaller executive committee actually manages and makes the decisions. It meets as often as monthly, and oversees the actions of all operating task groups, executes contracts in the name of the congress, approves disbursements, and directs the congress staff or secretariat.

Other committees have specific functions and responsibilities as outlined in the organization's bylaws or designated by the organizing committee. An excellent reference for detailed information about those functions is the *Manual for the Organization of Scientific Congresses* by Helena B. Lemp (see Resources).

Secretariat

The secretariat of an international congress should not be confused with an association's headquarters. The latter frequently has management responsibilities granted by the bylaws and is overseen by the governing body. Its staff members plan and manage the organization's conventions. A secretariat is more of an administrative body that might or might not want to be heavily involved in the planning and management of the congress, though it performs critical administrative and fiduciary roles. It also provides staff support to the executive committee and the operating committees, and serves as the administrative center for correspondence, purchasing, accounting, and disbursements.

The secretariat is managed by an administrative officer—a salaried professional who usually carries the title of executive secretary or secretary general. Under some congress arrangements, this position is filled by a professional congress organizer retained for the course of the event. Sometimes the international association maintains a permanent secretariat at its headquarters, which is responsible for all administrative duties during the planning phase before moving to the meeting site before the event begins. Another arrangement is to establish a satellite secretariat to support the executive committee on-site. This is particularly desirable when the congress is to be held at a destination remote from the permanent secretariat.

PLANNING CONSIDERATIONS

The planning process begins with a statement of objectives. If the meeting is one of a series of congresses held regularly but its venues alternate among member nationalities, objectives are likely to be defined in the organization's charter. Each meeting in the series should have other specific objectives. The objectives of an ad hoc event must be established by the organizers and clearly communicated to all participants.

Once consensus is reached on objectives and the decision is made to proceed with a congress, committees are organized and the planning group begins to address specific areas. Since languages and cultures at international meetings vary, the planners and staff need to understand how the differences affect meeting management functions. It is essential that you have effective communication between the secretariat and delegates, program committee and speakers, and presenters and delegates.

Demographics

An analysis of participant profiles determines factors influencing planning decisions. Consider these points:

- Organizational factors should be assessed. If all prospective delegates are members of the sponsoring organization, marketing and registration will be simplified. If not, additional time and budget allocations will be needed for market research.
- Socio-economic factors influence delegates' ability to afford transportation, registration fees, and housing.
- Cultural background and language fluency will determine the conference language and influence the program format, as well as food and beverage functions. Religion can also be a factor if the meeting dates conflict with religious observances important to many attendees.
- Attendance criteria should be assessed. Who will be invited? What are the requirements for eligibility? Will it be an open or a closed meeting?

Timetable

The planning group selects the meeting dates by analyzing preferred dates and taking into consideration events that might conflict or simultaneous events that might even boost attendance. Once registration deadlines are established, a planning schedule naturally evolves. Lead times for international events are longer than for domestic meetings: The average is two years, but substantially more lead time is needed as the number of attendees increases. The timetable must allow for the time-consuming process of having materials translated and then validated. Adequate time should be allotted for hindrances often encountered in international correspondence due to unexpected events (such as mail strikes and political unrest). E-mail and Web communication have somewhat lessened the impact of such delays, however.

Funding

A financial analysis forms the basis of the congress budget. Identify funding sources and address these questions: Will the congress be totally supported by registration fees? What other revenue sources are available? Sponsorships and grants? Subsidies? Exhibits? Will bridge funding be needed? From what sources? How will deficits be absorbed or surpluses distributed? Bridge funding (i.e., operating capital required for promotion and other expenses incurred prior to registration revenues) may come from several sources. The international association, if one exists, may underwrite organizational expenses. Funding may be provided by a patron, a corporation, a federation of associations, or even by a government agency of the host country as an incentive for holding the congress in that venue.

Venue

Selection of the domestic destination, hotels, and congress site for an international meeting should be based on the criteria presented in the preceding chapter. Attendance profile, facilities, and support requirements will influence the selection. Cities with large multicultural populations and a high percentage of bilingual staff in hotels and service industries have a distinct advantage. A key consideration may be to meet in a gateway city (one with an international airport) served by international carriers linking the delegates' originating cities. However, the availability of connecting flights to most major international gateways will determine whether or not you need to consider secondary venues.

PROGRAM CONTENT AND POLICIES

Initially, the program committee will have to prepare a tentative agenda and identify session formats for each day so that appropriate meeting facilities can be found. Subsequently, the committee attends to:

- Topics to be included and the session format for each.
- Selection and invitation of speakers, keynoter, and dignitaries; appointment of session chairmen or moderators; policy on their fees and/or expenses; complimentary registration for presenters.
- Calls for papers. Technical and scientific congresses follow a set protocol and policy when inviting speakers. The invitation includes a

request for a copy of presentations and abstracts of the topics to be presented. They must be submitted far enough in advance to allow time for translation, if needed, and reproduction for dissemination to delegates. The papers form the nucleus of the congress proceedings.

- Program support requirements (audiovisual equipment and staff, special staging or environment, special staff for security, room captains and aides, etc.).

Program design for multicultural and transnational meetings should reflect the organizers' concern for attendees who have traveled long distances. Adequate open or leisure time should be scheduled between sessions and at the end of the afternoon session so that delegates can meet with colleagues from other countries. Plan a free half-day on the second or third day and one or two open evenings. Formal sessions must follow the schedule precisely, remind speakers and session chairmen to adhere to the posted beginning and ending times.

The program committee should recognize that participating national and ethnic groups want to see their countrymen represented on the program. Speaker selection needs to reflect the international aspect of the event, but not all nationalities need to be represented. The program committee can create the appearance of multinational program participation in the designation of session chairmen, panelists, moderators, and event hosts.

LANGUAGE

English has become the *lingua franca* of international conferences, a fact most everyone acknowledges except perhaps the French. It is commonplace to see a Chinese scientist and a businessman from Bahrain carrying on a conversation in English. Nevertheless, it is necessary to designate the official language for the congress and arrange for translation of promotional and registration materials, handouts, papers, and proceedings. Plenary sessions will normally be in the conference language, but simultaneous interpretation (S/I) or concurrent interpretation may be needed for some attendees and some small-group sessions and social functions. In concurrent interpretation, the speaker pauses to allow interpretation—a preferred method for smaller sessions, but generally limited to a single interpretive language. Consecutive interpretation may be appropriate for plenary sessions where a significant number of attendees speak a tongue other than the official language, the conference is relatively small, and time constraints are minimal. Whatever the method, advise speakers that they are addressing a multinational audience and ask them to adapt their content and presentation techniques accordingly. Some guidelines were offered in the previous chapter.

Translation and interpretation services are expensive. Planners need to determine in what languages printed material will be translated and which sessions require S/I. Some associations routinely provide interpretation of major languages and offer S/I in other languages to those who require it. (In the latter case, a special supplement is added to the registration fee.) Interpretation is required if a prominent speaker is not fluent in the official language and their presentation is essential.

Language considerations influence other meeting planning areas. For example, in marketing the meeting, it is customary to produce brochures, Web content, and announcements in multiple languages, depending on what regions are involved. For European audiences, English, French, and German are customary. For Asian audiences, Japanese and Mandarin Chinese are advisable. Have multilingual staff members at hotels and registration, as well as at key functions, even if English is designated as the conference language. Simultaneous interpretation in three or four languages is needed if English is not the conference vernacular. Although program books are normally published in the host country's tongue, proceedings, handouts, and press releases might need to be translated into other languages.

Simultaneous interpretation normally requires teams of two people for each language, working in shifts of 15 to 30 minutes each. This skill is a demanding one, and strict professional codes govern their fees and working conditions. If there are not enough interpreters in a given city, make provisions in the budget for travel expenses as well as fees. The International Association of Congress Interpreters (AIIC) can offer advice (see Appendix A).

EXHIBITS

Where an exhibition is part of the congress, the organizing committee determines policy on the trade and technical exhibits and displays, eligibility of exhibitors, and responsibility for management, marketing, and promotion. The planning details are assigned to an exhibition committee that may, in turn, delegate specific planning tasks and management to an exhibition management company. In any case, the planning process covers fees, collection, and accounting; exhibit hours (decided in concert with the program committee); contract services and logistics; exhibitor attendance at sessions; and hospitality functions and activities.

Language concerns also impact exhibitions. If exhibitors from other countries are invited, they should be afforded the same considerations as delegates vis-à-vis language, protocol, and services. In fact, they may need more assistance than domestic exhibitors, since they may not be familiar with local exhibiting practices. Designate an official forwarding agent, experienced in receiving international shipments. Brochures, floor plans, and contracts need not be translated, but all weights, measurements, and dimensions should be expressed in metric as well as the imperial equivalent. Inform the exhibition service contractor about foreign exhibitors so that specialized equipment for electric current conversion will be available.

The following special services for multinational exhibitors and buyers facilitate interaction at the congress and beyond:

- An Export Products directory, organized by category
- Signs and badge codes that identify exhibitors seeking export sales
- A display of export product brochures in the international visitors area
- Visitor badge coding that identifies one's country of origin
- A reception for international buyers, hosted by export exhibitors

PROMOTION

Promoting the international event can be entirely a function of the secretariat, or shared with committees for registration and marketing. Marketing the congress entails the selection of foreign and domestic media, compilation of mailing lists, and identification of available promotional resources such as related events, publications, and trade shows. While recognizing the appeal and effectiveness of Web marketing, many show organizers regard Web-based promotion as an accessory to print and mail.

Direct mail marketing to other countries can be cost-effective when the printed materials are sent as a bulk shipment and subsequently mailed using a re-mail service. Most airlines offer this service; if an official airline has been named, check to see if it offers special rates. A foreign mailing service, a counterpart organization, or allied members in other countries can handle the mailing. Shipping camera-ready art and having the printing done locally may be advisable if there are high tariffs on printed material or if the mailing list has over a thousand names.

Publicity releases to the foreign trade or technical press provide a low-cost means of promoting the congress. Many of these publications will also include a registration form for a nominal charge. At the event, make special provisions for accrediting and accommodating the foreign trade press.

REGISTRATION

Registration procedures are normally part of the secretariat's function and are articulated in the organization's policy manual. The host organization of an ad hoc congress (and sometimes of the established ones) will assign some of that responsibility to a separate committee. Registration details and procedures for international meetings entail some special measures:

- *Registration fees.* Determine amount, acceptable currency, credit cards, collection and accounting, discounts, deadlines, penalties, and cancellation policies. If the secretariat is not located in the host country, registrants may be given the option of registering online by credit card or by mailing their forms and payments to the secretariat or the host committee registrar. As a convenience to attendees in large national blocks, organizers may arrange for fees to be paid to a designated national chapter or agency, which then forwards receipts in the appropriate currency.

- *Registration staff.* The personnel staffing the registration desks, information centers, and other key areas should be fluent in the languages of the main groups and be sensitive to cultural differences.

- *Forms and badges.* The staff that prepares registration materials should be aware that name forms vary across cultures. In some Asian countries, for instance, the surname precedes the given name(s). Registration forms must specify the surname or the family name, rather than the commonly used "last, first." Computer and Web-based registration systems must be programmed to accommodate such variations in storing and outputting names for attendee lists, rosters, and name badges. Planners should recognize that people in many cultural groups are uncomfortable with the use of nicknames on name badges. The registration form should ask for the individual's preferred form of address, giving examples such as "Mr. Zhang, Madam de Vries, Heinrich, Dr. Ellis, Prof. Yamato, Monique, or Mrs. Shamir." Special ribbons or badge codes that identify each visitor's country of origin are a nice added touch. NOTE: The use of "Ms." is essentially a Western practice. In many countries, women prefer either "Miss" or "Mrs." if a prefix is used.

- *Invitations.* Certain employers and national governments require that the delegates receive an official invitation to attend the congress. A form letter, personalized to the recipient, may be sent from the sponsor, secretary general, or chief executive. It outlines the objectives of the congress, the benefits to the attendee, and what the Chinese call "the rewards of world peace, friendship, and harmony."

- *On-site registration.* A clearly designated registration area that is staffed by multi-lingual registrars should be reserved for international delegates. Some organizations provide a lounge nearby where host members can meet and socialize with their counterparts from other countries.

CURRENCY

Most organizations holding meetings in North America will specify that fees are to be paid in United States or Canadian funds. In Europe and much of Asia and Latin America, where transactions in foreign currencies are commonplace, it is not unusual to designate the host country's currency as form of payment. In most European countries—and the list has expanded to include Eastern Europe—the Euro is standard currency for international events asking for all other transactions. The secretariat should be prepared to handle the processing of foreign remittances and bank drafts that are accepted as payment for conference fees, etc. (sometimes without identification). Organizers need to make sure that the hotels housing delegates are able to exchange foreign currency.

Some countries restrict their citizens from sending funds out of the country, even for pre-registration. The secretariat may decide to register such delegates and collect the fee on arrival.

PROTOCOL

Appropriate etiquette and decorum is essential at any international gathering of people from various cultures and backgrounds to avoid embarrassment or affront. The customs governing such behavior vary from country to country, but certain rules of protocol for international events have been developed. The United Nations has elaborate rules of procedure to facilitate interaction among people of different cultures. Many of these rules apply to meetings as well.

An international meeting may involve honored personages (HP) such as heads of state, ruling monarchs, governors, mayors, or high-ranking members of cabinets and military and religious organizations. There is a clear distinction between VIPs and HPs.

- VIPs are designated by organizations or occasions; "honored personages" are designated by title and status.
- VIP status recognizes the individual; HP status honors the offices.
- Anyone—even sports figures and entertainers—can be given VIP status. HP status implies high office.

If foreign dignitaries are expected to attend the event, contact the protocol officer of the appropriate consulate for information on forms of address, honors rendered, seating, order of precedence, and related courtesies.

Flags

It is customary at international conferences to display the flags of the countries represented by the delegates. Flags are normally arranged with the host country's colors at stage right and the others placed to the left (in alphabetical order, using the countries' names as spelled in English). Personal standards are displayed when royalty, heads of state, and high-ranking military officers participate. Contact their aides to arrange delivery and obtain instructions regarding proper positioning. Double check to ensure that no flag is positioned upside-down . . . it happens!

Honors and Ceremonies

Honor can be paid to arriving heads of state, dignitaries, and other HPs in a variety of ways: entrance and exit, salutes, anthems, processions, honor guards, greeting, escort, etc. These formalities are quite exacting; any departure from the norm is considered a breach of etiquette at best, and a diplomatic incident at worst. Consult with the appropriate protocol officer on these matters.

Order of Precedence

Rules of precedence govern the manner in which dignitaries enter the meeting room or dining facility, how they are seated, when and where they address the meeting, and how they depart. Here again, custom and tradition vary; consult the experts when the PCO is in doubt. There are, however, some general guidelines:

- *Arrival and departure.* The presiding officer greets the HP at the entrance to the facility if he or she is arriving by car, or in the pre-function area if the HP is already in the building. They enter the function room with the ranking HP at the presiding officer's right, followed by other HPs in order of rank, escorted by other officers of the sponsoring organization. The audience should rise and remain standing until the entourage is seated. The entourage may be preceded by a color guard carrying the appropriate standard and/or by a marching band. Departure follows the same pattern, but the HP may depart after the opening ceremonies or at the first break. The audience should again rise and remain in place until the honored guests have exited.

- *Form of address.* Verify the appropriate form of address with a consular officer or the HP's aide. Advise all officers and members who will be in contact with the personage of this form. Also advise media representatives if they are in attendance.

- *Seating.* The HP is seated to the right of the presiding officer; other dignitaries, in order of rank, are seated to the HP's right, alternating with escorts. If seated on the stage or at a head table, the presiding officer is seated at the center (or stage right of the lectern, if one is used). The ranking HP sits at the officer's right and the next-highest guest is seated on the left. The others alternate with their escorts from right to left. If spouses are seated at the head table, they are seated next to their husbands or wives.

- *Staging.* Guest dignitaries are introduced by the presiding officer and should address the audience from the lectern. If twin lecterns are used, the one at stage right is the position of honor. The introduction is made from the stage-left lectern.

Finally, all staff and officers should be briefed on protocol and cultural customs and taboos to avoid offending the guests and embarrassing the organization.

HOSPITALITY

There are a number of opportunities at international events to make visitors feel welcome and to promote interaction with their peers. A special lounge in the registration area is most appreciated. Some organizations will have a reception the day before the opening function, because they want to welcome people traveling great distances who tend to arrive two or more days before the event begins. Another welcome touch is to pair off visitors with officers, directors, or members of the host committee, who then take the responsibility of introducing them at social functions. Particular attention should be paid to the foreign trade press.

Review Chapter 14 for suggestions on special considerations for exhibition attendees (buyers) and exhibitors (exporters). Some show organizers provide a very popular service: Familiar with the high cost of excess baggage and the inconveniences related to airport security clearances, they offer to ship literature packets to the attendee's home city, a service subsidized by export exhibitors.

PCOs charged with the responsibility for organizing an international congress may sometimes feel that an awesome responsibility has been placed on their shoulders. Indeed it has! But with it comes the comforting knowledge that the organizations and companies involved have confidence in their ability to plan, manage, and successfully execute such an event. This is a recognition of their professional competence.

And that is the essence of professionalism!

Resources:

Lemp, Helena. 1979. *Manual for the Organization of Scientific Congresses.* New York: S. Karger AG.

Axtell, Roger. 1985. *Do's and Taboos Around the World.* New York: Wiley & Sons.

Copeland & Griggs. 1985. *Going International.* New York: Penguin Books.

Chesanow, Neil. 1988. *The World-Class Executive: How to Do Business Like a Pro Around the World.* New York: William Morrow.

APPENDIX A
Organizations in the Global Meetings Industry

Alliance of Meeting Management Consultants (AMMC) www.ammc.org

American Hotel and Motel Association (AH&MA) www.ahma.com

American Society of Association Executives (ASAE) www.asaenet.org

American Society of Travel Agents (ASTA) www.astanet.com

Asian Association of Convention Visitors Bureau (AACVB) www.aacvb.org

Association of Collegiate Conference and Events Directors International (ACCED-1) acced-i.colostate.edu

Association of Convention Marketing Executives (ACME) www.acmenet.org

Association for Convention Operations Management (ACOM) www.acomonline.org

Association for Conferences and Events (ACE) www.marrex.co.uk/ace

Association of Corporate Travel Executives (ACTE) www.acte.org

Association of Destination Management Executives (ADME) www.adme.org

Association Internationale des Palais de Congress (AIPC) www.aipc.org

Connected International Meeting Professionals Association (CIMPA) www.cimpa.org

Confederation of Latin American Congress Organizers (COCAL) www.bicca.com.br/cocal

Appendix A

Convention Industry Council (CIC) www.conventionindustry.org

European Association of Association Executives (ESAE) www.esae.org

Hospitality Sales & Marketing Association International (HSMAI) www.hsmai.org

International Association of Assembly Managers Inc. (IAAM) iacm.org

International Association of Conference Interpreters (AIIC) www.aiic.net

International Association of Conference Centers (IACC) www.iacconline.com

International Association of Convention and Visitor Bureaus (IACVB) www.iacvb.org

International Association for Exposition Management (IAEM) www.iaem.org

International Association of Professional Congress Organizers (IAPCO) www.congresses.com/iapco

International Congress & Convention Association (ICCA) www.icca.nl

International Special Events Society (ISES) www.ises.com

Meetings Industry Association (MIA – UK) www.meetings.org

Meetings Industry Association of Australia (MIAA) www.miaanet.com.au

Meeting Professionals International (MPI) www.mpiweb.org

National Association of Catering Executives (NACE) www.nace.net

National Speakers Association (NSA) www.nsaspeaker.org

Professional Convention Management Association (PCMA) www.pcma.org

Religious Conference Management Association (RCMA) www.rcmaweb.org

Society of Corporate Meeting Professionals (SCMP) www.scmp.org

Society of Government Meeting Professionals (SGMP) www.sgmp.org

Society of Incentive & Travel Executives (SITE) www.site-inti.org

Trade Show Exhibitors Association (TSEA) www.tsea.org

Travel Industry Association of America (TIA) www.tio.org

Union of International Associations (UIA) www.uia.org

World Travel & Tourism Council (WTTC) www.wttc.org

APPENDIX B
Industry Web Sites and Software

Product Category	Company	Web Site	Product Name or Description
Association Mgmt.	1st Priority Software, Inc.	www.1stprioritysoftware.com	Membrosia
Association Mgmt.	Amlink Technologies USA	www.amlinkevents.com	EventsPro
Association Mgmt.	AVECTRA	www.avectra.com	TASS-The Association Software System
Association Mgmt.	EKEBA International	www.ekeba.com	Complete Event Manager
Association Mgmt.	Peopleware, Inc.	www.peopleware.com	PeoplewarePro
Audio Conferencing	Conference Archives, Inc.	www.conferencearchives.com	ConferenceOnDemand
Audio Conferencing	Connex International	www.connexintl.com	Connex International
Badge Making	Avery Dennison	www.avery.com	LabelPro
Badge Making	PhotoBadge.com	www.photobadge.com	Asure ID Enterprise Edition
Badge Making	The Laser's Edge	www.badgepro.com	BadgePRO Plus
Communications	Association Network	www.theassociationnetwork.com	Event Express
Communications	Digitell Inc.	www.digitellinc.com	iPlan2Go
Communications	ExpoSoft Solutions, Inc.	www.exposoft.net	Product / Exhibitor Locator
Communications	FLASHpoint Technologies LLC	www.flashpointtech.com	FLASHfire Chats
Communications	Rockpointe Broadcasting Corp.	www.rockpointe.com	Video Conferencing
Communications	Tradeshow Multimedia (TMI)	www.tmiexpos.com	ShowMail—The Internet Message Center
Communications	WebEx Communications	www.webex.com	iPresentation Suite 4.0
Consultants/Speakers	Meeting U.	www.meeting-u.com	Speaker/Trainer
Consultants/Speakers	Meetingworks	www.meetingworks.com	Services
CVB Management	Newmarket International	www.newmarketinc.com	NetMetro Bureaus
Data Management	EventMaker Online	www.eventmakeronline.com	EventMaker
Data Management	Laser Registration	www.laser-registration.com	RegBrowser
Data Management	The Conference Exchange	www.confex.com	Online Abstract System
E-Learning	E-Conference, Inc.	www.e-conference.com	E-Conference, Inc.
E-Learning	PlaceWare, Inc.	main.placeware.com	PlaceWare Meeting Center 2000
E-Marketing	Cvent	www.cvent.com	Cvent
E-Marketing	ShowSite	www.showsitesolution.com	Interactive Event and ShowXpress
E-Marketing	thesmartpicture.com	www.thesmartpicture.com	Smart Picture for Events
Facility Management	CEO Software, Inc.	www.ceosoft.com	Scheduler Plus 2001
Facility Management	EventBooking.com	www.eventbooking.com	EventBooking.com

Appendix B

Category	Company	Website	Product
Facility Mgmt.	Network Simplicity	www.netsimplicity.com	Meeting Room Manager 2002
Facility Mgmt.	Resource Information & Control	www.riccorp.com	ConCentRIC'S
Global Web Portal	Comworld	www.comworld.net	Global events/sevices Web site
Groupware	Group Systems.com	www.groupsystems.com	Meeting Room, GSOnline
Housing	PASSKEY.COM, Inc.	www.passkey.com	Passkey.com ResDesk
Housing	ConventionNet	www.conventionnet.com	Visitor Housing
Housing	Pegasus Solutions Companies	www.pegs.com	Wyndtrac, LLC
Housing	Software Management, Inc.	www.softwaremgt.com	Housing 3000
Incentive Management	TimeSaver Software	www.timesaversoftware.com	Golf Trend Analyzer
Marketing	Data Tech SmartSoft, Inc.	www.smartsoftusa.com	Veri-A-Code
Meeting Management	123signup.com	www.123signup.com	123Signup Event Manager
Meeting Management	Dean Evans & Associates	www.dea.com	EMS Professional, Virtual EM
Meeting Management	Ambassadors International	www.ambassadors.com	Enterprise Event Solution 3.0
Meeting Management	gomembers inc.	www.gomembers.com	MeetingTrak Management
Meeting Mgmt.	Impact Solutions, Inc.	www.impactsolutions.com	MaxEvent
Meeting Mgmt.	ISIS Corp.	www.isisgold.com	ISIS Gold
Meeting Mgmt.	Meeting Expectations	www.meetingexpectations.com	Site Selection Services
Meeting Mgmt.	PC/NAMETAG	www.pcnametag.com	PC/Nametag Pro
Meeting Mgmt.	RegOnline	www.regonline.com	RegOnline Online Event Registration
Meeting Mgmt.	EventPro Software	www.eventpro-planner.com	EventPro Planner+D17
Program Content	Conf. Reports & Internet Services	www.conferencereports.com	Conference Reports and Internet Services
Registration	seeUthere Technologies	www.seeuthere.com	seeUthere Enterprise
Registration	b-there, a unit of Starcite, Inc.	www.b-there.com	b-there.com ERS (Event Registration System)
Registration	EventRegistration.com	www.eventregistration.com	The Event Assistant
Registration	International Conference Mgmt.	www.conference.com	Credit Card Manager
Registration	MeetingWare International, Inc.	www.meetingware.com	MeetingWare Registration
Registration	Worldwide Registration Systems	www.wwrs.net	Online Web-based registration
Resource Guide	Incentives & Meetings Intl.	www.i-mi.com	International venues
Resource Guide	Expoworld.net Ltd	www.expoworld.net	ExpoWorld.net
Resource Guide	Official Meeting Facilities Guide	www.omfg.com	OMFG.COM
Resource Guide	Bedouk International	www.bedouk.com	International venues
Room Diagramming	Event Software Corp.	www.eventsoft.com	3D Event Designer
Room Diagramming	Applied Computer Technology	www.expocad.com	Expocad VR2
Scheduling	Atlantic Decisions	www.ad-usa.com	Conference Room Manager
Scheduling	Meeting Maker, Inc.	meetingmaker6.com	MeetingMaker 6
Site Selection	BusinessMeetings.com Ltd.	www.businessmeetings.com	BusinessMeetings.com
Site Selection	MADSearch International, Inc.	www.madsearch.com	MADSearch.com
Site Selection	MeetingLocations.com	www.meetinglocations.com	Online Facility Search Database
Site Selection	HotelsOnline Directory	www.hotelsonline.com	HotelsOnline

Appendix B 367

Site Selection	Industry Meetings Network	www.industrymeetings.com	ProposalExpress
Site Selection	Market Stream, LLC	www.marketstream.com	STARdates
Site Selection	MeetingMakers	www.meetingmakers.com	MeetingMakers
Site Selection	MPBID.COM	www.mpbid.com	The Hotel Rooms Exchange
Site Selection	Starcite	www.starcite.com	Global Site Selection & Resources
Site Selection	Unique Venues	www.uniquevenues.com	Meeting Services Web site
Speaker Mgmt.	Walters Speaker Services World Class	www.walters-intl.com	Speakers
Speaker Mgmt.	Speakers/Entertainers	www.speak.com	Speakers
Surveys	Scantron Service Group	www.scantronservicegroup.com	Scanning
Surveys	Principia Products, Inc.	www.principiaproducts.com	Remark Office OMR, version 5.0
Surveys	SurveyConnect	www.surveyconnect.com	Survey Select Expert
Surveys	TRAQ-IT	www.traqit.com	TRAQ-IT
Surveys	Autodata Systems	www.autodata.com	Survey Plus 2000
Surveys	Creative Research Systems	www.surveysystem.com	The Survey System
Surveys	MarketTools, Inc.	www.markettools.com	Zoomerang
Surveys	Research Systems	www.surveyview.com	Surveyview
Trade Show Mgmt.	Acteva, Inc.	www.acteva.com	ExpoManager
Trade Show Mgmt.	HEMKO Systems Corp.	www.hemkosys.com	EMS-Exhibition Management System
Trade Show Mgmt.	iTradeFair	www.itradefair.com	Interactive Online Venues (IOV) software
Trade Show Mgmt.	Netronix Corporation	www.eshow2000.com	eshow2000
Travel Management	Double Eagle Services	www.doubleeagleservicesinc.com	TourTrak
Travel Management	GetThere.com	www.getthere.com	DirectMobile
Travel Management	Tr-IPS Services	www.Tr-IPS.com	Tr-IPS
Video Production	Premier Images	www.video11.com	Meeting/Exhibition Continuity
Virtual Trade Shows	Unisfair	www.unisfair.com	GMEP—Global Mass Event Platform
Web Conferencing	1st Virtual Communications	www.fvc.com	CUseeMe
Web Conferencing	Avistar	www.avistar.com	Avistar
Web Conferencing	Communicast.com	www.communicast.com	Communicast
Web Conferencing	ConferZone	www.conferzone.com	e-conferencing
Web Conferencing	EventCom by Marriott	www.marriott.com/eventcom	Global conferencing
Web Conferencing	HealthAnswers, Inc.	www.healthansersinc.com	Conference.CAST
Web Conferencing	iShow.com	www.ishow.com	iShow.com
Web Conferencing	Latitude Communications	www.latitude.com	Meeting Place
Web Conferencing	MindBlazer	www.mindblazer.com	MindBlazer
Web Conferencing	Netspoke	www.netspokc.com	iMeet, Inc.
Web Conferencing	Premiere Conferencing	www.premconf.com	Premiere Conferencing
Web Conferencing	WebEx Communications	www.webex.com	Multimedia communications
Web Conferencing	Winnov	www.winnov.com	Winnov
Web Conferencing	Wire One Technologies, Inc.	www.wireone.com	Wire One Technologies, Inc.
Web-Based Tools	ConventionPlanit	www.conventionplanit.com	Meetings Industry Link
Web-Based Tools	iNetEvents, Inc.	www.iNetEvents.com	iNetEvents Hosted Event
Web-Based Tools	Meetings on the Net	www.meetingsonthenet.com	Meetings on the Net
Web-Based Tools	Plansoft Corporation	www.plansoft.com	Internet Sales Support Solutions (SSS)

Index

A

AACVB. *See* Asian Association of Convention and Visitor Bureaus
ABA. *See* American Bankers Association
Abstracts, 277–278
Access, hotel selection and, 39
Accommodations
  costs, 91–92
  evaluation of, 294
  See also Hotels; Housing; Meeting rooms
Accompanying persons, 143
  fees for, 96
  See also Guest programs
Accounting, evaluation of, 294
ACE. *See* Association for Conferences and Events
ACEPLAN, 48
ACOM. *See* Association for Convention Operations Management
Acoustics, 181–182
Ad hoc committees, 3
Ad hoc congresses, 350, 356
Ad hoc teleconferencing, 210
Administration, international event, 323
Administrative and Management Society, 12

Administratorpy
  manager *vs.*, 12
  meeting planner as, 12
Adobe Acrobat, 208
Adult learning, 59
Advance Marketing Information Release, 111
Advance meeting announcement, 142–143
Advance registration, 141–142
Advance Registration Roster, 151
Agenda, pre-conference meeting, 239. *See also* Business agenda; Social agenda
Agent, 76, 77
AIIC. *See* International Association of Congress Interpreters
Air credits, 104
Air fares, 92, 102
Air freight, 342
Airlines
  concessions, 104–105
  fares, 92, 102
  negotiating with, 102–104
  planning air travel and, vi, 102
Airport layout, 42
Airport reception, 250–251
Air travel
  easing burden of, 108–109

369

370 *Meetings and Meeting Professionals*

international, 326–328
planning, 101–104
request form, 153
Allen, Fred, 32
Ambient light, 176
American Bankers Association (ABA), 23
American Express, 337
American Florist Marketing Council, 128
American Society for Industrial Security, 313
American Society of Association Executives (ASAE), 10, 48, 318
Amplification, 170–171
Angle of acceptance, 179
Animation software, 165
ANSI lumens, 175
APEX, 35–36, 84
APEX Initiative, 195, 217–218
Appetizers, 129
Application service providers (ASPs), 193
Architechnology, 184
Archival technology, 191, 192, 208–209
Artists, booking, 76–80. *See also* Entertainment
ASAE. *See* American Society of Association Executives
Asian Association of Convention and Visitor Bureaus (AACVB), 319, 321
Aspect ratio, 172–173
Assistant, 235
Association budget worksheet, 94
Association convention, staff organization for, 25
Association for Conferences and Events (ACE), 13, 48
Association for Conferences and Exhibitions, 318
Association for Convention Operations Management (ACOM), 13
Association of Briefing Program Managers, 184
Associations
computerized registration and, 147
fax solicitation and, 113
increase in international, 317–318
PCO and, 19
See also Multicultural events
Asynchronous learning, 6, 14
AT&T, 23
Attendance figures, 95–96
Attendance promotion, for exhibitions, 223–224
Attendance roster, 151
Attendees, 332
determining number/profile, 32
Attire, for social agenda, 284–285, 336
Audience, meeting, 3, 4
ensuring receptive, 74
food and energy levels of, 139–140
multicultural, 325–326
profile of for speaker, 73
Audience validation, 54–55
Audiovisuals
audio, 170–172
determining screen and image sizes, 177–179
equipment, 168–169
renting and shipping, 186–187
for international events, 330–331
media analysis and, 159–161
meeting with meeting producers, 161–162
needs, 279–283
for entertainment, 279–281
preventing glitches, 281–283
orders, 187
producing, 158–159

projection systems, 172–177
retention and, 157
staging with, 184–186
support for speakers, 73
surveying facilities for, 187–189
video
    applications, 168
    equipment and systems, 166–168
    at meetings, 165–166
visual design principles, 163–165
wireless technology, 169–170
Audiovisual seating, 180, 181
Auditing, 296–297
Automobiles
    international rules, 335
    rentals, 105, 109
AVW network, 183
Awards, 82–84
Axtell, Roger, 361

B

Badges, 151–152, 268–269
    computer-generated, 204–205
    designs, 268
    holders, 152
    international exhibit, 334
    multicultural event, 357
    press, 114
    security and, 307
    smart, 152. *See also* Smart Cards
Baggage
    handling, 335
    personal, 340–341
    security and check of, 232
Baksheesh, 343
Balancing, of meeting, 5
Ball, Corbin, 146
Ballrooms, 179
Bandwidth capacity, 183
    Web conference and, 215
Bank draft, 337
Banquet Event Order (BEO), 84

Banquets, 122–125
    gala, 125–126
    staging for, 186
Banquet seating, 270
Barclay's, 337
Bars, 286
Bartenders, 131
Beaded screens, 179
Bedouk Worldwide Directory, 319, 346
BEO. *See* Banquet Event Order
Berke, Robert, 147, 148
Beverages
    beverage plans, 132–133
    liquor liability, 134
    quality of, 131
    service and control, 131–133
    wine service, 126–127
    See also Food
Billing, speakers' fee, 71
Black tie, 284
Bluetooth Systems, 169
Boast, William, 5
Boca Raton, 36
Bonded registration staff, 247
Bonding, 323
Booths
    installation of, 230–231
    international exhibit, 334
    pricing, 226–227
    virtual, 234
Bottle, purchasing liquor by, 132–133
Breakfasts, 120–121
    buffet, 121
Breakout sessions, 60
    room setup, 270
Breaks. *See* Refreshment breaks
Breining, Terri, 26–27, 193–194
Bridges, 65–66, 214
Briefing
    program managers, 184
    speaker, 274–275
Brightness, projector, 175

Bristol-Myers Company, 24
Broadmoor, The, 36
Brochures
 destination, 335
 online, 113
Budget/budgeting, 34, 91–99
 controlling expenses, 92–95
 determining fees, 95–96
 exhibition, 97–98, 226–227
 hotel selection and, 40
 international events and, 323, 337–339
 major items, 91–92
 master account procedures, 253–257
 reconciling, 92, 98–99, 297, 298
 residual revenues, 99
 revenue projection, 96–97, 98
Buffets, 122, 286
 breakfast, 121
 dinner, 124–125, 126
 lunch, 121
 reception, 129
Bulk ordering, 129, 135
Bureau for Diplomatic Security, 313
Burrus, Daniel, 6
Buses, 107–109
Business agenda, 33, 34, 61–62, 195, 276–278
 abstracts, 277–278
 evaluation of, 294–295
 rehearsals, 277
 worksheet, 62
Business agendagram, 61
Business attire, 284
Business press, 112
Butler service, 122

C

Cairo Hilton, 136
Canadian Ministry of Trade, 333
Cancellation penalty, 97
Cancellation refunds, 97
Capacity, meeting environment, 180–181
Cardinal Communications, 113, 117
Cardioid microphone, 171
Career advancement, for meeting managers, 16
Carey, Tony, 65
Carnet, 338, 344, 348
Car rentals, 105, 109
Carving fee, 124
Cash bars, 133
Cathode ray tubes, 174
CCTV. See Closed-circuit television
Ceiling height, 181
Celebrity speakers, 76
Centering, of meeting, 5
Ceremonies, 359
Certificate of origin, 344
Certification, meeting management, 9, 14–16, 20
Certification in Meeting Management (CMM), 15
Certified Meeting Manager (CMM), 15
Certified Meeting Professional (CMP), 14
Certified Special Events Professional, 75
Charts, 164
Chase light, 280
Chat rooms, 198
Checklists
 daily duties, 262–263
 pre-departure, 236–238
 site selection, 49
Chef's Theme, 136
Chesanov, Neil, 361
Chief executive, access by PCO to, 21
Child care, 45, 288
Chrysler Corporation, 4
Citibank, 337
Classroom setup, 269, 270
Clinic, 60

Clip fasteners, 268
Closed-circuit television (CCTV), 165
CMM. *See* Certification in Meeting Management
CMM. *See* Certified Meeting Manager
CMP. *See* Certified Meeting Professional
Coat check, security in, 232
Code sharing, 326
Cognitive style, of meeting managers, 27
Collision/damage waivers, 109
Colloquium, 60
Colonial Williamsburg, 36, 123
Commercial invoice, 344
Committed capacity, 40
Committees, congress, 350–351
Communications
 data, 183–184
 electronic, 244–245
 expertise in, 11
 meeting as medium for, 36
 meeting environment and, 157–158, 180
 pre-meeting coordination of, 244–246
 procedures, 32
 skills for PCO, 16
 staging guide and, 242
 via e-mail, 207–208
 video and, 165–166
 voice, 183–184
 See also Audiovisuals
Community impact, 296
Community resources, 249–250
 security and, 309–310
Companion programs, 278–279
Compressed video, 212
Computer Aided Design software, 164–165
Computer data, simultaneous projection with video, 175

Computers, meeting professionals and, 192–194. *See also* Software
Conference, 60
Conference Associates, 283
Conference Management Program, 13
Conference management software, 194–195
Conference manager, vi
Conference seating, 184
Conferon, Inc., 27
Confirmation
 room, 42
 speaker, 67
Congresses, 349
 ad hoc, 350, 356
 committees, 350–351
 increase in international, 317
 organization, 349–351
 secretariat, 349–350, 351
Consecutive interpretation, 354
Continental Airlines MeetingWorks, 105
Continental theme, for refreshment break, 136
Contingency planning, 263–264, 303, 313
 revenue projection and, 97
Continuing education administration, 201
Controlling, manager *vs.* administrator, 12
Control numbers, 151
Convention and Visitors' Bureau, 114
Convention bureau, vi, 295
 housing options and, 149
 obtaining registration staff and, 247
Convention center, 220
Convention coordinator, vi
Convention Industry Council, 14, 134, 217

Convention Industry Council Manual, 120, 140, 343
Convention managers, 9
ConventionNet.com, 234
Conventions, vi
Convention services manager (CSM), vi, 45
Cooperative promotion, 114
Cornell University, 13
Corona Ware, 113, 117
Corporate budget worksheet, 93
Corporate meetings, staff organization for, 25
Corporate professional congress organizer
    access to chief executive, 21
    centralized meeting departments, 23–28
    functions of meeting manager, 21–22
    maintaining management credibility, 20
    management team and, 17–23
    See also Professional Congress Organizer
Corporations, PCO and, 19
Cost, teleconferencing and cost savings, 210
Couture, Gary, 138
CPE screen, 177
Credit Suisse, 337
Cross-lighting, 185
Cross rates, 338
CSM. *See* Convention services manager
Currency
    international events and, 323, 335, 358
    managing foreign, 337–339
    options, 338
Customs, 336, 340–344
    documentation, 343–344
    information, 347
    international events and, 323
Customs broker, 342

D

Daggett, Jim, 290
Daily duties, 262–263
Daily statements, 288
Dais, 185
Da-Lite Screen Company, 178
Dance entertainment, 76
Dance floors, 286
    estimating dance size of, 81
Data communication, 183–184
Data projectors, 171
Debriefing, 293–294
Decor
    meeting room, 128–129, 182
    table, 127, 128–129
Delegate, 235
Demographics, of multicultural events, 352
Demonstrations, 304–305
Departure plan, 289–290
    honored persons and, 359
Destination brochure, 335
Destination management companies (DMCs), 105–106, 320, 321, 328–329
    guest programs and, 279
    selecting, 106–107
Diagram books, 115
Diagrams, staging guide, 242
Digital animation, media analysis of, 160
Digital media, 192
Digital pager, 245
Digital video, 165
Dignitaries, seating, 128. *See also* Honored persons; VIPs
D-ILA. *See* Direct-Drive Image Light Amplifier
Dimmer, 281
Dinner entertainment, 76

Dinners, 122–125
  buffet, 124–125, 126
  gala banquet, 125–126
  themed, 123–124
Direct-Drive Image Light Amplifier (D-ILA), 174
Directional speakers, 171
Direct marketing, 112
  for multicultural events, 356
  See also Marketing
Distance learning, 14
Distribution analysis, of travel, 101
DLP (Digital Light Processor) projectors, 174
DMCs. *See* Destination management companies
DMD (digital micromirror device), 174
Documentation, 165
  conference, 292–293
  customs, 343–344
  international shipping, 342
  staff, 293–296
Doors, meeting room, 182
Do's and Taboos Around the World (Axtell), 361
Dow, Roger, 13
Dramatization, 165
Dress codes, 284–285, 336
Driveway access, security and, 232
DSL, 183
Dual beeper, 245
Dual spectrum lamps, 182
Duffy, Christine, 17, 319, 322
Duyff International, 320
DVDs, 167, 331

E

Early bird room rate, 1–2
Education, in professional meeting management, 13–14
Educational agenda, 195. *See also* Business agenda
Educational sessions, staging, 184–185
Edwards, Mauri, 11–12
EFCT. *See* European Federation of Conference Towns
Electrical needs, 182
Electronic communication, 244–245
Electronic whiteboard, 197
Ellipsoidal light, 280
E-mail, 244
  advance meeting announcement via, 142
  communication via, 207–208
E-mail promotional elements, 113
E-marketing, 207
Emergencies, 303–304
  medical, 304
  while abroad, 310–311
English, as international language, 354
Enhancements, 65
Enterprise-wide software, 199
Entertainment, 74–88
  awards and recognition, 82–84
  booking musicians/artists, 76–80
  communicating program details, 84–85
  estimating dance floor size, 81
  music for ambiance, 75–76
  needs, 33
  researching and selecting, 75–76
  staging for, 185–186, 279–281
  technical specifications, 80–81
  unions, 76–79
Equipment, shipping, 342–343
ESAE. *See* European Society of Association Executives
Ethics, of site inspections, 45–46
Ethnic theme, for refreshment break, 136
Etiquette, 322
Eurodollars, 338
Euromic, 320

376 *Meetings and Meeting Professionals*

European Federation of Conference Towns (EFCT), 319, 321
European Society of Association Executives (ESAE), 13
Evaluation questionnaire, 292–293
Event cancellation insurance, 47–48
event.com, 141
Event management, v-vi, 11
Event management software, 198–199, 365–67
    evaluating, 199–201
Event order, 84, 255
    sample, 258
Event planner, v
Event promotion. *See* Marketing
Event registration, 260–261. *See also* Registration
Event schedule, 84, 87–88
Event Solutions, 145
Executive committee, 350–351
Exhibit halls, 220
    security in, 232
Exhibitions, vi, 97–98
    budget and fiscal planning, 226–227
    decision factors, 219–220
    defined, 219
    evaluation of, 295
    exhibit prospectus, 224–226
    exhibit technology, 228–229
    exposition hotels, 221–223
    future of, 234
    in-house, 222–223
    installation phase, 230–231
    international event, 233, 331–334, 347
        attendee assessment, 332
        design dilemma, 333–334
        logistics, 332–333
        protocol, 334
    marketing, 223–224
    for multicultural events, 355–356
    on-site operations, 229–234
    production and operations, 227
    promoting attendance, 224
    Smart Cards and, 229
    venue selection, 220–221
    See also Booths
Exhibition service contractor, 227
Exhibitors
    briefing, 231
    registration of, 228
Exhibit prospectus, 224–226
Exhibit space marketing, 223–224
Expedia, 105
Expenses
    controlling, 92–95
    fixed, 92
    speaker, 71
    variable, 92
Experts, 69
ExpoPlusCCI, 48
Export declaration, 344
Export license, 344
Exposition. *See* Exhibitions
ExpSure Ltd., 48

F

Facilitators, meeting, 10, 21, 27–28
Facilities
    international event, 324
    requirements, 57
    See also Meeting rooms
Fares, air, 102
    discounts, 327
    negotiating, 103
Fast-fold screen, 177
Fax solicitation, 113
Federal Communications Commission, 113
Fees
    for accompanying persons, 96
    determining, 95–97
    registration, 96
    speaker, 71, 73
Fiber optics, 280
Film, media analysis of, 160

Financial analysis, 296–297
Fire emergency plans, 307
Fiscal management. *See*
    Budget/budgeting
Fiscal timetable, 255–257
Fixed expenses, 92
Flags, 358–359
FLASHpoint Technologies, 152
Flash software, 165
Floor plans, 244
    event registration and, 260
    meeting room, 42
*Flowers for Meetings &
    Conventions*, 128, 140
Fluorescent lighting, 182
Foire de Saint Denis, 332
Follow-spot, 280
Follow-up mailings, 113–114
Follow-up on site selection, 46–47
Font colors, for projected visuals,
    164
Food
    audience energy levels and,
        139–140
    breakfasts, 120–121
    bulk ordering, 129
    dinners and banquets, 122–125
    gala banquet, 125–126
    lunches, 121–122
    negotiating rates for, 33
    planning criteria for meals,
        127–128
    receptions, 129–131, 285–286
    refreshment breaks, 134–137,
        285–286
    table decor, 127, 128–129
    wine service, 126–127
    See also Beverages
Food guarantees, 137–138
"Foreign Exchange Information-A
    Worldwide Summary," 337
*Foreign Travel Immunization
    Guide,* 346
Formal attire, 284

Formats
    meeting, 34
    program, 59–61
    for speaker, 73
    video, 167
Forms of address, 322–323, 357, 359
Fortescue, Anthea, 283
Forum, 60
Forward contract, 338
Forwarding agent, 342
Foundation for International
    Meetings, 318
Fox, Doug, 234
Freight
    air, 342
    airline assistance with, 105
    ocean, 342
    rail, 342
    truck, 342, 343
French service, 122
Fresnell light, 280
Front office, evaluation of, 294
Functions, 119–140, 285–286
    beverage service and control,
        131–133
    breakfasts, 120–121
    dinners and banquets,
        122–125
    evaluation of, 294
    gala banquet, 125–126
    gastro-intellectual tract,
        119–120, 138–140
    guarantees, 137–138
    liquor liability, 134
    lunches, 121–122
    meeting agenda and, 119–120
    meeting management software
        and, 195
    off-site, 286–287
    planning criteria for meals,
        127–128
    purpose of, 119–120
    receptions and hospitality,
        129–131

refreshment breaks, 134–137, 285–286
room and table décor, 127, 128–129
wine service, 126–127
Funding, multicultural event, 353

G

Gala banquet, 125–126
GCI Financial, 337
General chairman, 350
General Electric, 19
General session, 59–60
Geneva Telecom, 332
Geographical area, site selection and, 37
George P. Johnson Company, 116
George Washington University, 13
Gifts, customs and, 340
Giuliani, Rudy, 74
Global meetings industry, organizations in, 363–364
Global professional congress organizer, 319
Godfrey, Arthur, 213
Going International (Copeland & Grigg), 361
Goldblatt, Joe Jeff, 74–75
Goodman, Ed, 183
Google, 202
Gordon, Myron, 4
Government regulations, international events and, 323
Graphic, teleconferencing and, 212
Gratuities, 297–300, 343
defined, 299
positions eligible for, 299
Grease, 343
Greenbriar, The, 36
Green meetings, 43
Ground operations, evaluation of, 295

Ground transportation, 101, 105–106, 246
buses, vans, limousines, 107–109
destination management companies and, 105–107
Grusich, Bill, 41, 49, 95
Guarantees, 285
meal, 137–138
Guest programs, 34, 278–279
Guidelines, speaker, 68, 72
Guide to Canada Customs, 347

H

Hamburg Convention Bureau, 322
Hannover Fairs, 332
Harris, Bruce, 27
HDTV, resolution, 174
Headings, event schedule, 84
Headquarters, 244
message center, 246
Headset microphones, 171
Health
information for international traveler, 346
records, 341–342
Health kick theme, for refreshment break, 136
Hedge, 323
Herbers, Dan, 116, 117
Hewlett Packard, 184
High-gain aluminum screen, 179
High Tea, 136
Hilton Hotels, 209, 260
Hollow square setup, 270, 271
Honored persons (HPs), 358
VIPS *vs.*, 358
Honors, 359
Hors d'oeuvres, 129, 286
Hosansky, Mel, 4
Hospitality, 129–131
for multicultural event, 360
Hospitality desk, 261

Hospitality suites, 130–131
Hotel registration, 260
Hotels
  exposition, 221–223
  international event, 324
  See also Housing
Hotel sales staff, 293
Hotel selection criteria, 39–41
House sound systems, 171
Housing, 149–150
  online systems, 206–207
  processing advance registrations, 151
  request form, 153
  speaker, 273–274
  Web-based options, 150
Housing bureau, 149
HPs. *See* Honored persons
Hudak, Richard, 306
Humor, 158

I

IAAM. *See* International Association of Assembly Managers
IACVB. *See* International Association of Convention and Visitors Bureaus
IAPCO. *See* International Association of Professional Congress Organizers
IBM, 192, 232–233, 260
ICCA. *See* International Congress and Convention Association
IDEA. *See* International Dance Exercise Association
Illustration, video, 165
Image height, 181
Image Magnification (IMAG), 165, 166
Image resolution, 172–173
Image sizes, determining, 178–179
Immigration, 340–344, 347
Incandescent lighting, 182
Incentive managers, 9
Incentives, vi
Incentives & Meetings International Workbook, 319
Independent conference consultants, vi
Independent hotel representatives, 41
Independent meeting planners, 9
Independent meeting professionals, 26–27
  computer technology and, 193–194
Individual folio, 253
In-house publications, 112
Innovating, manager *vs.* administrator, 12
Inoculations, 341–342
In-room exhibits, 222–223
Insurance
  international events and, 335
  liquor liability, 134
  meeting. *See* Meeting insurance
Interactive performances, 232
Interactive Web casts, 215
Intercom, 281
Inter-Continental Hotels, 128
International airlines, 326–328
International Association for Medical Aid to Travelers, 346
International Association of Assembly Managers (IAAM), 232
International Association of Congress Interpreters (AIIC), 355
International Association of Convention and Visitors Bureaus (IACVB), 318, 319
International Association of Professional Congress Organizers (IAPCO), 13, 26, 318
  criteria for hotels, 39–40

380 *Meetings and Meeting Professionals*

International Conference Resorts, 184
International Congress and Convention Association (ICCA), 13, 318
International Dance Exercise Association (IDEA), 148–149
International events, 6–7, 317–348
 audiovisual support, 330–331
 avoiding customs and immigration bottlenecks, 340–344, 3247
 carnet form, 348
 defined, 318
 destination criteria, 320–321
 disruptions, 313
 exhibiting abroad, 331–334, 347
 finding help, 319–320
 foreign currency and finances, 337–339
 global PCO, 319
 health information, 346
 hotels and facilities, 324
 international airlines, 326–328
 medical emergencies, 310–311
 metrics, 346
 National Tourist Office, 320–321
 planning for other cultures, 322–324
 preparing participants, 335–337
 program planning, 324–326
 protocol, 334
 security, 311–313
 simultaneous interpretation and, 216–217
 transnational events, 318–320
 using destination management companies, 328–329
 weather and safety, 311
 working with professional congress organizers, 329–330
 See also Multicultural events
International Exhibitors Association, 347
International SOS, 346
International Special Events Society (ISES), 13, 75
International Trade Administration, 347
Internet
 archiving the event, 208–209
 badges and ticketing, 204–205
 communication via, 207–208
 dedicated Web sites, 204
 growth of independent meeting professionals and, 27
 marketing using, 207
 meetings via, 191–192
 online housing systems, 206–207
 as planning tool, 202–209
 presentation technology and, 197–198
 registration using, 204
 research via, 202–203
 search engines, 202
 site selection using, 38–39, 203
 smart cards, 205–206
 virtual meetings, 214–216
 See also Web sites
Interpersonal style, of meeting managers, 27–28
Interpretation
 consecutive, 354
 simultaneous, 354–355
Interviews, 115
 random personal, 292
Invitations, to multicultural event, 357
ISDN, 183
ISES. *See* International Special Events Society

J

Joint Industry Council, 318
Jones, Jim, 17

K

King, Jeffrey, 134
Know Before You Go (U.S. Customs Office), 347
Kodak, 178
Kodak Projection Calculator, 188
KPMG International, 337
Kroll International, 313

L

Labels, 236
Labor disputes, 308, 313
Language, multicultural events and, 354–355
Laser light, 281
Lavaliere microphones, 171
Lavalier fastener, 268
Leadership speakers, 69
Lead-ins, 65–66
Learning
　adult, 59
　asynchronous, 6, 14
　online, 14, 99
　synchronous, 13
Lecterns, 185, 272, 360
Lecture, 60
LED screens, 166–167
Legibility of projected visuals, 164
Leko light, 280
Lemp, Helena B., 351, 360
Lenses, 176
Lenticular screens, 179
Letter of commendation, 300
Letter of credit, 323, 338
Lighting, 182
　banquet, 125
　educational session, 185
　entertainment, 185, 280–281
　for registration facilities, 248
　room setup and, 271
Limited power of attorney, 344

Limousines, 107–109
Liquid crystal display (LCD) projectors, 173–174
Liquor, purchasing plans, 132–133
Liquor liability, 134
Live theater, media analysis of, 160
Local services, 249–250
Loews Hotels, 306
Logistics, international event exhibit, 332–333
Long-Throw lens, 176
Lumens, 175
Luminescence, 172
Lunches, 121–122

M

Macromedia's Flash, 165
Mailing lists, rented, 114
Mailings
　direct, 112
　follow-up, 113–114
　See also Marketing
Mailing shells, 104
Making Meetings More Effective (Gordon), 4
Malaria, 341, 342
Management team, PCO and, 17–23
Manager
　administrator vs., 12
　meeting planner as, 12
Manual for the Organization of Scientific Congresses (Lemp), 351, 360
Mardi Gras break, 136
Marketing, 111–117
　conference marketing plan, 115–116
　cooperative promotion, 114
　direct, 112
　exhibition, 223–224
　follow-up mailings, 113–114
　initial announcement, 112–113

382 *Meetings and Meeting Professionals*

media analysis, 112
online, 207
publicity, 114–115
registration process and, 195
resources, 116–117
tips, 116
viral, 147
Marketing General Incorporated (MGI), 116, 117
Marriott Corporation, 13, 184, 209
Master accounts
 folio, 253
 monitoring, 269
 procedures, 253–257
 sample authorization, 254
 settling disputes over, 297
Materials, shipping, 342–343
Matte white screens, 179
McCormick Place, 332
McDonald, Tom, 6
McGettigan Partners, 17, 319
McLuhan, Marshall, 18
Meals. *See* Food; Functions
Media analysis, 112, 159–161
Media center, 266–267
Media kits, 114
Media liaison, 266
Media relations, 265–267
 evaluation of, 295
Media theaters, 232
Medical emergencies, 304
 while abroad, 310–311, 335
Meeting agenda, functions and, 119–120
Meeting and Exhibition Specification Guide (MESG), 36
Meeting departments, 23–28
 independent meeting professionals and, 26–27
 management of, 22–23
 manager *vs.* facilitator, 27–28
 organization and function of, 24–26

rationale for central control, 23–24
Meeting details, for speakers, 72
Meeting environment, 180–182
 acoustics, 181–182
 capacity, 180–181
 ceiling height, 181
 communication facilitation and, 157–158
 decor, 182
 doors, 182
 high-tech, 183–184
 lighting and electrical needs, 182
 voice and data communication, 183–184
 See also Audiovisuals
Meeting evaluation, 290–293
 areas to evaluate, 290
 computerized audience-response, 291
 course evaluation, 301
 documentation and tabulation, 292–293
 post-conference, 292
 program evaluation, 291–292
 written, 291
Meeting facilitators, 10
 meeting managers *vs.*, 21, 27–28
Meeting insurance, 47–49
 event cancellation, 47–48
 insurance plans, 48, 49
 professional liability, 48
Meeting management, v–vi
 expertise required, 11
Meeting management software, 198–201, 365–367
Meeting managers, v, 9
 key functions of, 21–22
 meeting facilitators *vs.*, 21, 27–28
 professional body of knowledge, 14–15

Index 383

See also Corporate professional congress organizer; Professional Congress Organizer
Meeting News, 145, 317
Meeting Plan, 195
Meeting planners, v, 9
  as managers or administrators, 12
Meeting planner timeline, 50–51
Meeting producers, 161–162
Meeting professionals, computers and, 192–194
Meeting Professionals International. *See* MPI
Meeting profile, 32, 33–34
Meeting prospectus, 35
Meeting rooms
  criteria for, 43
  inspecting, 43–44
  security in, 232
  setups, 269–273
    presentation area, 272–273
    room entrances, 271
    seating area, 271–272
  survey, 187–189
    sample, 189
Meetings, vi
  audience for, 3, 4
  automating the meeting process, 194–197
  criteria for success, 4–5
  in cyberspace, 191–192
  defined, 32, 33
  defining objective of, 4
  determining purpose of, 3
  ending, 66
  future of, 5–7
  green, 43
  initial announcement for, 112–113
  international. *See* International events
  as management tool, 18
  multicultural. *See* Multicultural events
  on-site, 238
  pacing, 5
  pre-conference, 238–240
  staff
    daily, 243
    on-site, 267
  technology and, 6
  types of, 22
  video at, 165–166
  virtual, 214–216
Meeting services, 45
Meetings Industry Association of Australia (MIAA), 13
Meeting Trak, 145
Meeting vignettes, 168
MeetingWorks, 105
Megatrends (Naisbitt), 5
Menus
  banquet, 125
  lunch, 122
Merck Pharmaceutical, 23
Merriam Webster, 33
MESG. *See* Meeting and Exhibition Specification Guide
Message boards, 197–198
Message center, 246, 261–262
Metrics, 346
Metric system, 334
Metropolitan State College of Denver, 13
MGI. *See* Marketing General Incorporated
MIAA. *See* Meetings Industry Association of Australia
MICE (meetings, incentives, conventions, and expositions), vi
Microlenses, 176
Microphones, 171–172
Microsoft Office, 145
Miller, Jack, 18
Mini-Olympics, 288

Mission statement, for meeting department, 22
Mixers
  microphone, 172
  sound, 281
Moderator, 275
Monitors, 166–167
  multiple, 166–167
Mordera, 343
MPI, 13, 48, 102, 128, 318
  Green Meetings Resource Guide, 48
MPI Foundation, 14, 27
  marketing information, 116–117
MS Project, 194
Multicultural audiences, 325–326
Multicultural events, 349–361
  congress organizations, 349–351
  currency, 358
  exhibits, 355–356
  hospitality, 360
  language, 354–355
  planning, 351–353
  program content and policies, 353–354
  promotion of, 356
  protocol for, 358–360
  registration, 356–357
  See also International events
Multimedia, media analysis of, 160, 161
Musco, Rodolfo, 15
Music, for ambiance, 75–76
Musicians, booking, 76–80
Muslim countries
  dress code, 284
  personal baggage and, 340

N

Naisbitt, John, 5–6, 317
National Association of Fleet Administrators, 147

National Passenger Traffic Association (NPTA), 103
National tourist offices (NTOs), 319, 320–321
Natural disasters, 307–308
NetMeeting, 214
Networking, 207–208
Networking outlets, 183
Networld, 320
News conference area, 267
News conferences, 115
Newsletters, 112
NPTA. *See* National Passenger Traffic Association
nTag, 205–206, 229
NTOs. *See* National tourist offices

O

Objectives
  defined, 4
  setting, 32, 33
Ocean freight, 342
Off-site functions, 286–287
Off-the-shelf software, 198
Omnidirectional microphone, 172
Online brochures, 113
Online learning, 14, 99
On-Line Publishers Associations (OPA), 99
Online registration, 145, 191
Online travel agencies, 105
On-site meeting, 238
On-site operations, 259–301
  audiovisual and staging needs, 279–283
  auditing and financial analysis, 296–297
  business agenda, 276–278
  daily duties, 262–263
  departure plan, 289–290
  gratuities, 297–300
  guest programs, 278–279
  media relations, 265–267

meeting evaluation, 290–293, 301
meeting room setups, 269–273
monitoring master accounts, 269
post-meeting procedures, 289–300
program management, 269–289
reception, 260–262
social agenda, 283–289
speaker support, 273–276
staff critique and documentation, 293–296
staff meetings, 267
tickets and badge control, 267–269
troubleshooting, 263–264
On-site registration, 141, 142, 357
 form for, 144
OPA. *See* On-Line Publishers Associations
Open Space Technology (OST), 60
Operational checks, 233
Orbitz, 105
Order of precedence, 359–360
Organizational profile, for speaker, 73
Organizational style, of meeting managers, 28
Organizing, manager *vs.* administrator, 12
Organizing committee, 350–351
Origination source, 167
OST. *See* Open Space Technology
Overflow, 165
Overhead lighting, 182
Overhead projection, 160
Owen, Harrison, 60
Oyez Training Ltd., 16
OzForex, 337

P

Pacing
 award ceremonies, 82
 meeting, 5, 65

program design and, 157
Packing list, 337
Pagers, 245
Panel discussions, 275
Papers, calls for, 353–354
Par cam light, 280
Participants, preparing international event, 335–337
PartnerWorld show, 232–233
Passports, 335, 341
Pass system, 231
Payment, for speakers, 252
PC-based event management software, 199
PCMA. *See* Professional Conference Management Association
PCMA. *See* Professional Convention Management Association
PC Nametag, 145
PCO. *See* Professional Congress Organizer
PCs, meeting professional use of, 192–194. *See also* Software
PDAs. *See* Personal digital assistants
Peopleware, 145
Peripheral systems, video, 167–168
Personal digital assistants (PDAs), 193, 232–233
 for staging guides, 241
Personnel roster, 240
Phrase book, 336
Picnic theme, for refreshment break, 136
Pin fasteners, 268
Pin spot, 280
Planning
 initial, 31–51
  meeting and the message, 36
  meeting insurance, 47–51
  meeting profile, 33–34
  prospectus, 34–36
  setting objectives, 33

site inspection, 41–47
site selection, 36–41
tasks, 31–32
manager *vs.* administrator and, 12
of multicultural events, 351–353
See also Pre-meeting coordination; Site inspections; Site selection
Planning International Meetings (ASAE), 346
Plansoft, 145
Plasma screen, 177
Plated service, 122
Platform, 185
Playback, 170
Plenary sessions, 59–60, 354
Pocket inserts, 268
Pointe Resort, 123
Police escorts, 273
Political speakers, 69
Polysilicon LCD projectors, 173–174
Posi-Pours, 132
Post-conference evaluation, 292
Posters, 112
Post-meeting procedures, 289–300
auditing and financial analysis, 296–297
departure plan, 289–290
gratuities, 297–300
meeting evaluation, 290–293, 301
staff critique and documentation, 293–296
Power of attorney, limited, 344
PowerPoint, 159, 163, 165
moving beyond, 164–165
Power strips, 182
PRA Destination Management, 106
Pre-conference meeting, 238–240
scheduling, 240
Pre-Conference Memorandum, 238
Pre-departure checklist, 236–238
Pre-meeting coordination, 235–258

communications, 244–246
community resources, 249–250
handling VIPs, 251–253
headquarters, 242–244
master account procedures, 253–257
pre-conference meeting, 238–240
pre-departure checklist, 236–238
reception plan, 250–251
registration facilities, 248
registration staff, 246–247
security and, 309
staff organization, 242–244
staging guide, 240–242
transportation, 246
See also Planning; Site inspections; Site selection
Premier Images, 210
Presentations
area setup, 272–273
materials, 253
specifics for speakers, 72
Presentation technology, 197–198
chat rooms, 198
message boards, 197–198
Presenters, 70, 325
rating, 291
surveying, 291–292
Press kits, 114, 265–266
Press releases, 356
Pressroom, 115, 265–267
setup requirements, 266–267
Price-Waterhouse-Coopers, 337
Private security services, 312
Producers, 76, 77, 78
for audiovisual productions, 161
meeting, 161–162
role of, 78–79
Production schedule, 161
sample, 162
Productivity, centralized meeting departments and, 23

Professional Conference Management Association (PCMA), 13
Professional Congress Organizer (PCO), v, 9
   function of, 330
   global, 319
   independent, 26–27
   international events and, 329–330
   maintaining management credibility, 20
   as part of organization, 17–28
   professionalism and, 9–16
   responsibilities regarding speakers, 73–74
   technology team and, 196–197
   See also Corporate professional congress organizer
Professional Convention Management Association (PCMA), 10, 318
Professional development, 16
Professionalism, 9–10
   definition of professional, 10–12
   emphasis on education, 13–14
   manager *vs.* administrator, 12
   meetings industry positions, 9–10
   professional development, 16
   recognition for professionals, 14–16
Professional journals, 112
Professional liability insurance, 48
Professional Meeting Management (Carey), 346
Professional speakers, 69
Program content, 55
   multicultural events, 353–354
Program design
   elements of, 54–55
   expertise in, 11
   international exhibit, 333–334
   multicultural meeting, 354

   pacing and, 157
Program details, communicating, 84–85
Program development, 53–68
   business agenda, 61–62
   facility requirements, 57
   program design, 57
      elements of, 54–55
      guidelines for, 63–67
   program outline, 57–59
   program sessions and formats, 59–61
   speaker guidelines, 68
   steps in, 55–57
Program elements, 69–88
   entertainment and special events, 74–88
   speakers and presenters, 69–74
Program enhancers, 76
Program evaluation, 291–292
Program formats, 59–61
Program management, 269–289
   audiovisual and staging needs, 279–283
   business agenda, 276–278
   guest programs, 278–279
   meeting room setups, 269–273
   social agenda, 283–289
   speaker support, 273–276
Program outline, 57–59
Program planning, international event, 324–326
Program sessions, 59–61
Program support, international event, 324
Projection surface, 176
Projection systems, 172–177
   designing artwork for, 163–164
   legibility of projected visuals, 164
Projectors, 166–167, 173–175
Promotion
   airlines and, 104
   evaluation of, 293

for multicultural events, 356
  See also Marketing
Promotion program, 33
Prompter signals, 276
Prospectus, 32, 34–36
Protocol
  flags, 358–359
  honors and ceremonies, 359
  international event, 322, 336
  international exhibits, 334
  multicultural event, 358–360
  order of precedence, 359–360
  for speakers, 73
Providential Mutual Insurance, 18
Provident Life Insurance
  Company, 5
Psycho-physiological relationship
  between food and mental activity, 119–120, 138–140
Public access
  to exhibitions, 222
  security in areas of, 232
Publicity, 114–115
  car rental firms and event, 109
  security and, 307
PZM microphone, 171

Q

Quicken, 91

R

Radde, Paul O., 270
Radios, 245–246
Rail freight, 342
Ralston-Purina, 23
Real-time desktop conferencing, 6
Rear-projection screens, 179
Reception, 34, 260–262
  event registration, 260–261
  of honored persons, 359
  hotel registration, 260
  message center, 261–262
  of speakers, 74, 273–274
Reception plan, 249, 250–251
Receptions, 129–131, 285–286
Recognition
  ceremonies, 82–84
  special, 297–300
Reconciliation, of budget report,
  92, 98–99
Recording, audio, 170
Recreational events, 287–288
Recreation highlights, 168
Reflective efficiency, of screens,
  179
Refreshment breaks, 65, 134–137,
  285–286
  low-budget, 135
  moderate budget, 136
  timing, 136–137
Refreshment station, 137
Registration, 34
  advance, 141–142
    processing, 151
  advance meeting announcement, 142–143
  automating, 145–147
    historical perspective on,
      147–149
  badges, 151–152
  databank, 195
  evaluation of, 293
  event, 260–261
  exhibit, 228–229
    exhibitors, 228
    visitors, 228–229
  facilities, 248
  forms, 143–144
    housing request and, 149
    sample, 154
  hotel, 260
  marketing and, 195
  multicultural event, 356–357
  online, 191, 204
  on-site, 141, 142, 144, 357
  procedures, 141–142

self-service, 260
software for, 145–146, 198–199
staff, 246–247, 357
Web-based, 146–147
Registration fees, 96, 357
early registration discount, 97
RegOnline, 141
Rehearsals, speaker, 277
Religious food restrictions, 122
Renting audiovisual equipment, 186–187
Reportage, 165
Requests for Proposals (RFPs), 33
elements of site selection RFP utility, 203–204
online, 38, 203
Residual revenues, 99
Resolution
image, 172–173
standard, 174
Retention
audiovisuals and, 157
visual design and, 163
Return on investment, automating meeting management and, 196–197
Revenue management, airlines and, 102–103
Revenue projection, 96–97, 98
Revenues, residual, 99
Reverse-text slides, 164
RFPs. *See* Requests for Proposals
Rigid RP, 177
Risk assessment, event cancellation insurance and, 48
Risk management, security and, 306–307
Roast, 83
Roller screen, 177
Room block splintering, 23–24
Room capacity, meal planning and, 127–128
Room captain, 275
Room chairmen, 275

Room decor, 128–129, 182
Room entrance setup, 271
Room setup, for meals, 128
Roscoe, Patti, 106, 107, 328
Rosten, Leo, 63
Rounds, 271
Round tables, 285–286
Rudkin, Dick, 24
Russian service, 122

S

Safety, 307–308
site inspection and, 44–45
weather and, 311
See also Security
Sales staff, meeting with at site inspection, 43
Schraeg, Michael, 17
Scientific program, 61, 276. *See also* Business agenda
SCMP. *See* Society of Corporate Meeting Professionals
Screens
determining, 178–179
LED, 166–167
placement in educational sessions, 185
reflective characteristics, 178–179
types of, 177
Search engines, 202, 203
Seating
banquet, 270
classroom, 269, 270
for educational sessions, 184–185
hollow square, 270, 271
at multicultural event, 359–360
rounds, 271
setup, 271–272
T conference, 270, 271
theater-style, 269, 270
U conference, 270, 271

SECAM system, 331
Secretariat, 336, 349–350, 351
Secret Service, 307
Security
  community resources, 309–310
  demonstrations, 304–305
  exhibit, 231–232
  general precautions, 309
  international event, 311–313, 336
  pre-conference planning for, 309
  risk management and, 306–397
  Smart Cards and, 229
  for speakers, 73
  travel, 312–313
Seekings, David, 65
Self-service registration, 260
Semi-formal attire, 284
Seminar, 60
Seminar on Professional Congress Organization, 13
Servers, number of, 131
Service, food
  level of, 126
  types of, 122, 127
Service charges, 300
  on beverages, 133
Service desks
  exhibit, 230
  registration, 248
Services, meeting management, 22
Session critique forms, 291
Shangri La, 136
Shaw, George Bernard, 263
Sheraton Hotels, 209, 213–214
Shipping
  materials and equipment, 342–343
    audiovisual, 186–187
  plan, 33
Short-throw lens, 176
Show acts, 76
SI. *See* Simultaneous interpretation

Signs, event registration, 260
Silberstein, Diane, 332
Simultaneous interpretation (SI), 216–217, 326, 354–355
Sir Stafford Fleming College, 13
Site inspections, 41–47
  checklist, 43
  ethics of, 45–46
  follow-up details and obligations, 46–47
  inspecting meeting rooms, 43–44
  meeting services, 45
  pre-inspection preparation, 41–42
  safety inspection, 44–45
  site inspection trip, 42–43
  surveying for AV, 187–189
Site selection, 32–33, 36–41
  automating, 194
  checklist, 49
  factors influencing destination, 37–38
  hotel selection criteria, 39–41
  international event, 320–321
  online, 38–39, 203
Sixth EEC VAT Directive, 339
Slides, 163, 281
  shipping, 343
Slide shows, media analysis of, 160
Smart badges, 152
Smart cards, 205–206
Social agenda, 33, 34, 143, 195, 283–289
  attire, 284–285
  daily procedures, 288–289
  off-site functions, 286–287
  receptions, meals, breaks, 285–286
  recreational events, 287–288
Social events, performers and, 80
Society of Corporate Meeting Professionals (SCMP), 13
Soft drinks, 135

Software
  animation, 165
  computer aided design, 164–165
  conference management, 194–195
  enterprise-wide applications, 199
  event-management, 198–199
    evaluating, 199–201
  exhibit registration, 228
  measuring effectiveness of, 201–202
  meeting management, 365–367
  meeting specific, 91
  off-the-shelf suite, 198
  PC-based event management, 199
  PC-based registration, 145–146
  registration, 141, 145–146
  shipping, 343
  Web-based registration applications, 199
Software Management Inc., 234
Sound console, 281
Sound systems, 170–171
Speaker clusters, 171
Speaker data, 72
Speakers, 69–74, 171, 252–253
  contracts, 71
  expenses, 71
  fees, 71
  guidelines, 68, 72
  information for, 71–72
  multicultural audiences and, 325–326
  for multicultural events, 353, 354
  PCO responsibilities regarding, 73–74
  professional, 69
  recognized experts, 69
  sample confirmation, 67
  seating, 128
  selecting, 70
  speakers' bureaus, 70–71
  travel arrangements for, 71
  treatment of, 251–252
  visual aids and, 163
Speaker support, 273–276
  reception and housing, 273–274
  session chairmen, 275
  speaker briefing, 274–275
  speakers' lounge, 274
Special effects, 281
Special events, 74–75
Special Events, Twenty-first Century Global Event Management (Goldblatt), 75, 85
Special event teleconferencing, 210
Specimen rates and charges bulletin, 255–256
  sample, 256
Split folio, 253
Spokesperson, 265
Sponsors
  for hospitality suites, 130
  for refreshment break, 136
Spot price, 338
Staff, 12
  international event, 324
  registration, 246–247
Staff critique, 293–296
Staff meetings, on-site, 267
Staff organization, 242–244
  for association convention, 25
  for corporate meeting, 25
Staff planning, 243
Stage directions, 79, 242
Staging
  with audiovisuals, 184–186
  for banquets, 186
  for entertainment, 185–186, 279–281
  meal, 128
  at multicultural events, 360
  needs, 279–283

preventing technology glitches, 281–283
Staging Guide, 195, 238, 240–242
   exhibit, 230
   maintaining, 242
   organizing, 241–242
Staging specification rider, sample, 86
Staging specifications, 80
Standards of professional conduct, 9
Starting Guide, 235
Statement of authority, for meeting department, 22–23
Strategic planning, 5
Stretch-screen, 177
Strikes, 308
Strobe light, 280
Successful Meetings magazine, 4, 39
Sumitomo, 337
Support services, 33, 35
   for international events, 324, 329
Surrogate address, 165
SVGA, 174
SXGA, 174
Sylvester, John, 309
Symposium, 60
Synchronous instruction, 13

T

Table cosmetics, 125, 127
Table decor, 127, 128–129
Table Deli, 122
Tabulation, of evaluations, 292–293
Task analysis, 32
Taxes, on beverages, 133
Taylor, Barry, 188
T conference setup, 270, 271
Technical knowledge/skills, of meeting managers, 28
Technical specifications, for entertainment, 80–81

Technology
   archival, 191, 192, 208–209
   exhibit, 228–229, 232–233
   future of, 217–218
   meetings and advances in, 6
   presentation, 197–198
   preventing glitches in, 281–283
   teleconferencing, 6, 209–212
   third-party services, 215–216
   videoconferencing, 211, 212–213
   video teleconference, 211
   Web cast, 211, 215
   Web conference, 211, 214–215
   See also Audiovisuals; Computers; Software
Technology Advisory Council, 217
Teleconferencing, 6, 209–212
   ad hoc, 210
   benefits, 210
   justification for, 213–214
   overview, 210–212
   truths/myths, 209–210
Telephone outlets, 183
Telephones, 245
Terminology, stage, 79, 242
Terrorism
   security and, 306–307
   virtual meetings and, 216
TFT projector, 173
Theater-style seating, 185, 269, 270
Theme, meeting, 31, 34
   reinforcing, 63–64
   sample, 64
Themed dinners, 123–124
Third-party services, 215–216
Tickets
   cash bars and, 133
   computer-generated, 204–205
   control of, 267–268
   meal, 138
Time Base Corrector, 167
Timelines

conference, 194
establishing, 32
fiscal, 255–257
marketing plan, 115–116
meeting planner, 50–51
multicultural event, 352–353
production schedule, 162
program design, 54
program development, 55–57
Time management principles, 235–236
Timing
 meeting, 5, 65
 for speaker, 73
Tip, defined, 299. *See also* Gratuities
Toffler, Alvin, 5, 6
Tourism Oriented Policing and Security (TOPS), 309
Tournaments, 288
Trade publications, 112
Trade shows, 219
 virtual, 216, 234
Train travel, 101
Transmission/streaming, 170
Transnational events, 318–320. *See also* International events; Multicultural events
Transparencies, 163
Transportation coordinator, 342
Travel agencies, 101–102
 online, 105
Travel agents, 9
Travel Assistance International, 346
Travelocity, 105
Travel security, 312–313
Travel/transportation, 35
 air. *See* Airlines; Air travel
 car rentals, 109
 cost of, 92
 distribution analysis of, 101
 ground. *See* Ground transportation

negotiating, 33
for speakers, 74
train, 101
Treasure hunts, 288
Treville, Rick de, 309, 313
Tripod screen, 177
Trouble desk, 261
Troubleshooting, 263–264
Truck freight, 342, 343
TV theme, 168
Two-by-eight principle, 180–181

U

Uconference setup, 270, 271
Unidirectional microphone, 171
Union of International Associations (UIA), 10, 317
Unions
 entertainment, 76–77
 expositions and, 222
 level of service and, 126
U.S. Department of Commerce, 333
U.S. Department of Homeland Security, 232
U.S. State Department, 310
Universities, meeting planning curriculum, 13
University-industry cooperation, 6
University of Hawaii, 13
UXGA, 174

V

Validation, program design, 54–55
Value-added tax (VAT), 323, 338
 recovery of, 339
Vans, 107–109
Variable expenses, 92
VAT. *See* Value-added tax
Vegetarianism, 122
Venues
 exhibition, 220–221

multicultural event, 353
See also Site selection
VGA, 174
Video
  applications, 168
  communication functions, 165–166
  digital, 165
  equipment and systems, 166–168
    peripheral, 167–168
  high-speed connections and, 183
  international events and differing standards, 330–331
  media analysis of, 160
  at meetings, 165–166
  monitors and projectors (LED screens), 166–167
  origination source, 167
  resolution, 174
  simultaneous projection with computer data, 175
Videoconferencing, 165, 192, 211, 212
  planning considerations, 212–213
Video (point-to-multipoint), 212
Video (point-to-point), 212
Video teleconference, 211
Viewing area, of screens, 179
VIPs, 251–253
  HPs *vs.*, 358
Viral marketing, 147
Virtual booths, 234
Virtual meetings, 214–216
Virtual trade shows, 216, 234
Virtual Web conferencing, 60
Visa Requirements of Foreign Governments (U.S. Bureau of Consular Affairs), 341, 347
Visas, 333, 335, 341
Visitors, registration of, 228–229
Vista International, 136
Visual design principles, 163–165
  beyond PowerPoint, 164–165
  designing artwork for projection, 163–164
  legibility of projected visuals, 164
Voice communication, 183–184
Voice pager, 245
Voice recognition, 202
Volunteers, registration staff, 247
Von Lehnsten, Dieter, 322

W

Weather, safety and, 307–308, 311
Web-based evaluations, 293
Web-based registration, 145, 146–147
  software, 199
Web casting, 99, 192, 211, 215
  interactive, 215
Web conferencing, 6, 60, 192, 211, 214–215
Web sites, 365–367
  advance meeting announcement via, 142
  dedicated event, 204
  Exhibit Contractor's, 226
  registration, 141
  venue, 191
  See also Internet
Welcome letter, 151
Western Barbecue, 123
Whiteboard, electronic, 197
WiFi standard, 169
Wine service, 126–127
  quality of, 131
Wireless communication, 191
Wireless microphone, 172
Wireless technology, 169–170
  benefits of, 169–170
Workbook, The (Incentives and Meetings International), 346
Work habits, of meeting managers, 28

Worksheets
  budget
    association, 94
    corporate, 93
  business agenda, 62
Workshop, 60
World-Class Executive, The
  (Chesanov), 361
Worldjam, 192
Wright, Andrew, 210

X

XGA, 174

Z

Zenith Corporation, 213
Zone pricing, 102
Zoom lens, 176